CHOOSING WAR

CHOOSING WAR

Presidential Decisions in the *Maine, Lusitania,* and *Panay* Incidents

Douglas Carl Peifer

OXFORD
UNIVERSITY PRESS

OXFORD
UNIVERSITY PRESS

Oxford University Press is a department of the University of Oxford. It furthers
the University's objective of excellence in research, scholarship, and education
by publishing worldwide. Oxford is a registered trade mark of Oxford University
Press in the UK and certain other countries.

Published in the United States of America by Oxford University Press
198 Madison Avenue, New York, NY 10016, United States of America.

Library of Congress Cataloging-in-Publication Data
Names: Peifer, Douglas Carl, author.
Title: Choosing war : presidential decisions in the Maine, Lusitania,
and Panay incidents / Douglas Carl Peifer.
Description: New York, NY : Oxford University Press, 2016. |
Includes bibliographical references and index.
Identifiers: LCCN 2016003097 | ISBN 9780190268688 (hardcover : alk. paper)
Subjects: LCSH: Presidents—United States—Decision making—Case studies. |
War and emergency powers—United States—Case studies. |
United States—Military policy—Decision making—Case studies. |
McKinley, William, 1843–1901—Military leadership. |
Wilson, Woodrow, 1856–1924—Military leadership. |
Roosevelt, Franklin D. (Franklin Delano), 1882–1945—Military leadership. |
Maine (Battleship) | Lusitania (Steamship) | Panay (Gunboat)
Classification: LCC JK558.P45 2016 | DDC 355.02/720973—dc23
LC record available at https://lccn.loc.gov/2016003097

9 8 7 6 5 4 3 2 1
Printed by Sheridan Books, Inc., United States of America

To
Lovers of history and international affairs
J. Carl and Doris Peifer, world travelers.

CONTENTS

PART THREE: The *Panay* Incident

PART FOUR: Anticipating the Unexpected

ACKNOWLEDGMENTS

My thanks go out to the many individuals who read portions of the book, debated the intricacies of coercion theory and naval diplomacy with the author, and engaged in the disciplinary jousting that distinguishes historians from social scientists studying the same topics. Special thanks go to John Geis, Gerhard Weinberg, Elizabeth Peifer, Mark Duckenfield, John Schuessler, Kevin Holzimmer, Nikolas Gardner, Robert Hanyok, David Alvarez, Alexander Lassner, and the anonymous outside readers who offered valuable insights. I very much value their comments and criticism even if I did not always heed all suggestions. Any errors or interpretive differences should be laid at my doorstep. I have been greatly enriched by the experience of working in a multidisciplinary, inter-service, and inter-agency setting where I could discuss and debate issues with fellow historians, international relations scholars, active-duty military officers from all the services, and international fellows from around the world. I am also deeply appreciative of the assistance rendered by Helen Lehman and Josephine Turner at the Muir S. Fairchild Research Information Center; David Colamaria of the Naval History and Heritage Center, the staff at the Library of Congress and the National Archives, and colleagues David Alvarez and Robert Hanyok from H-Net. Special thanks are due to Nancy Toff at Oxford University Press for her thoughtful editorial suggestions, which undoubtedly made the book more readable, organized, and focused.

My thanks go out to my family for their support and indulgence as I focused on presidential decision making, naval incidents, current affairs, and naval incidents past and present. As a fellow historian, mother to our four boys, and wife, Beth gave generously of her time and intellect as I subjected her to late-night discussions of the *Maine*, the *Lusitania*, the *Panay*, and the fruitful tensions between social scientists, historians, academics, practitioners, and policy-makers. Justin, James, Killian, and Fritz bring joy, energy, and a pride into my scholar's life.

Disclaimer

INTRODUCTION

NAVAL INCIDENTS AND THE DECISION FOR WAR

In his short masterpiece *The Historian's Craft*, the French historian Marc Bloch recounts a conversation with his friend Henri Pirenne about the historian's relationship with the past and present. Bloch and Pirenne, both scholars of the medieval period, rejected the proposition that the historian should confine his or her interests solely to the past, with Bloch contending that "the scholar who has no inclination to observe the men, the things, or the events around him will perhaps deserve the title . . . of useful antiquarian."[1] Bloch asserted that history connects the study of the dead and living, and while his essay focused on the techniques of historical observation, criticism, and analysis, he rejected words of caution that the historian should "spare Clio's chastity from the profanation of present controversy."[2]

Yet in the seventy years since Bloch wrote his thought piece (while serving as a reservist French staff officer assigned monotonous duties during the "phony war" that preceded Germany's lightning conquest of France in 1940), academic historians have by and large conceded the field of security studies to political scientists, international relations specialists, and other social scientists. Historians continue to connect the past to the present, but the focus of the profession has shifted from topics related to diplomacy, strategy, and military history to explorations of class, ethnicity, identity, memory, and meaning.[3] Social scientists, former government officials, and retired military officers dominate the halls of foreign and security policy think tanks, and journals such as *Security Studies, International Security*, and the *Journal of Strategic Studies* reflect disciplinary predilections that prioritize theory and parsimony over context, complexity, and the distinctiveness of time, place, and people. Social scientific methodologies overshadow historical analysis in contemporary debates about coercion and deterrence, the rise of China, the implications of proliferating anti-access and area denial weapon systems, and the Obama administration's efforts to shift U.S. strategic attention toward the Asia-Pacific region.

As a historian who has taught courses on strategy to senior military and government officials at one of the nation's war colleges for over a decade, I find Bloch's incitement to engage with matters of "present controversy" heartening. This book seeks to provide a historical perspective on what I view as an alarming but far from unlikely future scenario, namely that U.S. air and naval assets engaging in patrol, intelligence gathering, or freedom of navigation operations become entangled in some sort of small-scale incident that generates calls for escalation and retaliation. While I join my fellow historians in eschewing prediction, three strategic developments seem to make some sort of incident at sea (or in air and space) increasingly likely. The first concerns the rise of China, and unresolved territorial and economic claims in the East and South China Seas. Not a month goes by without another book or article addressing the challenges of accommodating a growing China within the international system, with a great deal of handwringing about the implications of expanding Chinese capabilities at sea, in the air, in space, and in cyberspace.[4] The midair collision between a Chinese fighter and U.S. EP-3 surveillance plane in 2001, China's harassment of Japanese aircraft and ships near the Senkaku/Diaoyu Islands in 2014, and its power diplomacy toward the Philippines and Vietnam in the South China Sea are worrying. The United States has announced that it intends to increase its presence in the region, and has strengthened ties with regional partners. Whether this calms troubled waters or sets the stage for future confrontations remains to be seen.

The second challenge is technological, namely the proliferation of what the military terms anti-access and area denial (A2/AD) weapons systems that will make it increasingly difficult for the United States to project power as it has since World War II. Military experts warn that operating U.S. ships and aircraft on and above disputed waters will become increasingly risky as new generations of long-range anti-ship and anti-aircraft missiles become available to both first- and second-tier powers, and as other powers develop capabilities to disrupt U.S. weapons systems dependent on space and cyberspace.[5] While China and Russia clearly have the most sophisticated network of A2/AD systems, proliferation of such systems to the Persian Gulf (Iran), the Mediterranean (Syria), and to other trouble spots makes the United States' traditional naval shows of force, aerial surveillance, and power projection from carriers and amphibious ships more dangerous and difficult.

The third development is the continued spread of radical jihadi terrorist groups throughout North Africa and the Levant, and into nations bordering the Indian Ocean. These groups have embraced suicide terrorism as a tool, transforming trucks, small boats, and civilian aircraft into low-tech but effective weapons. U.S. ships, embassies, and consulates make for convenient targets, as attested by the 1998 attacks on our embassies in Dar es Salaam and Nairobi, the October 2000 attack on the USS Cole, and most dramatically, the 2001 attacks on the World Trade Center and Pentagon. The United States has made great strides in hardening its embassies and instituting additional protective measures for its ships visiting ports overseas, but the threat of attacks by non-state actors employing explosive-laden small boats, wire-guided anti-tank missiles, and "man-portable air-defense systems" remains deadly earnest.

The academic security studies community, defense policy think tanks, and the Pentagon are all grappling with the challenges posed by China's rise, proliferating anti-access and area denial weapon systems, and maritime terrorism. One senses an awareness that naval diplomacy will become more risky in the future, but surprisingly little attention has been devoted to examining the historical connections between naval incidents and the decisions for war. I find this troubling, as a comparative analysis of incidents at sea underscores important questions that currently are neglected. Chief among these are whether naval incidents have generally resulted from miscalculation or intent; whether they arise more often from naval coercion or from the defense of rights; when and why specific naval disasters have escalated to war; and under what conditions previous U.S. administrations found it advisable to settle matters diplomatically despite the loss of life.

The subset of "incidents at sea" is particularly relevant to the United States, as both some of its earliest wars (the Quasi-War with France in the 1790s, the wars with the Barbary pirates, 1801–05, 1815) and more recent conflicts (U.S. escalation in Vietnam subsequent to the Gulf of Tonkin incident, 1964) were justified in part as responses to naval incidents. Yet naval incidents have not always nor immediately led to war—witness the awkward "undeclared war" pitting the U.S. Navy against the *Kriegsmarine* in the months before Pearl Harbor or the crippling of the USS *Stark* by an Iraqi F1 Mirage in 1987. Attribution uncertainty has complicated the matter further, as the Clinton administration discovered after the USS *Cole* (DDG-67) was rammed by a small boat packed with explosives while refueling in the port of Aden in October 2000. Multiple shadowy non-state groups initially claimed responsibility for the attack, and it required time and effort to trace the attack back to specific individuals within the al Qaeda organization.

Given the frequent yet ambiguous historical connection between naval incidents and military escalation, and given contemporary developments that make the maritime domain more dangerous, a study of how previous administrations have confronted crises stemming from the destruction of ships with Americans onboard is urgently needed. Historians and investigative commissions have written detailed analyses of the connections between particular episodes and subsequent wars, such as the sinking of the USS *Maine* and the Spanish-American War, or the Gulf of Tonkin incident and Johnson's Americanization of the Vietnam War in 1965. This study is unique in that it provides a comparative analysis of multiple cases, examining both incidents that led to war and others that did not. This approach is more typical of the political scientist than of the historian, but my aim is to provide a rich comparative historical analysis that prioritizes context, specificity, and historical detail over generalization, parsimony, and theoretical hypotheses. As an historian, I am wary of claims about testable, general propositions applicable across time and space, but I do believe a careful reading of history will inform when, why, and under what circumstances an incident at sea escalated from the diplomatic sphere to the military sphere. By providing a historical perspective of how three different U.S. administrations responded to naval incidents that had the potential to escalate from the diplomatic realm to the military sphere, this book aims to provide a window into presidential decision making. The three cases selected analyze how Congress, the press, and public opinion set parameters to presidential freedom of action. Strong presidents can shift the boundaries of what the nation views as an acceptable response to naval incidents, but the effort involved is substantial. The historical incidents examined here provide a sense of how context is critical in determining outcomes, and the book seeks to promote critical thinking on the part of future policymakers, practitioners, and the general public. As Frederick Jackson Turner remarked in 1891, "each age writes the history of the past anew with references to the conditions uppermost in its own time."[6] Ours is a time when shifting power relationships, disputes over maritime rights, overlapping exclusive economic zones (EEZs), the proliferation of anti-access/area denial weapon systems, and terrorism are making naval diplomacy an increasingly risky enterprise.

This rather modest agenda of studying the past to raise questions that have contemporary relevance, rather than mining it in order to produce theory and nomothetic (law-like) principles, stems from the quite different perspectives of historians and social scientists about the utility of generalization and the applicability of theory.[7] The political scientist, as Jack Levy explains in a marvelous essay on political science and history, seeks to abstract from the complexity of the world in order to derive theories that can "travel well" across time and space. He or she is less interested in the subtleties of particular cases than in forming and testing hypotheses that have broad validity across multiple cases, even at the cost of ignoring the unique, the unexpected, and the accidental.[8] Yet it is precisely by exploring the connections between domestic and international forces, between leaders and the public, and between cultures, personalities, and worldviews that one constructs a sophisticated, convincing, and multilayered understanding of reality. These variables cannot be held constant or factored out.[9] The historian recognizes that wars, revolutions, and diplomatic crises tend to have multiple interdependent causes, and understands that similar inputs may generate very different outputs depending on the context. Clausewitz recognized this nonlinear interaction among policy, violence, and chance in *On War* some two centuries ago. Most historians would concur with Stephen Pelz's assessment that "complex cases can be compared analytically, but they are unlikely to yield law-like explanations."[10] Hew Strachan, commenting that "the study of strategy has been largely divorced from the historical roots in which it first flourished," cautions that social scientists tend to select topics that prove or disprove a thesis rather than studying strategy and international relations in its historical context. He warns that studies devoid of context "obliterate the woof and warp of history, the sense of what is really new and changing as opposed to what is not."[11]

In a similar vein, Eliot Cohen advocates that would-be students of international relations and strategy acquire a historical mindset. What does this mean? All too often one encounters references to George Santayana's riff that "Those who cannot remember the past are condemned to repeat it."[12] Used carelessly, this admonition suggests that one can derive historical "lessons learned" that should guide contemporary decision making on issues of war and peace, diplomacy and coercion. Unfortunately, however, a "lessons-learned" approach often manifests itself as cherry-picking analogies from the past to support a contemporary agenda.[13] What Cohen has in mind is more subtle. He advocated studying the past in all its richness in order to understand the "essential elements of context and detail that make up a complex political-military situation." This embraces similarities and dissimilarities, intended actions and the accidental, patterns and the unique. It trains the mind to ask disciplined, critical questions. It provokes a degree of skepticism about overdependence on theoretical models *and* historical analogies. It prompts one to examine the assumptions and predictive qualities of both.[14]

While the above reflects the characteristic skepticism of historians about parsimonious international relations theories claiming to have general applicability, anyone writing a comparative history about certain *types* of events or *categories* of phenomena can profit from the social sciences. Comparative historians should structure their case studies in a clear and consistent manner, differentiating between necessary and sufficient causes, and ultimate and proximate factors. When appropriate, they should draw upon theory and models to provide analytical rigor, but they should not allow theory to become a blindfold or aperture that distorts and simplifies the historical record. While rejecting universal generalizations and categorical causation, historians should be bold enough to provide limited generalizations and identify contingent causes. Moreover, a comparative history should not hide its methodological plumbing within a narrative edifice, but to borrow an image from Gaddis, must expose its intellectual framework in the same manner that the designers of the Centre Pompidou in Paris placed ducts, escalators, and wiring on the outside of that building.[15]

What logic led to the selection of the *Maine*, *Lusitania*, and *Panay* incidents as case studies of presidential crisis decision making, and what methodology is employed throughout? One confronts such a plethora of peacetime naval and air incidents with the potential of escalation that narrowing the field is difficult. One might, for example, commence an analysis of naval incidents with references to the Ancient Mediterranean world, drawing upon episodes mentioned in the writings of Thucydides, Plutarch, and Polybius. One would have to study incidents between states and incidents between state and non-state actors, noting how the categories became blurred and indistinct at times. While tensions between Persia and the Greek city-states, between Athens and Sparta, and between Rome and Carthage involved incidents at sea prior to the open declaration of hostilities, a far more constant source of maritime trouble was the dependence of entire communities, and even kingdoms, on the capture and ransom of merchant ships, crews, and passengers. Cilicia and Illyria in particular were notorious for their trepidations, with Plutarch recording the story of how Julius Caesar was seized as a young man by Cilician pirates. He paid the ransom they demanded, and then organized an expedition to capture and crucify his former captors. This highlights the extent and pervasiveness of piracy, a practice not limited to rogue groups of outlaws but, additionally, sustained and supported by regional powers. The seizure of ships elicited both diplomatic protests and policing actions indistinguishable from war in their scale and ferocity.[16]

In a similar vein, one might turn to the early modern era and examine the interactions between state policy, piracy, and commerce warfare. A good many of England's famous sea captains, from Francis Drake to John Hawkins to Martin Frobisher, attacked and seized Spanish and French ships and property during periods when England was officially not at war, with Queen Elizabeth I rewarding rather than punishing them for their efforts. The French, the Dutch, and other powers likewise tolerated attacks on the shipping of others even during periods of truce, with the distinction between privateer and pirate often more theoretical than real.[17] Distinguished military historian Sir Michael Howard characterized warfare during this period as "war between merchants," though this downplays the dynastic and religious dimensions of the long struggle between Hapsburgs, Valois/Bourbons, Tudor/Stuarts, and the Dutch.[18] Yet at least along the Atlantic periphery, the characterization rings true, with the eighty-year Dutch War of Independence and the Protestant Revolution blurring religious, dynastic, and mercantile motives and resulting in continuous low-level maritime conflict even in the absence of official declarations of war.

Shifting one's gaze away from the West, one might analyze Zheng He's famous voyages (1405–1433 C.E.) through the South China Seas and into the Indian Ocean. His expeditions sought to display Ming China's power and over-awe the rulers of the various kingdoms and peoples visited in the course of seven expeditions. While Zheng's mission was not conquest and colonization, the bestowal and collection of gifts had a coercive element to it, as King Alakeshvara of the Ceylonese kingdom of Kotte discovered. Insufficiently mindful of Chinese interests and unintimidated by its fleet, Alakeshvara found his kingdom ravaged and himself in chains following a confrontation with Zheng.[19] While the specifics of the episode are hazy, coercive naval diplomacy has not been the exclusive preserve of the West, and one might draw upon naval incidents where Arab, Ottoman, Chinese, and Japanese governments blended diplomacy, force, and warfare in a manner modern theorists would term coercive.

The use of naval power as a diplomatic tool of coercion experienced a heyday in the nineteenth century, with the term "gunboat diplomacy" capturing the flavor of the period.[20] A host of technologies emerged in the nineteenth century that transformed warfare, from the use of railroads to the advent of the telegraph, from the mass introduction of rifled small arms to the development of the machine gun and quick action artillery.[21] On land and at sea, the narrow technological lead that separated Western militaries from those they encountered elsewhere steadily widened, leading British poet and writer Hilaire Belloc to exclaim in 1898 that "Whatever happens, we have got / The Maxim gun, and they have not."[22] Yet it was particularly in the area of naval technology that the West developed a decided advantage, with "gunboat diplomacy" becoming shorthand for Western coercive diplomacy and the limited use of force against less technologically developed societies.

American observers took note of the flexibility of "gunboat diplomacy," and during the 1880s the United States began to replace its outmoded post–Civil War wooden ships with a new generation of steel-plated modern warships, the so-called ABCD ships (the *Atlanta, Boston, Chicago*, and *Dolphin*).[23] Commodore Robert Shufelt sold the new steel navy to Congressman Morse of the House Naval Affairs Committee in terms of its utility in forcibly opening new trading opportunities:

> In pursuit of new channels the trader seeks not only unfrequented paths upon the ocean, but the unfrequented ports of the world. He needs the constant protection of the flag and the gun. He deals with barbarous tribes—with men who appreciate only the argument of physical force. . . . The man-of-war precedes the merchantman and impresses rude people with the sense of the power of the flag which covers the one and the other.[24]

Gunboat diplomacy led to war more often than its advocates recognized, with coercive diplomacy and limited shows of force escalating into substantial commitments of military power. The bombardment of Da Nang by two French warships in 1847, an action ostensibly taken to gain the release of French missionaries, achieved little other than to set the stage for the larger intervention a decade later that led to the French acquisition of Cochinchina (southern Vietnam). The appointment of a French admiral as its first governor illustrates how gunboat diplomacy all too often merged with the new imperialism of the late nineteenth century. Yet even in cases where annexation was not the objective of the intervener, gunboat diplomacy usually required more force, treasure, and bloodshed than we now remember. Commodore Perry may have opened Japan to trade in 1854, but keeping the door open required the combined intervention of nine British, three French, and five Dutch warships, along with a U.S. chartered steamer in 1864. Only after subduing the Chosu clan that controlled the Shimonoseki straits did the door stay open, with the limited use of force generating a reaction that toppled the shogunate and launched the Meiji Restoration.[25] Even a cursory examination of "gunboat diplomacy" reveals that the ability to shell ports, coastlines, and enemy shipping with impunity as often as not failed to achieve the desired political effects. Coercive diplomacy and limited violence worked best when the issue at hand did not affect core interests, when the targeted party had little popular backing, and when diplomacy and intervention did not seek regime change.

Gunboat diplomacy and its modern successors, carrier and airpower diplomacy, have proven so alluring because they promise risk-free interventions. James Cable, tallying the frequency to which the leading naval powers employed coercive naval force in some manner, finds that Britain used naval coercion almost fifty times between 1918 and 1945, with the United States taking the lead during the cold war and using some form of naval coercion over sixty times.[26] Most of the time, the costs to the coercer were low. But at times naval coercion has led to unanticipated difficulties, with ships showing the flag, collecting intelligence, and sending subtle diplomatic signals attacked and severely damaged or destroyed.

One might draw upon incidents at sea (or more recently in the air) from Caesar's time to the present, and from the perspectives as diverse as that of Phillip II of Spain dealing with Drake's depredations in the 1570s to that of a newly elected George W. Bush coping with the EP-3 incident in the spring of 2001. In order to provide a comparative, contextually rich examination of American presidential crisis decision making, I selected three naval incidents that shook the nation: the destruction of the USS *Maine* in 1898, the sinking of the *Lusitania* in 1915, and the aerial attack on the *Panay* in 1937. The three incidents involved three different administrations, with one of the incidents escalating to war, another establishing a red line that would trigger war if crossed, and the third resolved diplomatically. Two cases involve the sinking of large ships and the deaths of hundreds; the other, the destruction of an American gunboat with dozens of injured but few dead. Each case illustrates different principles, dynamics, and issues at stake, ranging from McKinley's failed attempt to use low-level coercive naval diplomacy to Wilson's defense of neutral rights, to FDR's effort to maintain an American presence in China at the height of American isolationism. Each incident had the potential to escalate, but each fell short of the threshold that compels a military response, such as Japan's attack on Pearl Harbor and al Qaeda's attacks on New York City and Washington, D.C., on September 11, 2001. Those attacks killed thousands of American citizens on U.S. sovereign territory, with little debate as to whether the United States needed to retaliate.

In the three cases examined, the American president had a choice of how to respond, with escalation and war only one of several options considered.

I restricted myself to those cases where we have a firm understanding of the dynamics of crisis decision making. There are numerous air and naval incidents of more recent provenance than the *Maine, Lusitania*, and *Panay* that one might examine. But while records related to the Gulf of Tonkin incident—the suspected attack on the destroyers USS *Maddox* and *Turner Joy,* which President Johnson used to gain congressional authorization to use force in Vietnam—have been declassified, many of the key documents related to more recent naval and air incidents remain classified. Only in November 2012, for example, did the National Security Administration release a tranche of documents related to North Korea's seizure of the USS *Pueblo* in 1968.[27] Government documents, cabinet discussions, and personal papers related to more recent incidents remain classified, rendering reconstructions of crisis decision making incomplete and tentative. One simply cannot delve into the decision-making processes responding to the Israeli attack on the USS *Liberty* (1967), North Korea's seizure of the USS *Pueblo* (1968), Iraq's attack on the USS *Stark* (1987), al Qaeda's attack on the USS *Cole* (2000), or more recent Chinese harassment of U.S. surveillance aircraft and ships with the same level of assurance as one can with the cases selected.[28] Constructing a comparative analysis of presidential crisis decision-making using recent air and naval incidents runs squarely into the obstacles of classification, sealed records, and self-serving leaks. In contrast, the three cases selected have been studied intensely for decades. The primary records are available, the memoirs and private diaries of all the key individuals are accessible, and most important, each event has been scrutinized by multiple generations of historians combing through the archives, assessing the accuracy of memoirs, reconstructing the flow of crisis decision-making, and challenging each other's interpretations. In each case examined, I was fortunate enough to stand on the shoulders of giants in the historical profession.

My work rests on meticulous, multi-volume analyses of the McKinley, Wilson, and Roosevelt presidencies; on hundreds of books about diplomacy, war, and coercion; and on dozens of books focused more tightly on the causes and consequences of the *Maine, Lusitania*, and *Panay* incidents. Whenever possible, I have attempted to examine the relevant primary correspondence and naval court findings. The aim of this book is not to write yet another exhaustive monograph on the causes of the Spanish-Cuban-American War, Wilson's drift from neutrality at the outset of World War I to Allied partiality by 1916, or Roosevelt's double-edged campaign against isolationists at home and the Axis powers abroad. Instead, the book seeks to provide a comparative analysis of presidential decision making in response to major naval incidents. It exposes the interconnections that have faded over time, and it assesses whether and how the incident altered the trajectory of American foreign policy.

Several additional considerations led to the selection of the *Maine, Lusitania,* and *Panay* incidents. I wanted to limit the study to the period after the United States emerged as a great power. Historians generally date this as beginning in the 1890s, associating the shift from regional actor to global power with the Spanish-American War. Only in the 1880s and '90s did American elites begin dreaming about acquiring a first-rate navy, with Alfred Thayer Mahan stimulating such ambitions with his publication of *The Influence of Sea Power on History* in 1890. The United States, moreover, was a very different country prior to the period selected. The powers of the federal government were far more limited, in particular during the period before the Civil War; the focus of most of its people was on continental expansion and agriculture; and the popular press such as it was had not gained mass circulation. By the 1890s, though, the United States had become a leading industrial power; Hearst and Pulitzer were transforming the media; and the Western frontier had disappeared.

In addition, diplomacy and naval operations prior to the invention of the telegraph and wireless had a very different rhythm before rather than after their advent. During the age of sail, communications between governments and far-flung ships took weeks at minimum, months in many cases. Governments had no choice but to delegate considerable autonomous powers of decision to navy captains, trusting that they would use their judgment to interpret broad directives in light of the changing situation at hand. While governments retained the prerogative of declaring war and crafting long-term strategy, those on scene had to manage crises as best they could within the parameters of the guidance they had received weeks before. By the late 1890s, wireless communications joined the telegraph in transforming crisis decision making, with Washington becoming more directly involved in crafting both short- and long-term responses. While satellite and Internet communications have accelerated the pace of communication in the last decades, the time lag between communications from Washington to ships and aircraft overseas is narrower if one compares 2020 to 1890 than if one compares 1890 to 1820.

Between 75 and 125 years separate us from the *Maine, Lusitania,* and *Panay* crises. This precludes the sort of experiential or remembered interaction with the past that the reader may have with the Global War on Terror, American interventions in the Middle East, or the cold war. But as I studied the period between 1890 and 1940, I came to recognize a dynamic that gives crisis decision making during this period contemporary relevance. During the cold war, the bipolar structure of the international system and the threat of nuclear war made minor naval and air incidents more prevalent and major confrontations more risky. Given the stakes at hand, the United States was willing to send aircraft over Soviet and Chinese airspace during the 1950s and early 1960s, only desisting once the risks became too high. It continued, however, to routinely send aircraft and ships on ISR (intelligence, surveillance, and reconnaissance) missions on the high seas and international airspace abutting the communist territories. On at least thirty-six occasions, Soviet, Chinese, and other communist regimes attacked American reconnaissance flights, with 264 Americans killed in action or declared missing as a result.[29] These low-level confrontations were quite prevalent during the 1950s and early '60s, but following the Cuban Missile Crisis and several near collisions at sea in the late 1960s, the Soviet Union and the United States signed an agreement on the "Prevention of Incidents On and Over the High Seas" (INCSEA agreement) in 1972.[30] The bipolar nature of the international system and the risks of nuclear war *increased* the need for surveillance and *decreased* the willingness to escalate when individual aircraft or ships were damaged, downed, sunk, or seized. The United States and the Soviet Union eventually developed mechanisms to dampen the risks that unintended incidents would escalate into major confrontations, from instituting a "hot line" linking the White House to the Kremlin, to the signing of the INCSEA agreement. These safeguards were not present during the period 1890–1940, with power more dispersed, red lines less explicit, and escalation less risky than during the cold war. One might add that these safeguards are absent in many of today's hot zones, with the emerging multi-polar configuration of power blurring the red lines and altering the calculations about regional conventional escalation.[31]

While we are apt to interpret and understand crisis decision making with the benefit of hindsight, it is well to remember that the actors involved drew upon their remembered past. It is striking how often the *Maine* and *Lusitania* came up in discussions related to the *Panay,* but hardly surprising. Franklin Delano Roosevelt's personal military adviser, Admiral William Leahy, cut his teeth outside Santiago Harbor in 1898. The American ambassador to Japan in 1937 reacted to news that the *Panay* had been sunk by telling his staff to pack their bags, recalling his experience as first secretary in the American embassy in Berlin when the *Lusitania* was destroyed. And an overwhelming majority of senators and representatives were determined in the 1930s that the United States would not repeat the perceived mistakes of twenty years earlier, passing neutrality legislation that tied the president's hands.

This brings us back to Cohen's admonition to nurture a historical mindset. Strict analogies, "lessons learned," and theoretical generalizations can mislead as often as they inform. But by understanding the "essential elements of context and detail that make up a complex political-military situation," we can better evaluate how former decision makers reacted to crisis situations. This equips us with the tools to scrutinize the rationale and logic for deploying the "big stick" of naval power in an era when others are building shields and slingshots. We may well have to strengthen our presence in crisis areas around the world, but we need to be able to think critically about appropriate responses if and when things go awry.

The USS *Maine* entered Havana harbor on the morning of January 25, 1898, passing Morro Castle to port.

Naval History and Heritage Command, Photo Archives, Photograph NH 48619

1   THE *MAINE* INCIDENT

THE INCIDENT

As dawn broke on the clear Tuesday morning of January 25, 1898, the USS *Maine* sighted the Cuban coast as it approached Havana. The *Maine*, a second-class battleship commissioned less than four years earlier, bristled with a primary battery of four ten-inch guns, a secondary battery of six six-inch guns, fifteen smaller rapid-fire guns, and four Gatling machine guns. It had been ordered to Havana ostensibly to pay a courtesy call, though the timing of the visit—less than two weeks after serious rioting shook Havana—made many doubt the U.S. government's characterization of the port call as nothing more than a "purely friendly matter." The State Department had received clearance for the visit from Spanish authorities the previous day, but the *Maine*'s commanding officer, Captain Charles Sigsbee, took precautions in the event that local authorities might be unwelcoming: while most of the crew were topside in their dress uniforms and the *Maine*'s turrets were aligned amidships in a nonthreatening manner, Sigsbee had stationed ammunition and gun crews at the ready. As the ship neared the harbor entrance over which loomed the historic Moro Castle and the still-functioning Forteleza de San Carlos de la Cabaña, there was anxiety about whether the *Maine* would be peppered with rifle and artillery fire or received in a friendly manner. The peaceful approach of a Spanish pilot boat dispelled this initial trepidation. The *Maine* took on the harbor pilot, Julian Garcia Lopez, who guided the ship safely through the narrow channel, recommending that Sigsbee moor the *Maine* near the Spanish cruiser *Alfonso XII* and a visiting German training ship, the *Gneisenau*. Shortly thereafter, a Spanish naval lieutenant came onboard to welcome the Americans. Sigsbee rendered and received the customary gun salutes, and then began the expected round of courtesy calls to senior civil and military authorities in Havana.

The McKinley administration went to great lengths to portray the *Maine*'s visit as nothing more than the resumption of friendly naval visits to Cuban ports. It followed an interlude during which the U.S.

Navy had suspended port visitations after the outbreak of armed rebellion in Spain's "ever faithful isle" in 1895.[1] Secretary of the Navy John D. Long vented in his journal that American newspapers were attempting to "discover some hidden meaning" behind the visit when none existed. Captain Sigsbee recalled that "all visits were made without friction and with courtesy on both sides."[2] The subsequent twenty days gave little cause for concern. Sigsbee showed off the ship to various official parties, attended dinners ashore, and even accepted the invitation of the acting Spanish governor general to attend a bullfight at the Plaza de Toros in nearby Regla. The atmosphere in Havana, the administrative and military epicenter of Spanish rule in Cuba, was tense as Spain struggled to find a way out of an unwinnable war against Cuban revolutionaries without acceding to their demand for independence. Sigsbee wisely restricted his crew to the ship and allowed only small parties of officers into the town. Aside from some scowls and one vaguely threatening flyer, the Americans experienced no overt hostility.[3] The port visit seemed on the verge of becoming one of those unremarkable, unremembered episodes of naval diplomacy, when on February 15, precisely three weeks after the *Maine* made fast to buoy 4 in Havana harbor, catastrophe struck.

Captain Sigsbee sat in his port cabin finishing a letter to his wife shortly after taps had sounded when he recalled "a bursting, rending, and crashing sound or roar of immense volume . . . followed by a succession of heavy, ominous, metallic sounds" and a "trembling and lurching motion of the vessel, a list to port, and a movement of subsidence."[4] Lieutenant John J. Blandon, standing watch on the quarterdeck, recalled a dull, sullen roar followed by a sharp explosion that seemed to emanate from the port side forward. A shower of "missiles of all descriptions, from huge pieces of cement to blocks of wood, steel railings, fragments of gratings and all the debris that would be detachable in an explosion" rained down, with a chunk of cement striking him in the head and causing him to fall.[5] Within minutes, the quarterdeck was awash with water. Lieutenant George Blow was below decks in his cabin when the *Maine* blew up. He rushed toward the nearest ladder but found the door blocked. "In pitch darkness, with explosion following explosion, and expecting each second to be blown into the air, or drowned by the inrushing water, I found the other door and reached the ladder," wearing only trousers and undershirt.[6]

Captain Frederick Teasdale, master of the British bark *Deva,* made fast to the wharf at Regla some 700 yards from the *Maine,* testified that he had been in his cabin when he heard a tremendous explosion. He "rushed on deck, and was on deck just in time to see the whole debris going up in the air. The stuff ascended, I should say, 150 or 160 feet up in the air." One of the passengers aboard the *City of Washington,* a steamship moored in the harbor, was about to sit in a deck chair and enjoy the night air when he "heard a shot, the noise of a shot. I looked around and saw the bow of the *Maine* rise a little, go a little out of the water. It couldn't have been more than a few seconds after that noise, that shot, than there came in the center of the ship a terrible mass of fire and explosion, and everything went over our heads, a black mass. We could not tell what it was. It was all black. Then we heard the noise of falling material. . . . After we saw that mast go up, the whole boat [*Maine*] lifted out, I should judge, about two feet. As she lifted out, the bow went right down. . . . We stood spellbound."[7]

In the first minutes after the explosion, surviving officers and crew tried to grasp what had happened. Sigsbee initially thought the ship might be under attack, and ordered sentries to be posted. He and others made their way toward the stern of the ship and began to organize damage-control efforts. The ship was listing heavily and fires had broken out amidships. Spare ammunition in the pilot house began to cook off. Sigsbee ordered the forward magazines to be flooded, only to receive a report that the entire front of the ship was already under water. The executive officer, a lieutenant, and a cadet moved forward to assess the situation. Sigsbee and others noticed dozens of white shapes bobbing in the water, and as their eyes adjusted to the dark, realized that dead and wounded men had been thrown into the water by the force of the explosion. The ship's lifeboats were lowered immediately, but of the fifteen boats onboard, only three—the barge, the captain's gig, and a whale boat—remained intact. These were put into the water, tasked with rescuing those trapped forward of the fires or floating in the water. Father John Patrick Chidwick, the ship's chaplain, described the scene:

The forward part of the ship was ablaze by now and up from the waters and from the ship came the heart-rending cries of our men, "Help me! Save me!" From the quarterdeck, I gave them absolution and, climbing to the poop deck, I saw and heard the Captain who was moving up and down, shouting his orders above the terrible din. I called on the men to mention the name of Jesus, and again and again I repeated the absolution. . . . I only hope that our men heard it.[8]

The nearby Spanish cruiser *Alfonso XII* and the American merchant steamer *City of Washington* dispatched their lifeboats to help rescue survivors. Onboard the *Maine*, Captain Sigsbee began to realize that saving his ship was beyond hope: water was fast rising, pumps were submerged, the fire main destroyed, and "air could be heard whistling through the doors and hatches," indicating that the *Maine*'s watertight compartments were failing under the pressure of inrushing water.[9] The effort shifted from damage control to rescuing survivors. After receiving assurances that all the wounded who could be found had been transferred to the *Alfonso XII*, the *City of Washington*, or shore, the survivors remaining onboard stepped into lifeboats and shoved off. Captain Sigsbee was the last to depart. He proceeded to the *City of Washington*, and after checking that his wounded sailors were being cared for, sent the following telegram to the commander-in-chief at Key West in the early-morning hours of February 16.

> Commander in Chief, *Key West*:
> *Maine* blown up in Habana harbor at 9.40 last night and destroyed. Many wounded and doubtless more killed or drowned. Wounded and others on board Spanish man-of-war and Ward Line steamers. Send lighthouse tender from Key West for crew and the few pieces of equipment above water. None has clothing other than that upon him. Public opinion should be suspended until further report. All officers believed to be saved; Jenkins and Merritt not yet accounted for. Many Spanish officers, including representatives of General Blanco, now with me to express sympathy.
> SIGSBEE[10]

As muster rolls and the coming of morning light slowly made clear, the casualties aboard the *Maine* were even worse than Sigsbee had initially anticipated. The *Maine*'s designers had followed existing convention, and situated the crew berthing in the forward section of the ship and the officer cabins aft. The explosion that sank the *Maine* devastated the front end of the ship, shearing the bow from the rest of the ship but for the keel and a portion of the starboard bottom plating. Most of the crew not on watch had been in their berthing. The explosion pancaked the crew's quarters, with only boatswain's mate Charles Bergman and coal-passer Jeremiah Sheah somehow surviving. Of the *Maine*'s 328 enlisted crew, 250 died at the scene, 8 died later from wounds, and 54 were injured. Only 16 enlisted men emerged physically unscathed. The officers' contingent, housed in the aft section of the ship, was more fortunate. Two of the twenty-two officers onboard at the time of the explosion (Jenkins and Merritt) died at the scene. Many of the injured suffered horribly from burn wounds, impact lacerations, and the like. Over the course of the next day, these survivors were transported from the *City of Washington* and *Alfonso XII* to two hospitals in Havana, where the Spanish staff, in the words of Sigsbee, "was most considerate and humane. They did all they habitually did for their own people, and even more."[11]

The destruction of the USS *Maine* transformed what might have been a routine demonstration of naval diplomacy into an international crisis of the first order. Secretary of the Navy John Long noted in his journal that he had received

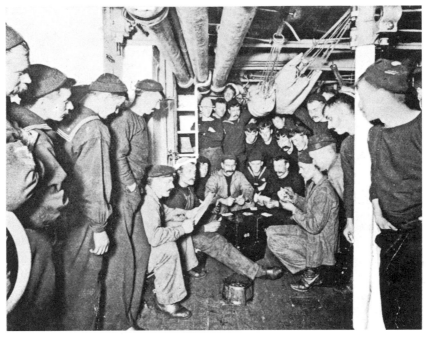

The *Maine*'s enlisted men playing cards and reading during off-duty hours, sometime between 1895 and 1898. The explosion flattened the enlisted berthing space, instantly killing 250 of the ship's 328 enlisted sailors.
Naval History and Heritage Command, Photo Archives, Photograph NH 46729

news of the event at half past one in the morning, commenting that "This is a most frightful disaster, both in itself, and with reference to the present critical condition of our relations with Spain."[12] He immediately sent Commander Francis W. Dickens to the White House to inform President William McKinley. Dickens later recalled, "The President came out in his dressing gown. I handed him the dispatch which he read with great gravity. He seemed to be very deeply impressed with the news, handed back the dispatch to me, and took it again, two or three times, expressing great regret that the event had happened, particularly at that time."[13] McKinley understood that with the coming of dawn, the American public and Congress would be in an uproar over the sinking of the *Maine*. He was not mistaken. By 2:10 A.M., copy editors at Joseph Pulitzer's *New York World* had received word from their correspondent in Cuba that the *Maine* had been destroyed. The paper broke the story that morning. Not to be outdone, William Randolph Hearst instructed his editors that "There is not any other big news. Please spread the story all over the [front] page. This means war."[14] Less than twenty-four hours after the USS *Maine* was sunk, the *Evening Journal* trumpeted in oversize block letters:

CRISIS AT HAND
Cabinet in Session; Growing Belief In

SPANISH TREACHERY

From the start, two questions dominated the deliberations about how to react to the sinking of the USS *Maine*. What caused the explosion, and who was to blame? Secretary Long confided in his journal the day after the disaster that "There is intense difference of opinion as to the cause of the blowing up of the *Maine*. . . . My own judgment is, so far as any information has been received, that it was the result of an accident."[15] His assistant, Theodore Roosevelt, wrote confidentially to a Harvard classmate that same day that he believed "The *Maine* was sunk by an act of dirty treachery on the part of the Spaniards; though we shall never find out definitely, and officially it will go down as an accident."[16] The Navy quickly organized an official Naval Court of Inquiry; but even before the appointment letter to its board members had been issued, the yellow press began to make inflammatory assertions concerning both the cause of and culpability for the explosion. On February 17, the banner headlines of the *Journal* proclaimed in large bold capitals that DESTRUCTION OF THE WAR SHIP *MAINE* WAS THE WORK OF AN ENEMY. In a smaller font, the paper asserted that "Naval officers unanimous that the ship was destroyed on purpose," with an illustration showing how a Spanish mine had destroyed the ship.

The appointment letter to the Naval Court of Inquiry directed its members to inquire into all circumstances attending the *Maine*'s loss; report whether its loss was in any respects due to fault or negligence on the part of any officers or members of the crew; report on the cause or causes of the explosion; and record any information as to persons not connected with the U.S. Navy who, in its opinion, were responsible for the explosion and loss of the ship. The court convened on February 21, 1898, devoting twenty-three days to interviews, analysis, and deliberation. On March 19, four members of the board provided McKinley a confidential briefing of the court's forthcoming report, though there is good reason to believe that McKinley had a general sense of the direction of the court's investigation well before this.[17] Throughout this period, newspaper reporters made every effort to finagle insights into the proceedings, but the members of the naval court maintained a stern silence. The court formally adjourned on March 21, forwarding its findings and associated interviews up the chain of command. The White House received the final formal report on Thursday evening, March 24. The cabinet and top military advisers digested its findings the next day, and the president transmitted the full report to Congress on Monday morning. Much to the administration's chagrin, a synopsis of the report was leaked to the press shortly before the president's official transmission; readers of Monday's early paper were cognizant of the court's findings hours before Congress received the full report.[18] The Naval Court of Inquiry concluded that, while no evidence was obtainable as to what person or persons were responsible for the *Maine*'s destruction, the *Maine* had been sunk by the detonation of a submarine mine that caused the partial explosion of two or more of her forward magazines.

Much of the literature on the sinking of the USS *Maine* has focused on the three official inquiries into the cause of the dramatic explosion that ripped the ship apart and killed more naval personnel than would the subsequent Spanish-American War. Twelve years after the initial Naval Board of Inquiry (dubbed the Sampson Board, after its senior member) issued its findings, the *Maine* was raised out of the muck of Havana's harbor by means of a cofferdam, and a second Naval Court of Inquiry, the Vreeland Board, was convened. The Vreeland Board was able to draw on a much more extensive examination of the physical evidence, in that the water surrounding the *Maine* had been pumped out of the cofferdam and investigators could examine, measure, and photograph the wreck in detail. The Vreeland investigation concluded that the earlier board had erred in regard to the location of the initial external triggering detonation, but reiterated that some sort of external detonation had most likely caused the larger, catastrophic internal explosion of the forward magazines which sank the ship.[19]

Some sixty years later, Admiral Hyman Rickover, USN, commissioned a third analysis. The Rickover report contradicted earlier inquiries, asserted that a fire in the *Maine*'s forward coal bunkers had triggered the magazine explosion, and claimed that "there is no evidence that a mine destroyed the *Maine*."[20] The Rickover report has become the standard interpretation of the event, yet the matter remains contested. On the centenary of the *Maine*'s destruction, *National Geographic* commissioned a fourth technical analysis of the matter by the respected engineering firm Advanced Marine Enterprise. It drew upon computer models not available in the 1970s, and asserted that "it appears more probable than was previously concluded that a mine caused the . . . detonation of the magazines."[21] The Naval History and Heritage Command reflects the prevalent view that while a "definitive explanation for the destruction of the *Maine* remains elusive," evidence of a mine remains "thin and . . . based primarily on conjecture."[22]

Although the findings of the initial Naval Court of Inquiry have faced a great deal of scrutiny ever since they were released, there is no evidence that administration officials sought to influence the court during its investigation or to steer it toward any particular conclusion. Rickover suggested that the board should have called upon more technical experts, and suggested that a number of these had reservations about its conclusions.[23] Yet most Americans held that the inquiry was thorough, meticulous, and fair in contrast to their dismissive perception of the simultaneous Spanish inquiry as perfunctory and "false."[24] Few believed that the board had entered its deliberations with foregone conclusions, and a good many influential figures anticipated that the board would determine that an accident had caused the *Maine*'s destruction.[25] The board's findings pulled the rug out from under the feet of this group, and accelerated the deterioration of relations between Spain and the United States.

Following the release of the Naval Court of Inquiry's findings, interactions between the United States, Spain, and the Cuban rebels moved along a trajectory that culminated in the military intervention of the United States in the Cuban War of Independence. Before examining whether and how the *Maine*'s destruction contributed to U.S. intervention, one needs to step back and ask why the *Maine* was sent to Havana in the first place. Was the *Maine* an instrument of coercive diplomacy, and if so, why did the McKinley administration employ such an instrument when the previous administration had deliberately suspended naval port calls in order to avoid some sort of incident? What was the United States' interest in Cuba before the sinking of the *Maine*, and what purpose did the dispatch of the vessel to Havana seek to promote?

CONTEXT

THE CUBAN INSURRECTION, AMERICAN PERCEPTIONS, AND THE CLEVELAND ADMINISTRATION'S POLICY

Americans had long been interested in Cuba; influential figures ranging from Thomas Jefferson to James Buchanan had daydreamed about incorporating the island into the United States during the pre–Civil War period. On two occasions these flights of fantasy matured into serious diplomatic overtures to Spain about purchasing the island, but on both occasions Spanish officials indignantly rejected these offers.[26] Spaniards dubbed Cuba the "ever faithful isle" because it had not broken away during the Wars of Liberation that reduced Spanish holdings in the Western Hemisphere to Cuba and Puerto Rico, but the epithet rang hollow by the 1890s. Cubans had staged a ten-year-long rebellion against Spanish rule from 1868 to 1878, and the outbreak of renewed rebellion in the island in 1895 initially excited little public interest in the United States.[27]

Five factors acted in combination to transform the Cuban question from a niche concern for most Americans to one that generated heated discussions even in the barbershops and front parlors of Main Street Peoria. The first was the success of the rebel forces. During the Ten Years' War, Spanish forces had largely contained rebel forces to Cuba's mountainous far eastern provinces of Santiago de Cuba and Puerto Principe, leaving the wealthy sugar plantations of Matanzas and Havana and the tobacco plantations on the western end of Cuba in Pinar del Río barely affected by the uprising. Few American interests were endangered, and during an era when Reconstruction efforts were fading in the United States, the high proportion of Afro-Cubans in rebel ranks soured interventionist sentiment among that segment of the American public that had been most keen to acquire Cuba during the 1840s and 1850s—southern white plantation owners. Following the February 1895 *grito de Baíre* ("cry of Baíre"), which marked a renewed effort to expel Spain and gain Cuban independence, rebel forces successfully invaded central and western Cuba. Máximo Gómez, the rebels' military commander-in-chief, adopted a strategy of targeting the Cuban economy so as to bring the economy to a halt. He directed that all plantations were to be totally destroyed, and that those who continued to work in sugar factories be treated as traitors.[28] This time the governing Spanish-born *peninsulares*—rich Creole planters—and foreign investors were to feel the weight of war; and while rebel forces were incapable of defeating Spanish forces in conventional battle, they adopted the classic guerrilla strategy of wearing down superior forces with constant hit-and-run attacks.[29] By January 1896, rebel forces operated throughout Cuba, and the island's sugar and tobacco industries had been seriously damaged. The frustrations of the Spanish forces battling the rebels are evident in the description that one Spanish military officer offered of the *mambises* (Cuban guerrillas):

> They ride incessantly here and there, and when their horses are tired, they seize any they come across. They frequently rest during the day, and march at night, in as light order as possible, carry only a hammock, a piece of oilcloth, cartridges, machete and rifle. They live by marauding. The country people feed them and help them so far as they can, and where these insurgents don't find sympathy, the machete, the torch, and the rope are good arguments. . . . They always run after firing, and if pursued, they leave a small body charged with firing on their pursuers, while the main body advances rapidly and then stops, and by circling around, get to the rear of our troops and harass them. . . . Such are the insurgents of Cuba, and their ways of fighting.[30]

In addition to fighting better than they had in previous rebellions, the Cuban rebels were much better organized politically. Much of the credit for this should be given to José Martí, poet, revolutionary thinker, and political strategist. For much of the decade before the *grito de Baíre* sounded in the military phase of Cuba's War of Independence, Martí visited Cuban exile communities throughout the United States, Central America, and the West Indies. He and other exiles established dozens of local revolutionary committees and raised funds in support of a free Cuba. At the grassroots level, he organized Cuban tobacco factory workers in Key West, Tampa, and elsewhere on the Gulf Coast, combining organizational efforts in support of strikers with appeals for small donations to sustain the cause. At the institutional level, Martí organized a political party, the *Partido revolucionario cubano* (Cuban Revolutionary Party) to plan, coordinate, and mobilize support for an independent Cuba.[31] Headquartered in New York and with offices in Philadelphia and elsewhere, the party council arranged public meetings, published a newspaper, and engaged in what we now call "information operations" to solicit support for *Cuba Libre*.

Capitalizing on the initial success of the military offensive in Cuba, revolutionary Cubans drafted a constitution and established a government. Tomás Estrada Palma, head of the New York junta of the *Partido revolucionario cubano*, was designated Delegate Plenipotentiary and Foreign Representative of the Cuban Republic. He and other representatives of the Cuban Republic, unrecognized by the U.S. government and still often referred to as members of the Cuban junta by the U.S. press, continued the work of the *Partido Revolucionario Cubano*. They raised funds and outfitted more than seventy filibustering expeditions to Cuba, staged Cuban-American fairs, organized "Sympathy Meetings" throughout the country, and sponsored hundreds of lectures, speeches, and educational events. They contacted non-Cuban U.S. citizens, and encouraged the formation of a Cuban League composed of Americans sympathetic to the Cuban cause. Not content with such grassroots activism, the junta established a legation in Washington, D.C., to convince influential Washington figures to support the cause of Cuban independence. In addition, the legation in Washington and the headquarters in New York directly engaged the U.S. press, providing news from Cuba at no cost to American newspapers. New York's reporters could drop by the junta's headquarters to receive the latest "news" from Cuba, with the Cuban Legation in Washington providing the same services to the D.C. press corps, congressional staffers, and any others desiring information about events in Cuba.[32] Spanish censorship and clumsy efforts to control the news percolating out of Cuba only played into the hands of the junta and its supporters in the United States.

Careful political organization, a sophisticated information campaign, and military success in the field resulted in a sustained interest about developments in Cuba on the part of the American press. While the argument that the "yellow press" drove McKinley to war has fallen out of favor, even those who point out that the rabid, sensationalist, and interventionist tone of Joseph Pulitzer's *New York World* and William Randolph Hearst's *New York Journal* was not representative of papers in the American heartland acknowledge that press coverage of the Cuban Revolution was extensive in the three-year period before American intervention.[33] Though we lack the sort of sophisticated public polling data to quantify American public opinion during this era, almost all the memoirs and journals from the time convey a sense that the American public had become enthralled by developments in Cuba. One might link this interest with the frontier's closure, the search for a new national purpose, or the need for new export markets, but a more persuasive argument is that the public was interpreting the Cuban Revolution through an American lens. The Cuban junta's efforts to convey a narrative of freedom-loving Cubans struggling against corrupt and oppressive European control resonated with a wide spectrum of the American public. While mainstream papers of the heartland were more circumspect about direct American intervention, opinion ran overwhelmingly in favor of the Cuban insurgents and against the Spanish military effort. This third factor—the pro-Cuban tilt of both the yellow and the mainstream press—was accentuated by the methods that Spain employed to fight the Cuban Revolutionaries.

Spanish authorities found that containing and defeating the Cuban rebels was more difficult than anticipated following the outbreak of renewed armed rebellion in February 1895. Spain sent one of its most esteemed generals, Arsenío Martínez de Campos, to the island in April and increased the number of Spanish troops posted to the island from 30,000 to 150,000 by March 1896.[34] General Campos had combined military force with negotiation to end the earlier Cuban revolution of 1868–1878, and the Spanish government hoped the aged general might repeat the feat. Yet Campos was utterly unsuccessful in suppressing the effort, and by December rebel forces had broken out from eastern Cuba and were torching plantations and farms on the outskirts of Havana itself. Campos wrote privately to the Spanish prime minister in July that the insurgency was impossible to defeat using conventional methods; Spain would have to resort to harsher methods, such as forcibly relocating civilians, seizing hostages, and shooting captives if it hoped to crush a rebellion reflecting widespread antipathy to Spanish rule. Campos indicated that he was unwilling to resort to these methods, warning that they would cause "horrible misery and hunger" that Spain would be powerless to relieve.

In January 1896, Campos stepped down under pressure from *peninsulares* in Cuba who were frustrated by his inability to protect the rich plantations that were the mainstay of the economy. American newspapers had covered the uprising in Cuba over the past year, exposing Spanish fecklessness and inefficiency.[35] Following the appointment of Valeriano Weyler in February 1896, a new theme became dominant: that of Spanish brutality.

Spanish brutality and Cuban suffering became an intertwined fourth dimension that raised the issue of Cuba from one that interested only a small segment of the U.S. population—chiefly Cuban Americans, those with investments in the island, and expansionists eager to raise America's profile in global affairs—to one that attracted a much wider spectrum of the public. Shortly after arriving in Cuba, General Weyler issued the first of several "reconcentration" orders meant to deprive Cuban insurgents of one of their key strengths—the support they received from the rural population in the form of food, livestock, and information. He ordered that all people in designated zones were to relocate to protected zones adjacent to garrisoned towns and cities, thereby abandoning farms, livestock, and homes. They had eight days to do so. Local authorities were to provide shelter and protect "cultivation zones" set aside for these refugees to sustain themselves.[36]

Initially limited to the eastern provinces of Santiago, Puerto Principe, and the adjacent district of Sancti Spíritus in Santa Clara, the order was gradually expanded to embrace Pinar del Río, Havana, Matanzas, and the rest of Santa Clara. While Weyler's order may have made sense from an amoral operational perspective, as the British and Americans resorted to similar schemes in South Africa, the Philippines, Malaya, and Vietnam, it generated a humanitarian and public relations disaster. Rural families were driven from their holdings by pro-government militias and forcibly marched to designated urban centers protected by Spanish garrisons. When they arrived, they found that local authorities were incapable of housing and feeding the rural influx, often providing refugees with only the most primitive shelter, such as warehouses and sheds lacking basic sanitation facilities. Food soon became scarce, and ragged women and children begged in the streets of every city. Disease decimated the weakened *reconcentrados*. Reports poured into the United States from private individuals and U.S. consular officers about the appalling conditions in Cuba, and the American press labeled the Spanish governor general "Butcher Weyler."

A growing sense of outrage about what was taking place in Cuba spread throughout the United States. The yellow press, the Cuban junta, and American jingoes seized upon the crisis for their own purposes. Accounts of Cuban suffering and Spanish frightfulness confronted the public daily. The *New York World* stirred the passions of its readers with an article lead (May 17, 1896) that bellowed "Blood on the roadside, blood in the fields, blood on the doorsteps, blood, blood, blood. The old, the young, the weak, the crippled, all are butchered without mercy."[37] While a number of correspondents noted that Cuban insurgents had provoked countermeasures by burning plantations, executing government sympathizers, and extracting supplies from the rural population, the *World*'s character ization of the Spanish policy as "murder by starvation" and "the extermination of a people" (May 9, 1897) was not that far off.[38] A recent study relying on Spanish archival records concludes that fully half the *reconcentrados* in Pinar del Río perished, with the estimated number of civilian casualties in Cuba numbering some 170,000 out of a prewar population of some 1.7 million. While that figure was not the 300,000 dead reported by Consul Fitzhugh Lee to Washington, it was enormous.[39] Former congressman William Calhoun undertook a fact-finding mission for the incoming McKinley administration in June 1897, and his words convey a sense of the devastation. He described the general conditions in the countryside:

> I travelled by rail from Havana to Matanzas. The countryside outside the military posts was practically depopulated. Every house had been burned, banana trees cut down, cane fields swept by fire, and everything in the shape of food destroyed. I did not see a house, man, woman or child, a

horse, mule, or cow, nor even a dog. . . . The countryside was wrapped in the stillness of death and the silence of desolation.[40]

As for the unfortunate *reconcentrados*, their condition made his "heart bleed for the poor creatures. . . . We saw children with swollen limbs and extended abdomens, that had a dropsical appearance; this, I was told, was caused by want of food."

The interaction between insurgent and counterinsurgent strategies—the former designed to bring the Cuban economy to a standstill by torching plantations, sugarcane factories, and other sources of wealth while the latter sought to deprive the insurgency of its popular support by concentrating the rural population in towns and cities under Spanish control—proved catastrophic to Cuba's civilian population. Both rebels and government forces blurred the lines between combatant and noncombatant, and while the Cleveland administration made a point of apportioning blame to both sides, the American public became increasingly hostile to the Spanish war effort in Cuba. The Cuban junta, the Cuban League, and the Hearst and Pulitzer papers urged that the United States at a minimum recognize that a state of belligerency existed in Cuba, thereby conferring on Cuban rebels the same rights and responsibilities as those accorded to the Spanish government. More broadly, the sense that something must be done began to spread across the United States as it became apparent that neither side in Cuba could force the other to concede.[41]

The Cuban Revolution broke out during Grover Cleveland's second term in office. Cleveland was a conservative, pro-business "Bourbon" Democrat, opposed to high tariffs, Free Silver, and imperialism. He and his secretary of state, Richard Olney, did not allow themselves to be swept along by popular opinion favoring the Cuban insurgents. When Tomás Estrada Palma, the junta's plenipotentiary, secured a meeting with Olney, he received the stern admonishment that the insurgent strategy of attacking Cuba's economy should be known for what it was, arson.[42] The administration had little desire to be dragged into foreign entanglements, and as a whole it favored the status quo in Cuba. Having just concluded a contest of will with Great Britain over Venezuela and concerned that Wilhelmine Germany's imperial ambitions might veer toward adventurism in the Caribbean, the Cleveland administration saw little benefit to replacing long-established Spanish rule over Cuba with the uncertainties of a potentially unstable, independent Cuba.[43]

Despite the Cleveland administration's reluctance to become entangled in the Spanish-Cuban war, the emerging public sentiment that something must be done politicized "the Cuba question." Members of the House and Senate felt compelled to take up the issue. The Senate Foreign Relations Committee led the way in January 1896, with the majority of the committee resolving that since a state of war existed in Cuba, the United States should accord both sides the rights of belligerents while maintaining "strict neutrality"; a minority of the committee pushed to go further, resolving that the president should offer Spain the friendly offices of the United States for the purpose of recognizing Cuban independence. Over the subsequent weeks, as senators debated the two versions of the resolution, submitted amendments, and eventually approved a bipartisan resolution which was passed to the House, the contours separating Senate from House and Congress from the Executive became clear. Congress as a whole wanted to move more vigorously than the administration, with the Senate content to merely bestow equal belligerent rights to both parties while the House pushed for recognition of Cuban independence. The Cleveland administration wished to do neither.

Political pressure on the administration continued through the last year of the Cleveland presidency, exacerbated by two persistent sources of tension. The first concerned the fate of Americans in Cuba who had run afoul of Spanish authorities. By the late nineteenth century, a number of Cubans had become naturalized Americans, with many maintaining homes, businesses, and associations on both sides of the Florida straits. As Spanish authorities cracked down on dissent and revolutionary activity, more than eighty Americans were arrested in the two years following the outbreak of the Cuban Revolution.[44] The American consul in Havana and the State Department found that they were constantly drawn into investigations and appeals related to the fate of arrested Cuban Americans.[45] The American press portrayed these arrests, detentions, and court cases as assaults on the dignity of the United States, with sensationalist papers prone to ignoring all evidence of guilt or complicity. Press reports of Spanish mistreatment of incarcerated Americans—in particular the death of a Cuban-American dentist, Ricardo Ruiz—stoked anti-Spanish sentiment. President Cleveland attempted to explain to Congress and the American public that many of the arrested Americans were "Cubans at heart and in all their feelings and interests" and conceded that in a number of cases, these naturalized Americans might have crossed the boundary between sympathizing with and actively participating in the rebellion.[46] Nevertheless, his administration was duty bound to protect American citizens in Cuba, and the occasionally haughty or perfunctory cooperation of Spanish officials was irksome.

A related matter, that of filibustering—organizing private military expeditions from the United States—likewise threatened to poison Spanish-American relations. The Cuban junta and American sympathizers relentlessly sought to aid the rebellion by smuggling men, arms, and equipment to the island. Spanish officials, as so often is the case when fighting insurgencies, preferred to blame the ongoing rebellion in Cuba on outside agitators and the influx of weapons to the island rather than confront the internal sources of Cuban discontent. They had some cause for disgruntlement: the United States was the point of origin for more than seventy filibustering expeditions during the period 1895–98, with thirty-one U.S.–based vessels more or less continuously engaged in ferrying arms, money, and volunteers to the insurgents.[47] The United States responded to Spanish protests by noting that it was doing what it could; the Cleveland administration invested considerable sums of money establishing new bases in Florida and along the Gulf Coast for the Treasury Department's Revenue Cutter Service, the forerunner of the U.S. Coast Guard. U.S. Revenue cutters and the U.S. Navy did far more to stop the flow of military supplies into Cuba than did their Spanish counterparts; the United States intercepted thirty-three filibustering expeditions, whereas the Spanish stopped only five.[48] The Cleveland administration's efforts to stymie private support of the Cuban Revolution were unpopular both in Congress and among the wider public. Furthermore, prosecuting filibusters proved a difficult and protracted endeavor. Early court rulings defined filibustering in such terms that prosecutors had to overcome an exceedingly high legal hurdle; convictions were infrequent, sentences short, and fines low. Later rulings made conviction more likely when infractions of U.S. neutrality laws were blatant, but expedients such as shipping men and weapons separately to rendezvous points outside U.S. territorial waters complicated prosecution. The judiciary gradually moved toward interpreting the law in a manner that might have deterred future infractions of U.S. neutrality laws, but the time lag between the apprehension of suspected filibusterers and their conviction was protracted. The owner of the ship *Laurada*, for example, was charged with filibustering for attempting to ship arms and men to Cuba in August 1896. He was found guilty, condemned to two years in prison, and fined five hundred dollars. He appealed, and by the time the final appeal was overruled, the Cleveland administration had departed the scene and the McKinley administration was on the verge of sending the USS *Maine* to Havana.[49]

Despite these mutual aggravations, the Cleveland administration sought to avoid conflict with Spain and adopted a cautious, nonprovocative policy. This is particularly clear if one looks at its responses to the persistent entreaties for some sort of naval intervention by the American consul general in Havana, Fitzhugh Lee. By the fall of 1895, the administration sensed that Spain was incapable of rapidly suppressing or containing the Cuban Revolution. President Cleveland and Secretary of State Olney had selected Lee for the position in April 1896, as it seemed that he possessed all the qualities they needed for their representative in Havana. Lee had risen to the rank of major general of the cavalry in the Confederate army, suggesting he had the military expertise to evaluate the state of hostilities; he had been governor of Virginia, suggesting he had executive experience and would be able to offer insights on the efficiency and effectiveness of the Spanish administration; and as a conservative Southern Democrat, it was assumed that he shared the administration's preference for stability over change in Cuba. While one can debate Lee's qualities on the first two counts, on the last he fell afoul of expectations, displaying a cavalry officer's preference for action over inaction and for intervention rather than mediation.

Two weeks after arriving in Cuba, Lee reported that the possibility of some sort of compromise between the Spanish government and the Cuban rebels was nonexistent; sensing victory, the rebels were uninterested in settling for autonomy in exchange for dropping their insistence for full independence. The Spanish, for their part, were in no mood to negotiate. Lee suggested that the United States offer to buy the island from the Spanish, later elaborating that the situation in Cuba was like "a huge volcano . . . which must in the near future produce an eruption." By mid-July, Lee was advocating that the United States should recognize Cuban independence even if it brought about a state of war with Spain, since such a war would be "short and decisive." He suggested that the administration should station an

Consul General Fitzhugh Lee repeatedly urged Presidents Cleveland and McKinley to exert pressure on the Spanish government by dispatching U.S. warships to Cuba.
Naval History and Heritage Command, Photo Archives, Photograph NH 48273

American warship with marines at Key West in the event that it became "necessary to protect the consulate and the lives of Americans from mob violence."[50]

Cleveland and Olney rejected Lee's recommendation that they position an American warship close to Cuba. Cleveland explained to his secretary of state in July 1896 that he "did not want now anything of that kind made a convenient excuse for trouble with Spain." The consul nevertheless revisited the concept of using U.S. naval forces to apply pressure on Spain in February 1897, recommending that the United States "demand the release of all American prisoners suffering and lingering in the prisons and jails" of Spanish Cuba. Should the United States' demand be rejected, Lee asserted that the country had an obligation to take action, inquiring "How many war vessels Key West or within reach, and will they be ordered here at once if necessary to sustain demand?" Lee's concept reflected ideas that he had shared privately with Postmaster General William Wilson while on leave the previous December, when he had grumbled that all one needed to do to end Spanish barbarities in Cuba was to blockade Cuban ports and cut the cable to Madrid. Yet his willingness to employ "naval diplomacy" in support of his efforts to secure the release of Americans in Cuba did not resonate with the secretary of state, who again sought to deflect him from provocation, carefully inquiring whether the Americans in question were naturalized Cubans and asking for details about the circumstances of their arrest and detention. Lee chafed at the Cleveland administration's caution. His reply to Olney verged on daring the secretary of state to recall him: "If action [the dispatch of U.S. warships] not indorsed, remedy in your hands and you should not hesitate to employ it."[51] Olney ignored both the request to send warships and Lee's bluster. The Spanish release of the arrested American who had prompted Lee's latest call for gunboat diplomacy calmed matters as the Cleveland administration entered its final weeks in office.

By this point, Cleveland and Olney had lost confidence in their "man in Havana." Lee clearly favored a more vigorous policy than they believed was appropriate, and he seemed enamored with gunboat diplomacy. His impatience with Spanish mistreatment of U.S. citizens, his revulsion over the human costs of war in Cuba, and his willingness to combine diplomacy with implied threats were not out of line with mainstream U.S. opinion. Yet Cleveland and Olney preferred a less aggressive diplomatic stance, and the Spanish—for reasons that had nothing to do with U.S. entreaties—began to publicly embrace the idea of instituting reforms in Cuba.[52] While Cuba took a back seat to the issue of free silver in the hotly contested election of 1896, the Republican Congress eagerly returned to the matter in December. Shortly before Christmas, the Senate Foreign Relations Committee agreed on a resolution acknowledging the independence of Cuba and advising the president to use America's friendly offices with Spain to bring the war to a close. The House was eager to approve the resolution, but supporters of the measure had the wind taken out of their sails when Secretary of State Olney coolly noted to the press that only the executive—the president— had the authority to recognize a state.[53]

The outgoing Cleveland administration refused to bow before congressional and public pressure to recognize Cuban independence, fully aware that such a step would be tantamount to declaring war with Spain. Charles H. Grosvenor of Ohio warned his colleagues in the House, "I think I see everywhere all along the line a disposition to provoke hostilities and to bring about a condition that will ruin us all." Cleveland recognized that American patience with the state of affairs in Cuba was running short. His last annual message to Congress cautioned Spain that, "It cannot be reasonably assumed that the hitherto expectant attitude of the United States will be indefinitely maintained." Elaborating, he counseled the Spanish government that it needed to end the contest in Cuba "either alone and in her own way, or with our friendly cooperation."[54]

William McKinley assumed the presidency with full knowledge that Congress would surely revisit the Cuban question in the near future if he failed to move toward a resolution of the issue. McKinley had not made Cuba a significant component of his 1896 bid for the presidency, and at the start of his campaign he put off questions about Cuba by blandly noting, "I most politely decline to go on record. At this time I do not care to speak about it."[55] His 1897 inaugural address discussed the economy, bimetallism, tariffs, and civil service reform but made no mention of Cuba, instead reminding listeners that in general "War should never be entered upon until every agency of peace has failed; peace is preferable to war in almost every contingency."[56]

Many analyses of the Spanish-American War conflate the causes and outcome of the war. They overemphasize the significance of ideological, cultural, and economic factors, and downplay the role that miscalculation, policy failure, and chance play.[57] Proximate causes are glossed over in favor of alleged underlying or ultimate causes, with insufficient attention given to the question of whether these ultimate causes were necessary or sufficient in themselves, absent the confluence of discrete triggering events and policy decisions. Clearly navalism, a search for new markets, a sense of Anglo-Saxon superiority, anxiety about American masculinity, and expansionist reveries predated the Spanish-American War. All these factors help explain the prosecution and outcomes of the war. Yet as adequate and sufficient causes for American intervention in the ongoing Cuban-Spanish War, they fall short. Throughout 1897, Roosevelt, Lodge, and other jingoes fretted that President McKinley sought to avoid war, and feared that his policies might rob them of the chance to test the New Navy, acquire overseas holdings, and at least for Roosevelt, test his manhood. The business community and Wall Street, far from pushing the president toward war and empire, instead quietly backed McKinley's hope that the Cuba question might be settled through conflict resolution and mediation.[58] Diplomatic historian Ernest May once remarked that McKinley "led his country unwillingly toward a war that he did not want for a cause in which he did not believe." His conclusion, though challenged in the interim, remains sound.[59] John Offner's recent impressive analysis of primary records expands upon the May thesis, and rebuts revisionist narratives that suggest the war was inevitable and resulted from awakening imperial ambitions in the United States. Offner concludes that none of the belligerents wanted an American intervention in Cuba.[60] That intervention nonetheless took place stems more from the choices, decisions, and the forces at play during the fall and winter of 1897–98 than from long-term underlying U.S. naval, market, or imperial ambitions.

McKinley sought to steer a middle course on Cuba, placating the jingoes within his own party by appearing to be more proactive on Cuba than the Cleveland administration had been while simultaneously derailing efforts in Congress that would offend Spanish sensibilities. He secured the release of American citizens detained or arrested in Cuba without initially resorting to "naval diplomacy"; he sidetracked or ignored repeated congressional resolutions granting the Cuban Republic belligerent rights; and he sent a note to the Spanish government calling for a revocation of Spain's reconcentration orders in Cuba. He dispatched a new minister to Spain, Steward Woodford, instructing him to do all he could to obtain a peaceful resolution to Spanish-American differences while reiterating in much sharper tones to the Spanish government that America would "take such steps as its Government should deem necessary" if no progress was made on the Cuba question.[61] Though there is no indication that McKinley wanted war, a careful look at his diplomacy shows that he was willing to back diplomatic demands with veiled threats, and had not ruled out the resort to force should declaratory pressure be insufficient.

McKinley's willingness to back diplomatic negotiations with subtle and implied threats of force suggests that May's thesis requires some refinement. While McKinley may not have wanted war, he diverged from the Cleveland administration's policy by adding coercive ingredients to his diplomacy. The language and terminology of modern coercion theory provides a useful tool for assessing McKinley's diplomacy.[62] Coercion theorists blur the boundaries between peacetime diplomacy and war, subsuming both the threat and use of force under the overall mantle of coercion.[63] Yet a distinction should be made between employing threats to convince an opponent to do something (or cease doing something), and actually employing force to do so. The latter should be recognized for what it is, war. McKinley did not want war, and he hoped that the mere threat of war would suffice to accomplish his objective. The concept of "coercive diplomacy" comes close to capturing McKinley's willingness to employ subtle, understated, but implied threats of force.[64] McKinley sought both to deter and to compel Spain. He sent protests demanding that Spanish authorities release Americans detained in Cuban prisons, and he insisted that they do more to alleviate the situation of the unfortunate *reconcentrados* dying in Cuba. He appealed to Congress for money to aid Americans in Cuba, and subsequently persuaded Spain to open Cuban ports to the delivery of food and medicines to desperate *reconcentrados* as well. Most directly, in September 1897 he directed his minister to Spain, Stewart Woodford, to inquire—"in the most courteous form and with most friendly purpose"—whether the time had not arrived for Spain to put an end to the war in Cuba. Spain was advised to find some arrangement of settlement "honorable to herself and just to her Cuban colony and to mankind," with the United States offering its good offices should they be useful. To ensure that Spain understood that protracted warfare was not an acceptable course of action, Woodford warned that "Spain's inability [to restore peace on its terms] entails upon the United States a degree of injury and suffering which can no longer be ignored."[65] The diplomatic clock was ticking, though courtesy dictated against setting a time limit or specifying the consequences for Spain should it ignore the president's offer, advice, and warning.

McKinley's more assertive tone appeared to bear fruit. By December 1897, the last Americans incarcerated or facing charges had been released or expelled from Cuba. Disputes related to filibustering had been largely resolved, and Spain apologized for incidents at sea where Spanish vessels had mistakenly intercepted or fired upon U.S. merchant ships. Most strikingly, Spain revoked its *reconcentrado* edicts, repudiated Weyler's counterinsurgency strategy, and recalled the general to Spain. These Spanish concessions had more to do with internal Spanish politics (the conservative prime minister Antonio Cánovas del Castillo was assassinated by an Italian anarchist in August, with Práxedes Mateo Sagasta of Spain's Liberal Party taking charge in October) than with external pressure, but McKinley believed that his tougher—though "most courteous and friendly"—diplomacy was bearing fruit.[66]

Nevertheless, McKinley's assertive diplomacy fell short in several essential areas if one considers the prerequisites for successful coercive diplomacy. While McKinley clearly desired that the new Spanish government should embark on a course of action that previous governments had spurned—that is, "make proposals of settlement honorable to herself and just to her Cuban colony and mankind"—he gave no indication of what such a settlement might entail. McKinley backed his demands with such veiled, opaque threats that the consequences of Spanish inaction were unclear. Using the diplomatic language of the era, McKinley informed the Spanish government that "should his [McKinley's] present effort be fruitless his duty to his countrymen will necessitate an early decision as to the course of action which the time and the transcendent emergency may demand."[67] What the Spanish were to make of this is unclear. Successful coercive diplomacy springs from clear objectives, a sense of urgency, strong leadership, domestic support, and clarity concerning the precise terms of settlement.[68] McKinley's diplomacy—persuasive with a whiff of compellence—lacked both clarity and precision.

A subtle shift from purely persuasive diplomacy to gentle coercion can be detected in the McKinley administration's embrace of naval diplomacy. McKinley's secretary of the navy, John Long, recorded in his private journal that in the first meetings of the new administration, "consideration was given to the suggestion to dispatch a man-of-war to Havana." The administration deferred the matter, preferring not to "arouse the suspicion that the United States was applying pressure" on Spain.[69] This was in line with the preceding Cleveland administration's policy, as was Washington's negative response to Consul General Lee's request to send an American warship to Havana in June 1897.[70] Yet when Lee again raised the issue in late November, asking that at least two warships be sent to Key West so that he might call upon them should the situation in Havana deteriorate, the McKinley administration met him halfway by sending the USS *Maine* to Key West. While welcoming the new Spanish government's conciliatory gestures, Lee assessed that Spain's promise of autonomy no longer sufficed. He feared that Havana might be wracked by disturbances as many loyalists found compromise (autonomy) objectionable while those sympathetic to the Republic would no longer be satisfied with anything short of full independence. To make this point utterly clear, Cuban General Gomez threatened to shoot anyone in the ranks willing to settle for autonomy, executing an envoy sent by Weyler's successor to discuss conflict termination on the basis of Cuban self-government and autonomy.

The administration surely knew that Spanish agents would inform Madrid that the United States had sent a battleship to Key West. In addition, shortly before Congress broke for its winter recess, the administration announced that the North Atlantic Squadron would resume to its former practice of holding winter drills and squadron maneuvers off the Keys.[71] The administration assured the Spanish government that the measure was a return to normalcy, but coming on the heels of McKinley's annual message to Congress, in which he alluded to taking "further and other actions" should the Spanish government veer away from "the new order of things to which she stands irrevocably committed," the signal was clear.[72] Even as the administration downplayed press speculation that it was prepared to back its diplomatic protests with forceful action, the Navy Department was instructing the commander of the European Station to retain until further notice all sailors whose enlistment was expiring.[73]

The British diplomat Sir James Eric Sydney Cable captures the subtleties of naval coercive diplomacy better than anyone, and his work on gunboat diplomacy provides an additional set of concepts helpful to understanding McKinley's use of naval diplomacy in early 1898. Cable held that naval power could be used in four different ways to support diplomacy. It could be used as a definitive force that created or removed a fait accompli. It could be a purposeful force that aimed to change the policy or character of a target government. It could be used to buy breathing space or increase the range of options available to policymakers, a role he termed "catalytic force." Lastly, one could use naval power as expressive force meant to send a political message.[74]

McKinley's decision to send the *Maine* to Havana sought neither to create a fait accompli nor to change the policy of the new Spanish government. Instead, it sought to reinforce and render irrevocable the Liberal government's change of course. Much of McKinley's first annual message to Congress had been an overview of progress on the Cuba question. McKinley noted that Spain had recalled Weyler, that it had revoked its reconcentration orders, and that no Americans remained under arrest or in confinement in Cuba. McKinley urged Congress to give the Sagasta government the opportunity to demonstrate its commitment to negotiating a "righteous peace, just alike to the Cubans and to Spain, as well as equitable to our interests." While a careful assessment of divergent Cuban and Spanish aspirations might have revealed that neither side was willing to lower its own goals sufficiently to meet the other side's threshold criteria for settlement, McKinley's strong faith in the efficacy of arbitration led him to believe that a mutually acceptable settlement of Cuban-Spanish differences remained a possibility. McKinley stayed open to the possibility of a settlement whereby Spain retained some sort of sovereignty but ceded self-government to the Cubans—as long as such a scheme was acceptable to both sides.[75]

McKinley sought to avoid American intervention except as a last resort. He wanted a peaceful resolution to the conflict but reserved the right to use force should it be necessary. He sent the *Maine* to Havana to buy time (catalytic force) and to reinforce the political message (expressive force) that he had communicated to Congress: the war in Cuba must end. The ambiguities of this demand would come home to roost after the *Maine*'s destruction.

The reaction of Spanish officials in Washington, Madrid, and Cuba to McKinley's dispatch of the *Maine* makes it quite clear that they understood the subtext of the ship's friendly visit. The impetus for McKinley's foray into naval diplomacy was the outbreak of rioting in Havana on Wednesday, January 12, 1898. Three Havana papers had published articles critical of various Spanish officers associated with the departed General Weyler, with one charging that Cuban *Voluntarios* (pro-Spanish Cuban militia) had embezzled army funds for their own purposes. These allegations enraged Weyler's supporters and loyalists opposed to autonomy, with off-duty officers, soldiers, and militia members among the crowds that torched the offending newspapers' offices. Mob demonstrations escalated into widespread rioting throughout Havana, with crowds of pro- and anti-Weylerites assembling at points to jeer at one another. Consul General Lee feared the mobs might direct their wrath at the consulate and American businesses, though the shouts and slogans he heard were directed against Weyler's successor and the Liberal government in Spain rather than against the United States.

The *Maine* was already stationed at Key West in the event that Lee deemed it necessary to send for a U.S. warship to protect the consulate, American lives, and American property in Havana. Lee and Sigsbee were in daily communication, with the two devising a primitive code to circumvent Spanish eavesdropping at the telegram office. If the consul included the phrase "two dollars" in a telegram, Sigsbee was to prepare the *Maine* for departure within two hours. If Sigsbee read the phrase "vessels might be deployed elsewhere," he was to sail to Havana without further notice.[76] Lee, in short, had the independent authority to order the *Maine* to Havana should he need immediate assistance.

Lee's reaction to the riot on January 12 was to put the *Maine* on alert, and to ask Spanish authorities in Havana whether they required American assistance in restoring order.[77] The offer was declined, and after careful consideration, Lee judged it best not to send for the ship in the face of the Spanish response. He cabled Washington that the situation appeared under control, and advised that the sudden appearance of an American warship might aggravate the situation. He assessed that a growing number of Spanish officials were beginning to see advantages to accepting America's good offices as a mediator. Rather than push the matter, it might be best "to let matters progress in that direction rather than for the U.S. to insist upon being heard at once on this question. One method may bring trouble and perhaps some bloodshed. The other may reach the same results by peaceful paths."[78]

Lee's judgment was sound, but pressure was building in the United States for more action. The Havana riots were catnip to the American press, which exaggerated the extent of disorder in Havana. The *Journal* ran a banner "Next to War with Spain," while the *World* exclaimed "Riots in Havana mean REVOLUTION."[79] Secretary of the Navy Long lamented in his journal that "there is an utter recklessness with regard to the statements of facts or the ascertainment of truth. The wildest rumors are gathered from the outside, or concocted in a reporter's brain, and are printed, with headlines and pictures, as actual occurrences. The whole tendency is to sensationalism and the exploitation of the circulation of the newspaper."[80]

Congress again began to clamor for speedier action on Cuba. Democrats led the charge, pushing for immediate action while the president's Republican majority, which had previously cudgeled the Cleveland administration for its lethargy, now was put in the uncomfortable position of supporting McKinley's request for patience. The Republican House leadership felt under siege, with junior members reporting that their constituents wanted action. In order to buy time, the chairmen of the House Foreign Affairs Committee and its subcommittee on Cuba delivered speeches that reinforced McKinley's December message. They argued that the president deserved more time, and they pointed out that the U.S. Navy had ships close at hand when and if the president decided to "take the next step."[81] It is hardly surprising that most newspaper reports focused on the speeches' references to intervention rather than their intended purpose: the plea for patience.

Sending a ship to Havana would serve both to placate jingoes in the House and Senate and reinforce McKinley's message to Spain that time was of the essence. On January 21, Lee again requested that a U.S. warship be sent to Havana. While the situation in the city had been brought under control, with Spain's governor-general reinforcing the city garrison with thousands of Spanish troops, Lee still felt that matters remained extremely volatile. He feared that another round of unrest was inevitable given the hostility of loyalists to Spain's scheme of creating an autonomous Cuban government. The presence of an American battleship in Havana harbor might deter plots to overthrow Weyler's successor in Cuba, and in the event that Spanish authority collapsed, a landing party from the ship could protect the U.S. consulate and assorted ill-defined interests.[82]

Lee's request put the administration in a delicate situation. If the administration ignored the request and riots did indeed result in the death or destruction of American lives or property in Havana, all hell would break loose in Congress. On the other hand, Spain would surely interpret the uninvited arrival of a U.S. warship as a hostile intervention, and the president wished to avoid military confrontation with the Sagasta government. He understood that Spain had come a long way toward meeting American demands, and he wanted to give its government the opportunity to test the viability of its scheme to end the war on the basis of a political settlement that granted Cuba autonomy and self-government while retaining Spanish sovereignty. Secretary of the Navy John Long—who harbored no ill will toward the Spanish government and shared none of his assistant's bellicosity—raised the issue of timing with the president and Assistant Secretary of State William Day.[83] He argued that it would be better to schedule a port call with Spanish acquiescence when things were quiet rather than send an uninvited ship to Cuba during a crisis. McKinley and Day concurred. On the morning of January 24, Day casually raised the concept of resuming port visits with Spain's minister to the United States, Enrique Dupuy de Lôme.

The minister had just recently cautioned Day that America's naval diplomacy was unwelcome, encouraging the insurgency. Yet he had little choice but to respond positively to Day's general proposition that naval visits between Spanish Cuba and the United States should be resumed. The Americans seized on the opening, and informed de Lôme that very same day that the *Maine* had been ordered to Havana. De Lôme was displeased to hear that a battleship was en route to Havana, blustering about war. But when told that the administration was intent on sending the ship, he calmed down and put the best face on the matter.[84] In order to avoid humiliating the Spanish, both sides decided to portray the decision as mutual, with the Spanish cruiser *Vizcaya* invited to reciprocate by visiting New York in the near future.

For months, Consul General Lee had been agitating for a show of the American flag in Havana, but the pace of developments caught him by surprise. Lee received a telegram from the State Department on January 24 directing that he make arrangements for the *Maine*'s arrival the next day. Despite his role in initiating the visit, Lee advised that it be postponed for six or seven days so that he could lay the groundwork. He proceeded to the governor-general's palace, where news of the *Maine*'s imminent arrival was unwelcome. Spanish authorities suggested that there was an ulterior purpose to the visit, and asked that it be delayed until they received instructions from Madrid. If, they remarked, the visit was for purely friendly purposes as the Americans claimed, then a delay would be unimportant.[85] Washington declined both requests for delay, noting simply that orders had already been given and that the *Maine* was on its way.

The *Maine* steamed into Havana harbor on the morning of January 25, less than twenty-four hours after Day first broached the topic of naval visits with the Spanish minister in Washington. In Madrid, the minister of state was notified of the visit by the U.S. minister to Spain some twelve hours after the *Maine* dropped anchor in Havana harbor.[86] While McKinley, Day, and Long might claim that the visit was merely a resumption of routine and mutual naval visits to one another's ports, the Spanish understood that it was more. Dispatching the *Maine* to Havana sent a signal, though what that signal was and to whom it was directed were not particularly clear. Spain's representative in Washington recommended that the Spanish government portray the visit as an indication of support for the Liberal government's reformist agenda. The Cuban junta, pro-Cuban congressmen, and the yellow press interpreted the visit as the first step toward an American intervention in the Spanish-Cuban War, with a pro-Cuban senator noting that "the people of this country [the United States] were exultant that the power of the United States was to be made manifest."[87] Yet publicly and privately, the administration stuck to its line that the port call was a purely friendly matter and a resumption of customary relations.

Members of Congress were delighted by news that the *Maine* had been sent to Havana. The American press trumpeted the arrival of the ship as a signal of American strength and determination. The Spanish press was less enthused about the visit, portraying it as an affront to Spain that only served to encourage Cuban insurgents in their obstinacy. Sigsbee noticed that beneath the veneer of formal courtesy and strict adherence to protocol, his Spanish hosts were less than pleased with a naval visit they had not requested but could not reject without diplomatic incident. Spain, after all, had not protested when Imperial Germany sent its officer-training ship, the SMS *Gneissenau*, to Cuba the week before.

During the *Maine*'s protracted port call, Spanish authorities acted properly, if coolly. Protocol was strictly followed, from the exchange of gun salutes to formal visits to and from the governor-general and Spanish naval officials. Yet Sigsbee noticed that few Spanish officers saw fit to accept social invitations to visit his wardroom, and he detected occasional dark glances when out and about town. He dismissed a threatening flyer that characterized the American visit as a humiliation and insult, seeing it directed as much against the reformist Spanish

The USS *Maine* was a 6,682-ton second-class battleship commissioned in September 1895. The ship's port visit to Havana was stretching into a fourth week when the *Maine* exploded on February 15, 1898.

Naval History and Heritage Command, Photo Archives, Photograph NH 60255-A

government as against the United States. Consul general Lee had received similar material on previous occasions, and dismissed such flyers as the pathetic protests of bitter loyalists who recognized that their domination of the Cuban government and economy would soon end.

John Long, the secretary of the navy, noted that the administration initially intended that the *Maine*'s port visit should be brief. In addition to dispatching the *Maine*, the United States had sent the cruiser *Montgomery* on a port visit to a different Cuban port. The administration hoped that the simultaneous port visits would underscore the United States' keen interest in a rapid settlement of the Cuban problem. Once the vessels were in Cuba, it became difficult to extricate them without undermining this message. Fitzhugh Lee, the American consul general, cautioned against pulling out the *Maine* without replacing the ship with another American warship, preferably a first-class battleship. This assuredly would have upped the ante, but events took another course. Three weeks to the day after arriving in Havana, the *Maine* exploded in the harbor.

McKinley attempted to use naval diplomacy as a lever internationally and domestically. Internationally, he ordered the Atlantic Squadron to its exercise grounds off the Keys and sent two ships to Cuba to make it very clear to Spain that time was running out. His coercive diplomacy, or more precisely, his use of catalytic and expressive force, supported his policy of increasing the pressure on Spain. McKinley was imprecise about what course of action Spain needed to take, neither asking that it grant Cuban independence nor insisting that autonomy was an inadequate basis for settling differences with the Cuban insurgents. A number of McKinley's advisers grew increasingly skeptical of autonomy as an acceptable settlement, succumbing to Fitzhugh Lee's negative assessment of the scheme and the Cuban junta's rejection of it. Yet in January 1898, the president still wanted to provide the Spanish the opportunity to test the viability of their approach. Domestically, sending the *Maine* to Havana furnished McKinley with a similar breathing space, placating the members of his own party who increasingly feared that the Democratic minority would use the government's go-slow policy on Cuba as a cudgel to court public opinion. The administration was able to contain the pressure to intervene in Cuba even after the *Maine*'s explosion, arguing that one needed to let the Naval Court of Inquiry complete its investigation before jumping to conclusion. From February 15, the day the *Maine* exploded, until March 28, the day that McKinley shared the court's findings with Congress, an unreal state of suspended animation seemed to descend on Washington. Thereafter, the pressure to act increased exponentially.

THE IMMEDIATE REACTION

THE PUBLIC, THE PRESS, CONGRESS, AND THE BUSINESS COMMUNITY

McKinley had to take note of three broad audiences as he crafted his response to the *Maine* catastrophe. First, he had to respond to public opinion, shaping it if he could and directing it when possible. Second, and more directly, he had to deal with Congress, recognizing that its members demanded action even if they were divided concerning what action was needed. Lastly, as a pro-business Republican, McKinley needed to consider the fears, desires, and preferences of Wall Street and business leaders. McKinley did not perceive of the Cuban junta as a partner or audience that merited consideration as he crafted his response: he held that diplomacy was the intercourse between governments, and focused his attention on the Spanish government. For McKinley, Cuba was the object of intergovernmental dialogue between the United States and Spain, not a participant in the process. The American public, the American press, Congress, and the business community had a greater role in shaping McKinley's decisions than did the Cuban people. After all, he was elected by the former and responsive to the latter two; while sympathetic to Cuban suffering, the president felt that neither he nor his administration was beholden to Cuban nationalists.

Public opinion in the United States ran strongly in favor of the Cuban insurgents and against Spain. From the outset of the rebellion, the American press had focused on Spanish brutality and incompetence. The *New York Times* informed its readers in January 1897 that "Every mail from Cuba brings tales of massacres of innocent women and children, and of the most unheard torture."[88] The Cuban junta went to great lengths to shape American opinion, arranging Cuban sympathy meetings, sponsoring public lectures and readings, distributing pamphlets, and publishing a paper. It staged a "Grand Cuban-American Fair" at Madison Square Garden in May 1896, and followed up on the success of the event by sponsoring similar affairs in other major American cities.

While measuring public opinion during this period is difficult, given the absence of the sort of opinion polls now available, one can gauge opinion by looking at the editorial pages of the dozens of papers published in regions outside New York's hotbed of Hearst-Pulitzer sensationalism. Midwestern papers strongly supported the concept of Cuban independence, with the main difference of opinion centering on how to achieve this objective. [89] Papers in the South, Plains states, and other regions outside the New York–Washington orbit likewise were hostile to Spanish war efforts and favorably disposed to Cuban rebels, filibusterers, and the suffering *reconcentrados*.[90] Letters, diaries, and the flood of volunteers eager to serve in the Spanish-American War indicate that war fever began to grip the public as McKinley pondered his course of action following receipt of the Naval Court of Inquiry's report.

The Hearst and Pulitzer papers had capitalized on public opinion by running lurid, grim stories of the situation in Cuba since 1895. They had played upon pre-existing hostilities toward European meddling in the Americas, amplifying perceptions of Spaniards as cruel, oppressive, racially inferior, unstable, and impotent.[91] McKinley paid little attention to the lurid journalism of the Hearst-Pulitzer papers, but they were important in sharpening and focusing public opinion in general. One example of this was the *Journal*'s campaign to save Evangelina Cisneros, a seventeen-year-old Cuban beauty imprisoned by the Spanish for supporting the Cuban Revolution. One of Hearst's reporters had stumbled on her story while in Havana, and the *Journal* transformed Cisneros into a symbol of Cuban martyrdom. Hearst organized a petition drive enlisting American women in a campaign to free Evangelina, with Clara Barton, Mrs. Mark Hanna, Mrs. Jefferson Davis, McKinley's grandmother, and reportedly ten thousand other women from all segments of society petitioning for her release. The story and petition drive illustrate how Hearst tapped into preexisting sympathy for the Cuban insurgents, provided a face and a narrative that personalized Cuba's trauma, and then sought to capture public interest by direct action. Here as elsewhere, Hearst was not content with reporting events in Cuba—his papers personalized Cuba's suffering and created storylines to captivate the public. After whipping up sympathy for Evangelina, Hearst hired a handsome blond adventurer to free her, with the *Journal* devoting gallons of ink to the story when the improbable rescue succeeded. Secreting the girl out of Cuba, the Hearst empire then staged mass rallies and receptions for her in the United States, with cheering crowds greeting the bewildered young girl upon her arrival in New York.[92] Given public interest, other newspapers had little choice but to cover the Evangelina story. While the sensationalism of the Hearst and Pulitzer press coverage of Cuba did not reflect a nationwide phenomenon, their stories and anti-Spanish spin were echoed in less belligerent tones in regional markets as well.

Public opinion did not dictate the course of McKinley's policy toward the Cuban question during the crucial period after the sinking of the *Maine*, but it did set limits on the range of options the president might pursue. Outrage over Cuban suffering coupled with distrust of Spain made inaction or an open embrace of Spain's autonomy scheme difficult. The de Lôme letter scandal, unfolding during the interval between the *Maine*'s arrival in Havana on January 25 and its explosion on February 15, exacerbated anti-Spanish sentiment further.

Sometime after McKinley's December 1897 State of the Union address, Enrique Depuy de Lôme, Spain's minister to the United States since 1895, wrote an injudicious private letter to a friend of his in Havana, José Canalejas. In it, he characterized McKinley as a weak political operator (*politicastro*) pandering to public opinion and unduly deferential to the jingoes of his party. De Lôme indicated that he had little confidence in the autonomous government recently established in Cuba by Spain's governor-general, and dismissed negotiations with Cuban rebels as "a waste of time." A Cuban sympathizer, most likely a clerk handling Canalejas correspondence, read the letter and realized how damaging it could be. He passed the letter to Cuban contacts in New York. The Cuban junta used the letter with devastating effect, turning it over to Hearst's *Journal,* which scooped its competitors by publishing a deliberately inflammatory translation of the letter under the headline "The Worst Insult to the United States in Its History." Other papers subsequently published the letter as well, with editorials across the board condemning it as insulting and duplicitous. The administration had enjoyed a reasonable working relationship with Depuy de Lôme up to that point, and might have been willing to accept his explanation that the letter had been strictly personal and its contents distorted in translation had the matter been kept out of the press. But press coverage and public outrage made the letter a matter of state. Confronted in person by Assistant Secretary of State Day, de Lôme admitted the authenticity of the letter. The administration thereupon insisted that he be recalled, asking the Spanish government to distance itself from his remarks and express its regrets. The Spanish government bowed to these demands, and as a consequence, Spain's most experienced interlocutor in Washington was on his way home in disgrace when the *Maine*'s explosion brought Spanish-American relations to a crisis point.

The threefold sequence of the de Lôme scandal, the *Maine*'s destruction, and the Naval Court's findings served to undermine those who argued publicly against American intervention. Many regional papers had little sympathy for Spanish rule in Cuba, but a good many opposed direct American intervention in the Spanish-Cuban war until February-March 1898. The reasons varied, ranging from concern about the Spanish Navy to fear that tropical disease would ravish American forces on Cuba, to trepidation about European intervention. Anti-intervention papers argued that the costs of war would be high and the benefits low. Yet over the course of February and March, many of the papers that had hitherto cautioned against intervention quietly shifted their position.[93] The public and press clamor for action grew stronger following the *Maine*'s destruction.

Judge magazine's April 1898 cover admonished its readers that "Peace in Cuba under Spanish rule is worse than hell."

Library of Congress, Prints and Photographs Division, LC-USZ62-75560

If public opinion and the influence of the press set boundaries on the president's freedom of action, Congress's role in pressuring the president to act was more direct. The Republican-dominated Congress had been relentless in pressuring McKinley's Democratic predecessor, Grover Cleveland, to take a stronger line on Cuba, and McKinley's allies in Congress found it challenging to constrain their colleagues from proposing measures that the president felt were provocative and unwise. Over the course of 1895–97, pro-Cuban congressmen presented sixty-one resolutions on the Cuba issue. Senators Cannon of Utah and Mason of Illinois submitted resolutions recognizing Cuban belligerency after the *Maine*'s arrival in Cuba. Cannon complained that McKinley's naval diplomacy was accomplishing little:

> It has been no answer to the American people to send the *Maine* to Cuban waters. For twenty-four hours the people of this country were exultant in the thought that the power of the United States was to be made manifest, but almost instantly there was a revulsion of feeling, because, instead of the *Maine*'s appearing as a friend of the Cubans, it was made to appear that the visit of that war vessel was in compliment to Spain and the flag of the United States was dipped to the banner of the tyrant. It is no answer to the American people to send the fleet to Key West.[94]

Instead, Cannon argued that McKinley had the power to force conflict termination in Cuba simply by recognizing a state of belligerency. McKinley and Cleveland had both argued that recognizing a state of belligerency in Cuba would do little to help Cuban nationalists and might well drag the United States into a conflict with Spain. Pro-Cuban congressmen found this line of reasoning increasingly hollow. Cannon claimed that "the President of the United States can by a pen stroke stop the barbarities in Cuba, free the people, and relieve the island from burdens which it sustains." He insisted that Cubans had already won their independence in the field, and he maintained that once the United States recognized a state of belligerency, Spain would have little choice but to withdraw. Even as the *Maine* still swung undisturbed around its mooring buoy in Havana on February 9, pro-Cuban congressmen pushed the president to do more. Cannon captured the exasperation and impatience of the Cuba Libre faction on the hill as follows:

> What hand is it that stays William McKinley from signing his name [to a resolution recognizing Cuban belligerency]? What whispers is it that say to him, "Wait?" . . . We have waited while Americans in prison have been starved and tortured and assassinated. We have waited . . . until all American property on the island and commerce with the island have

been destroyed. We have waited until war itself has ended and until starvation has begun. Our cup of waiting is full.[95]

The cup threatened to run over once the *Maine* exploded, but McKinley and the congressional leadership successfully argued that public opinion and congressional action needed to be suspended until the Naval Court of Inquiry concluded its investigation. The week before it forwarded its results to McKinley, Senator Redfield Proctor of Vermont gave a speech that galvanized Congress.

Senator Proctor came from the same branch of the Republican party as had McKinley, favoring the gold standard, high tariffs, and a cautious, pro-business foreign policy. He had broached the topic of undertaking an independent fact-finding mission to Cuba with the president in early 1898, and had received letters of introduction to Fitzhugh Lee in Havana from the acting secretary of state. He went to Cuba shortly after the *Maine*'s explosion, but his purpose was not to micromanage the ongoing naval investigation but, rather, to assess the general situation in Cuba. He spent some time in Havana, but most of his travel focused on the rural areas and minor towns of Cuba's four western provinces.

Rising to address the Senate, Proctor began his speech quietly, explaining that his fact-finding mission had been entirely unofficial, undertaken in part because he suspected that the press had exaggerated the conditions in Cuba. His conclusions, based on interviews with businessmen and consular officials in Cuba, painted an extremely grim picture. Suffering, despite the revocation of Weyler's reconcentration order, remained widespread. Proctor estimated that out of a population of 1.6 million, two hundred thousand Cubans had died from starvation and disease. Deaths in the street, he noted, were common, and consular officials had informed him that one could find emaciated corpses in the marketplaces each morning, as starving *reconcentrados* tended to crawl there "hoping to get some stray bit of food from the early hucksters." As for the political situation, Proctor viewed it as "Cuban against Spaniard," with practically the entire population in sympathy with the revolution save for the Spanish-born population of perhaps 200,000. Only a handful of people supported the Spanish governor-general's concept of autonomous Cuban self-rule under Spanish sovereignty; the Cuban population believed the offer was too little and Spanish-born loyalists feared that it would undercut their political, social, and economic position in Cuba. Proctor concluded his speech by noting that he was refraining from arguing for or against any particular policy choice, but simply wanted to communicate the conditions as he had observed them. As for the *Maine*,

To me the strongest appeal [for action] is not the barbarity practiced by Weyler nor the loss of the *Maine*, if our worst fears should prove true, terrible as are both these incidents, but the spectacle of a million and a half of people, the entire native population of Cuba struggling for freedom and deliverance from the worst misgovernment of which I ever had knowledge. . . . [I]t is not my purpose at this time, nor do I consider it my province, to suggest any plans. I merely speak of the symptoms as I saw them, but do not undertake to prescribe. Such remedial steps as may be required may safely be left to an American president and the American people.[96]

Proctor's speech, delivered in an unemotional, matter-of-fact tone, was as critical as the subsequent report of the Naval Court of Inquiry in setting the boundaries for presidential decision making on Cuba. Within Congress, it moved the momentum toward action in a way that the dozens of resolutions and speeches by pro-Cuban congressmen had not. Coming from a conservative, pro-business Republican, the speech undercut hopes that Spanish concessions and American aid had turned the corner on the humanitarian crisis. It made clear that Spanish offers of Cuban autonomy enjoyed little support on the island, opposed by both Cuban nationalists and Spanish loyalists. The speech aroused public opinion on the eve of the publication of the long-anticipated court finding. Widely quoted, both in summary and in lengthy excerpts, the speech confirmed that humanitarian conditions remained abysmal and it emphasized that nothing short of independence would satisfy the Cuban people. Public and editorial opinion, already generally hostile to Spanish policies in Cuba, became ever more insistent that something needed to be done, pressuring McKinley to move faster and more forcefully than he had in 1897.

Proctor's speech and McKinley's transmission of the Naval Court of Inquiry findings finally brought Congress's "cup of waiting" to the point of overflow. Jingoes in McKinley's own Republican Party feared that the Democratic minority might seize the Cuba issue, and chafed at the president's restrained Cuba policy. Once the Naval Court of Inquiry concluded that the *Maine* had exploded as the result of an initial detonation outside the ship's hull, McKinley found it extremely difficult to restrain Congress. In the Senate, all but one senator on the Foreign Relations Committee favored voting for Cuban independence. In the House, Speaker Reed's efforts to buy the president additional time proved extremely unpopular. Two days after McKinley forwarded the findings of the Naval Court of Inquiry to Congress, more than one hundred House Republicans threatened to join Democrats and force a vote on Cuba. McKinley's secretary of war, Russell A. Alger, worried that if McKinley waited much longer, he would ruin himself and "the Republican Party by standing in the way of the people's wishes. Congress will declare war in spite of him. He'll get run over and the party with him."[97]

Starving Cubans at Matanzas, ca. 1898. The claim that hundreds of thousands of Cuban civilians were suffering grievously as a consequence of Spanish counterinsurgency policies was accurate, with stereographic cards such as this pricking the conscience of the American public.
Library of Congress, Prints and Photographs Division LC-USZ62-75981

If the public, press, and Congress were factors that McKinley had to consider in crafting his policy toward Spain and Cuba after the *Maine*'s destruction, the business community was an audience near and dear to the president's heart. Indeed, during his election campaign, William Jennings Bryan had caricaturized McKinley as a tool of big business, making much of his long and close association with Mark Hanna. A fellow Ohioan, Hanna had made millions in the coal, steel, railroad, and newspaper industries, and had served as McKinley's campaign manager during the tumultuous campaign of 1896. McKinley's connection to Hanna was personal and close, reflecting a worldview that extolled capitalism, private enterprise, and the conviction that what was good for business was good for the country.

The financial and business communities stood against intervention until the multiple crises of January–March 1898 transformed the environment in which the "system makers"—the elite who determined decisions in industry, finance, and government—operated.[98] While a number of second-tier investors with plantations, mines, and other assets on the island favored American intervention during the heady early days of the Cuban Revolution, the captains of American industry and the men McKinley admired—John D. Rockefeller, George Pullman, J. P. Morgan, shipbuilder William Cramp, and Wall Street bankers—cautioned against intervention until the tides of public and congressional opinion threatened to overwhelm the president's policy of prudence, patience, and graduated pressure on Spain.[99] Mark Hanna, McKinley's confidante, viewed Roosevelt, Lodge, and other jingoes as dangerous zealots, dismissing

T.R. as an immature cowboy ignorant of the needs of business and overeager to embroil the United States in foreign adventures that would impede economic recovery. Searching for evidence of the baleful influence of Wall Street bankers and Gilded Age industrialists, even Walter LaFeber admits that American industrialists and bankers began to push for intervention only in March 1898.[100]

There are two possible explanations for this crucial change of heart on the part of the industrialists, businessmen, and bankers whom McKinley held in high esteem. One explanation is that these powerful men decided to push for U.S. intervention precisely because the Cubans were on the cusp of winning their own independence without U.S. assistance. The United States, so goes the reasoning, intervened to forestall Cuban land redistribution programs and to protect U.S. investments in Cuban tobacco, sugar, and mining enterprises. This explanation downplays the significance of the *Maine* incident, the impact of the yellow journalism of the Hearst and Pulitzer press groups, and the humanitarian posturing of American congressmen, religious leaders, and public lecturers. The United States intervened in Cuba in 1898 because powerful groups in the United States feared the consequences of a free Cuba and sought to protect their economic interests. These bankers, businessmen,

The memorial parade for victims of the USS *Maine* wound down Pennsylvania Avenue, with the outline of the Capitol barely visible in the background.
Library of Congress, Prints and Photographs Division LC-USZ62-41794

and investors used public outrage about the humanitarian crisis in Cuba to intervene in the Cuban-Spanish conflict in order to forestall Cuban reform programs and secure U.S. commercial interests. The McKinley administration sought to replace Spanish rule over Cuba with American control of the island's resources. The *Maine* incident provided an excuse for intervention, but other excuses would have been found even if the Maine had not been blown to pieces.[101]

An alternative explanation is that the United States intervened because it feared that the conflict in Cuba might drag on for months absent some sort of American intervention.[102] Proponents of this view argue that the Spanish military was not on the verge of collapsing. While Spain's offer of autonomy was unattractive to Cuban rebels, the insurgents were in no position to capture Havana, Santiago, or any of the island's major ports and towns. Spain seemed determined to hold on to the island even if it was willing to grant Cubans more control over their own affairs. The Spanish government was in the midst of mustering another contingent of troops to dispatch to Cuba in the hope that rebels might eventually embrace political offers of autonomy and amnesty as had happened in 1878. Far from crumbling, the situation in Cuba was stabilizing into a protracted military standoff where neither side held the upper hand. The Cuban Revolution was not on the verge of victory in January 1898. Desertion was on the rise, and a smattering of mid-level officers had gone over to the Spanish side.[103] While demoralized, Spanish troops retained the ability to stubbornly defend Cuba's key ports and cities, as well-equipped American troops would find out to their surprise in July.[104] The struggle had become one of exhaustion, with neither Spain nor the Cuban insurgents able to force the other side to agree to the terms they sought. Given mounting public pressure and a rambunctious Congress that was threatening to take matters into its own hands, America's business elites came to the conclusion that intervention was preferable to interminable war. The weight of opinion in American business and financial sectors ran against intervention until the crises of February–March 1898. The sinking of the *Maine*, Proctor's Senate speech, and the findings of the Naval Court of Inquiry changed their calculus. Absent the catastrophic destruction of the *Maine* and the loss of 260 American lives in Havana harbor, the business community would have supported a policy of graduated diplomatic coercion short of war.

If McKinley's intent had been to buy time by using naval diplomacy to increase pressure on Spain and to pacify domestic jingoes, the outcome of his decision to send the *Maine* to Havana was the opposite. The combined effect of the *Maine*'s explosion, the Proctor report, and the release of the Naval Court of Inquiry's finding was to shorten the time line of American diplomacy. The public, press, Congress, and U.S. industrialists and bankers all pushed for action by late March 1898. Yet McKinley as president determined the form and manner of America's response.

THE PRESIDENT DECIDES, CONGRESS ASSENTS, AND A NEW ERA IS BORN

McKinley had inched toward intervention in Cuba in December 1897, pressing Spain to allow the delivery of American humanitarian assistance free of charge and insisting that the American Red Cross, rather than Spanish officials, supervise the distribution of donated food, clothing, and medicine. In January he had dispatched the *Maine* to Havana and ordered the North Atlantic Squadron to conduct exercises off Florida. In early February, the administration postponed the *Maine*'s departure, heeding Consul General Lee's advice that the ship needed to stay in Havana until another American warship could relieve it. These indications of American interest were framed in terms of friendly assistance and the normalization of relations with Spanish Cuba, consistent with McKinley's December message to Congress that "[Spain] should be given a reasonable chance to realize her expectations and to prove the efficacy of the new order of things."

During the interim between the *Maine*'s destruction and McKinley's receipt of the Naval Court of Inquiry report, McKinley asked for calm and patience from Congress and the American public. In the interval, he received a number of disquieting reports that suggested that more vigorous action might be necessary to force a settlement. From Madrid, he had reports that the Spanish government was hardening its position, fearful that further concessions might lead to the overthrow of the government and monarchy. The Spanish press had its counterparts to Hearst and Pulitzer's yellow press, as Spanish papers lambasted the Sagasta ministry as weak, feminine, and submissive (a "*gobierno femenino*"), and urging it to stand up to the arrogant demands of the greedy Yankees.[105]

The Sagasta ministry, which had come to power only because of the unexpected assassination of the Conservative prime minister Cánovas the previous August, was beset by rivals willing and eager to topple the government, with Carlist detractors intent on replacing Spain's young monarch as well. Given these realities, America's minister to Spain warned Washington that, given the choice between war with the United States and domestic revolt, the Sagasta government preferred "the chances of war, with the certain loss of Cuba, to the overthrow of the Dynasty."[106] The Sagasta ministry seemed to be preparing for the contingency of war with the United States, putting out feelers about purchasing Brazilian cruisers under construction in England and dispatching a small flotilla of torpedo boats and destroyers toward Cuba. Assistant Secretary of the Navy Theodore Roosevelt fretted that "Month by month the Spanish Navy has been put into a better condition to meet us," and urged a more proactive policy on his superiors.[107]

From New York and Cuba, McKinley received additional reports confirming that Cuban nationalists were uninterested in settling their conflict with Spain on the basis of autonomy. They held out for full independence. Senator Proctor had verified these assertions, and while McKinley remained averse to recognizing the Cuban Republic in any form, his faith in an arbitrated settlement was diminishing. Responding to a suggestion from the former American minister to Turkey that Turkey's titular but fictitious suzerainty over Egypt might serve as a model for the future relationship of Cuba to Spain, McKinley remarked privately, "We will have great trouble in satisfying the insurgents or in getting them to agree to anything—they are even more difficult than Spain to deal with."[108]

Most unsettling, by late February McKinley had good reason to believe that the Naval Court of Inquiry would reject explanations that posited internal causes for the explosion of the *Maine*'s forward magazine and its subsequent destruction. Consul General Fitzhugh Lee communicated to Washington on February 22 that divers had found evidence pointing toward an external triggering detonation, and that American reporters in Havana had soon picked up on the story. Lee provided further elaboration the next week, again pointing to the likelihood that the Naval Court would conclude that the initial detonation setting off the explosion of the *Maine*'s magazines had come from outside, rather than inside, the ship. While the court's proceedings were closed, Lee was resourceful, and his dispatches to Washington reflected the prevalent view of the American community in Havana. Whether he received informal updates of the court's proceedings, or more likely, gathered news from divers, newsmen, or those interviewed by the court, is unknown.[109] Whatever the case, by early March McKinley understood that he needed to speed up his coercive diplomacy with Spain, intensifying the dialogue with Madrid while preparing for war, should Spain prove intransigent.

McKinley explored a number of options for achieving his objectives without recourse to war. He resurrected the old scheme of buying Cuba from Spain, already tried and rebuffed or abandoned by the Polk, Pierce, and Grant administrations decades before.[110] The reaction of those senators to which he confided the scheme was one of skepticism; none entertained any enthusiasm for annexing the island, as its inhabitants spoke a different language and would be culturally difficult to absorb into the body politic. If the concept involved purchasing the island in order to grant independence, they queried, why spend the money when Cubans stood on the verge of achieving their own independence? Exploring another avenue, McKinley had his contacts inquire whether the Cuban junta's earlier offer to pay Spain for independence still stood, receiving an affirmative answer. Yet when McKinley's minister to Spain broached the topic of Spain's selling the island, he received a pointed reply that Spain's queen regent "would prefer to abdicate her regency and return to her Austrian home rather than be the instrument of ceding or parting with any of Spain's colonies."[111]

Even while exploring the efficacy of financial incentives to induce Spain to grant Cuban independence, McKinley began to prepare the American military for confrontation should force be necessary. In early March, McKinley signaled that the chairman of the House Appropriations Committee, Joseph G. Cannon, should introduce a bill asking Congress to appropriate $50 million for national defense. McKinley told Cannon, "I must have the money to get ready for war. I am doing everything possible to prevent war but it must come, and we are not prepared for war."[112] Congress moved rapidly, and both houses approved the bill unanimously on March 9. The effect in Madrid was dramatic. Stewart Woodford, the U.S. minister to Spain, reported that the bill "has not excited the Spaniards— it has stunned them."[113] He described the mood in governing circles as despondent and pessimistic, in sharp contrast to the jingoist tones of the Spanish press.

On March 19, four members of the Naval Court of Inquiry discreetly briefed the president about what he should anticipate when he received the formal report at the end of the week. The results were as expected: the court concluded that the loss of the *Maine* was not in any respect due to fault or negligence on the part of any of the ship's officers or crew; the ship had been destroyed by a submarine mine, which caused the partial explosion of two or more of her forward magazines. The president received the full report on the evening of Thursday, March 24. He and the cabinet considered the report the next day and deliberated over the weekend. On March 28, he transmitted the report to Congress, noting that he had communicated its findings to the Spanish government and would advise Congress of the results.

Spain's chargé d'affaires in Washington had warned Madrid that a great deal rested on the outcome of the U.S. Naval Court of Inquiry into the disaster. He advised that "if it declares that the catastrophe was due to an accident, I believe I can assure your Excellency that the present danger will be over, but if, on the contrary, it alleges that it was the work of a criminal hand, then we shall have to face the gravest situation."[114] He gauged the report's impact accurately.

The day after McKinley received the final report, Assistant Secretary of State Day shared the administration's desired end state with the American minister to Spain. First, Spain had to revoke the reconcentration order and maintain the Cuban people until they could support themselves; and second, Spain needed to offer the Cubans full self-government with reasonable indemnity.[115] When queried by Woodford if "full self-government" meant independence or encompassed some sort of nominal Spanish sovereignty over a self-governing Cuba, Day replied that full self-government meant Cuban independence.[116] Perhaps to soften the blow, Day instructed Woodford to determine if several things could be done:

> First. Armistice until October 1. Negotiations meantime looking for peace between Spain and insurgents through friendly offices of President United States.
>
> Second. Immediate revocation of reconcentrado order so as to permit people to return to their farms, and the needy to be relieved with provisions and supplies from United States cooperating with authorities so as to afford full relief.
>
> Add if possible:
>
> Third. If terms of peace not satisfactorily settled by October 1, President of the United States to be final arbiter between Spain and insurgents.
>
> If Spain agrees, President will use friendly offices to get insurgents to accept plan. Prompt action desirable.[117]

The discrepancy between the clear, unambiguous set of goals that Washington communicated to its minister in Spain and the more ambiguous, less strident terms that it instructed its minister to communicate to the Spanish government was intentional but unfortunate. McKinley and Day believed that an open demand for independence would leave Spain no choice but to opt for war, and they hoped that the less confrontational demand that Spain accept binding American arbitration might enable the Sagasta government to terminate the war with honor. But they misjudged the Spaniards. The Spanish press and public were intensely hostile to the idea of the United States determining the future of Spain's "ever-faithful isle," and the Sagasta government opted to play for time and postpone the unacceptable. It sought to appease the McKinley administration by revoking reconcentration orders in western Cuba (March 31) and proclaiming an armistice in Cuba (April 11). It simultaneously sought to rally other European powers to support Spain. The Spanish government discovered that European sympathy for Spain did not translate into European support for Spain; the furthest that European powers would go was to present a joint note to the United States and Spain on behalf of Austria-Hungary, France, Germany, Great Britain, Italy, and Russia, calling for moderation and negotiation over the situation in Cuba. It was hardly the response Spain desired.

Lastly, the Spanish clung to the notion that Cuban rebels might be won over to a settlement based on Cuban autonomy under Spanish sovereignty. Although the Cuban junta in New York, Gómez's Cuban Liberation Army in the field, and the self-proclaimed government of the Cuban Republic all sought to disabuse the Spanish government of the notion that a compromise settlement was still acceptable, Spanish officials remained firmly convinced that autonomy could succeed if the United States supported the concept. Woodford conveyed the Spanish position to McKinley by recounting a conversation Woodford had with a well-known Spanish merchant. Woodford remembered that the Spaniard had insisted:

> Spain had done all she could do or expect to do in recalling Weyler, in sending Blanco [Weyler's successor as Governor General in Cuba], in abandoning the policy of reconcentration, in establishing legitimate warfare, in rescinding tobacco edicts . . . in offering full pardon to all rebels . . . the great majority of the white people of Cuba had accepted autonomy. The rebellion is now confined almost entirely to negroes [*sic*]. . . Autonomy, with real self-government of Cuba by Cubans, can and will succeed if the United States will openly advise it and place the moral power of the United States on the side of autonomy.[118]

On March 18, the Spanish minister for the colonies, Segismundo Moret, asked Woodford to inquire whether McKinley would be willing to "advise the insurgents to lay down their arms and accept autonomy." Woodford chided Moret that the Spanish government had turned down the president's offer to act as an intermediary the previous fall. If Spain now wanted to draw upon the good offices of the United States to end the insurrection, it needed to give the United States a "very free hand" and recognize that "the Spanish flag can not give peace."[119]

McKinley misjudged the cultural and symbolic significance of Cuba to Spain as he explored various options to settle the conflict without intervening militarily. The Spanish government was unwilling to grant independence to Cuba or sell the island to the Americans. The Spanish likewise did not understand the strength of pro-Cuban public and congressional opinion in the United States. The idea that McKinley should openly advise Cuban rebels to lay down their arms was preposterous in light of both popular and congressional opinion.

McKinley knew this, his minister to Spain understood this, and Moret probably realized this. Yet the request is revealing: despite three years of warfare, the Spanish remained convinced that the Cuban rebellion was dependent on outside aid and encouragement. They simply could not accept the notion that most Cubans favored independence over any sort of association with Spain.

McKinley stalled for time after forwarding the findings of the Naval Court of Inquiry to Congress. He hoped that Spain might respond favorably to the conditions Woodford had proposed on March 25, and he wanted to give diplomacy a chance. On April 4, Consul General Lee in Havana asked McKinley to delay delivering any statement on Cuba so as to allow American citizens and diplomats on the island to leave. McKinley used Lee's cable as an excuse for postponing his message to Congress for an additional week. He forwarded his long-awaited declaration on Spanish-American relations to Congress on April 11, more than three weeks after he was first briefed on the findings of the *Maine* inquiry.

McKinley's message to Congress left even the president's closest supporters dissatisfied. McKinley did not call for war, but merely for authorization to take measures to secure a full and final termination of hostilities in Cuba and the

McKinley and his cabinet had to deal with steadily mounting pressure from Congress to "do something about Cuba" throughout the fall and winter of 1897, with interventionist sentiment reaching a fever pitch after the Naval Court of Inquiry concluded its investigation.
Library of Congress, Prints and Photographs Division LC-USZ62-96543

establishment of a stable government on the island. Most controversial, both at the time and in retrospect, was McKinley's persistent reluctance to acknowledge the role of Cuban leaders in resolving the conflict in Cuba. Pro-Cuban congressmen and senators had anticipated stronger action, either in the form of recognizing the Cuban Republic or at a minimum some sort of declaration granting Cuban forces the status of belligerents. McKinley disappointed them on both counts. The rather academic, pedantic message continued to advise against granting Cuba belligerent status, and it rejected recognizing the "so-called Cuban Republic" as an independent entity. McKinley explained that doing so would have secondary effects, in that the Cuban Republic would then be entitled to approve, disapprove, and even direct the form and manner of American intervention.

Once viewed as a cautious and indecisive president overwhelmed by events, McKinley is now generally credited with having successfully navigated the currents of public and congressional pressure in directions amenable to his political instincts. This view of McKinley as manipulator and master strategist leads some to contend that the president's equivocal attitude to the Cuban Republic was due to a long-term agenda of replacing Spanish rule over Cuba with U.S. hegemony. Yet simpler explanations suffice: McKinley believed that the immediate recognition of Cuba would lead to war; he desired additional breathing room to explore a diplomatic resolution to the crisis; and he sought to retain maximum freedom of action. Successive presidents from Woodrow Wilson to Bill Clinton to George W. Bush to Barack Obama have exhibited similar reticence about allowing allies and insurgent groups to determine the timing, conduct, and resolution of American military interventions.[120]

McKinley noted at the close of the message that he had received information that the queen regent of Spain had directed her governor-general in Cuba to suspend hostilities in Cuba, though details remained unknown. He explained that he had "exhausted every effort to relieve the intolerable conditions of affairs which is at our doors," and now awaited congressional action. He was prepared to execute the obligations imposed on him by Congress. McKinley understood that Congress had been chomping at the bit for weeks. He did not ask for war, but he did ask for the power to take measures to secure a full and final termination of hostilities. This was coercive diplomacy in its essence: if the gentle nudges of naval diplomacy had been insufficient to convince Spain to speedily end the war in Cuba, perhaps explicit demands backed by the open threat of force might convince the Sagasta ministry to be reasonable.

Congress had been waiting for the president's message. Senator Lodge recalled, "for more than a week a draft of a resolution to be passed by Congress had been in existence," though no one knew who drafted it.[121] Given the remarkable similarities between the resolution and the president's message, one can surmise that the White House had been consulted, with Speaker of the House Thomas Reed most probably its author. But Congress had no intention of rubber-stamping the resolution. In the House, Democrats pushed for an immediate recognition of the insurgent government, only to be overruled by the Republican majority. In the Senate, a cross-party majority likewise favored recognizing the Cuban Republic, with McKinley's allies struggling in both houses to gain support for a resolution consistent with the president's message. The House and Senate resolutions differed in form and language, passing back and forth between the chambers and exposing the deep differences of opinion.

Yet slowly, the president's allies gained ground. After laboring through the night and into the morning hours of April 19, Congress passed a joint resolution resolving that the people of Cuba are and of a right ought to be free; demanding that Spain relinquish its authority over Cuba and withdraw its land and naval forces; and empowering the president to use the entire land and naval forces of the United States to enforce these resolutions. To placate the numerous supporters of the Cuban Republic on both sides of the aisle in both chambers, a fourth paragraph (known as the Teller amendment) specified that the United States disclaimed any disposition or intent to exercise sovereignty, jurisdiction, or control over Cuba except for the pacification thereof. Once this was accomplished, it pledged to leave the government and control of the island to its people.[122]

The reaction in Spain to the congressional resolution was immediate and predictable. On the same day that McKinley signed the joint resolution, the Sagasta government convened the Spanish Cortes. Sagasta presented a passionate defense of Spanish policy, listed American provocations to date, and promised that his government would defend Spanish territory no matter the costs. The next day, Spain broke diplomatic relations with the United States, and McKinley ordered the naval blockade of Cuba. On April 23, 1898, Spain declared war on the United States. Congress reciprocated, backdating the start of war to April 21 for good measure.

AFTERMATH, CONSEQUENCES, AND REFLECTIONS ON THE *MAINE* INCIDENT

Did the destruction of the USS *Maine* in Havana harbor on February 15, 1898, cause the Spanish-American War? The question seems clear and forthright, but to answer it one has to address levels of causation. Was the destruction of the *Maine* in and of itself a sufficient cause to propel the McKinley administration to war? No. The United States had long been interested in Cuba, and the outbreak of the Cuban Revolution in 1895, the manner in which it was waged, and the reaction of the American public and Congress were necessary preconditions for the war hysteria that erupted in the United States in February–March 1898. Yet to argue that American intervention was inevitable, that McKinley would have intervened absent the *Maine*'s destruction, is problematic, as are all counterfactuals. Clearly McKinley adopted a more insistent stance on Cuba than had his predecessor, making demands, employing naval diplomacy, and ratcheting up the pressure on Spain. Senator Proctor would still have witnessed miserable conditions in Cuba, and his report to Congress would still have elicited indignant demands to do something from the press, the public, and pro-Cuban congressmen even if the *Maine* had never been sent to Havana.

But that had been the case throughout 1897, particularly during the period when "Butcher" Weyler had been driving Cuban peasants into zones of concentration; the president had protested, pressured Spain, but held back. Whether mounting public outrage, fanned by the press and the Cuban junta, and congressional party politics—in particular Republican fears that Democrats might seize upon the Cuba issue in the next elections—were in and of themselves sufficient to push McKinley into war is a proposition unknowable. We have difficulty even assessing what occurred with certainty, let alone what might have been.

Arguments that Mahanian navalism, imperialist daydreaming, capitalism's thirst for new markets, and anxiety about manhood caused the Spanish-American War overshoot their mark. If Assistant Secretary of the Navy Teddy Roosevelt was all agog about Mahan, battleships, and expansion, his superior was not. Too much attention has been devoted to T.R.'s self-aggrandizing account of his importance in preparing the U.S. Navy for war and too little to Secretary of the Navy Long's central role. Likewise, while Henry Cabot Lodge became a tremendously powerful spokesperson for the New American Empire, we should not forget that in 1896, Mark Hanna—McKinley's confidante, campaign manager, and a representative of the millionaire capitalist-industrialist club—could ask Lodge "Who in hell are you?" before telling him to "plumb go to hell" while Hanna's circle crafted the Republican platform.[123] And Hanna, appointed to the Senate vacancy following McKinley's election, had voted against U.S. intervention in Cuba in 1897.

This is not to say imperialist and navalist aforementioned undercurrents were not operating in late-nineteenth-century America, and that they would not have surfaced at some point. But they were not the causes of the Spanish-American war. A careful look at McKinley's Spanish policy through January 1898—in particular his naval diplomacy—indicates that McKinley by no means sought to engage Spain in a war in order to reap colonies, dependencies, and naval stations. Instead, one sees gradualism, conservatism, and an aversion to war. Reflecting back on the tumultuous events of 1898, McKinley mused in May 1899 that had he been left alone, he could have concluded an arrangement with the Spanish government for the peaceful withdrawal of Spanish troops from Cuba. Congress, under the impression that the country demanded war, had left him no choice.[124] How long McKinley could have held back from intervention had the *Maine* left Havana earlier, or had he never sent the ship to show the American flag, one cannot know. What one can conclude is that the *Maine*'s destruction acted as an accelerant, pushing McKinley to war earlier than would have been the case absent the death of 260 American sailors.

How might McKinley's diplomacy have played out if the timetable under which he operated in February–April 1898 had encompassed months rather than weeks? The prospects for the success of an autonomous Cuba under Spanish rule seemed poor, and Cuban forces were not poised to drive the Spaniards from Cuba militarily. American intervention might still have occurred, but later. In the interval, autonomy might have succeeded (doubtful), the Spanish people might have tired of the conflict (uncertain), or some unanticipated event on a par with the assassination of Spain's conservative prime minister by an Italian anarchist in August 1897 might have altered the political landscape of Cuba, Spain, or the United States. Looking back, we know what did not happen. But looking forward, the Spanish policy of delay, appeal (to Europe's powers), and appeasement may not have seemed as hopeless to Spanish officials as it appears in retrospect.

McKinley's reputation has increased over time as scholars have analyzed his wartime leadership. McKinley sought and gained funding for the war well before it began, and the U.S. Navy was well positioned for the lopsided victories it achieved in Manila Bay and off Santiago. He directed the war effort firmly, using modern technology and the equivalent of a war room to track, coordinate, and supervise the operations of his military commanders. Lastly, he outmaneuvered anti-imperialists in Congress, industry, and in the public, achieving a peace settlement that reflected his preferences for Cuba, the Philippines, and Puerto Rico.

Yet if one considers McKinley's goals and preferences before the war, the record is less impressive. McKinley sought to use naval diplomacy and coercion short of war to push Spain toward settling the Cuban issue. McKinley sought to use expressive and catalytic naval power to send a political message and to buy time in December 1897 and January 1898. The *Maine*'s destruction and the subsequent interaction of domestic forces in the United States pushed McKinley along a path he had not intended to follow. The success of McKinley's wartime leadership should not hide the failure of McKinley's prewar coercive diplomacy. War unleashed forces that McKinley and Cleveland had held at bay. Key figures of the "system making" elite that dominated government, finance, and industry had opposed war prior to the *Maine* incident, but once war appeared inevitable, they succumbed to the temptations of empire.

The arrival of a large passenger ship such as the *Lusitania* attracted considerable attention. This peacetime photograph (September 1907) shows the liner warping to dock in New York harbor.

Library of Congress, Prints and Photographs Division LC-USZ62-55380

2 THE *LUSITANIA* CRISIS

THE INCIDENT

Shortly after noon on Saturday, May 1, 1915, the passenger ship RMS *Lusitania* cast off from Pier 54 of New York Harbor, bound for Liverpool. As always, there was a crowd of well-wishers at the pier bidding it farewell, for the departure of a large transatlantic liner remained quite a social event. First-class passengers traveled in a style reminiscent of the Gilded Age, with millionaire Alfred Vanderbilt, inspirational publicist Elbert Hubbard, and theater producer Charles Frohman among the 290 wealthy travelers who booked first-class passage aboard the liner.[1] A far larger contingent booked second-class passage, as 601 men, women, and children crowded into the ship's 145 second-class cabins. The *Lusitania* was designed to lodge more than one thousand third-class passengers, but the ongoing war in Europe had slowed the stream of poorer workers migrating to or returning from the New World to Europe. Though the ship could accommodate 1,186 third-class passengers, only 370 people booked third class for the voyage. If one adds to the passenger list the 688 members of the ship's crew, its five band members, three stranded British merchant seamen, and three stowaways discovered after departure, the *Lusitania* carried almost two thousand people.[2] The great majority, some 80 percent, held British passports, though a considerable number were residents of Canada or Ireland. There were almost two hundred Americans on the *Lusitania*, with smaller contingents of Russians, Swedes, Persians, Greeks, and French adding a multinational dimension to the ship's passenger list. The passengers consisted largely of businessmen, families returning home or visiting relatives on the other side of "the pond," a number of doctors and nurses headed for the Western Front, and 129 children accompanying their parents across the Atlantic. The outbreak of war in Europe the previous August had caused much trepidation among transatlantic travelers, but that May Day, the *Lusitania* carried more passengers than on any of its other eastbound voyages since the Great War had begun some eight months earlier.[3]

In hindsight, one wonders at the nonchalant attitude that many passengers affected concerning the dangers of booking passage aboard a

British liner headed into a maritime war zone. While British shipping losses to date had been downplayed by the Admiralty, rumors abounded among the dockworkers and crew that Germany intended to sink the *Lusitania*. A number of passengers even received threatening telegrams warning them against traveling on the ship.[4] The morning of departure, a notice from the German embassy, originally scheduled for publication the previous Saturday, appeared in many New York papers. The warning, in some cases posted directly beneath the Cunard departure times, read:

NOTICE!

Travellers [*sic*] intending to embark on the Atlantic voyage are reminded that a state of war exists between Germany and her allies and Great Britain and her allies; that the zone of war includes the waters adjacent to the British Isles; that, in accordance with formal notice given by the Imperial German Government, vessels flying the flag of Great Britain, or any of her allies, are liable to destruction in those waters and that travelers sailing in the war zone on the ships of Great Britain or her allies do so at their own risk.

IMPERIAL GERMAN EMBASSY
Washington, D.C. 22nd April 1915[5]

Passengers who inquired about the danger were reassured by Cunard representatives that there was no risk whatsoever. One later recalled that he had been told that travel aboard the ship was "perfectly safe, safer than the trolley cars in New York City."[6] To allay any misgivings, Cunard's general agent in New York issued a statement the next day: "The truth is that the *Lusitania* is the safest boat on the sea. She is too fast for any submarine. No German war vessel can get her or near her. She will reach Liverpool on schedule time and come back on schedule time."[7]

If passengers had misgivings, most adopted a stiff upper lip; only five canceled their reservations and booked passage on another ship.[8] For first- and second-class passengers, travel aboard the *Lusitania* promised both comfort and luxury. Tickets for first- or "saloon class" accommodations ranged from $140 at the low end to $4,000 for one of the two elite Regal Suites, a considerable sum considering that the average American worker of the period earned around $20 a week. In return, first-class ticketholders were wined and dined, with attentive stewards catering to their every need. The first-class dining room featured white tablecloths and crystal glasses, a grand dome supported by Corinthian columns, and potted greenery. The wood-paneled lounge boasted comfortable armchairs under a stained-glass ceiling, with smoking, music, and reading rooms set aside for society's upper crust.[9] Should walking the grand stairway that stretched six decks prove too onerous, first-class passengers could avail themselves of two elegant grillwork elevators. Second-class accommodations, at $50 per person, rivaled those of first-class aboard older ships, with public drawing rooms and a well-designed if not sumptuous dining room featuring a domed ceiling.[10] Third-class passengers made do with less opulent facilities, but they too were provided with clean, functional common areas for smoking and sitting, in addition to a large dining room that served generous portions of high-quality food. In short, the *Lusitania* provided its passengers with what one might expect at a top-notch hotel, with the added attraction of deck promenades to view the sea. En route to New York, the *Lusitania*'s passengers and crew had "eaten their way through 40,000 eggs, 4,000 pounds of fresh fish, two tons of bacon and ham, 4,000 pounds of coffee, 1,000 pineapples, 500 pounds of grapes, 1,000 lemons, 25,000 pounds of meat, nearly 3,000 gallons of milk, over 500 gallons of cream, and 30,000 loaves of bread."[11] Her eastbound passengers looked forward to a similar gastronomic extravagance, with shipboard entertainment ranging from musical performances to bridge tournaments, to badminton shuttlecock.

A labyrinth of galleys, bakeries, pantries, laundry rooms, and storerooms manned by a victualing department of more than three hundred waiters, barkeepers, stewards, cooks, butchers, bakers, barbers, and pursers supported the ship's mission of providing swift, comfortable transatlantic travel to paying passengers. Twenty-five coal-fired boilers supplied steam to four Parsons turbines that could propel the ship to a maximum of 26 knots, though for reasons of economy Cunard had shut down one of the boiler rooms, reducing the ship's top speed to 21 knots. The engineering department, numbering 313 men, was the largest department. Feeding the boilers with coal was a labor-intensive, grimy, backbreaking task, and the coal-dust-encrusted trimmers, firemen, and greasers who kept the liner running worked deep in the bowels of the ship in stifling heat. The deck crew of sixty-nine, by contrast, worked topside maintaining the ship's lines, lifeboats, paintwork, and nautical gear when not at watch. Displacing 38,000 tons and measuring 787 feet in length, the *Lusitania* would have dwarfed the American battleship *Maine* (displacement 6,789 tons, length 324 feet) and was larger than the "super Dreadnought" battleships that were the mainstay of the British and German fleets then confronting each other across the North Sea.

The *Lusitania*'s captain, William Thomas Turner, gave no indication that he was overly concerned about the U-boat menace, commenting that "It's the best joke I've heard in many days, this talk of torpedoing the *Lusitania*."[12] Turner was a crusty sailor, having gone to sea at thirteen. He had "learned the ropes" as a youngster aboard various sailing ships, joining Cunard in 1883 and ascending to command Cunard's prestigious passenger steam ships by dint of hard work. He had a reputation for good ship handling and sound navigation, and did not suffer fools gladly. Yet despite his reputation as a sailor's sailor, Turner put little emphasis on abandon-ship drills. The *Lusitania*, in contrast to the *Titanic*, was equipped with enough lifeboats to accommodate all passengers and crew, but the daily boat drills were "a pitiable exhibition" according to one of the passengers. At the sound of a siren, eight members of the crew would assemble at one of two designated lifeboats, and at the command of the boat officer, they would climb into the boat. They would sit down, dress oars, and then, on command, get out of the boat. No effort was made to practice lowering or launching the lifeboats, a task that required considerable skill as the ship was equipped with old-fashioned block-and-tackle davits that necessitated manually releasing the fore and aft fall lines of the boat at the same rate. One of the ship's firemen admitted that his mates had "no idea of how to get the boat away, lower the boat, or . . . pull the oars or any damn thing."[13] Presumably the deckhands would know. As for the passengers, several of them grew so perturbed that no abandon-ship drills had been held that, on the third day out of New York, they approached Captain Turner to inquire whether it might not be advisable to do so. Turner reassured them that he would ask the first officer to schedule a drill, but as the *Lusitania* neared the German war zone on the morning of May 6, none had been held.

In accordance with Admiralty orders, Turner did take some precautions upon entering the danger zone. He swung out all twenty-two of the ship's lifeboats and directed that the ship be darkened. While nothing untoward occurred during the day, shortly before 8:00 P.M. the *Lusitania* received a signal from the Admiralty warning "Submarines active off south coast of Ireland."[14] Three additional wireless messages, one repeated six times, followed over the course of the night, reiterating the threat. These should have sufficed to make even the most self-confident captain anxious. As a precaution, Turner ordered that the lookout watch be doubled at dawn, stationing two sailors in the forecastle, one off each bridge wing, and two in the *Lusitania*'s crow's nest.

Around 8:00 A.M., the *Lusitania* entered a fog bank and Turner slowed the ship to 18, then 15 knots, directing that the bridge sound the ship's fog horn every minute in accordance with peacetime practice. Around eleven, the fog lifted and the *Lusitania*'s speed was increased back to 18 knots. Contrary to Admiralty guidance, Turner plotted a course that took the *Lusitania* far closer to the Irish coast than was necessary.[15] He did not order the ship to zigzag, nor did he bring it up to the maximum speed available with one boiler room out of operation. Turner later explained that he wanted to arrive at the entrance to Liverpool harbor at full tide so that he would not have to wait for a pilot to negotiate the passage across sandbars the next morning.[16]

One can only conclude that Captain Turner was overly complacent as the *Lusitania* began its final leg of the transatlantic journey and headed into the Irish Sea on May 7, 1915. Britain and Germany had been at war with one another since

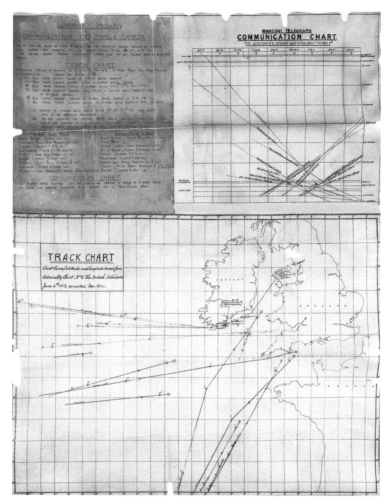

These two charts, compiled for the Board of Trade (Mersey) Inquiry, show the *Lusitania*'s position at the time of the attack, along with the tracks and signal transmissions of other inbound and outbound merchant traffic.

UK National Archives, ADM 116/1416

August 1914, and Germany had warned that as of February 18, enemy merchant vessels found within the war zone it had declared around the British Isles would be subject to destruction "without it always being possible to avoid danger to the crews and passengers."[17] Whether Turner simply did not believe that anyone would intentionally target a passenger ship carrying women, children, and third-country neutrals, or whether he simply could not grasp the vulnerability of even the largest ship to torpedoes is unclear. In the period since the *Lusitania* departed New York, German U-boats had sunk thirty-two merchant ships, five of them off the southern entrance to the Irish Sea.[18] At 11:52—almost an hour after the *Lusitania* emerged from the fog bank that had prompted Turner to slow the ship—Turner received a wireless signal from the Admiralty indicating "Submarines active in southern part Irish Channel. Last heard of twenty miles south of Coningbeg Lightship." The *Lusitania* was heading into dangerous waters. At 12:40, Turner received an additional coded message warning "Submarines five miles South of Cape Clear proceeding west when sighted at ten a.m."[19] Turner may have calculated that by this point the *Lusitania* had passed Cape Clear, but being the careful navigator that he was, he ordered the ship closer to the Irish coast so he could take a four-point fix off a promontory called the Old Head of Kinsale. Once in sight, Turner altered course to starboard and ordered the ship to maintain course and speed so he could take bearings off the lighthouse.

Kapitänleutnant Walter Schwieger, peering through the periscope of the U-20, could hardly believe his luck. Unbeknownst to Turner, the U-20 had been stalking the *Lusitania* for forty minutes. Schwieger recalled his reaction as the *Lusitania* came to starboard: "I saw the steamer change her course again. She was coming directly at us. She could not have steered a more perfect course if she had deliberately tried to give us a dead shot."[20] At 2:10 P.M. GMT, when the distance between the U-20 and the *Lusitania* had closed to 700 meters, Schwieger ordered the release of one torpedo. His war diary described the effect of the torpedo's impact:

> Clear bow-shot from 700 meters. . . . Torpedo hits starboard side close abaft the bridge, followed by a very unusually large explosion with a violent emission of smoke (far above the foremost funnel). In addition to the explosion of the torpedo there must have been a second one (boiler or coal or powder). The superstructure above the point of impact and the bridge are torn apart, fire breaks out, a thick cloud of smoke envelopes the upper bridge. The ship stops at once and very quickly takes on a heavy list to starboard, at the same time starting to sink by the bow. She looks like she will quickly capsize. Much confusion on board; boats are cleared away and some of them lowered to the water. Apparently considerable panic; several boats, fully laden, are hurriedly lowered, bow or stern first and at once fill with water.[21]

Schwieger's detached, matter-of-fact diary entry does not capture the terror, confusion, and agony that unfolded onboard the *Lusitania* over the next twenty minutes. The U-20's torpedo slammed into the ship just as many of its passengers were finishing lunch, lingering in one of the dining rooms for conversation, or taking a promenade on deck to catch some sea breeze. A good number of those topside saw the telltale bubbles of the incoming torpedo before feeling its impact. One of the strollers recalled that "It made a noise like a million-ton hammer hitting a steel boiler"; another topside passenger described the sound as "the most dreadful explosion the world has ever heard"; and a third who had been below decks described the torpedo's impact as "a dull, thud-like, not very loud but unmistakable explosion."[22] Many described a second, larger explosion that raised a geyser of water, steam, debris, and fragments of wood and iron high up into the air, with the wreckage then raining down on the decks. The ship took on a sharp list to starboard, making movement difficult.

Although crewmembers had been assigned to specific lifeboats, the passengers had not been, as Cunard management deemed the idea impractical.[23] As the *Lusitania* began to list, some passengers scrambled to retrieve life jackets stowed in their quarters while others hurried topside without them. The second-class dining room was filled to capacity, and as people realized what had happened, a mad rush ensued to reach the stairs. Husbands became separated from wives and parents from their children in a desperate attempt to reach safety. Adding to the terror and confusion, the *Lusitania* lost all electricity within minutes, rendering the interior of the ship utterly dark. One can only imagine the horror experienced by the ship's engineering crew in the pitch-black engine and boiler rooms, by the galley staff in kitchens tilting crazily, or by passengers lost in the maze of passageways and stairways. One of the bellboys recalled that he could hear the screams of a group of butchers stuck in one of the service elevators. They knew they were trapped, and the sound of their banging and screaming was ghastly. The *Lusitania*'s beautiful first-class elevator became a death cage, wedged between decks, its passengers unable to open the door or squeeze out of its ornate metal grillwork.[24] A passenger on the boat deck described the emergence of steerage passengers from one of the stairwells: "They were white-faced and terrified; I think they were shrieking; there was no kind of order." Reaching the stairs had been a matter of survival of the fittest. "The strongest got there first, the weak were pushed aside. Here and there a man had his arm around a woman's waist and bore her along with him ... there were no children to be seen ... no children could have lived in that throng."[25]

Reaching the boat decks did not guarantee survival, as the ship's sharp tilt to starboard made it difficult to launch the lifeboats. On the starboard side of the ship, the lifeboats dangled as much as eight feet away from the ship, and crewmembers had to either load the boats at an angle or encourage people to jump out to the lifeboats. On the port side, the lifeboats dangled into the ship, and crewmembers had to push them outward before attempting to lower them across the *Lusitania*'s exposed hull, from which bolts projected. Of the *Lusitania*'s twenty-two large wooden lifeboats, only six were successfully launched. Others tumbled to the sea, sank because of misplaced plugs, or could not be lowered because of the ship's tilt.[26]

The *Titanic* had taken more than two and a half hours to sink after striking an iceberg in 1912. The *Lusitania*, though equipped with more watertight compartments, disappeared under the sea in eighteen minutes after U-20's torpedo hit its starboard side. As the ship had been making way at the time it was struck, it continued to move forward while sinking, leaving a debris trail of lifeboats, bodies, deckchairs, and assorted flotsam that stretched for two miles. Hundreds of people were crowded onto the afterdecks as the liner began slipping under the water. Sixteen-year-old bellboy Ben Holton later recalled a "mighty crescendo of screams and cries of fear [that] . . . died away to a whisper."[27] Shortly after the mighty ship disappeared under the waves, a huge broiling bubble of air, boat parts, corpses, and half-drowned swimmers erupted out of the sea. One survivor remembered a "deep lingering moan that rose, and which lasted for many moments after the ship disappeared. They who were lost seemed to be calling from the very depths."[28]

The crew of the *Wanderer of Peel* witnessed the *Lusitania*'s final moments, and the small fishing boat rushed to the scene but was soon filled to the gunwales with survivors and could take no more onboard. While the day was bright and sunny, the water off the Irish coast was icy, and many survivors perished from exposure or drowned waiting for rescue. For two hours, the *Peel* did what it could before a small flotilla of tugboats, fishing trawlers, and torpedo boats from Kinsale and Queenstown (now named Cobh), Ireland, joined the rescue attempt. Over the course of the afternoon and through the night, rescuers pulled survivors out of the water and from the overcrowded lifeboats; one rescuer described corpses that floated among the wreckage "as thick as grass."[29] Many were particularly distressed by the small lifeless bodies of children bobbing like dolls in the water and by the dead mothers still clasping their lifeless infants in their arms.

The living were taken to various hotels, boardinghouses, and other accommodations throughout Queenstown, while the dead were taken to three temporary morgues set up in the town hall. Survivors desperately looked for lost spouses, missing children, best friends, and parents, grimly checking the rows of dead bodies to see whether their loved ones were there. Bodies would wash up along the coast for weeks, and identifying the dead became ever more difficult with time. The toll was terrible: of the 1,960 men, women, and children who embarked on the *Lusitania* in New York, only 764 survived; of the 129 children onboard, only 35 survived. The mortality rate for infants approached 90 percent. Among the dead were 128 American civilians.[30]

The reaction in Britain, Canada, and the United States to the *Lusitania*'s destruction was one of shared horror, revulsion, and indignation. For weeks, newspapers ran heart-wrenching stories about the tragedy, with many including sketches and photographs of the dead and missing.[31] The Cunard Line and local authorities faced an overwhelming task, coping with hundreds of shivering, shocked survivors with nothing other than the wet clothes they wore. Survivors, many injured, had to be fed, clothed, healed, and provided with emergency travel funds, even as authorities sought to identify the dead and missing. The emotional toll was tremendous, as survivors desperately sought information about missing husbands, wives, and children. Initial recovery efforts collected some 100 corpses from the sea, and dozens more washed up along the Irish coast in various states of decomposition for the next two months. Almost a thousand bodies were never recovered. As accounts of the tragedy spread, outrage swelled, with mobs in Liverpool, Manchester, and other major British cities venting their anger by attacking shops, restaurants, and hotels with German-sounding names. The reaction in Canada was identical, and the mayor of Victoria, British Columbia, was forced to declare martial law to prevent rioting.[32] The American press and public, while deeply divided about the war in Europe, roundly condemned the brutality of the attack. The New York *Nation* editorialized that

> Germany ought not to be left a moment's doubt how the civilized world regards her latest display of "frightfulness." It is a deed for which a Hun would blush, a Turk be ashamed, and a Barbary pirate apologize. To speak of technicalities and the rules of war, in the face of such wholesale murder on the high seas, is a waste of time. The law of nations and the law of God have been alike trampled upon. . . . And so must the German Government be given to understand that no plea of military necessity will now avail it before the tribunal on which sits as judge the humane conscience of the world.[33]

The *Lusitania* disaster soon became encrusted with conspiracy theories. What were the key investigations that examined the disaster, what controversies still swirl around the incident, and how have the multiple forensic dives to the *Lusitania* wreck, along with new research into the archives, informed our understanding of the tragedy?

The two naval boards that examined the USS *Maine*'s destruction have been subject to much criticism, and most modern analyses now echo Admiral Rickover's 1976 contention that the Sampson and Vreeland boards misdiagnosed the cause of the *Maine*'s destruction.[34] There is no analogous controversy about the cause of the *Lusitania*'s destruction, as dozens of witnesses saw the trail of the U-20's incoming torpedo and the German government claimed credit for the attack, coolly noting that it had warned against traveling through the war zone it had established. The *Kölnische Volkszeitung*, mouthpiece of the Catholic Centre Party, gleefully editorialized that "The sinking of the *Lusitania* is a success of our submarines which must be placed beside the greatest achievements of this naval war . . . with joyful pride we contemplate this latest deed of our Navy. It will not be the last."[35]

While none disputed that the *Lusitania* had been attacked by a German submarine, questions immediately arose about whether the liner had been adequately warned by the Admiralty; why Turner had not steered a different course or zigzagged; whether the captain and crew had been negligent in their preparations for and execution of abandon-ship procedures; whether the ship carried troops, munitions, and explosives; and why the Royal Navy had not provided some sort of escort given the known dangers.[36] Many of these legitimate questions were taken up in three official inquiries into the sinking of the *Lusitania*: the Kinsale coroner's inquest (May 8–10, 1915), the Mersey Board of Trade Inquiry (June 15–July 17, 1915), and the Mayer Liability Trial (April–August 1918).

The gentler critics of the *Lusitania* investigations note that Britain was engaged in a life-and-death struggle with Imperial Germany, empathizing with those charged with conducting inquiries in the midst of war. They excuse the tendency to ignore information that might have worked to Britain's disadvantage as the understandable prioritization of national interests over the full, public disclosure of all facets of the disaster. Harsher critics portray the second, official examination as little more than a whitewash and cover-up.[37] Regardless of how one characterizes the investigations, it is clear that British authorities influenced the outcome of the official *Lusitania* inquiry to a greater extent than did U.S. officials in the case of the 1898 Naval Court of Inquiry into the sinking of the *Maine*. The British government deliberately withheld certain information, selectively managed the witness list, and encouraged statements conducive to reaching desired conclusions.[38]

The first inquiry convened less than twenty-four hours after the liner went down. For decades, Irish nationalists had chafed at Ireland's subsidiary status as part of the United Kingdom of Great Britain and Ireland, invoking local rights whenever possible. Kinsale's coroner, sympathetic to the Irish nationalist cause, seized upon the town's ancient privileges as an independent authority to convene a coroner's jury composed of local shopkeepers and fishermen. He subpoenaed Turner and a number of survivors, subjecting the captain to some sixty questions pertaining to the cause of death of three male and two female corpses that Kinsale fishermen had delivered to his care. The coroner wanted to complete his inquest before British authorities intervened, acidly commenting that the Admiralty was as "belated on this occasion as they had been in protecting the

Lusitania against attack."[39] Nonetheless, the verdict of the inquest, soon widely disseminated in papers on both sides of the Atlantic, captured the indignation that the attack generated even among those not favorably disposed to the British crown. The Kinsale inquest concluded:

> We find that the said deceased died from their prolonged immersion and exhaustion in the sea . . . owing to the sinking of the R.M.S. *Lusitania* by a torpedo fired without warning from a German submarine. That this appalling crime was contrary to international law and the conventions of civilized nations, and we therefore charge the officers of the said submarine and the Emperor and Government of Germany, under whose orders they acted, with the crime of willful and wholesale murder.[40]

British authorities sought to stop Kinsale's hastily convened coroner's inquest, noting that a proper, duly organized inquiry would take place shortly. Britain's Merchant Shipping Act required that the Board of Trade conduct formal inquiries into major maritime accidents or losses involving British shipping. The formal investigation into *Lusitania*'s loss, known as the Mersey Inquiry, constitutes the second, much more extensive official examination of the cause of the *Lusitania*'s destruction and culpability for it. The investigation took place in London from June 15 to July 1, 1915, headed by the Board of Trade's wreck commissioner, John Charles Bigham (Baron Mersey).[41] The British government ensured that its top legal experts, Attorney General Sir Edward Carson and Solicitor General Sir Frederick Smith, ably represented its interests. The inquiry met in six sessions, calling upon thirty-six witnesses and drawing upon documents furnished by the Cunard Company and the Admiralty. In addition to Carson and Smith, attorneys representing the Board of Trade, the Cunard Company, the Canadian government, various passengers, the National Union of Sailors and Firemen, and the Marine Engineers Association had the opportunity to cross-examine witnesses. Only counsel for the government and Cunard were allowed to attend the two closed ("in camera") sessions that drew upon classified Admiralty instructions and wireless messages.

Britain's Board of Trade provided Lord Mersey with twenty-one questions to frame the proceedings, ranging from findings of fact (What was the total number of passengers on board? Were there any troops onboard? What cargo had she on board and where was it stowed) to rulings on conduct and responsibility (Was any loss of life due to any neglect by the master of the *Lusitania* to take proper precautions? Does any blame attach to him for such loss?).[42] While much of the inquiry was devoted to analyzing when Turner had received warnings about the danger of U-boat attacks, and whether he had followed

Admiralty instructions to steer a mid-channel course, avoid headlands, and zigzag, the investigation did not address the sensitive issue of whether the Royal Navy should have provided an escort for the liner, given the known danger of submarine attacks.

The British government was very concerned that the investigation remain focused on German frightfulness rather than British negligence. The Admiralty appears to have done all it could to shift blame from itself and onto Captain Turner. Lord Mersey, though discreetly informed that the Admiralty had no objections to censuring Turner, decided that doing so would detract from the investigation's main thrust, spotlighting the brutality of Germany's attack on a passenger liner carrying almost two thousand civilian men, women, and children. Ancillary matters such as Turner's conduct, the poor training of the crew, the cause of the secondary explosion, and the absence of Royal Navy escorts were brushed to the periphery or ignored entirely. Lord Mersey, presenting the court's findings, sought to drive home that the party responsible for the loss of life had been the German government—not the Cunard Line, not the Royal Navy, and certainly not the British government. In summarizing the inquiry's findings, Mersey affirmed the attorney general's opening charge that, under the circumstances and conditions that prevailed, the destruction of the *Lusitania* constituted "a deliberate attempt to murder the passengers on board that ship."[43]

Though a number of the court's findings have held up to postwar scrutiny—in particular its assertion that the *Lusitania* was unarmed, carried no troops, and had no secret load of high explosives—the Mersey Inquiry's dubious contention that the *Lusitania* had been struck by two torpedoes illustrates how the British government was willing to manipulate evidence.[44] The Royal Navy, through the efforts of its highly classified decryption center in Room 40 of the Admiralty, knew that U-20 had fired only one torpedo.[45] Yet the British government found it more convenient to attribute the second explosion that many survivors recalled to a second torpedo attack rather than to prolong the inquiry by examining alternative explanations, some of which might raise troubling questions about the ship's cargo.[46] The Admiralty did not share this information with the court in the closed sessions, nor were any of the numerous survivors who maintained that only one torpedo had struck the ship called to the witness stand.

Few survivors, however, cared deeply whether the *Lusitania* had been struck by one or two torpedoes. More disturbing to them was the inquiry's conclusion that the *Lusitania*'s captain and crew had shown competence, skill, and good judgment throughout. This simply did not conform to their fresh, vivid memories of the ship's final eighteen minutes. Survivors gathered at Caxton Hall to hear the verdict reacted with astonishment, with murmurs of a "whitewash" soon rumbling among those most angry over the chaos and confusion they had

Captain William Thomas Turner was an experienced mariner who had joined the Cunard Line in 1878, receiving his first command in 1903. Known for his gruff demeanor, Turner proved a tempting target for Admiralty scapegoating during the Mersey Inquiry.

Library of Congress, Prints and Photographs Division LC-DIG-ggbain-19067

experienced.[47] These allegations soon spread, particularly among survivors and heirs suing Cunard for damages. German propagandists and sympathizers did all they could to stoke uncertainty about the impartiality and completeness of the Mersey Inquiry, finding a receptive audience within Germany and among segments of the population of the most powerful neutral power, the United States.

Survivors and heirs to those who perished in the *Lusitania* disaster initiated legal proceedings against Cunard even before the Mersey Inquiry had begun its work, and the inquiry's findings did nothing to derail private efforts to seek some sort of compensation for pain, suffering, and loss. In the United States, some sixty-seven individuals and groups initiated lawsuits against Cunard, seeking compensation for a hodgepodge of grievances ranging from negligence on the part of the captain and the crew to allegations that Cunard, unbeknownst to them, had secretly placed troops and explosives onboard the *Lusitania* and thereby put their lives at risk. These latter allegations derived from rumors fed and spread by German sympathizers in the United States, and they were dropped once the sixty-seven proceedings were consolidated into a group action lawsuit.

This group action lawsuit, known as the Mayer Liability Trial, constitutes the third and last official inquiry into the cause of and culpability for the *Lusitania's* destruction. Given that the United States was still neutral when lawyers for the claimants began to gather witness statements and documents, it is hardly surprising that the British government refused to share information from the Mersey Inquiry's "in camera" sessions during which classified matters such as Admiralty instructions to merchant shipping and wireless warnings to the *Lusitania* had been analyzed. Despite this limitation, lawyers for the claimants compiled an impressive case file, supplementing the printed evidence from the open sessions of the Mersey Inquiry with sworn statements and depositions from thirty-three British and thirty-seven American witnesses. In addition, the plaintiff's lawyers obtained written responses from the Cunard Company to some seventy-nine questions. Captain Turner, who had moved on to command the *Ivernia* (torpedoed in January 1917) and then the *Mauretania*, endured his third round of questioning. Legal preliminaries started in 1915, when most Americans still wanted no part in the ongoing war in Europe; by the time the consolidated case came to trial in August 1918, the United States had been at war with Germany for sixteen months and the public mood had changed dramatically.

Judge Mayer's verdict reflected the pervasive anger at Germany's conduct of its war at sea. Judge Mayer cleared the Cunard Company of any responsibility and negligence, despite various witness statements that claimed watertight compartments had not been shut, portholes had been open, and efforts to launch the lifeboats had seemed clumsy and chaotic. While sympathetic to survivors and heirs, Mayer reminded them that only one party should be held responsible for the loss of life and property, and that was Germany. Quoting Lord Mersey, Mayer concluded that "The whole blame for the cruel destruction of life in this catastrophe must rest solely with those who plotted and with those who committed the crime." Well aware that claimants would be disappointed that they were to receive nothing for their loss and suffering as a result of his ruling, Mayer reassured the claimants that "when the time shall come, [the United of America and her Allies] will well remember the rights of those affected by the sinking of the *Lusitania*, and will see to it that reparation shall be made for one of the most indefensible acts of modern times."[48]

The three official inquiries shaped Anglo-American opinion on both sides of the Atlantic as newspapers quoted testimonies, printed inquiry excerpts, and publicized court findings. Perhaps of equal significance, however, was the struggle unfolding outside the courtrooms to establish the narrative of what had happened and why. British and German newspapers provided entirely different interpretations of the incident to their reading publics. British papers and periodicals emphasized Hunnish barbarity, while their German counterparts, after initially celebrating the *Lusitania*'s destruction as a great accomplishment, expressed sorrow for the loss of innocent lives but justified the act. German papers echoed the government's position that the *Lusitania* had been armed and carried war munitions. In addition, German papers sought to shift responsibility for the loss of civilian lives from the U-boat commander and the German government to Cunard and the British government.

Both governments attempted to bend opinion in the United States in their direction, with the German government devoting a great deal of effort to counteracting the perceived pro-British bias of the American press and of its political elite. As part of this effort, the German government and sympathetic German Americans offered up a number of arguments to dampen American outrage. This struggle for the sympathy of the American public generated myths and conspiracy theories that have persisted for decades. Apologists for the German attack raised four main questions about the *Lusitania* during the war, with versions of these questions resurfacing for the next hundred years. First, was the *Lusitania* armed, and did deck guns render it an armed merchant cruiser subject to destruction? Second, was the *Lusitania* carrying war materials to Britain, and did the presence of undeclared high explosives cause the ship to sink so rapidly? Third, was the *Lusitania* carrying troops from Canada to the United Kingdom, in effect making it a legitimate target of war? Lastly, did Churchill, the Admiralty, or the British government welcome the ship's destruction in the hope that it would bring the United States into the war as an ally? More provocatively, did the Admiralty deliberately withhold information from Captain Turner, and was the absence of Royal Navy destroyer escorts indicative of some sort of nefarious British plot to poison relations between the United States and Germany?

Within Germany, conservatives, centrists, and liberals alike shared the conviction throughout the war that the U-20's attack on the *Lusitania* had been justified. The notion that the ship had been armed and carried troops or munitions became pervasive in wartime Germany and persisted for decades thereafter. Overseas, particularly in the United States, the German government and its representatives sought to dispel anger at the sinking of a passenger liner by casting doubt on the ship's civilian character. German Americans, Irish Americans, and others immune to the Anglophilia that prevailed in the East Coast establishment proved particularly receptive to conspiracy theories. Midwestern Progressives such as Robert La Follette never abandoned the notion that the Wilson administration had deliberately misled the American public about the *Lusitania* disaster. More recently, these questions figure prominently in sensationalist new documentaries, articles, and books purporting to reveal the "dark secrets of the *Lusitania*."[49]

British and German secrecy, misinformation, and messaging made separating fact from fiction difficult in the midst of a world war. A trickle of survivor accounts appeared during the conflict, followed by a deluge of memoirs and histories written by politicians, ambassadors, and admirals after its conclusion.[50] By the late 1920s, a noticeable subgenre appeared in Britain and the United States that sought to re-examine the war from the other side of the hill and humanize the "barbarous Hun." Writing in 1928, Lowell Thomas, a popular American journalist and bestselling author, felt free to refer to the U-20 as a jolly, mirthful boat "loud with laughter and rollicking fellowship."[51] This would have been unthinkable a decade earlier, and by the end of the 1930s, it would strike the public as tone-deaf to British merchant seamen once again "in peril on the sea."

With the passage of time, the raw emotional toll of the incident receded from memory, and by the mid-1960s, records long sealed in the British archives began to become available.[52] A number of engaging narratives of the *Lusitania*'s final voyage appeared before this, but the British government's reticence to make public Admiralty files from the First World War fed conspiracy theories. Even after the release of those files, the proclivity to advance provocative, unsupported, and conjectural notions about the *Lusitania* persisted.[53]

Yet we know much more about the incident than once was the case, thanks to well-researched books that draw upon government records, company files, the official investigations, and collections of survivor accounts.[54] In addition, since the 1990s, several well-funded diving expeditions have explored the wreck of the *Lusitania*, with Gregg Bemis indefatigable in his quest to unravel the full story of the ship's rapid demise. These forensic dive expeditions have deployed the latest underwater video and salvage technologies, ranging from remotely controlled submersibles equipped with lights and cameras to miniature manned submarines, to lightweight atmospheric diving suits that enable the diver to stay on station for hours. We now have startlingly clear, crisp images of the wreck's exterior, though the starboard side where the torpedo hit lies embedded in the ocean floor.[55] Bemis's 2011 dive expedition broke previous boundaries, successfully sending a small, remotely piloted submersible "video ray" into the interior of the ship.

Turning to the first question—whether or not the *Lusitania* was armed—we can say with certainty that the ship was not armed. Rumors that the *Lusitania* had been equipped with secret deck guns began circulating in the German-American press shortly after the *Lusitania*'s destruction.[56] No evidence has ever been produced to disprove Captain Turner's sworn statements that the ship was unarmed. Dozens of survivors provided sworn statements to the Mersey Inquiry and Mayer Liability Trial attesting that they had seen no guns aboard the ship. Photographs and a short film taken as the *Lusitania* was leaving New York reveal no signs of deck guns. Furthermore, the dive expeditions of 1993, 1994, 2008, and 2011 have uncovered no sign of deck guns, concealed or otherwise. As to allegations that the British somehow cleverly stowed away guns below decks with the intent of attaching them to preinstalled mounting rings embedded in the ship's deck, it beggars belief that a crew lacking proficiency in the lowering of lifeboats would be capable of hauling guns stored below decks, installing them on cleverly disguised mounting rings, and operating them once danger loomed.[57] The only discernible protective measures taken as the *Lusitania* approached Germany's declared war zone on May 6 was to swing out the lifeboats and darken ship.

The myth of the *Lusitania*'s deck guns endured long after the close of World War I because it did not appear entirely preposterous, as details about the contractual relationship between the Cunard Company and the Royal Navy began to emerge. In 1903, the British government had furnished Cunard with a £2.6 million low-interest loan for the construction of the *Lusitania* and *Mauretania*, along with an annual operating subsidy. In exchange, Cunard agreed to certain naval construction specifications, with the 1907 blueprints of the *Lusitania* indicating that mounting rings for guns should be installed in the deck.[58] Sir Julian Corbett, who wrote the naval sections of Britain's official history of the Great War, noted that at the outset of the First World War the Admiralty planned to outfit the *Lusitania* and eight other liners with naval guns, deploying them as "armed merchant cruisers." The Admiralty, after considering the high costs of operating the *Lusitania* and *Mauretania*, released both ships back to Cunard, but apparently did equip the remaining passenger ships with naval guns.[59] Further obscuring the matter, there is evidence that the Admiralty had previously used Cunard liners to transport large-caliber guns purchased in the United States, and was in the midst of arming a number of merchant ships with guns in the spring of 1915.

This program, known as the Q-ship program, sought to entrap German U-boats adhering to the conventions of cruiser warfare, luring the U-boats into range and then sending them to the bottom of the sea using concealed naval guns and trained gun crews.[60] German agents quite likely had some inkling of these developments, and Berlin was eager to acquire more information. Shortly after departing New York harbor, the *Lusitania*'s master-at-arms discovered three German-speaking stowaways, one with a camera, hiding in one of the ship's pantries. Their identity has never been established, as the master-at-arms was unable to free them from confinement before the ship went down. They were most probably German agents who had slipped onboard looking for some sort of incriminating evidence.[61] This suggests that the German government suspected that the *Lusitania* carried guns or munitions, but the suspicion was unfounded. One can say with certainty that despite persistent German claims to the contrary, the *Lusitania* carried no naval guns, mounted or otherwise.

This raises the second question that swirls around the *Lusitania*, namely whether the ship carried munitions and in effect used its civilian passengers as human shields. The German government chided President Wilson that the *Lusitania* had been no ordinary unarmed merchant ship. It claimed that "on her last trip the *Lusitania*, as on earlier occasions, had Canadian troops and munitions on board, including no less than 5,400 cases of ammunition destined for the destruction of brave German soldiers who are fulfilling with self-sacrifice and devotion their duty in the service of the Fatherland. . . . [T]he [Cunard] company quite deliberately tried to use the lives of American citizens as protection for the ammunition carried."[62]

There has never been any dispute that the *Lusitania* carried munitions. Per law, Cunard was required to file a cargo manifest with the (customs) collector of the port of New York. On April 30, the day before the *Lusitania* was scheduled to depart, Captain Turner dropped by the customs house to swear that the one-page manifest delivered was a full and truthful representation of cargo laden. The list was short, listing thirty-five separate consignments ranging from meat to shoes to machine parts.[63] This initial listing did not include munitions, but on May 5, four days after the *Lusitania* had left harbor, Cunard officials turned in a detailed, twenty-four-page supplemental manifest. Among the items included in the supplemental manifest were 4,200 cases of rifle ammunition; 1,248 cases of three-inch shrapnel shell casings; 18 cases of fuses; 184 cases of military accoutrements (haversacks, pouches); 400 cases of machine tools; and consignments of copper, aluminum, and foodstuffs purchased by the British government.[64]

The full supplemental manifest was published by the *New York Times* the day after the *Lusitania*'s destruction, and though the British government sought to characterize the ship's cargo as "general" and "of the ordinary kind" during the Mersey Inquiry, it acknowledged that "about 5,000" cases of cartridges were stowed in the ship's forward cargo spaces. The use of supplemental manifests was not uncommon, reflecting last-minute deliveries of meat, fresh produce, and other cargo. It may seem disingenuous that Cunard only listed munitions in the supplemental manifest it filed four days *after* the *Lusitania* had left port, but if Cunard had sought to mislead U.S. officials, it would have refrained from listing them at all. Cunard probably delayed disclosing some of its more sensitive cargo until the *Lusitania* was clear of dockyard disturbances, the machinations of German sympathizers, and time-delaying inspections by the U.S. Neutrality

Squad charged with enforcing America's few export regulations. Overall, the British government sought to downplay the significance of the *Lusitania*'s cargo. Yet if one does the math, as German-American editors soon did, it is beyond dispute that the *Lusitania* carried more than 4 million rounds of small-arms ammunition (.303 caliber) and nearly 5,000 shrapnel shell casings. The *Lusitania*'s primary function remained carrying paying civilian passengers across the Atlantic in style and comfort as before the war. But packed in its limited cargo compartment were sufficient munitions to kill thousands of German soldiers.[65]

The Mersey Investigation and the Mayer Liability Trial duly recognized that the *Lusitania* had been carrying munitions, and the presence of munitions was never denied by Cunard or the British government. The British government minimized their significance, and emphasized that Cunard had observed U.S. regulations prohibiting passenger liners from transporting explosives "likely to endanger the health or lives of the passengers or the safety of the vessel." The U.S. Department of Commerce and Labor had tested whether it was safe to stow small-arms ammunitions onboard passenger ships in 1911, and had ruled that they could be safely transported without restriction. Cunard therefore did not violate U.S. law in packing millions of rounds of small-arms cartridges among the crates of fur, boxes of candies, and stacks of copper ingots.[66] As for loading shrapnel shell casings, fuses, machine tools, and vital metals such as copper and aluminum, this was perfectly legal under U.S. law so long as passenger ships refrained from transporting assembled munitions, explosives, and other highly volatile material. American dockworkers were openly and legally loading tons of explosives, shells, finished guns, armor plate, and other war matèriel to the tune of millions of dollars onto British freighters in the spring of 1914. New York's port collector remarked that there were "dozens of ships sailing from the port of New York during that period with larger consignments of small-arms ammunition and other military supplies."[67]

In short, Cunard and the British government never denied shipping munitions and contraband. Their insistence was only that they had complied with U.S. law and did nothing to endanger the lives of the passengers embarked on the *Lusitania*. Within days of the incident, German sympathizers in the United States began to challenge the latter claim, asserting that the *Lusitania* had carried high explosives, chemicals, or other volatile material not listed on the manifest. These high explosives, so went the claim, caused the secondary explosion that doomed the *Lusitania*. Variants of these allegations linger on, fed by odd entries on the manifest and by speculation that shipments identified as cheese, furs, and oysters might have been something more sinister.[68]

One cannot rule out the possibility that there was more to the *Lusitania*'s cargo than what was listed on the manifest. One can, however, test hypotheses concerning the second mysterious explosion for feasibility, drawing upon physical evidence obtained through forensic dives, laboratory tests, and computer simulations. In 2011, Gregg Bemis, who first purchased a share of the *Lusitania* wreck in 1968 and has since become its sole owner, sought to settle the question once and for all. He funded an elaborate eight-day dive to the wreck and contracted the Lawrence Livermore National Laboratory (LLNL) to conduct a test of the major theories explaining the cause of the ship's rapid sinking. The field study, equipped with a two-person submersible, a one-person lightweight atmospheric diving apparatus, a team of tech divers (deepwater scuba experts), and a remotely piloted, unmanned video underwater vehicle, found 0.303 cartridges scattered in and around the *Lusitania*. Bemis's team attempted to cut an opening into the hull of the ship to examine the cargo area itself, but the effort proved unsuccessful. The team was able, however, to pilot its small, remotely controlled "video ray" into another hole in the hull, penetrating well into the interior of the ship. The submersible's camera captured images of hundreds of rounds of small-arms ammunition in the cargo area, but other than some bent girders, discovered no evidence substantiating that there had been a massive explosion in the cargo area. After eight days of diving and tens of thousands of dollars, the field study confirmed only what was already known: the *Lusitania* was carrying large quantities of small-arms ammunition. The physical evidence uncovered at the wreck site to date can neither confirm nor disprove competing theories pertaining to the second explosion.[69]

Bemis asked scientists at LLNL to subject the four most likely theories about the secondary explosion to scientific scrutiny. He may have hoped the Livermore team would lend its weight to his conviction that explosives played a role, but made no attempt to suppress findings when they pointed in the other direction. After rigorously testing four hypotheses, the scientists ruled that the most likely cause of the secondary blast was a boiler explosion associated with the onrush of cold ocean water into the boiler room. The boiler explosion would have produced a dramatic plume of steam, debris, and deck material, but would have done little structural damage to the ship. Scientists ruled out an alternative hypothesis, that aluminum powder had caused the second explosion, as inconsistent with eyewitness accounts. Controlled tests showed that an aluminum-powder explosion would have produced an intense flash of white light, yet none of the survivor accounts make mention of such a flash. As for the theory that coal dust might have caused the second explosion, the Livermore team concluded that a coal-dust explosion would have lacked the force to throw materials sky-high, as per survivor accounts. Lastly, the Livermore scientists tested the hypothesis that the torpedo detonated high explosives within the *Lusitania*, a theory that has persisted for over a century. They concluded that high explosives, whether packed into shrapnel cases or hidden in barrels labeled oysters, would have exploded almost immediately after the torpedo's detonation. Survivors, however, recalled a ten- to twenty-second time interval between the torpedo's detonation and the second explosion. John Maienschein, director of the Energetic Materials Center at the Livermore National Laboratory, commented that he found the high-explosives scenario "highly unlikely."[70]

In addition to the explosives tests, Livermore scientists ran computer simulations analyzing what damage a single torpedo might have caused. Their digitized model of the ship incorporated 3 million digital points of reference. After running the simulation, the lead scientist concluded, "I am confident the torpedo caused catastrophic damage that was fatal to the ship. No ambiguity about that in my mind."[71]

The *Lusitania* carried munitions and war supplies, and these were duly recorded on the manifest at the time. The most likely explanation for the catastrophic loss of life is that the U-20's torpedo hit precisely the right spot to sink the pride of the Cunard Line in less than twenty minutes. Chance, Clausewitz's third factor in conceptualizing war, played a key role in the ship's demise. Had the fog not lifted when it did, the *Lusitania* would have passed undetected that May day in 1915. Had Turner not brought his ship closer to land and held a steady course while taking a navigational fix, it would have been impossible for U-20 to launch its torpedo. And had Schwieger pulled the launch trigger just seconds later, his torpedo would have struck the *Lusitania* farther back toward its stern, and the ship would have remained afloat longer.

A third charge common to conspiracy theories about the *Lusitania* is that the liner carried a contingent of Canadian troops who came onboard disguised as civilians. One wonders why the British and Canadian governments would go to the trouble of sending Canadian troops to New York City rather than Halifax, subjecting them to possible internment, if detected, for transportation across the Atlantic. The German government levied this charge in its note to Wilson of May 28, 1915, and as with allegations concerning deck guns and high explosives, the allegation lingered on for decades. New York's collector of port, Dudley Field Malone, sought to nip the matter in the bud in his lengthy official report to the U.S. Secretary of the Treasury three weeks after the *Lusitania*'s destruction. He firmly asserted that the ship "did not have Canadian troops or troops of any nationality on board," and remarked that he and his inspectors had not seen any passengers who even looked like they might be military men in civilian clothing. Numerous survivors affirmed that they, too, had seen no signs that any fellow passengers might be military men traveling in civilian garb. During the Mersey hearings, Captain Turner responded under oath to the question "Were there any Canadian troops on board?" with a firm "None whatever."

Speculation to the contrary has focused on unaccompanied male passengers of Canadian origin. The Canadian Department of National Defence responded to a query in the 1970s as to whether any of the men who fit this category and had perished that day were soldiers. It responded that they were not. Given that none of their families, dependents, or heirs has over the course of decades ever claimed any survivor benefits, one can say with near certainty that there were no troop contingents on the *Lusitania*.[72] Some of the male passengers did indeed hold reserve commissions, others were returning from convalescent leave in Canada, and a number of the female passengers were nurses bound for hospitals in Britain and France. But despite German efforts to obscure the character of the ship by alleging that it carried troops, the evidence clearly contradicts this claim.[73] The *Lusitania* was an unarmed passenger ship, carrying no troops but transporting munitions unbeknownst to its passengers.

The last charge common to conspiracy theories then and now is that Winston Churchill and "Jacky" Fisher, First Lord and First Sea Lord of the Admiralty, respectively, somehow connived to create the incident in the hope of drawing the United States into the war. Churchill and Fisher were bombastic, forceful, and compelling figures each of whom had a brutal streak to their character. Assigned as Britain's naval delegate to the First Hague Peace Convention in 1899, Fischer lectured his fellow delegates that "moderation in war is imbecility," exclaiming that "If you rub it in both at home and abroad that you are ready for instant war with every unit of your strength in the first line, and intend to be first in and hit your enemy in the belly, and kick him when he is down, and boil your prisoners in oil (if you take any!), and torture his women and children, then people will keep clear of you."[74] Churchill, initially smitten with Fisher's forcefulness, determination, and color, adopted similar tones in speech and correspondence, coolly informing Walter Runciman at the Board of Trade in February 1915:

> It is most important to attract neutral shipping to our shores in the hope especially of embroiling the U.S.A with Germany. The German formal announcement of indiscriminate submarining has been made to the United States to produce a deterrent effect upon traffic. For our part we want the traffic—the more the better; and if some of it gets into trouble, better still.[75]

Fisher and Churchill's bombast, coupled with nagging questions about the incident, soon gave rise to suspicion that the Admiralty, Churchill, and others in the British government were somehow complicit in the disaster. German agents and sympathizers did their best to stir up these rumors, but one cannot attribute misgivings solely to German misinformation. On May 15, a week after the *Lusitania*'s destruction, former Democratic congressman Richard P. Hobson of Alabama published a letter in the *New York Tribune*. Hobson, a naval hero of the Spanish-American War and a recipient of the Congressional Medal of Honor, suggested that his fellow Americans should think twice before allowing another naval incident to propel them into war. He reflected that "There could be no possible motive for Germany wishing to destroy American lives. In fact, Germany sought by extraordinary warning not to destroy American lives. . . . On the other hand, there is a full motive for England wishing such a tragedy—the motive for thrusting America into war with Germany." Hobson, no Midwestern German American, levied a series of questions that he found baffling: "Knowing that German submarines were operating in the south of the Irish coast, why did not the British Admiralty, which controlled the *Lusitania*'s movements, order her to use the uninfested route around the north of Ireland? . . . How could a torpedo sink such a ship in twenty minutes? . . . Why was there no protecting convoy in the danger zone?"[76]

Hobson's suspicions, soon picked up and disseminated in German-American newspapers throughout the United States, persisted in many circles long after the war.[77] The truth is far more mundane. If the Admiralty was guilty of anything, it was of complacency, a tendency to focus more on fleet operations than on the protection of merchant shipping, and the over-compartmentalization of intelligence. One can detect signs of cover-ups in logbooks, records, and correspondence, with the intent to protect the Royal Navy's reputation. Several historians have studied the matter intensely, with an expert on British naval intelligence remarking that "if there was a plot by Winston and his advisers to engineer an encounter between U-20 and the *Lusitania*, it left an enormous amount to chance. . . . [A]n encounter between the U-boat and the liner depended on the thousand-to-one chance of the U-boat being . . . within a few hundred yards and on a bearing for an attack."[78] Churchill and Fisher were gamblers, but the communications between the two after the *Lusitania* sank convey surprise, anger, and fear rather than satisfaction. Churchill and Fisher were furious over the *Lusitania*'s destruction; Fisher commented privately, "I hope that Captain Turner will be arrested immediately after the enquiry whatever the verdict. . . . No seaman in his senses could have acted as he did." Churchill recommended pursuing the captain "without check."[79] One can charge the British Admiralty with negligence and cover-up, with Churchill and Fisher eager to shift blame and preserve their reputations. Soon Fisher and Churchill would be gone from the Admiralty because of a fiasco even larger than the loss of the *Lusitania*—the debacle at Gallipoli.

The sinking of the *Lusitania* was a human tragedy, separating mothers from their babies, fathers from families, and friends from one another in a brutal, chaotic scramble for survival. Numerous witnesses recalled the selfless conduct of ship stewards seeking to bring passengers up from below; of individuals such as the millionaire Alfred Vanderbilt, who calmly helped load others into lifeboats and remained on the ship as it went down; and of strangers who offered up their life jackets in a last salute to Edwardian notions that women and children should be spared the horrors of war. Others never forgot the scenes and sounds of horror they experienced, from the desperate cries of people trapped in engine rooms to the moans of hundreds clinging to flotsam after the ship went down. The overwhelming majority of passengers and crew were subjects of the British Crown, with Canadians, English, Irish, Scots, and Indians among the dead. The next-largest contingent was American, with Russians, Swedes, Persians, and others also at the receiving end of U-20's torpedo attack. Although the event touched many nationalities, diplomats soon focused on the reaction of the most powerful neutral power still unaligned with the warring alliances that were struggling for supremacy. In the spring of 1915, the leaders and people of the United States viewed the Great War as a distant struggle that did not directly involve them or the nation's interests. The *Lusitania* incident shook this conviction, with Colonel Edward House, Woodrow Wilson's confidante and adviser, writing the president the day after the attack that "America has come to the parting of the ways, when she must determine whether she stands for civilized or uncivilized warfare. We can no longer remain neutral spectators."[80]

AMERICAN NEUTRALITY, AUGUST 1914–MAY 1915

When war broke out in Europe in August 1914, the reaction in America had been one of shock, and for most, surprise. One North Carolina congressman described the onset of war as akin to "lightning out of a clear sky . . . the grim reality of it stuns you."[81] The large majority of the population was sympathetic to the Entente rather than the Central Powers, focusing on the conflict being waged on the Western Front rather than on the Eastern dimensions of the struggle. Many Americans perceived the struggle as one pitting British and French liberal democracy against German militarism and autocracy, with most convinced that the world would be a better place if the former rather than the latter prevailed. As for the immense struggles in the East between the Russian, Austro-Hungarian, German, and Ottoman empires, Americans followed newspaper accounts of the movements of their vast armies but few other than those with roots in the region cared deeply about the outcome.[82] Colonel House's characterization of Americans as "neutral spectators" before the sinking of the *Lusitania* is not far off the mark, but it needs some qualifications.

During the first year of the war, the American public fell into three groups in terms of their attitude toward the Entente and Central Powers. The largest group of Americans was moderately pro-Allied.[83] This group had been shocked at Germany's violation of Belgian neutrality in August 1914, had cheered on French and British forces desperately seeking to stop the forward momentum of the German steamroller in August and September, and had been appalled by lurid stories of German brutality against Belgian and French civilians. Their ardent pro-Entente sympathies had dissipated somewhat in the fall and winter of 1914, as they became aware of the complexities of the war's origin, and as irritation increased over British restrictions on neutral trade and shipping. Increasingly prone to apportioning a share of blame to both sides for the outbreak of war, this group retained sympathy for the Allied cause but believed there was no compelling case why the United States should join the slaughter taking place on faraway battlefields. Most preferred an Allied rather than a German victory, but they thanked their God and good fortune that America had no stake in the struggle.

A second, smaller group believed that the United States did indeed have an interest in the outcome of the war. These pro-Allied extremists did not yet advocate direct American intervention, but they were convinced that Germany alone was to blame for the war. The ongoing struggle in Europe, in their view, pitted right against wrong, freedom against slavery, and democracy against autocracy.[84] Many who fell into this category were Anglophiles educated in the English tradition at prep schools like Groton, exposed to notions of Anglo-Saxon solidarity, and imbued with Whiggish perspectives on history and governance.[85] They were disproportionately Episcopalian, Presbyterian, or Methodist in faith and worldview, and while the group was far smaller than the group of pro-Allied moderates, they occupied influential positions in business and finance (J. P. Morgan), government (Henry Cabot Lodge, Henry L. Stimson), law, the publishing industry (George Haven Putnam), and academic circles. The prominent author and editor William Dean Howells, nicknamed the "Dean of American Letters," captured the perspective of this group in a piece he wrote for the *North American Review* in May 1915, titled "Why":

> After these nine months of the manifold murder in Europe begun by Germany, we who hold her guilty of all the harm that can flow from the largest evil let loose upon the world may fitly take stock of our reasons and convictions, not so much as against Germany as in favor of England and France, and especially England. Why do we still believe as powerfully in her cause as at the first? It is easy to say because it is the cause of liberty, of humanity, of Christianity; that it is something like a last hope of mankind; that if it fails civilization will no longer be free in Europe or America. . . . One wishes to count and recount one's convictions, to repeat again that the party of the Allies is the party, above everything, of peace, the party of hope, of the equal right to life, liberty, and the pursuit of happiness, of everything endeared by the Declaration and guarded by the Constitution.[86]

This ardently pro-British viewpoint was a minority perspective at the beginning of 1915, but it found outlet in influential newspapers and periodicals ranging from the *New York Times* to *The Nation,* from *Harper's Weekly* to Teddy Roosevelt's *Outlook.* Recognizing that the great majority of Americans had little appetite for becoming involved in the war, few pro-Allied extremists argued for any sort of direct American intervention. Only after the Allied disasters at Gallipoli, the Somme, and

Verdun did this group begin to realize that more than sympathy, lines of credit, and American munitions would be needed to roll back Germany's armies.

The third group, much smaller than the pro-Allied camp as a whole but probably numerically as strong as the extremist Allied supporters, were those who favored a German victory or at least some sort of comeuppance to the British Empire. Among this group, or more properly, these assorted groups—disparaged by the outspoken Theodore Roosevelt as "hyphenated Americans"—were German Americans, Catholic Irish Americans, Jewish Americans, and to some degree the Scandinavian Americans of the upper Midwest. It is easy to forget how widespread and organized was the German-American community before America's entry into World War I. During the war, anti-German feeling resulted in the renaming of hundreds of towns and communities, the closure of German-language newspapers and schools, and the dissolution of German *Vereine* (clubs and civic organizations), which had been a staple of German-American community life for decades. Numbering over 8 million in the census of 1910, Americans of German ancestry or origin could be found from the mid-Atlantic seaboard to the Texas hill country, with New York, Philadelphia, Cincinnati, Chicago, St. Louis, and Milwaukee all supporting major German-language newspapers and periodicals. German government efforts to portray the war as a defensive response to Russian aggression, French revanchism, and British intrigue found a receptive audience in the German-American community, with papers such as the *New Yorker Staats-Zeitung*, the *Illinois Staats-Zeitung,* and the English-language, pro-German *The Fatherland* seeking to counteract what they viewed as the pro-British bias of the mainstream press. As a whole, the American public tended to see German Americans as industrious, hardworking, and well educated, and if few were swayed by pro-German arguments, the counter-narrative of the German-American community acted as a brake to pro-Allied extremism.[87]

Lining up with the German-American community in questioning whether the British Empire and its allies represented the "cause of liberty [and] . . . a last hope of mankind" were Catholic Irish Americans and the Jewish-American communities. Many Irish Americans nursed a sense of grievance that bordered on hatred of the British Empire, associating English rule with starvation, oppression, and racial arrogance. The Irish-American community, while smaller than the German-American community at 4.5 million, had gained considerable political power in Boston, New York, and other East Coast cities. The German-Jewish community, as well as the larger Yiddish-language Jewish community that traced its origins to areas ruled by the tsar, preferred Imperial Germany to tsarist Russia: while right-wing parties in Germany spouted anti-Semitism, at least they did not engage in the sort of violent pogroms that had made life perilous and difficult for Jews living in the East. Lastly, the Scandinavian communities of the upper Midwest tended to be more receptive to German perspectives than the U.S. population as a whole, with many favoring policies such as an arms embargo on both sides in order to keep the United States out of the war.

The American public, in short, was deeply divided in its sympathies toward the Entente and Central Powers in the period before the *Lusitania*'s destruction. In November 1914, the *Literary Digest* canvassed more than 350 newspapers, reporting that 46 percent of editors identified themselves as sympathetic to the Allied cause and 49 percent expressed no leanings in either direction.[88] The majority of the population harbored pro-Allied sympathies, but only a segment of this majority was outspoken and uncritical in its support for the British and French. A well-organized minority, making up around 15 percent of the population, favored the German cause. But whether pro-Allied or pro-German, the vast majority preferred to stay out of the war. As a correspondent for the London *Nation* remarked in October 1915, months after the *Lusitania* incident,

> The strongest sentiment in the United States of today is not anti-German but anti-war, not pro-Ally but pro-peace. There is nothing Americans desire more fervently than to keep out of the present ghastly struggle. They regard Europe as rattling madly back into barbarism, while they themselves are the sole depositories of sanity and civilization. . . . They look down upon us as the victims of dynastic ambitions, diplomatic plots, and an anti-democratic dispensation, and they thank their stars that in America they are exempt from the conditions which have produced so appalling a catastrophe.[89]

How, then, did American neutrality, or more precisely the desire to be a spectator rather than a participant in the Great War, express itself in terms of policy and action during the period before the sinking of the *Lusitania*? Did Wilson live up to his initial message to the American people after the outbreak of war, warning them against "passionately taking sides" and cautioning that "The United States must be neutral in fact as well as in name [and] . . . impartial in thought as well as in action" lest the country become "divided in camps of hostile opinion, hot against each other"?[90] What sort of policies did the Wilson administration pursue during the period preceding the *Lusitania*'s destruction, and based on these policies, what conclusions can one reach regarding the impartiality of Wilson and his advisers?

One can gain a sense of the trajectory of U.S. foreign policy during the period before the *Lusitania*'s destruction by looking at five areas of decision making: policies related to loans and finances, policies related to the sale of military goods and munitions, an initiative to establish a government-owned merchant marine, and the response of the Wilson administration to British and German naval and maritime war measures. While endeavoring to maintain strict neutrality, administration policy resulted in outcomes that favored the British in three of these areas, while tilting against British interests in two.

Turning first to the issue of loans and finances, initial U.S. decisions endeavored to be as strictly neutral as Wilson's August 1914 message promised would be the case. Shortly after the outbreak of war in Europe, J. P. Morgan & Company asked the State Department whether it had any objections to Morgan's floating a loan to the French government for the sum of $100 million. The State Department's counselor—a position created in 1909 to provide the secretary of state with advice on treaties, international law, and interstate negotiations—informed the secretary that neither international nor U.S. law prohibited U.S. financial institutions from making private loans to belligerent governments, concluding that the department would be following precedent if it gave a green light to the request. The "Great Commoner" William Jennings Bryan, whom Woodrow Wilson had appointed secretary of state in 1913 because of his loyal following in Democratic circles, ignored counselor Robert Lansing's legal exposition. Bryan had accepted the offer to become secretary of state in the hope of diminishing the likelihood of war, and he had spent his first seventeen months in office trying to negotiate a series of conciliation treaties calling for "cooling off" periods before the resort to war. Mocked by the Eastern press as a naïve "fathead" whose evangelical piety, prohibitionist sentiments, and fondness for the Chautauqua adult education lecture circuit betrayed an embarrassing provincialism and lack of sophistication, William Jennings Bryan brushed aside Lansing's analysis of what was legal and instead made a case for what was right.[91] Bryan informed Lansing that while the "precedents were all in favor of such loans. . . . I thought they violated the spirit of neutrality because money, being able to purchase all other contraband materials, was in effect the worst contraband."[92] Bryan warned Wilson that if American financiers became involved in raising money for belligerents, then future U.S. policy would be subjected to lobbying by "powerful financial interests" seeking policies favorable to securing their investments. Bryan secured the president's permission to issue a statement that the U.S. government believed authorizing loans to belligerent states would be "inconsistent with the true spirit of neutrality."[93]

Market forces soon put pressure on the administration's commitment to maintaining this "true spirit of neutrality" in financial matters. The American economy had entered a severe recession in 1913, and the outbreak of war disrupted normal peacetime trade. Steel mills were operating at half capacity, unemployment in the industrial sector was climbing toward 15 percent, and prices for key agricultural goods were plummeting.[94] By October, State Department officials were warning Bryan and Wilson that a continued ban on loans and credits would drive Britain and France to place orders for war matèriels with Canada, Australia, Mexico, or Argentina. Caught between a principled stance that threatened to undermine an already faltering economy and an embarrassing reversal of policy, the administration found a loophole: Americans banks were indeed prohibited from making loans, but the administration had no objections if U.S. banks arranged lines of credit that would enable belligerents to purchase goods and services from the United States. This change of policy opened the door for massive Allied orders for raw materials, agricultural products, and industrial goods. The administration pointed out that the Central Powers might likewise place orders with American firms, but given Britain's determination to disrupt German imports, the opening of lines of credit favored the Entente powers in reality regardless of protestations that they were theoretically strictly neutral. By May 1915, the Entente powers had secured American lines of credit exceeding $170 million, while Germany had secured $10 million.[95]

If the Wilson administration employed a degree of sophistry in differentiating between war loans and lines of credit, it was quite forthright in a second policy arena that likewise tended to favor the Entente, namely the sale of war matériel and munitions. Wilson's proclamations of neutrality and his appeal to the people of the United States in August 1914 left many businessmen and traders scratching their heads, particularly his admonition that all Americans should avoid "every transaction that might be construed as a preference of one party to the struggle before another."[96] Given that neutral powers had previously felt free to sell war material to belligerents, with Germany doing so during the Boer War and Britain during the Russo-Japanese War, inquiries soon began to arrive in Washington as to what the administration's policy entailed: were American businesses to refrain from selling war material (contraband), or were they free to do so as long as they understood that such material could be intercepted and confiscated by belligerent powers under international law? The administration felt compelled to clarify its policy in a public circular issued by the secretary of state in October. The new guidelines stated that in view of the many inquiries the State Department was receiving from American merchants and businesses,

> . . . generally speaking, a citizen of the United States can sell to a belligerent government or its agent any article of commerce which he pleases. He is not prohibited from doing this by any rule of international law, by any treaty provisions, or by any statute of the United States. It makes no difference whether the articles sold are exclusively for war purposes, such as firearms, explosives, etc., or are foodstuffs, clothing, horses, etc., for the use of the army or navy of the belligerent . . .

It is true that such articles as those mentioned are considered contraband and are, outside the territorial jurisdiction of a neutral nation, subject to seizure by an enemy of the purchasing government, but it is the enemy's duty to prevent the articles reaching their destination, not the duty of the nation whose citizens have sold them. If the enemy of the purchasing nation happens for the time to be unable to do this that is for him one of the misfortunes of war; the inability, however, imposes on the neutral government no obligation to prevent the sale.[97]

While issued under Secretary of State Bryan's signature, the statement reflects the legalistic reasoning of counselor Lansing more than the "common-sense" perspective that Bryan usually brought to bear. Legal precedents rather than the "spirit of impartiality and fairness" framed the response. U.S. citizens were free to sell arms, munitions, and war goods to whomever they wanted, as neutral parties had done so in the past and law allowed it; if only one side to the conflict benefited from the unrestricted export of war matériels manufactured in the United States, that was simply the fortune of war and the consequence of superior British sea power.

The administration, in short, tended to interpret neutrality in strictly legal terms, with occasional intercessions by the secretary of state and the president when those legal rights seemed too far out of line with the spirit of neutrality. When Wilson forwarded to Lansing at the State Department letters from critics who pointed out that his policies in effect favored the Entente, Lansing replied that "Law was the sole measure of neutrality. . . . If the Government, as a matter of policy, advocates neutrality beyond the legal requirements, it cannot rightfully be called to account for infractions of these extra-legal restrictions, since it has no power to prevent or to punition their violation."[98] Lansing's legal interpretation resonated with the president, a scholar of constitutional governance.

Recognizing that the administration was unwilling to curb the export of arms and munitions without a legal requirement to do so, the German-American community began to organize in December 1914 to pass laws that would embargo the export of contraband to belligerents. Shortly before Christmas, four embargo bills were introduced by members of Congress representing Nebraska, Missouri, and Iowa. The German- and Irish-American communities mobilized letter-writing campaigns, delivering huge bundles of mail supporting the embargo bills. Advocates for an embargo staged mass meetings in almost all the large cities of the United States, flooding papers with letters to the editor explaining that U.S.-manufactured cannons, munitions, and war goods were sustaining the war in Europe. The German embassy did all it could to encourage the movement. In response, pro-Allied editors, politicians, and journalists, supported to the fullest by British representatives in Washington, New York, and elsewhere, did what they could to counter the effort.[99] A survey by the *Literary Digest* in January 1915 revealed that editorial opinion was deeply divided: out of 440 editors who responded to the *Digest's* survey, 244 opposed an arms embargo, 167 favored it, while 29 sat on the fence.[100] The administration, in short, had considerable leeway: if it had desired a law that would have provided legal justification for restricting arms and munition exports, it could have mustered support for the embargo. It did not. The administration instead endeavored to kill the embargo bills. On the advice of the administration, both the Senate and House refused to move embargo bills out of committee, effectively killing them in January and February 1915.

Had the war in Europe been of short duration or even a matter of one or two years, the strict legalism of the Wilson administration in defense of the American right to sell munitions to belligerents and neutrals would have elicited only minor resentment in Germany and among its supporters in the United States. But as the war dragged on with no end in sight, the reality that Britain and France could draw upon American manufacturers for guns, shells, and munitions while Germany could not even import foodstuffs struck German supporters as partial and not neutral. An advertisement by the Cleveland Automatic Machine Company that appeared in a weekly trade journal on May 6, 1915, exacerbated this sense of grievance, drawling cries of outrage from German editors and members of the Reichstag. Promoting the advantages of its munitions, the Cleveland Automatic Machine Company boasted that

> The timing of the fuse for this shell is similar to the shrapnel shell, but it differs in that two explosive acids are used to explode the shell in the large cavity. The combination of these two acids causes terrific explosion, having more power than anything of its kind yet used. Fragments become coated with these acids in exploding and wounds caused by them mean death in terrible agony within four hours if not attended to immediately. From what we are able to learn of conditions in the trenches, it is not possible to get medical assistance to anyone in time to prevent fatal results. It is necessary to immediately cauterize the wound if in the body or head, or to amputate if in the limbs, as there seems to be no antidote that will counteract the poison.[101]

The issue of American arms exports slowly poisoned German-American relations. Had the Cleveland Automotive Machine Company placed its advertisement five months earlier, Germany's supporters in the United States might have used the callous advertisement to buttress the public campaign for laws prohibiting the sale and export of arms, munitions, and war matériel to belligerents. Yet widespread outrage over the *Lusitania's* destruction on May 7 silenced public discussion about arms embargoes. As Germany's ambassador confided to Berlin, efforts to sway American opinion in Germany's favor suffered a catastrophic setback with the sinking of the passenger liner. He counseled that Berlin needed to understand that German "propaganda in this country has, as the result of the *Lusitania* incident, completely collapsed."[102]

If decisions by the Wilson administration in the areas of finance and the export of war matériel favored the Entente powers in practice if not by design, a failed maritime initiative by the Wilson administration showed that the president was willing to proceed with policies he felt important even in the face of vociferous British objections. This third policy initiative has faded into obscurity as Wilson failed to secure congressional passage of the program. It nonetheless remains important as a window into the president's thinking about American freedom of action, British efforts to control the flow of trade, and the role of international law in foreign policy.

At the outset of the First World War, more than 90 percent of U.S. exports were carried by foreign-flagged vessels, with the Entente controlling close to 80 percent of the global merchant fleet once British sea power had driven Germany's substantial merchant marine from the seas.[103] The president concluded that the United States urgently needed to increase the size of its own merchant marine. Wilson realized that he could hardly count on British shipping to sustain American trade with important neutrals, let alone support its right to continue supplying Germany and Austria-Hungary with materials of a nonmilitary nature, such as cotton and foodstuffs. Wilson's response to the shortage of American merchant vessels shows that the administration was willing to overrule British protests when American interests seemed at stake. It reveals a degree of flexibility in interpreting how international law should be applied.[104]

Wilson shared his concerns about an impending shipping shortage with key Democratic congressional leaders at the outset of the war, encouraging them to introduce legislation that would allow foreign owners to reflag their vessels more easily. The Ship Registry Act passed through both houses of Congress rapidly, and the president signed it into law on August 18, 1914. The Ship Registry Act sought to persuade U.S. owners of foreign-flagged vessels to reflag their vessels as American, but the new tonnage failed to offset the loss of available shipping that had resulted from the incapacitation of the world's second-largest merchant fleet, that of Germany. German vessels with a total carrying capacity of more than 500,000 tons sat idly in American ports as German owners feared their ships would be seized by the Royal Navy if they ventured into international waters. Wilson sought to purchase these ships in order to increase the size of the U.S. merchant marine. This more ambitious scheme was introduced in Congress as the Ship Purchase Bill. It envisioned establishing a corporation under federal control, which would purchase and operate merchant vessels. The bill stalled in Congress in October, but Wilson supporters reintroduced it when Congress reconvened in December 1914.[105]

For Wilson, passage of the Ship Purchase Bill became a test of presidential leadership with political ramifications at both domestic and international levels. Domestically, the Republican minority in the Senate, led by Senators Henry Cabot Lodge of Massachusetts and Elihu Root of New York (who had served as secretary of war under presidents William McKinley and Theodore Roosevelt), deemed the scheme a harbinger of state socialism. Root characterized it at "wholly unrepublican, un-American, and destructive of the principles upon which our free government has been built up and maintained."[106] Wilson, for his part, viewed passage of the bill as a test of progressivism. He charged that his Republican opponents were "employing the most unscrupulous methods of partisanship and false evidence to destroy this administration," with the political struggle in the Senate nothing less than a "war to save the country from some of the worst influences that ever debauched it."[107] The political struggle in the Senate escalated into multiday filibusters, midnight votes, threats of special sessions, and presidential bullying. Wilson scolded Democrats wavering in their support of the bill that "If a man will not play in the team, then he does not belong to the team." Despite all his efforts, Wilson failed to secure passage of the bill before the 63rd U.S. Congress adjourned in March 1915.

The failed Ship Purchase Bill reveals much about Woodrow Wilson's rocky relationship with the Senate, and it provides insights into his foreign policy during the first year of U.S. neutrality. Wilson was ready and willing to ignore British objections when he deemed them contrary to American interests. For Britain, the Ship Purchase Bill was a danger that threatened to undermine one of the signal accomplishments of the Royal Navy, its successful effort to sweep German commerce from the high seas.[108] The British Admiralty was determined to use British sea power to strangle Germany economically, and it feared that if the United States purchased German merchant vessels and reflagged them, then these vessels might be used to supply Germany with food, cotton, and other non-contraband goods.

The British Foreign Office was initially inclined to accept the inevitable, but the Admiralty and Coordinating Committee on Trade and Supplies were insistent that the initiative be vigorously opposed. Churchill at the Admiralty demanded that the Foreign Office exert "very great pressure" on the United States, using "every means and influence at our disposal," including full publicity to derail the American initiative.[109]

Wilson's Ship Purchase Bill raised hackles in London because it threatened to undermine a strategy that Britain had pursued from the start of the war—that of using Britain's superior sea power and favorable geographic position to bring Germany to its knees economically.[110] Wilson's dogged insistence that Congress pass the bill shows that he was willing to deviate from the legal advice provided by Robert Lansing and the Joint State and Navy Neutrality Board when he deemed national interests to be at stake.[111] Well aware that London was being selective in observing the latest iteration of maritime law, the Declaration of London, Wilson understood that the British could indirectly control U.S. trade by virtue of their near monopoly of the shipping trade. He wanted an alternative, reassured the British that newly acquired German merchant ships would be used only to trade with other neutral states, and applied maximum pressure on Congress to pass the bill. The scheme ran aground on the shoals of Republican opposition, surreptitiously encouraged by Britain's ambassador, who was on very close terms with both Henry Cabot Lodge, leader of the opposition in the Senate, and ex-president Theodore Roosevelt, who continued to have considerable sway in Republican circles. Had the bill passed, the ongoing diplomatic row between Britain and the United States about freedom of the seas would surely have become even more acrimonious.

This leads to the fourth area of American policy and decision making—namely, the response of the Wilson administration to Britain's tightening economic war against Germany. Britain had for centuries used its navy and Britain's fortunate position athwart European trade routes to impose economic costs on its enemies in times of war, driving their merchant vessels from the sea and controlling their access to key imports. As it became increasingly clear in the first decade of the twentieth century that Germany was becoming a rival and threat, Admiralty planners began to explore what economic warfare might look like in the industrial age. By 1909, the contours of a strategy emerged: Britain, much as it had done against the Dutch in the seventeenth century, would cripple the German economy by starving it of imports and undermining its financial stability. At the start of the war, the Royal Navy would drive German shipping from the seas, seize German merchant ships at sea, and bottle up those that sought refuge in neutral ports. British shipping companies, whose dominance would become even more pronounced once the German merchant marine was incapacitated, would be prohibited from trading with Germany and neutral powers would be discouraged from doing so. This could be accomplished in a number of ways, ranging from denying insurance to shippers who violated British guidance to withholding coaling rights, to offering incentives that would encourage neutrals to export their products to Britain.[112] As a last resort, the Royal Navy could inspect, detain, and otherwise prevent neutrals from supplying Germany with the essentials necessary to sustain its economy and military. The concept was explored in 1907, developed as an Admiralty paper the following year, and forwarded for further examination to a subcommittee of the Committee of Imperial Defence headed by Lord Desart, Hamilton John Cuffe, of the Treasury Department in January 1911. Following almost two years of study, Lord Desart presented the findings of his subcommittee to the Committee of Imperial Defence (CID) in December 1912. Attending the CID meeting were nine cabinet-rank ministers, indicative of the importance attached to the matter. Lord Desart informed Britain's political leadership that economic warfare was indeed viable and, if implemented in full, would have devastating effects on the German economic and financial systems. He cautioned the committee, however, that it must be prepared to face loud protests from neutral powers, including the United States.[113] The committee reacted positively to the presentation, discussed its implications at length, and endorsed the concept. By 1914, economic warfare had emerged as a central tenet of British strategic planning in the event of war with Germany.[114] Those who suggest that the Admiralty had no strategy beyond destroying the German High Seas Fleet have it very wrong. Admiralty supporters had been studying how to use the Royal Navy, the City of London, and Britain's domination of shipping and maritime insurance to wage economic warfare against Germany since 1906. With the onset of war in August 1914, the Admiralty and the Coordinating Committee on Trade and Supplies moved to implement the strategy.[115]

British leaders anticipated that economic warfare would cause a diplomatic uproar because it ran counter to the trajectory of international law as developed at The Hague Conferences of 1899 and 1907 and the London Naval Conference of 1909. At all three conferences, national delegations from around the world gathered together to hammer out the laws of war, with an emphasis on minimizing the impact of war on civilians, noncombatants, and neutral parties. Naval and maritime law had a long pedigree dating back hundreds of years, but disagreements had invariably surfaced when it came to interpreting the definitions and associated rights and responsibilities pertaining to concepts such as the blockade, the right of capture, the rights of neutrals, and the distinction between goods that had a military purpose (contraband) and those that had no military purpose. Disagreement over these issues had driven the United States into a Quasi-War with France in 1798–1800, contributed to the War of 1812, and created tension between Great Britain and the United States during the American Civil War.

Animated by a desire to hammer out agreements on these matters so as to minimize conflict between belligerents and neutrals, protect peaceful commerce, and promote the common welfare, the British government had invited delegations from all the major European powers, as well as the United States and Japan, to London in December 1908. First Sea Lord "Jacky" Fisher fumed that the inevitable result of conferences such as this was that Britain would give up its advantages without adequate concessions from others. Eyre Crowe of the Foreign Office recorded that the First Sea Lord had bluntly told him that, in the event of war, "our commanders would sink every ship they came across, hostile or neutral, if it happened to suit them. He [Fisher] added, with characteristic vehemence, that we should most certainly violate the Declaration of Paris and every other treaty that might prove inconvenient." Blasting preliminary discussions with senior cabinet members regarding Britain's position on blockades and neutral rights, Fisher confided to one of Britain's leading naval journalists in November 1908 that

> We were discussing yesterday for the international conference on Dec 1ˢᵗ the laws of blockade as desired to be altered by everyone except England (as all are weaker on the sea!). They asked what should be the decision. I replied "make all the infernal fuss you can to get something elsewhere out of them quid pro quo but it don't signify a 'tinkers damn' what laws of blockade you make. *'MIGHT IS RIGHT'* & when war comes we shall do just as we jolly well like! *No matter what your laws are!* We've got to win and we ain't going to be such idiots as to keep one fist tied behind our back! There's a law against sinking neutral merchant ships but we should sink them-everyone! We can pay two or three millions indemnity afterwards if willing but we shall have saved about 800 millions in getting victory & getting it *speedily* & so on." But these worms don't understand it & and looked at me as a wild lunatic.[116]

Given British determination to use sea power to economically strangle Germany, and given the hostility of the Admiralty's First Lord and First Sea Lord, Winston Churchill and "Jacky" Fisher, toward the efforts to limit war, it is hardly surprising that the United States and Britain were at loggerheads over neutral rights by the fall and winter of 1914–15. At the outset of the First World War, the U.S. State Department sent inquiries to all the belligerents as to whether they would abide by the guidelines developed during the London Naval Conference. Although the treaty had been signed by all in attendance, it had not yet been ratified by all and therefore had not yet entered into force. Both the House of Commons and the U.S. Senate had debated and approved the text of the declaration, but Conservatives in the House of Lords successfully blocked its passage. Nonetheless, the State Department sought to persuade all belligerents that "acceptance of these laws . . . would prevent grave misunderstandings" and expressed the earnest hope that all parties to the conflict would accept rules developed at the London Naval Conference. The German and Austro-Hungarian governments indicated their willingness to abide by the declaration so long as their opponents did the same; the British government hedged, explaining that it had "decided to adopt generally the rules of the declaration in question, subject to certain modifications and additions which they judge indispensable to the efficient conduct of their naval operations."[117]

The modifications of the Declaration of London cast an increasingly dark shadow on Anglo-American relations by the winter of 1914–15. The declaration had sought to hammer out rules reflecting generally recognized conventions governing war at sea. Twenty-one articles set out the rights, duties, and responsibilities relating to blockades, twenty-three defined rules governing contraband goods, seven focused on the treatment of captured neutral vessels, two discussed the rules governing the transfer of belligerent vessels to neutral flags, and a dozen pertained to other assorted issues.[118] Article 65 specified that the provisions of the declaration had to be treated as a whole, as otherwise each signatory would simply insist that those rules that favored it be honored and those rules that it found inconvenient be ignored.

The Admiralty had warned the British government that if it accepted the Declaration of London without change, the rules set forth would rob Britain of one of the key advantages of superior sea power: the ability to inflict economic pain on an enemy. As the British government began to make unilateral modifications of rules specifying which goods could be confiscated if destined for enemy territory and which goods were not subject to confiscation under any circumstances, tensions arose. Cotton, metallic ores, agricultural and mining equipment, and nitrates and phosphates, for example, had been listed as items that could not be included in the category of contraband, as were foodstuffs, grain, clothing, and fuel not "destined for the use of the armed forces or of a government department of the enemy state."[119]

By Order of Council, the British government began to chip away at the rights of neutrals to continue to trade goods "not susceptible for use in war." The British moved cautiously despite the Admiralty's hope for an early and ruthless implementation of economic warfare. The British Orders-in-Council of the fifth and twentieth of August 1914 applied the doctrine of continuous voyage to several classes of goods that had both military and civilian purposes.[120] This meant that food, forage, railroad equipment, and communication gear, along with clearly military goods such as small arms, guns, shells, ammunition, and military supplies, could be seized and confiscated by Britain if destined ultimately for Germany.[121] While it was careful not to employ the term "blockade" given the legal definitions of the term, British policy aimed to bring the German war economy to a standstill by depriving it of imports, including materials transshipped through neutral ports such as Rotterdam.

The American reaction was measured, seeking to resolve the matter without resort to formal diplomatic protests. As Robert Lansing, the State Department counselor and its second in command, explained in a seven-page legal analysis sent to the American ambassador in Britain, accepting the British Order-in-Council of August 20 would in effect concede that American trade with other neutral countries was subject to interference at Britain's pleasure. In addition, Lansing explained, "The United States has always insisted that foodstuffs are legitimate articles of commerce and that mere destination to an enemy port is not of itself justification for their seizure of confiscation."[122] The United States relayed its grave concerns to the British informally and confidentially, hoping that quiet diplomacy would persuade the British to alter their policies.

The British replied reassuringly that their sole purpose was to "prevent the enemy from receiving food and materials for military use and nothing more," noting that the British government had never ratified the Declaration of London. Shortly thereafter, the British government informed the Americans that copper, lead, iron ore, rubber, and hides—items specifically designated as non-contraband by the Declaration of London—had been added to the list of contraband goods that would be confiscated if bound for Germany. Once again, London reassured the U.S. administration that its sole purpose was to "restrict supplies for German army and to restrict supply to Germany of materials essential for making of munitions of war."[123]

A series of consultations ensued between the State Department and Foreign Office, with Lansing pushing the British to accept the Declaration of London, going so far as to point out that the treaty allowed signatories to modify lists of items designated absolute and conditional contraband. Curiously, Lansing did not revisit his earlier point that the United States had a right to export foodstuffs directly to Germany, instead focusing mainly on America's right to continue trading with other neutrals subject to the accepted convention that military materials (contraband) could be confiscated if their ultimate destination was Germany. The British attempted to appease the U.S. administration by forwarding a draft of a proposed new Order-in-Council consolidating and modifying the orders of August 4, August 20, and September 21. Yet while the British presented the new Order-in-Council to the Americans as an effort to take their objections into consideration, the document in effect asserted that Britain would interdict the flow of both military matériel (contraband) and dual-use goods (conditional contraband) bound for Germany directly or indirectly.

Lansing prepared a detailed dossier of British violations of American rights along with a draft protest note for the president's consideration. Wilson, on the advice of Colonel House, decided against lodging a formal protest. He instead directed House to take up the matter with the British ambassador in Washington, with the upshot that the American ambassador in London discussed the matter with the British foreign minister on an informal and confidential basis.[124]

Walter Page, the American ambassador in London, grew exasperated at the barrage of instructions, legal arguments, and objections to British Orders-in-Council that he received from Washington. Page used his prerogative of direct access to the president to forward the following telegram for Wilson's consideration. It clearly situates Page among the group of pro-Allied extremists. Wilson worried that his ambassador had lost touch with U.S. public sentiment. Page telegraphed:

> For the President:
>
> Present controversy about shipping. I cannot help fearing we are getting into deep water needlessly. The British Government has yielded without question to all our requests and has shown a sincere desire to meet all our wishes short of admitting war materials into Germany. That it will not yield. We would not yield it if we were in their place. Neither would the Germans. The English will risk a serious quarrel or even war with us rather than yield. This you may regard as final. . . . This is not a war in the sense we have hitherto used the word. It is a world clash of systems of government, a struggle to the extermination of English civilization or of Prussian military autocracy. . . .
>
> The question seems wholly different here from what it probably seems in Washington. There it is a more or less academic discussion. Here it is a matter of life and death for English-speaking civilization. It is not a happy time to raise controversies that can be avoided or postponed. Nothing can be gained. . . . I recommend most earnestly the substantial acceptance of the new Order-in-Council or our acquiescence with a reservation of whatever rights we may have . . .
>
> Page[125]

Wilson and Lansing instructed the American ambassador to once more approach the foreign ministry with a plea that Britain accept the Declaration of London without reservations. The Americans were politely rebuffed. By the end of October, the Wilson administration abandoned its attempt to ground neutral rights on the declaration. Absent a general acceptance of the Declaration of London by all belligerents, no universal agreement existed specifying what constituted contraband and what did not. Belligerents simply made their own determination of what goods they would confiscate, subject only to the power and willingness of neutral countries to contest their exercise of sea power. Over the following months, the Royal Navy seized American goods and detained

American cargoes. In each case, the State Department protested the matter, but proceeded to resolve seizures and detentions on a case-by-case basis.

In November, when the British Admiralty declared the whole North Sea a war zone, the Americans said nothing.[126] The declaration was without legal precedent and had no grounding in law, but the British reassured neutral shippers that designated safe shipping lanes remained open. Step by step, the Admiralty extended its control over neutral shipping, first narrowing the list of what they might carry to other neutral powers and then restricting their movements in the international waters of the North Sea. The United States protested through diplomatic channels, but it lodged no formal notes of protest and made no public demands.

As the Admiralty began to enforce the Orders-in-Council more rigorously in November and December, American exporters and shippers began to clamor for a more muscular response. A week before Christmas, Secretary of State Bryan forwarded a draft note of protest to Wilson for his consideration. It laid out the case that British policy threatened to destroy American commerce with the neutral countries of Europe, and renewed U.S. objections to British interference with neutral shipping. The president returned the draft to Bryan with the comment that it was "too abrupt." Bryan and Lansing labored to soften the language of the note without detracting from the strength of the protest.[127] The revised protest was dispatched to Ambassador Page in London the day after Christmas, with Page delivering the note to the Foreign Office on December 28. In courteous terms, the note reminded the British government that "commerce between countries which are not belligerents should not be interfered with by those at war unless such interference is manifestly an imperative necessity to protect their national safety." It reassured the British government that the United States appreciated the "momentous nature" of the ongoing war, but insisted that "the present policy of His Majesty's Government toward neutral ships and cargoes . . . constitutes restrictions upon the rights of American citizens on the high seas which are not justified by the rules of international law or required under the principle of self-preservation."[128]

Newspapers in both the United States and Britain got wind of the protest note, which the *New York Tribune* characterized as a "sharp protest" and formal warning that the United States would "no longer tolerate unwarranted interference with American commerce on the High Seas.[129] Seeking to dispel rumors of an impending Anglo-American diplomatic crisis, Wilson held a press conference where he informed reporters that the note had contained no threats and that he did not intend to force the issue with Britain.[130] It is hardly surprising, therefore, that the British made no concessions in response to the American protest. After the war, Foreign Minister Sir Edward Grey revealed that the objective of his diplomacy had been to "secure the maximum of blockade that could be enforced without a rupture with the United States," elaborating that the "blockade of Germany was essential to the victory of the Allies, but the ill-will of the United States meant their certain defeat. . . . It was better therefore to carry on the war without blockade, if need be, than to incur a break with the United States about contraband."[131]

One wonders whether Wilson could have loosened the British blockade if he had pressed harder, as he did with the Germans. Wilson believed that he was acting impartially to both sides, but even his private secretary, William Tumulty, thought otherwise. Tumulty recalled that during the fall and winter of 1914–15, a stream of representatives from the Northwest, Midwest, and Southern states all urged Wilson to take a more vigorous stance against the British blockade because it was hurting farming, meatpacking, and cotton interests. When Tumulty raised the matter after dinner one evening, Wilson became animated and assured his private secretary that

Woodrow Wilson's private secretary, Joseph Tumulty, would later wonder whether the president should have taken a more vigorous stance against the tightening British blockade in the fall and winter of 1914/15.
Library of Congress, Prints and Photographs Division
LC-DIG-hec-16830

I am aware of the demands that are daily being made upon me by my friends
for more vigorous action against England in the matter of the blockade;
I am aware also of the sinister political purpose that lies back of many of
these demands. Many senators and congressmen who urge radical action
against England are thinking only of German votes in their districts and
are not thinking of the world crisis that would inevitably occur should there
be an actual breach at this time between England and America over the
blockade.... I have gone to the very limit in pressing out claims upon
England and in urging the Foreign Office to modify the blockade....
England is fighting our fight and you may well understand that I shall
not, in the present state of the world's affairs, place obstacles in her way.
Many of our critics suggest war with England in order to force reparation
in these matters. War with England would result in a German triumph.
No matter what may happen to me personally in the next election, I will
not take any action to embarrass England when she is fighting for her life
and the life of the world.[132]

Two test cases in January and February 1915 laid bare Wilson's reluctance to
do anything more than protest British infringements of American neutral rights.
At the height of the debate over Wilson's Ship Purchase Bill, a Michigan busi-
nessman named Edward Breitung purchased one of the German steamers in-
terned in American ports, registering the vessel, the *Dacia*, under the American
flag and loading it with raw cotton. Breitung initially planned to ship the cotton
directly to Bremen, as he had a right to do under international law. Responding
to a State Department suggestion, Breitung altered his plan and instead asked
for clearance to unload the shipment of cotton at Rotterdam. The scheme clearly
conformed to the administration's stated position regarding neutral rights, forcing the State Department to take up the matter with the British.

Yet the British were unyielding, well aware that if they allowed the *Dacia* to
proceed, the fabric of their economic warfare strategy might begin to unravel.
The British offered instead to buy the shipment of cotton directly, but warned
that they would seize the *Dacia* if it proceeded to Rotterdam with its cargo
of cotton for Germany. Though Wilson did not back down about the right of
Americans to conduct unrestricted business with neutrals in non-contraband
goods, he avoided spelling out the consequences if Britain carried out its
threat. Luckily for both parties, the French intercepted the vessel, buying its
cargo and interning the *Dacia* while a French naval prize court adjudicated the
ship's ultimate disposition. The diplomatic consequences for the French were
minimal.[133]

The second case touched an even more sensitive nerve than the right of
American merchants to ship cotton to neutral ports. In January 1915, German

sympathizers, funded and supported by the German embassy, chartered the American-built and flagged ship *Wilhelmina* to ship foodstuffs directly to Germany. The British had declared food a conditional contraband—that is, something used to support the German military—on the rather weak premise that the German government had become involved in distributing foodstuffs in the civilian sector. The German embassy responded that the German government was prepared to guarantee the *Wilhelmina*'s cargo be used solely to feed German civilians, yet when the Americans took up the matter with the British, they were rebuffed and told that the ship would be violating British Orders-in-Council if it proceeded.[134] The Wilson administration again asserted that it had the right to ship foodstuffs to German civilians, and sought to assuage British concerns that American food exports might land in the field kettles of the German military by proposing a number of schemes to prevent this. The British rejected the proposed solutions. When the British seized the *Wilhelmina* as it docked in Falmouth en route to Germany, the United States merely protested the ship's seizure and began negotiating for its release. None of *Wilhelmina*'s cargo of food made it to its intended destination.[135]

Wilson's biographer, Arthur Link, bends over backwards to portray Wilson as strictly neutral in thought and deed throughout this period, pointing out that in public utterances and in state papers, Wilson took pains to be impartial. Yet to argue, as Link does, that a more vigorous assertion of American rights as a neutral would have been unneutral, as it would have deprived Britain of the advantages of superior sea power, is disingenuous.[136] A policy of strict neutrality would have defended American rights against both British and German infringements. Yet Wilson had no desire to become another Madison and push the issue of American rights so far as to lead to a rift in relations with Great Britain. Deep down, Wilson sympathized with Britain's plight and was unwilling to threaten the beleaguered island during its time of trial. This predisposition became even more apparent once Wilson began to deal with a new threat to American neutral rights at sea—that posed by Germany.

Throughout the fall and winter of 1914–15, the major irritant to U.S. relations with the European belligerents had been Britain's effort to use its naval predominance to cut off German imports and exports. Germany repeatedly drew the attention of the U.S. government to British violations of neutral rights and maritime law during the first six months of the war, but given that German armies had blatantly violated Belgian neutrality in August 1914, these German appeals to international law rang hollow. The British, in enforcing their maritime policy of strangulation, were careful to assuage American sensibilities when possible by offering compensation, by suggesting that the measures were more limited than was the case, and by redirecting U.S. exporters toward the much larger Entente markets. Although the American response of protest, discussion, and inaction did not signal an acceptance of the British policy, it did convey that the United States was unwilling to back its demands with threats of a diplomatic breach or an embargo of war materials. The United States reacted to Germany's declaration of a zone of maritime warfare around the British Islands much more forcefully, in part because Germany's resort to submarine warfare threatened American lives, whereas the British Orders-in-Council only impinged on American trade. The Wilson administration's response to Germany's declaration of unrestricted submarine warfare around the British Islands provides a fifth prism for assessing Wilson's neutrality prior to the *Lusitania*'s destruction, and a yardstick by which to measure how the disaster impacted administration policy.

The German Admiralty had not envisioned using the submarine as a platform for economic warfare at the start of World War I, devoting far more thought and capital to building Admiral von Tirpitz's *Risikoflotte* ("Risk Fleet") of heavy battleships, which were meant to deter, dissuade, and impress Great Britain. The German Admiralty had not yet fully grasped the strategic short-sightedness of von Tirpitz's concept by the close of 1914, but as Britain slowly mopped up German overseas naval squadrons and surface raiders while simultaneously clamping down on German imports and exports, a sense of frustration began to mount among German naval officers.

The submarine seemed to offer a way to strike back at Britain—in particular after German U-boats proved that they had the range, endurance, and weapons to wage a campaign against merchant shipping. Already in October 1914, the German commander of submarines, Hermann Bauer, recommended unleashing his handful of submarines against British shipping in order to demonstrate that Germany could retaliate against British measures that threatened Germany with economic strangulation.[137] The German chief of the Admiralty, Admiral Hugo von Pohl, initially thought Bauer's proposal was too radical, but following Britain's designation of the North Sea as a war zone in November 1914, von Pohl became an enthusiastic convert to the idea. The fact that Germany had only a handful of U-boats capable of operating against Britain's vital Atlantic sea lines was brushed aside as unimportant: once Germany demonstrated its willingness and ability to sink shipping in designated areas, the threat of sinking would drive away neutral shipping and send maritime insurance rates sky-high.[138]

Once von Tirpitz embraced the concept, the coast was clear for the German Admiralty to push unrestricted submarine warfare on an ambivalent Kaiser Wilhelm II. German Chancellor Theobald von Bethmann-Hollweg, fearful that unrestricted submarine warfare would alienate important neutrals such as Norway, Sweden, the Netherlands, and the United States, initially convinced Wilhelm II against endorsing the concept. But after blocking unrestricted submarine warfare for weeks, Bethmann-Hollweg succumbed to pressure from the German navy in early February. Wilhelm II authorized the new form of war shortly thereafter.[139]

Germany framed its imposition of an "area of war" around Britain in February 1915 as a retaliatory response to Britain's Orders-in-Council. The German government noted that Britain had declared the whole North Sea an area of war, in violation of international law; that it was ignoring conventions differentiating among contraband, relative contraband, and non-contraband goods; and that it aimed to completely paralyze the German economy and starve the German people. The German government pronounced that it had brought these violations of international law to the attention of neutrals, and charged them with lodging only rhetorical protests that in effect acquiesced to British violations of international law. In response, Germany claimed it had no choice but to retaliate. "Just as England has designated the area between Scotland and Norway as an area of war, so Germany now declares all the waters surrounding Great Britain and Ireland including the entire English Channel as an area of war" where all enemy merchant ships would be subject to destruction. Germany warned neutrals against entrusting crews, cargoes, and passengers to enemy merchant ships, and advised them that while German naval forces had instructions to avoid violence against neutral ships insofar as they were recognizable, "it cannot always be avoided that neutral vessels suffer from attacks intended to strike enemy ships."[140]

Though one might think that Wilson and his advisers would have anticipated some sort of German reaction to the tightening British distant blockade, the German declaration came as a shock. The idea that German submarines would so flagrantly violate the accepted conventions of naval warfare appalled them. Recent German provocations, such as the attempt of a German reserve officer to blow up a Canadian Pacific Railway bridge in Maine on February 2, had already watered the seeds of distrust.[141] Wilson tasked Lansing with preparing a reply, since Bryan was out of town. Lansing forwarded a draft note to Wilson, describing Germany's proposed course of action as a "wanton act unparalleled in naval history."[142] Wilson personally reworked the draft over the weekend, and after showing his revised message to the secretary of state the following Monday, directed that it be dispatched as soon as possible. The American diplomatic dispatch requested that the German government carefully consider the consequences of its proposed course of action, warning that

> the sole right of a belligerent in dealing with neutral vessels on the high seas is limited to visit and search, unless a blockade is proclaimed and effectively maintained. . . . To declare or exercise a right to attack and

destroy any vessel entering a prescribed area of the high seas without first certainly determining its belligerent nationality and the contraband character of its cargo would be an act so unprecedented in naval warfare that this Government is reluctant to believe that the Imperial Government of Germany in this case contemplates it as possible. . . . If the commanders of German vessels of war should . . . destroy on the high seas an American vessel or the lives of American citizens, it would be difficult for the Government of the United States to view the act in any other light than as an indefensible violation of neutral rights which it would be very hard indeed to reconcile with the friendly relations now so happily subsisting between the two Governments. If such a deplorable situation should arise . . . the Government of the United States would be constrained to hold the Imperial German Government to a strict accountability for such acts of their naval authorities and to take any steps it might be necessary to take to safeguard American lives and property and to secure to American citizens the full enjoyment of their acknowledged rights on the high seas.[143]

The message, while framed in the diplomatic niceties of the period, was harsh and uncompromising. Britain, when interfering with American trading rights, had been gently chided in December to alter its way lest its actions "arouse a feeling contrary to that which has so long existed between the American and British peoples." Germany, on the other hand, was held to "strict accountability" and threatened with severe consequences if it persisted with its proposed response to a tightening British blockade.[144]

The American response to the German announcement rejected the contention that the United States, as a neutral power, had in any way acquiesced to British infringements on neutral trade. As if to prove the point, Bryan seized upon the suggestion of the German ambassador that Germany might revoke its order implementing a military zone around Britain in exchange for Britain's lifting its blockade of foodstuffs bound for Germany. British fears that food imports might be diverted to the German military could be addressed by establishing some sort of American supervisory agency, like the one in occupied Belgium.[145] Wilson authorized Bryan to bring up the idea of mutual concessions with Berlin and London. The German government responded positively, with the minor caveat that "other raw material used by the economic system of noncombatants including forage" be included alongside food stuffs. Overplaying its hand, the German government also asked whether "some way could be found to exclude the shipping of munitions of war from neutral countries to belligerents on ships of any nationality."[146]

Not wanting to appear intransigent, the British foreign secretary responded to the identical American proposal by indicating that, while he personally thought the suggestion acceptable, he would have to discuss the matter with the cabinet before answering definitively. This reassuring mask of reasonableness completely hoodwinked Wilson's personal representative, Colonel Edward House, and the U.S. ambassador in London, Walter Page. All the evidence suggests that Grey welcomed the German declaration of submarine warfare, as it provided the pretext for putting the final plank of Britain's strategy of economic strangulation in place: the complete interdiction of all commerce bound to and from Germany and Austro-Hungary. On February 6, Grey commented to a friend that "The contraband difficulty was greatly relieved by Germany's having announced a blockade of England and that she will sink ships trying to run it, drowning the crews! This will enable England to do ditto to Germany but to guarantee not to murder the crews."[147] Even as Grey was asking for time to present the American proposal to the cabinet, he and his French counterpart were working up a joint declaration prohibiting all trade with Germany.[148] The declaration further impinged on American and neutral trading rights, but as Grey anticipated, the British could point out that their measures, in contrast to those of Germany, did not kill crews and passengers.

The reaction of the U.S. press, nonetheless, was furious, with Hearst's *New York American* thundering that in 1812 the United States had gone to war over such matters.[149] The British and French declaration put an end to Bryan's plan. After considering sending a very harsh protest to the British regarding its imposition of a total blockade on Germany, Wilson and Bryan instead settled on a lengthy note that laid out the American position, reserved the right to enter a protest or demand should American rights be violated, and informed Great Britain that the United States would expect full reparations for every act violating neutral rights.[150] The communication was hardly a ringing defense of American rights; instead, it reflected Wilson's weary recognition that "they [the British] are going to do it [impose a blockade] no matter what representations we make."[151] Writing to a friend, Wilson vented that "Together, England and Germany are likely to drive us crazy."[152]

In March 1915, Wilson was unwilling to push maritime trading disagreements with Britain to the point of rupture. As the month neared its end, the German sinking of the British passenger liner *Falaba* forced Wilson to decide whether he should pursue a more vigorous defense of U.S. rights when Germany violated them. Could American losses be resolved through protest, compensation, and reparation, as he reluctantly was doing with Britain, or did the loss of lives and the sinking of ships require a sterner response? The president's initial response to Germany's declaration of unrestricted submarine warfare had been to warn Germany that if its naval commanders sank American ships or killed Americans traveling on the high seas, the U.S. government would have little choice but to view such acts as an "indefensible violation of neutral rights which it would be very hard indeed to reconcile with the friendly relations." Wilson may have missed the crucial distinction between warning Germany against sinking American ships and insisting that all Americans traveling through the war zone remain free from harm. German commanders could reasonably be expected to avoid sinking American ships, but how they could guarantee the safety of American citizens traveling on British ships was unclear, short of refraining from attacking these as well.[153] On March 28, as the small passenger steamer *Falaba* steamed out of the Irish Sea bound for West Africa, Wilson's implied blanket protection for all Americans was put to test. The U-29 signaled the *Falaba* to stop, and after giving chase to the vessel, torpedoed it after providing only a short time for passengers to take to the lifeboats. The German captain may have feared that the *Falaba* was radioing for help, but whatever the cause, the attack was brutal, killing more than one hundred passengers and crew. Many were still in the midst of abandoning the ship when the torpedo struck, with one of the British passengers taking poignant pictures of the chaotic last minutes. Among the dead was Leon Thrasher, a U.S. mining engineer bound for the Gold Coast (present-day Ghana).

The sinking of the *Falaba* received significant coverage in the U.S. press, ranging from indignant cries that the U.S. government confront German "Barbarism run mad" to articles that took pains to provide the German perspective of the incident as well.[154] At the State Department, Lansing and Bryan grappled with the appropriate response. Lansing, while laying out various options, clearly favored a firm response. His draft message of protest was harsh, with the counselor explaining to Secretary of State Bryan that if the president decided to make a protest, he "did not see how we can say it in a pleasant way. We are dealing with a tragedy. It seems to me that we must assert our rights, condemn the violation and state the remedy which we expect. If we do this without evincing a firm determination to insist on compliance, the German Government will give little heed to the note."[155] Americans taking passage on belligerent merchant vessels, the counselor commented, were entitled to rely on the established rules of visit and search, and should not be exposed to greater dangers than the rules impose.

Bryan took a broader view of the matter, cautioning that Britain's arming of merchant vessels had complicated matters, and urging the president to consider the larger picture. Bryan understood that while American arms exports to Britain were legal, the perception that the administration was favoring the British was gaining strength both domestically and abroad. Bryan advised the president to look beyond the strictly legal aspects of the particular case, and respond in a manner that reflected the sentiments of the whole country. And in this regard, Bryan wrote to Wilson:

> I am sure that the almost unanimous desire of our country is that we shall not become involved in this war and I cannot help feeling that it would be a sacrifice of the interests of all the people to allow one man, acting purely for himself and his own interests, and without consulting his government, to involve the entire nation in difficulty when he had ample warning of the risks which he assumed.[156]

The president, after acknowledging that both Bryan and Lansing had made compelling arguments, took time to ponder the matter. His cabinet was divided, with Secretary of War Garrison Lindley and Treasury Secretary William Gibbs advocating a hard line, while Secretary of State Bryan and Secretary of the Navy Josephus Daniels counseled moderation.[157] For ten days, he grappled internally about what the response of the United States should be. On April 20, he outlined the contours of a note, forwarding his thoughts to Bryan in the form of a suggestion. In essence, it advised Germany to abandon the use of submarines against merchant vessels since submarines could not observe the safeguards and precautions associated with cruiser warfare. The "whole thing" (submarine warfare) was not only contrary to law, but in opposition to humanity, fair play, and the rights of neutrals. Raising the ante, Wilson proposed that the American note of protest should rest "on very high grounds,—not on the loss of this single man's life, but on the interests of mankind."[158]

Wilson's suggested course of action so alarmed Bryan that he felt compelled to state his reservations more forcefully while Lansing began to draft the formal protest note. Bryan argued that the note Wilson proposed would inflame hostile feeing against the United States in Germany because it diverged quite markedly from the administration's attitude toward Allied infractions. Bryan observed:

> If we oppose the use of the submarine against merchantmen we will lay down a law for ourselves as well as for Germany. If we admit the right of the submarine to attack Merchantmen but condemn their particular act or class of act as inhuman we will be embarrassed by the fact that we have not protested against Great Britain's defense of the right to prevent foods reaching non-combatant enemies. We suggested the admission of food and the abandonment of torpedo attacks upon Merchant vessels. Germany seemed willing to negotiate but Great Britain refused to consider the proposition. I fear that denunciation of one and silence as to the other will be constructed by some as partiality.[159]

Bryan observed that Germany had warned neutrals that it intended to sink enemy merchant vessels around Great Britain, and commented that Thrasher had knowingly taken a risk by traveling on a belligerent vessel. "Our people," Bryan continued, "will, I believe, be slow to admit the right of a citizen to involve his country in war when by exercising ordinary care he could have avoided danger."[160]

Bryan's heartfelt appeal made a deep impression on Wilson and led him to reconsider the matter. Perhaps, Wilson said, it was not necessary to make formal representations in the matter at all. Two new incidents now caused additional delay and complication. On April 29, a German plane attacked a small American tanker, the *Cushing*, as it neared the Dutch coast with a cargo of petroleum. Two days later, U-30 attacked and damaged another American tanker, the *Gulflight*, some fifteen miles east of the Isles of Scilly off the tip of Cornwall. Initial reports on both incidents were sketchy, and the State Department required several days to ascertain the facts and decide how to respond. Three weeks had gone by since Lansing had laid out two alternatives for consideration. The United States, Lansing commented on April 7, should either warn Americans generally to keep out of the German war zone, if on board a merchant vessel which was not of American nationality, or hold Germany to a strict accountability for every American life lost by submarine attack on the high seas. Bryan favored the former, Lansing the latter. But Wilson had done neither, agonizing over the diverging assessments and recommendations of his subordinates. This dithering and indecision so worried the German ambassador to the United States, Count Bernstorff, that he had taken it upon himself to place notices in major newspapers warning American citizens about the dangers of booking passage aboard Allied ships transiting Germany's declared war zone. Lansing was affronted by this initiative, while Bryan thought Bernstorff was seeking to avoid incidents by placing the notice in the press. Initially scheduled to appear in the press on Saturday, April 24, because of a production snafu the notice instead appeared the next week, on the morning the *Lusitania* was set to sail. Wilson had not yet decided whether to confront Germany or to seek some sort of accommodation as he had with Britain. The sinking of the *Lusitania* on May 7 forced his hand.

THE IMMEDIATE REACTION

Americans of all walks of life reacted to the news of the *Lusitania*'s sinking with stunned disbelief, followed by anger at the brutality of the act. The reading public had been following news of the Great War with detached interest for months, but the sinking of the *Lusitania* enraged people hitherto unconcerned by Europe's agony. The event evoked images of the earlier *Titanic* disaster, yet it seemed even worse because it had been deliberate and calculated. It appeared not just callous but also barbaric. The attack ignored the distinction between combatants and non-combatants, between civilians and military personnel. More than one hundred Americans had perished—short of the three hundred American sailors who died or were grievously wounded when the USS *Maine* went down, but horrifying because they were innocent civilians. And in an age that still held to notions that women and children were off-limits when it came to waging "civilized" war, the incident seemed an appalling breach of ethics.

Veteran reporter Mark Sullivan, writing more than a decade after the event, remarked that almost to a man and woman, everyone he interviewed for his popular history *Our Times* (1926) recalled vividly where they were and what they were doing when they heard of the disaster. The *Lusitania* may have been a British liner and most of its passengers had been British, but its loss nonetheless imprinted itself on the American national consciousness in the same way that Pearl Harbor, the assassination of John F. Kennedy, and the terrorist attacks of 9/11 would do for subsequent generations.[161]

The first reports of the *Lusitania*'s sinking reached Washington, D.C., in the early afternoon of Friday, May 7; both the president and the secretary of state heard of the calamity via press bulletins and newsmen. Bryan hurried back to the State Department to read the official reports of the incident, which came in shortly after 3 P.M. By evening, information began to arrive that the ship had sunk with heavy loss of life. Wilson received the news without comment, taking a long walk through the rainy streets of Washington to clear his head. The next day, he deliberately stuck to his normal routine of morning golf followed by a three-hour ride through the countryside. Wilson wished to convey a sense of calm and deliberation, waiting until after dinner before releasing a statement reassuring the American people that he shared their distress and was considering very earnestly what course of action to pursue.[162]

Over the course of the weekend, the State Department gathered facts and began drafting recommendations for Wilson to evaluate. The day after the incident, the State Department asked the Treasury Department whether the *Lusitania* carried any contraband or ammunition and whether the ship was armed. Treasury forwarded the response of the port collector at New York, who explained to his superiors that "practically all her [the *Lusitania*'s] cargo was contraband of some sort," noting that among the goods carried by the *Lusitania* were 1,250 cases of shrapnel and 2,400 cases of cartridges shipped by the Remington Arms Company.[163] Later that day, the American ambassador to Great Britain telegraphed that "The freely expressed unofficial feeling is that the United States must declare war or forfeit European respect," a view he clearly shared.[164] On May 9, the department received grim news from its consul in Cork that "persons not listed as either survivors or identified dead are missing and almost certainly dead. . . . Rough weather has prevented recovering bodies. . . . More to follow."[165] Secretary of State Bryan took the unprecedented step of skipping church that Sunday as he and Lansing sought to gather the facts and develop recommendations for the president.

Woodrow Wilson had appointed William Jennings Bryan as his secretary of state because of Bryan's stature in the Democratic Party and in recognition that the "Great Commoner" resonated with the populist, agrarian constituency of the party. Yet as crises unfolded in Mexico and in Europe, Wilson came to rely increasingly on the carefully argued position papers that he received from the State Department's counselor, Robert Lansing, and on the evaluations of his trusted confidante and presidential counselor without portfolio, Colonel Edward House. Wilson had dispatched House to Europe for a second extended round of consultations with British, French, and German leaders in January 1915. After an extended stay in London, followed by shorter visits to Paris and Berlin, House was back in Great Britain when the *Lusitania* was sunk.[166] House's mission had been to see whether the United States could help bring about some sort of negotiated peace, but his reaction to the liner's destruction underscores his growing disposition toward open intervention. Telegraphing the president on May 9, House recommended:

> An immediate demand should be made upon Germany for assurance that this shall not occur again. If she fails to give such assurances, I should

William Jennings Bryan was derided by much of the East Coast establishment as a populist teetotaling naïf out of his depth as secretary of state.
Library of Congress, Prints and Photographs Division LC-DIG-ggbain-11437

inform her that our government expected to take whatever measures were necessary to insure the safety of American citizens. If war follows, it will not be a new war but an endeavour to end more speedily an old one. Our intervention will save rather than increase the loss of life. America has come to the parting of the ways, when she must determine whether she stands for civilised or uncivilised warfare. Think we can no longer remain neutral spectators.[167]

Colonel House could weigh in from abroad, but it was to Bryan and Lansing that Wilson turned for more direct counsel as he deliberated how to respond. Their advice diverged. Bryan's first instinct was to warn the president that the *Lusitania* had been carrying ammunition, and to recommend that ships carrying contraband should not be permitted to carry passengers. "Germany," explained Bryan, "has a right to prevent contraband going to the allies and a ship carrying contraband should not rely upon passengers to protect her from attack—it would be like putting women and children in front of an army."[168] Lansing strongly disagreed. He pointed out that "hundreds of Americans" had traveled through Germany's war zone on British ships since February, and he insisted that since the United States had not advised them against doing so, American citizens had the right to expect that their government would "stand behind them in case their legal rights were invaded." Warning Americans against booking passage on belligerent ships now, Lansing felt, would be both untenable and a serious mistake.[169]

Lansing's position, developed in a series of memoranda forwarded through Bryan to the president, was that the presence of munitions did not relieve German naval commanders of the responsibility of stopping the *Lusitania* and allowing passengers time to safely disembark into lifeboats before sinking the ship. The German ambassador's extraordinary step of directly warning Americans against traveling through its declared war zone did not absolve the German government of responsibility for an act that violated the principles of law and humanity. The German government, wrote Lansing, should have communicated directly to the U.S. government, which then should have decided whether to warn its own citizens of the same. The conduct of the German ambassador in publishing the warning, Lansing exclaimed, had been an "indefensible breach of propriety [and] an insult to this Government."[170]

The only course of action, he argued, was for the U.S. government to demand that the German government disavow and apologize for the act, punish the officers guilty of committing the offense, acknowledge liability, promise just indemnity, and take such measures that will ensure "the safety of the lives of American citizens on the high seas." Lansing maintained that Americans were entitled to travel through Germany's announced war zone even on board British merchant ships and liners carrying munitions. The only excuse for sinking a merchant ship without first inspecting its cargo and providing civilians with the opportunity to take to the lifeboats was if the vessel was armed or if it was escorted by belligerent warships.[171]

Lansing's recommendation, in short, was that Wilson demand that Germany abandon its declared intention to sink without warning Allied ships operating in the war zone Germany had imposed around the British Isles. Lansing was simply advising the president to hold firm to the position he had staked out in February. Since then, the *Falaba, Cushing*, and *Gulflight* incidents had challenged the American position. The sinking of the *Lusitania* made some sort of response imperative. Wilson could dither no longer. Three paths seemed to present themselves. Wilson could confront Germany while accommodating Britain; confront both Germany and Britain with equal vigor; or accommodate his administration to the unfortunate reality that both Britain and Germany were violating American neutral rights with little regard to American protests.

Did the *Lusitania* disaster unite a divided American public, creating public pressure on the president to defend American rights even at the cost of possible war with Germany? Did the press play a similar role as it had in 1898, with voices for intervention and action using the crisis to drown out more moderate voices? Did Congress, as it had in 1898, urge the president forward, threatening to take action if he would not? Put differently, did the sinking of the *Lusitania* reshape the contours of the domestic environment in which Wilson operated, or did it remain largely the same despite the shock of the event?

The reaction to a speech that Wilson presented to an audience of fifteen thousand at Philadelphia's Convention Hall the Monday after the *Lusitania's* demise provides a sense of public opinion, and more pointedly, how Wilson initially misread it. Wilson had spent the weekend in deliberate fashion, carrying on with his regular routine. He did not call his cabinet together for a crisis session, nor did he speak directly to Bryan, Lansing, Daniels, or any member of Congress.[172] On Monday, he was scheduled to give a speech in Philadelphia celebrating the naturalization of four thousand immigrants. He declined to reschedule the event, and instead remained in seclusion. That evening, waxing eloquent about the ideals of their new nation to his audience, Wilson declared:

> The example of America must be a special example. The example of America must be the example not merely of peace because it will not fight, but of peace because peace is the healing and elevating influence of the world and strife is not. There is such a thing as a man being too proud to fight. There is such a thing as a nation being so right that it does not need to convince others by force that it is right.[173]

Wilson's speech, coming on the heels of the *Lusitania's* destruction, was widely perceived as signaling what the administration's response might be. Few found it satisfactory. Pro-Allied extremists such as Theodore Roosevelt frothed with indignation, lambasting Wilson as a weakling and coward who was trolling for the votes of "hyphenated Americans," "flub dub," and pacifists. Drilled by reporters the following day about what he meant, Wilson backtracked, claiming that "I was expressing a personal attitude, that was all. I did not have in mind any specific thing. I did not regard that as a proper occasion to give any intimation of policy on any special matter."[174]

Wilson distanced himself from his remarks because they struck the wrong tone. Americans were outraged as reports of dead babies, drowning women, and desperate men filled their newspapers. Across the spectrum of opinion, editors condemned the German attack as barbaric, incredible, and unacceptable. The reaction of Americans to speeches by Bernhard Dernburg of the German Information Service was so hostile that the German ambassador felt compelled to advise Berlin to recall him rather than further inflame American opinion. Dernburg's efforts to rationalize or justify the attack provoked rather than assuaged the sensibilities of his audience. Oswald Garrison Villard, a well-respected journalist known for his anti-imperialist stance and neutralist sympathies, explained to a German friend that "it is no longer possible for the bulk of the papers to deal with judicial minds with the situation. . . . When I think of the *Lusitania* and our innocent women and children lying at the bottom of the sea as the result of that dastardly crime, I see red."[175] And this from an American who had been born in Wiesbaden, admired German culture, and went out of his way to understand the German perspective. Comparing the public's reaction to that of 1898, a prominent university president remarked, "There was no flash of passion, no stampede of thought as marked the destruction of the *Maine* in '98, but rather a sort of stunned amazement that such bold savagery and ferocity could mark the public policy of any great nation."[176]

The public's pervasive sentiments of shock and anger did not translate into the shrill cries for intervention, as had been the case in 1898. Scholars who have

The insufficiently apologetic German response to Wilson's first *Lusitania* note elicited this cartoon commentary from the *New York Herald* on May 29, 1915: Here lie "the facts."
Library of Congress, Prints and Photographs Division
LC-USZ62-105673

examined the thousands of editorials that decried the *Lusitania*'s destruction find that less than one out of one hundred called for an American declaration of war.[177] Instead, most editorials demanded some sort of German apology, disavowal, and compensation for loss and suffering. Likewise, rudimentary polls of congressional sentiment revealed that only one senator and three representatives were clamoring for intervention and war. Dozens remarked that the incident did not and should not become a cause for war. This sentiment was particularly marked in the Midwest; Nebraska's governor commented that 90 percent of his constituents thought that the matter might be settled by arbitration. Britain's ambassador in Washington warned London against expecting much more than protests from the Americans despite press uproar: "The general feeling here in the United States," he advised, "is that the United States Government ought to keep out of it [the war]. . . . I don't think that the American people taken as a whole have even contemplated for an instant coming to the help of the Allies or of intervening unless they are absolutely obliged to do so. . . . The long and the short of the matter is that we must count on ourselves for success or failure and that we must not expect help from this continent."[178]

Public opinion, press commentary, and congressional sentiment had all exerted intense pressure on President McKinley to act forcefully in 1898, particularly after the Naval Court of Inquiry concluded that the *Maine* had been sunk as a result of an external explosion. President Wilson, in contrast, had the luxury of crafting an American foreign policy response to the *Lusitania* incident free of such intense domestic pressure. The American public, while deeply divided in sympathy for and against the war's belligerent parties, remained strongly noninterventionist. The press, while critical of Wilson's "too proud to fight" rhetoric, pushed for something more, but few editors advocated the threat of military force to compel Germany to abandon its submarine campaign. Even had they done so, Wilson would have been indifferent, having consciously abandoned the habit of reading the papers in December 1914 in order to "hold excitement at arm's length."[179] On Capitol Hill, the 63rd Congress had concluded its business weeks before the *Lusitania* incident occurred, and the 64th would not convene for months. Intervention had not yet become a partisan issue, and rabid pro-Allied extremists remained a minority voice in both parties in May 1915. Wilson enjoyed incredible freedom of action, and while willing to hear out others, he was extremely confident in his own intellect and judgment. His secretary of war, who later resigned over policy differences, caustically commented that Wilson's "overpowering self-esteem left no place for common counsel of which he talked so much and in which he did not indulge at all."[180] Wilson did not relish extended discussions and cabinet deliberations, preferring instead to read memoranda, consider written reports, and form his own conclusions in isolation. Lansing's carefully reasoned legal analyses resonated with Wilson far more than did the "commonsense" musings of the secretary of state. More broadly, Wilson tended to think deductively, abstracting from general notions to policy decisions. This mode of reasoning proved resistant to compromise, counterarguments, and sentiment.[181]

WILSON'S RESPONSE
AND BRYAN'S DEPARTURE

As Wilson pondered his response and pored over the memoranda, letters, and telegrams he was receiving from Bryan and Lansing at the State Department, Colonel House in London, and his ambassador in London, he worked in solitude, pounding out a draft protest note to Germany on his own typewriter. On Tuesday, May 11—four days after news of the *Lusitania*'s destruction arrived in Washington, D.C.—Wilson convened his cabinet to discuss the matter. He began the session by reading House's strongly worded cable from London, in which he had advised Wilson that he needed to decide whether America stood for civilized or uncivilized warfare. Wilson then reviewed the situation, read the draft of the note he proposed to send, and elicited comments.

Wilson's draft informed Germany that the lives of non-combatants could under no circumstance be put at jeopardy, even if traveling onboard enemy merchant ships suspected of carrying contraband. International law was quite specific. Germany was obliged to stop, verify the nationality of a ship, and conduct a search for contraband prior to seizing or sinking the ship. "The lives of non-combatants, whether they be of neutral citizenship or citizens of one of the nations at war, cannot lawfully or rightfully be put in jeopardy by the . . . destruction of an unarmed merchantman." Wilson acknowledged that following these rules was a "practical impossibility," conceding that it was not feasible for German submarine officers to surface, board merchant ships at sea, inspect their papers, and for German submarines to surface, dispatch inspection teams to examine whether a merchant ship was carrying contraband, and if they were, leave a "prize crew" onboard with instructions to bring the vessel into port where its contraband cargo could be legally confiscated. Since these requirements could not be met, there was only one conclusion to reach: Germany should entirely abandon its efforts to wage commerce warfare using submarines.[182] The matter, Wilson went on, could not be settled with expressions of regret and offers of reparations. Nations that resort to war to settle disputes, he scolded, had no right to subordinate the rights of neutrals to the supposed or even actual needs of belligerents.

Wilson's proposed note to Germany doubled down on the American note of February, not just asserting that American ships and American individuals had the right to move anywhere they wished on the high seas but also expanding the scope of the American position to insist that the lives of belligerent noncombatants likewise could not "lawfully and rightfully be put in jeopardy." While cognizant of the German government's claim that Berlin had resorted to submarine warfare in retaliation for measures adopted by its enemies, Wilson gave no hint that he would confront Britain over its Orders-in-Council. He simply rejected the validity of Germany's retaliatory campaign of submarine warfare, pointing out that it violated all notions of fairness, reason, justice, and humanity. Reluctant to spell out precisely the consequences for Germany should it continue to disregard American rights, Wilson concluded with a vague warning that the American government would "not omit" taking such actions as it deemed necessary to safeguard its rights.[183]

As Wilson laid out his thinking to his cabinet, those with strong pro-Allied sentiments were pleased. No one in the cabinet believed that the *Lusitania*'s destruction merited a response that might escalate to war, but opinions were divided over whether Wilson's draft struck the right tone. Secretary of War Garrison warned that the note might indeed lead to a rupture of relations, but Wilson disagreed, claiming that a strong line generally causes an aggressor to back down. Bryan, supported by Postmaster General Burleson, continued to hold out the hope that differences could be settled by arbitration. The cabinet discussed Wilson's proposed response for three full hours, and once it became clear that Wilson was unwilling to compromise, the cabinet endorsed Wilson's note unanimously.[184]

Bryan left the session a deeply troubled man. Over the course of the next several days he sought to re-engage the president and moderate a course of action he feared would lead to war. Bryan forwarded Wilson's draft to Lansing for final polishing the morning after the extended cabinet session, and after returning the revised note to the White House, he took the liberty of sending an additional suggestion to the president. Concerned that Wilson might be backing Germany into a corner, Bryan suggested issuing a statement that disputes that do not yield to diplomatic treatment could be settled after peace is restored. Wilson answered that he would think over the proposal overnight.

Wilson responded to Bryan the next day, indicating that while he did not want to provide a formal statement, he thought there might be merit to tipping off reporters that his administration had not ruled out the possibility of submitting differences to arbitration. Bryan was delighted with the response, informing

Lansing of the president's intent and sending instructions to the American ambassador in Berlin to pass on the press statement at the same time he delivered the formal U.S. note of protest. What followed was one of the most unusual displays of backchannel maneuvering ever displayed. Lansing, who indicated to Bryan that he approved of the two-track initiative, immediately contacted Secretary of War Garrison without Bryan's knowledge. Garrison in turn contacted Wilson's personal secretary (akin to today's White House chief of staff) Joseph Tumulty, asking him to discuss the matter directly with Wilson.

With Burleson at his side, Tumulty rushed into the president's office, visibly distraught and excited. Tumulty urgently advised Wilson against issuing any sort of special statement or providing Germany with any off-the-record reassurances. The public, claimed Tumulty, would raise a "terrible howl" and Wilson's domestic opponents would lambaste him as a "double dealer."[185] Burleson and Tumulty were clearly tuned in to the domestic, political ramifications of appearing weak, but one wonders in hindsight whether their political antennas were not overly sensitive. Shrill partisan voices such as Theodore Roosevelt, Henry Cabot Lodge, Elihu Root, and other pro-Allied Republicans would certainly have attempted to use any weakness on the part of the president to discredit him, but a careful assessment of the broader public sentiment gives little indication that Bryan's unofficial reassurances would have had significant domestic costs. The great majority of telegrams pouring into the White House favored a firm yet peaceful resolution to the matter.[186]

The German government did itself no favors with its tone-deaf response to the *Lusitania* incident. Its ambassador to the United States, Count Johann von Bernstorff, telegraphed the German Foreign Office on May 9, strongly urging that Berlin express some sort of regret for the death of so many Americans.[187] The ham-fisted apology issued by the German Foreign Office the following day did little, however, to conciliate an angry American public. After briefly expressing deepest sympathies for the loss of American lives, the German apology justified submarine attacks as necessary to counter British restraints on trade. Germany insisted that the *Lusitania* had been carrying munitions, claimed that practically all British merchant vessels were armed, and put full responsibility on England for any loss of life. Adding insult to injury, moreover, the apology included the suggestion that the Americans had only themselves to blame in that "Americans felt more inclined to trust English promises rather than pay attention to warnings from the German side."[188]

On Saturday, May 15, eight days after the *Lusitania* was sunk, the American ambassador to Berlin formally delivered the American response to the *Falaba, Cushing, Gulflight,* and *Lusitania* incidents to German foreign minister Gottlieb von Jagow. Its substance adhered closely to the draft that Wilson had hammered out on his typewriter over the weekend and discussed with his cabinet on Tuesday. Ambassador Gerard's account of the German reaction was not encouraging. Von Jagow read the American note, chuckling to himself. He commented to Gerard, "Right of free travel on the seas, why not right of free travel on land in war territory?" Ambassador Gerard telegraphed Washington that he felt quite positive that Germany would not modify its declared policy of sinking belligerent ships without warning. It was only a question of time, in his view, before another American ship was sunk or American lives were lost.[189] Over the next several days, Gerard sent a series of additional telegrams underlining the seriousness of the situation. He requested authority to advise Americans to leave Germany (May 17), reiterated that the German government would not bend, and forwarded summaries of various newspaper editorials conveying the German perspective. Gerard indicated that all classes, especially Germans of position such as bankers, editors, and officials, agreed that "enemy ships carrying munitions of war should not be made immune from submarine attack by [the] fact that they carry American passengers."[190]

Having sent a stern note to Germany, Wilson faced the decision whether he should follow up on his earlier protests to Britain as well. Since early April, the number of incidents in which Britain had intercepted or disrupted American trade with neutrals had steadily increased. On the eve of the *Lusitania* incident, American exasperation with Britain reached a new high. Writing to Colonel House in London in early May, Secretary of the Interior Franklin K. Lane confided that "The English are not behaving very well. They are holding up our ships; they have made new international law. . . . There is not a man in the Cabinet who has a drop of German blood in his veins. . . . Two of us were born under the British flag. Yet each day we boil over somewhat at the foolish manner in which England acts."[191] Bryan in particular felt strongly that Washington needed to protest against British infractions of American rights if it was doing so with Germany. Wilson weighed the idea of sending a parallel note of protest to Britain, but decided against doing so. He explained to Bryan that he did not wish to "make it easier for Germany to accede to our demands by turning in similar fashion to England."[192] The phrasing was unfortunate. What Wilson most probably meant was that he did not want to concede any linkage between American diplomacy toward Britain's violation of international law and its demand that Germany abandon submarine warfare. Doing so would only reward the Germans.

Germany responded to the U.S. note of protest concerning the *Falaba, Gulflight, Cushing,* and *Lusitania* incidents toward the end of May. It ignored the central thrust of the American note, which called on Germany to abandon submarine warfare due to the inherent difficulty of observing the legal conventions of stop, search, and seizure. Instead, Germany assured the United States that it had repeatedly given explicit instructions to its forces to avoid attacking neutral vessels, and explained that such attacks as had occurred were mistakes brought on by British misuse of neutral flags. If neutral vessels came to grief through no fault of their own, the German government was willing to pay indemnities once the facts of each case were established. As for the *Lusitania*, the German government noted that it had already expressed deep regret to neutral governments for the loss of the lives of their nationals resulting from the ship's sinking. Germany wished, however, to bring certain information to the attention of the American government. It claimed that it had reliable information that the *Lusitania* had masked guns on board mounted under decks, that British ships had orders to ram submarines, and that the *Lusitania* carried Canadian troops and ammunition on board. There can be no doubt, the note claimed, that that rapid sinking of the *Lusitania* was primarily due to the explosion of ammunition ignited by the torpedo's impact. Germany recommended that the American government carefully examine these facts, and begged to reserve a final statement of its position until it received a reply from the American government.[193]

The German reply evaded the central thrust of the American note of protest. A number of its assertions, particularly that the *Lusitania* carried Canadian troops and was armed, were contradicted by survivor accounts and did not stand up to scrutiny. But these were side issues. The essential shortcoming of the German note is that it sidestepped Wilson's main demand: that Germany cease using submarines to attack merchant ships. Germany indicated that it would be willing to pay indemnity costs for neutral vessels accidentally destroyed, and offered to submit disputed cases to arbitration by an international commission of inquiry. But it gave no indication that it was willing to abandon its campaign against British commerce.

On June 1, Wilson called together his cabinet to discuss the German response. He indicated that he wanted a full and free discussion, opening the doors to the heated debate that ensued. Secretary of War Garrison recommended that Wilson simply demand to know whether Germany accepted the principle underlying the American position, asserting that if it did not, there was nothing further to discuss. Someone else then asked whether a note of protest would also be sent to Britain. At this, Secretary Bryan jumped into the discussion. He passionately exclaimed that he had been advocating such a course of action all along, and blurted out that "You people are not neutral. You are taking sides!" Wilson cut off Bryan's outburst, sharply interjecting, "Mr. Secretary, you have no right to make that statement. We are all honestly trying to be neutral against heavy odds."[194] Bryan's closest ally in the cabinet, Secretary of the Navy Josephus Daniels, held his tongue and did nothing to support the secretary of state.

Commenting on Secretary of State Bryan's resignation, the *Chicago Daily News* portrayed Wilson as a resolute eagle perched on a nest titled "Firm Foreign Policy" while Bryan is shown as a gentle dove flying away from approaching trouble.
Library of Congress, Prints and Photographs Division LC-USZ62-84053

The session broke up with no consensus. The president, meeting with the German ambassador the next day, reaffirmed that he viewed the issue as one of humanitarian principle, with indemnity for losses suffered a secondary issue. Wilson sought nothing less than a total cessation of submarine warfare. Perhaps to soften the blow, Wilson promised that he would press England to abandon its blockade of foodstuffs if Germany abandoned submarine warfare, a bargain he had been unable to broker less than a week before.

The divide in the State Department between Lansing and Bryan came to a head following the stormy cabinet meeting. Wilson sent a polite note to Bryan requesting that he forward an outline of the answer the United States should make to the German reply. Curiously, he asked that Bryan also send Lansing's response to the same question. Their responses could not have been more different. Lansing compiled a nineteen-page memorandum, refuting every point the German note had raised and insisting that the United States should not give an inch. Bryan dispatched several shorter memoranda to the president, addressing the particulars but focusing more on the broader ramifications of policy decisions. His key concern was to keep the United States from slipping into war, and he could not see why the United States, having in effect tolerated British infractions of American trading rights, should stake out a maximalist position with regard to Germany.

He summarized his position in a note to Wilson on June 5, laying out three recommendations that he begged the president to consider most seriously. First, Bryan urgently pressed that the American response make some sort of reference to an arbitration of differences, a scheme the secretary of state had been pushing for years. Second, he advised that some sort of step be taken to prevent passenger ships from carrying ammunition before sending a reply to Germany. Last, Bryan again recommended that Wilson protest British interference with U.S. trade before sending a second note to Germany. Bryan reminded Wilson that he had been on the verge of doing so before House had dissuaded him.[195]

Wilson firmly rejected each of Bryan's recommendations. For Bryan, sending a note of protest to Britain was essential if the United States wished to be viewed as even-handed. For Wilson, doing so would weaken the American protest to Germany and decrease the likelihood of resolving Anglo-American differences. For Bryan, arbitration offered the best path for settling differences. For Wilson, the matter was one of principle and law; while one might reasonably delay and arbitrate financial claims of indemnity, one could not put off protecting American lives and rights. More broadly, though Bryan defended the rights of American manufacturers to sell munitions to whomever they chose, he found it unreasonable to demand that Germany cease attacking British merchant ships carrying munitions if Americans were onboard. Wilson had appeared sympathetic to the idea of warning U.S. citizens from traveling on belligerent ships in late April, but after the *Lusitania* disaster he felt that any such warning would be perceived as a sign of weakness.

Wilson's second *Lusitania* note incorporated Lansing's legal and factual refutations of German explanation of the *Cushing, Gulflight, Falaba*, and *Lusitania* incidents. Wilson brushed aside "circumstances of detail" when discussing the *Lusitania*; "Whatever be the other facts, the principal fact is that a great steamer, primarily and chiefly a conveyance for passengers, and carrying more than a thousand souls who had no part or lot in the conduct of the war, was torpedoed and sunk without so much as a challenge of warning, and that men, women, and children were sent to their death in circumstances unparalleled in modern warfare." The United States, Wilson asserted, was not merely protesting about rights of property and privileges of commerce; it was "contending for nothing less high and sacred than the rights of humanity."[196]

As the contours of Wilson's second *Lusitania* note became clear, Bryan agonized over what to do. He had repeatedly advised the president to couple protests against German submarine warfare with protests against British naval interdiction of trade, only to be ignored. He had advised Wilson to warn Americans against traveling through the war zone on belligerent vessels, only to be told that the time was not right. He felt strongly that the United States could avoid confrontation with Germany by settling differences through arbitration after the passions of war dissipated, only to discover that his president was convinced that the American response needed to be firm and without any hint of compromise. On the morning of June 8, 1915, Secretary Bryan submitted his resignation. Bryan explained that he could not sign the note that Wilson was preparing to send to Germany, stating that while he and Wilson had the common goal of finding peaceful solutions to the problems arising out of the use of submarines against merchantmen, they were in fundamental disagreement about the methods to be employed. Wilson accepted the resignation that afternoon with deep regret and a feeling of personal sorrow. The next day, Bryan met with his friend and ally in the cabinet, Josephus Daniels, who berated him for having resigned without consulting Daniels beforehand. Yet Daniels made no move to do the same, preferring to provide private counsel to the president from within the administration than public critique from without. Acting Secretary of State Lansing dispatched Wilson's second *Lusitania* note to the American ambassador in Berlin for delivery to the German government the day after Bryan's resignation.

AFTERMATH, CONSEQUENCES, AND REFLECTIONS ON THE *LUSITANIA* CRISIS

Bryan's departure removed one of the key players who had counseled Wilson to find a way to de-escalate tensions with Germany, whether by advising Americans against traveling through Germany's war zone or by settling differences through arbitration. The dispatch of Wilson's second *Lusitania* note did not escalate into an immediate breach of relations as Bryan feared, but it did set the trajectory of Wilson's future policy related to German submarine warfare. The secretary of state's resignation constituted a turning point. Wilson's rejection of Bryan's recommendations signaled a willingness to confront Germany even at the risk of war. Within months, two additional German attacks on British liners, the *Arabic* on August 19 and the *Hesperian* on September 6, brought relations between Germany and the United States to a crisis state.

This drift toward war was precisely what Bryan had feared. In his first public statement after his resignation, Bryan laid out for the American public the argument he had been making within the administration:

> Why should an American citizen be permitted to involve his country in war by traveling upon a belligerent ship when he knows that the ship will pass through a danger zone? The question is not whether an American citizen has a right under international law to travel on a belligerent ship; the question is whether he ought not, out of consideration for his country, if not for his own safety, avoid danger when avoidance is possible. It is a very one-sided citizenship that compels a government to go to war over a citizen's rights, and yet relieves the citizen of all obligations to consider his nation's welfare. . . . [E]ven if the Government could not legally prevent citizens from traveling on belligerent ships, it could, and in my judgment should, earnestly advise American citizens not to risk themselves of the peace of their country, and I have no doubt that these warnings would be heeded.[197]

Yet for Wilson, the matter had become greater than a protest about the loss of American lives. Wilson based his policy on international law, justice, and humanity. In his mind, he was not defending the rights of a handful of American passengers, or even the rights of the thousands of Allied civilians who lost their lives when the passenger liners *Lusitania, Arabic,* and *Hesperian* went down. He was defending the rights of humanity.

In the short term, Wilson's policy resulted in the near break in relations with Germany followed by a highly unstable compromise solution to German-American differences that endured only so long as the German government held back from reinstituting unrestricted submarine warfare. Unbeknownst to Wilson and his advisers, the German government had been deeply divided when it evaluated the German navy's proposal to declare a war zone around Britain in February 1915. The policy had seemed too risky to the German chancellor, the Foreign Office, and to its ambassador in Washington, Count Johann von Bernstorff. Germany's chancellor had given his assent only under intense pressure, and once it became apparent that Wilson was not backing down, Chancellor Bethmann-Hollweg sought to re-engage the matter with the Kaiser as soon as he had gathered additional allies to support him. Bethmann-Hollweg convinced the chief of the German General Staff, General Erich von Falkenhayn, that Germany's policy of unrestricted submarine warfare threatened to bring the United States into the war. In the period between the American first and second *Lusitania* protest notes, Chancellor Bethmann-Hollweg persuaded the Kaiser to order the German navy to refrain from attacking neutral shipping, with a supplementary order directing it to avoid sinking large passenger ships of any nationality. Both Grand Admiral von Tirpitz (secretary of state of Naval Cabinet) and Vice Admiral Gustav Bachmann (chief of the Admiralty Staff) objected strenuously, and when their objections were overruled, requested permission to resign their posts. The Kaiser refused, reprimanding his truculent admirals that "The gentlemen are to obey and to remain! This is nothing but a military conspiracy!"[198]

The German government did not communicate these restrictions to the Americans or to its own public, simply hoping that the instructions would avoid future incidents. Wilson's second note prompted the German government to explore whether Wilson would back down from his grand claim to stand for the rights of humanity and settle for concessions that protected American ships, American citizens, and non-combatants traveling on passenger liners. Working closely with the U.S. ambassador in Berlin, the German government proposed that American ships would not be hindered in the prosecution of legitimate shipping and that the lives of American citizens on neutral vessels would not be put in jeopardy. In order to ensure that Americans could travel through its war zone in safety, the German government indicated that it would instruct its forces to permit the free and safe passage of American passenger steamers made recognizable by special markings, and if this was insufficient, grant the same guarantee of free and safe passage to neutral passenger liners flying the American flag and marked in similar fashion. Should this still be insufficient, up to four enemy passenger liners might be offered the same terms of safe conduct so long as the American government guaranteed that they would not be used to transport contraband. The German government was not, however, willing to "admit that American citizens can protect an enemy ship through the mere fact of their presence on board." This was akin, the German government explained, to claiming that American civilians should be free to traipse through localities of war on land in the confident expectation they would not be harmed.[199]

Ambassador Gerard had assisted the Germans in crafting these proposals aimed at minimizing future clashes, and he was taken aback by Washington's intransigence. In reply to a feeler he sent to Washington outlining the German proposals, he was granted permission to convey unofficially that the president was determined not to surrender or compromise in any way the rights of the United States or of its citizens as neutrals.[200] Wilson's third and final note dealing with the *Lusitania* held firm to the position he had staked out, again asserting that the United States would not consent to any abatement of its fundamental rights due to circumstances. Germany's suggestion that American-flagged passenger ships receive special treatment was rejected because agreeing to such a compromise would, by implication, concede Germany's right to attack other merchant ships without abiding by the conventions of stopping, searching, and embarking prize crews. The only hint of flexibility in Wilson's response was that he backed away from his insistence that Germany abandon submarine warfare entirely. Instead, if Germany practiced submarine warfare in such a way as to conform to international law, a suggestion that Wilson had judged a practical impossibility two months earlier in his first *Lusitania* note, then the chief cause of offense would be removed from German-American relations. Any repetition by German commanders of acts that violated American rights, the note warned ominously, would be regarded as deliberately unfriendly. As for Germany's incessant complaints that the United States had done little to uphold its rights against British violations, Wilson responded that the government of the United States would continue to contend for freedom of the seas, from whatever quarter violated, without compromise and at any cost.[201]

The reaction in Germany to Wilson's third note was almost universally negative. The Kaiser angrily noted in the margins that it was "Immeasurably impertinent!" and "Unheard of!" The right-wing press was infuriated. Even liberal editors found it confrontational and threatening in tone. The *New York Times* reported that the consensus in Germany was that President Wilson had just brushed aside German proposals and offered no constructive suggestions of his own. Across the spectrum of the German press, the widespread conviction prevailed that Germany should stay its course; the *Morgen Post,* for example, concluded, "There is a boundary to the concessions we can make. This boundary is Germany's self-respect and self-preservation."[202] In Britain, on the other hand, the note was commended from every quarter for its firm tone, dignity, and forcefulness, with many papers interpreting it as a practical ultimatum to Germany. The *Daily News* was particularly insightful, commenting that "The very nature of the submarine campaign makes it extremely difficult to avoid the offense which Wilson has indicated will be regarded as final. . . . A single intractable submarine commander may now destroy in a few seconds the flimsy fabric which is all that remains of official German-American friendship."[203]

The *Daily News's* commentary proved prescient. Shortly after dispatching Wilson's third *Lusitania* note, Lansing—now secretary of state—requested that German ambassador Bernstorff pay him a call. According to Bernstorff, Lansing informed him that if Americans again lost their lives through the torpedoing of a merchant ship, war could not be avoided. The United States would write no further notes.[204] Consequently, when Washington and Berlin became aware on August 19 that U-24 had sunk the 5,801-ton White Star Liner *Arabic* south of Ireland with the loss of forty-four lives, including those of two Americans, a crisis ensued. The British liner had been heavily involved in shipping contraband, as the Democratic-leaning New York *World* reported on August 20, but U-24 had not stopped, inspected, and allowed all its passengers to take to the lifeboats as international law demanded. Lansing, always the stickler for legalities, noted that the vessel had been westbound and therefore probably was not carrying contraband at the time it was attacked. Wilson finally realized the cul-de-sac his policy had created. Turning in anguish to his trusted counselor Colonel House, he wrote, "I greatly need your advice what to do in view of the sinking of the *Arabic*. . . . Two things are plain to me: 1. The people of this country count on me to keep them out of the war, 2. It would be a calamity to the world at large if we should be drawn actively into the conflict." He brought up the idea of writing to England in "very definite terms" to see whether Britain would rescind its Order in Council, presumably in exchange for Germany's abandoning its submarine campaign without loss of face. House was taken aback, and replied, "Our people do not want war, but even less do they want you to recede from the position you have taken. Further notes would disappoint our own people and would cause something of derision abroad. In view of what has been said, and in view of what has been done, it is clearly up to this Government to act." As for the idea of simultaneously confronting Britain, House advised Wilson to settle

Woodrow Wilson found Robert Lansing's meticulous, carefully crafted analyses of international law more to his taste than the less disciplined notions of common sense and fairness that framed William Jennings Bryan's recommendations.

Library of Congress, Prints and Photographs Division
LC-DIG-hec-03947

the conflict with Germany before taking on the British. Bolstered by House's response, Wilson remained resolute and took the plunge.[205]

On August 22, a high official in the administration informed the press corps that if it became apparent that Germany had deliberately ordered the attack on the *Arabic*, the administration would break diplomatic relations with Germany. It would recall Ambassador Gerard and all the American consuls from Germany, and send the German ambassador back home. If appropriate, the president might even call Congress back into session in order to ask for funds to expand the fleet, increase the size of the army, and strengthen coastal defenses.[206] The message was clear. Wilson understood that the country did not want war and was not prepared for war. He nonetheless was willing to publicly threaten to break relations with Germany in the hope that the threat would convince Imperial Germany to back down.

Wilson's threat worked. The Kaiser had secretly ordered his forces to avoid sinking large passenger liners without warning before the *Arabic* incident, and now expanded his order to encompass all passenger ships. He dismissed the German chief of admiralty, Admiral Bachmann, and humiliated von Tirpitz by withdrawing his right of direct access. Responding to pressure from Washington, the German government publicly revealed the limitations it had imposed on its commanders, pledging that passenger liners would be sunk only after warning and after passengers had time to take to the lifeboats. When that proved insufficient, the German government gave further assurances that neutral merchant ships, including American ones, would be exempt from interference except when carrying contraband, and then would only be subject to destruction "under the conditions laid down by the international code concerning maritime war."[207] For all intents and purposes, Wilson had achieved the objective laid out in his third *Lusitania* note. Germany was pledging that it would observe all the regulations associated with international law when dealing with neutral ships and passenger liners. Only in one area did the German concessions fall short of what Wilson demanded: Germany did not extend the commitment to observe war-prize rules to attacks against belligerent merchant ships. This would prove an issue the next year, but as summer turned to fall in 1915, Wilson's firm stance appeared vindicated. On September 18, the new chief of the German Admiralty decided to withdraw all U-boats from the English Channel and southwestern approaches rather than wage war within the boundaries imposed from above.[208]

In 1916, a renewed effort by the German navy to use submarines to attack without warning enemy merchant ships other than passenger liners resulted in another German-American crisis. Wilson again threatened to break relations if Germany did not accede to his demands. A German submarine, observing the French passenger liner *Sussex* near the port of Dieppe, misidentified the liner as a troopship and attacked the ship without warning. The *Sussex* was carrying some 325 passengers, including twenty-five Americans. The impact of the torpedo killed and injured eighty people, wounding four Americans. Lansing's initial draft note blasted the German government for the "wanton and indiscriminate slaughter of helpless men, women, and children," accusing it of reverting to a spirit of barbarism "which has no thought for human life and causes the innocent and defenseless to suffer even more grievously than those who bear arms." Lansing pressed the president to sever relations, and only Germany's coerced pledge to avoid attacking *any* passenger ships and observe war-prize rules when attacking *all* merchant ships avoided a diplomatic rupture.[209]

Wilson twice brought the United States to the brink of war with Germany, in fall 1915 and spring 1916, over a stubborn defense of neutral rights. His administration did indeed protest British infractions quite vigorously, and at times put forth suggestions that Britain opposed. But Wilson never threatened Britain with either ultimatums or sanctions. William Jennings Bryan resigned because he feared that Wilson's diplomacy was one-sided and would allow a handful of American citizens to recklessly drag a nation of millions into war. Bryan's common sense rejected the notion that the United States should threaten Germany with war in defense of the right of American citizens to travel undisturbed anywhere on the high seas on merchant ships of any flag. After resigning as secretary of state, Bryan took to the lecture circuit to make his case. Speaking before tens of thousands at Madison Square Garden in June and at the San Francisco Exposition in July 1915, Bryan argued that the question before the nation was not one of rights, but one of reason. Should the United States feel compelled to send one hundred thousand brave Americans to their deaths, he thundered, because a little more than a hundred took ships that they ought not to have taken into danger zones that they fully understood? If in time of war the government had the right to compel a son to leave his mother and risk his life, then was it not reasonable that in times of peace the same government could say to its citizens that they should not drag their country into war by taking unnecessary risk?[210]

Bryan's argument enraged that section of the governing establishment, the press, and the public that had come to identify strongly with the Allied cause. From London, the Anglophile American ambassador Walter Hines Page fumed in a letter home that "Of course he's [Bryan] a traitor: he always had a yellow streak, the yellow streak of a sheer fool." In Louisville, Kentucky, "Marse" Waterson of the *Courier-Journal* editorialized that "Men have been shot and beheaded, even hanged, drawn, and quartered, for treason less heinous. He [Bryan] commits not merely treason to the country at a critical moment, but treachery to his party and its official head." Republicans, who had always branded Bryan's populism as radical rabble-rousing, believed that Bryan might unleash the dangerous force of prairie pacifism. Former President Taft commented that "Bryan as usual is an ass, but he is an ass with a good deal of opportunity for mischief."[211] Most East Coast newspapers and Republican-leaning outlets throughout the nation found Bryan's argument craven, naïve, and dangerous. Yet many Midwestern newspapers commented favorably on Bryan's analysis, with the Hearst newspapers who had previously lambasted Bryan as a sell-out to Allied and business interests now celebrating his common sense.

Bryan's vision of neutrality was a powerful force in mid-1915, but as Germany backed down from open confrontation, Wilson's star rose domestically and Bryan's fell. The German government once again did itself no favors, leaking confidential communications, mismanaging espionage efforts, and sponsoring acts of sabotage in a country where public opinion was still very much in flux.[212] Bryan and other pacifist voices increasingly found themselves associated with "hyphenated Americans" who could not be trusted. Wilson, on the other hand, seemed to present a middle course between Bryan's pacifism and those who advocated for intervention. Capitalizing on this perception, Senator Ollie James of Kentucky reminded his fellow Democrats at their convention in June 1916 that "Without orphaning a single American child, without widowing a single American mother, without firing a single gun or shedding a drop of blood, he [Woodrow Wilson] wrung from the most militant spirit that ever brooded above a battlefield the concession of American demands and American rights." Bryan, who had feared that Wilson's diplomacy would drive the United States into war and who opposed Wilson's efforts to increase military spending, returned to the fold by 1916. At the same convention, crowds demanded that Bryan be given the forum, and the "Great Commoner" mended bridges by reminding all assembled that while he had differed with Wilson over diplomatic methods, they had both shared the same end goal: keeping the country out of war. Bryan reminded a cheering audience that "It was a Democratic President, supported by a Democratic Senate and House who has thus saved the country the horrors of that war."[213] After having brought the country twice to the brink of war, Wilson found that one of the most effective election slogans during the campaign of 1916 was "He kept us out of war."

If Wilson's policy toward Germany's U-boat warfare was successful in the short term, causing the Germans to back down and rallying the American public behind the notion that firmness had protected American rights while keeping the nation out of war, it was less successful in the medium term. One cannot assert that Wilson's firm line against unrestricted submarine warfare led to war in April 1917. It was Germany's decision to resort to unrestricted warfare in January 1917, after multiple warnings from the United States, that more than any other factor pushed Wilson over the brink. Germany's ambassador to the United States recognized that a resumption of unrestricted submarine warfare would lead to war, and repeatedly counseled Berlin against resuming its campaign. Germany's leaders nonetheless took a calculated gamble in 1917 to resume unrestricted submarine warfare, fully expecting that Wilson would break relations and assuming that the United States would eventually enter the war. At the Pless Conference in January 1917, the German Kaiser, the chancellor, and its military leaders carefully considered a navy study and concluded that a renewed campaign of unrestricted submarine warfare would bring Britain to its knees before American troops and supplies could be brought to bear.[214] They made this decision even as Wilson was attempting to broker a negotiated peace. Though the prospects for Wilson's peace initiative were poor, Germany's leaders timed their announcement with supreme indifference to American feelings. Germany's political and military leaders provoked the United States into war at a time when public sentiment was still undecided. Even after Germany resorted to unrestricted submarine warfare, Wilson agonized for almost two months before asking Congress to declare war against Germany. In the interim, the German government blundered both diplomatically and in the prosecution of the U-boat campaign, sending an extremely ill-conceived proposal to Mexico (the Zimmerman Telegram) for an alliance should the United States declare war on Germany, dangling the prospect of territorial gains in Texas, New Mexico, and Arizona as an incentive.[215] And as if to emphasize that the door was shut to some type of modus vivendi in the maritime sphere, German submarines sank the Cunard passenger liner *Laconia* on February 25 and U.S. merchant ships *Vigilancia, City of Memphis, Illinois,* and *Healdon* in mid-March. Abandoning the idea of armed neutrality, on April 2, 1917, Wilson advised Congress to declare war on Germany. By a vote of 82 to 6 in the Senate and 373 to 50 in the House, Congress formally declared war on Germany on April 6.[216]

Germany's resumption of undeclared submarine warfare in February 1917 stands out as a strategic miscalculation of the first order. Yet if Germany deliberately crossed the red line that Wilson drew with full knowledge that its action would put the American president in the position of having to break relations or lose all credibility, it nonetheless is true that Wilson was the one who drew that red line. He might, as Bryan had wanted, have warned Americans against traveling into the German war zone on British ships, particularly ships carrying contraband. He might, as the second German note suggested, have limited his demands to the right of American ships to pass unmolested, working out some sort of arrangement whereby U.S. ships could be readily identified via markings or by other arrangements. This would have entailed confronting Britain over its use of false flags and would have had domestic costs. Much of the East Coast press derided Germany's proposal as an arrogant demand that Uncle Sam paint its ships with barbershop stripes. He might, as German Americans demanded, have restricted the export of munitions or used the threat of an embargo to pressure Britain to roll back its blockade of foodstuffs. The record suggests that Germany was quite open to some sort of maritime bargain in early 1915. We cannot know whether Britain would have yielded to stronger pressure, but foreign minister Grey's postwar comments seem to indicate that it would have. More broadly, Wilson might have cast his policy in terms of American interests and American rights rather than in the loftier terms of universal rights and principles. This would have opened differences to arbitration, a scheme near and dear to Bryan's heart. One wonders, however, about what sort of compensation the United States could have expected from a victorious Germany.

In the short term, Wilson's firm policy forced Germany to back down, kept the United States out of war, and strengthened Wilson's domestic political position. In the medium term, it increased the likelihood of war, with the promise to keep the nation out of war resting on the slender reed of grudging German acquiescence to American demands it deemed unreasonable. Germany's leaders based their decision to resume unrestricted submarine warfare on strategic calculations and not popular opinion, but the decision enjoyed widespread support. The German government made its decision not in the face of popular opinion but with the public's enthusiastic backing. A few brave individuals stood up against the pressure, but once Ludendorff and the army came around to the navy's position, it became virtually impossible for the German chancellor to resist pressure to unleash the U-boats. By the winter of 1916–17 the German populace was eating turnips as Britain's blockade began to bite with a vengeance.[217]

German proponents of unrestricted submarine warfare found it easy to manipulate public resentment of the British blockade, of American exports of guns and munitions, and of Britain's use of Q-ships, false flags, and ramming to argue that the gloves must come off. After the war, German Admiral Arno Spindler would conduct a remarkably candid assessment of the German U-boat campaign and conclude that German submarines in the Mediterranean had been effective even when observing the limitations imposed by international law. He suggested that Germany should have contented itself with waging limited submarine warfare.[218] But perceptions shape reality and by late 1916, the German government, its military, and much of the public believed that Wilson's restrictions were undermining the effectiveness of their naval war on British commerce. Bryan may have been wrong about the timing, but the inevitable clash he foresaw played itself out in the spring of 1917.

The long-term consequences of Wilson's response to the *Lusitania* disaster consisted of two diametrically opposed currents. First, Wilson's response established the trajectory for what became known as Wilsonianism or liberal internationalism. Rather than justify his opposition to German policies in realist terms related to the global balance of power and the threat that growing German power posed to the Monroe Doctrine in South America and the Caribbean, Wilson claimed to be pursuing a policy of strict neutrality. His stated objective was not to contain Germany or aid Britain but, rather, to defend universal principles of fairness, justice, and right. Wilson did not limit the protests he lodged with Germany to the loss of American lives and the destruction of American property; he objected to the essence of unrestricted submarine warfare because it killed non-combatants of other nationalities as well. Wilson claimed to speak for wider, universal rights, drawing upon long-established national perceptions of America as a city upon the hill and an example for others. He would enunciate his vision more fully in his January 1918 Fourteen Points speech, and his cherished concept of a League of Nations that promised to render realpolitik a thing of the past. Subsequent presidents might step back from Wilson's soaring goals, but beginning with Franklin Roosevelt, American presidents have framed their foreign policy goals in terms of values, as well as interests.

The second current that emerged in reaction to Wilson's U-boat diplomacy was a delayed reemergence of many of Bryan's notions. The belief that loans to the Allies, the manufacture and export of arms and munitions, and the presence of

Americans onboard belligerent merchant ships led to America's intervention in World War I gained strength in the 1920s and became widespread by the 1930s. Unsurprisingly, these notions were particularly strong in those sections of the United States that had a heavy concentration of German Americans and in those agrarian areas where Bryan had never been dismissed as a fool and a clown. By the 1930s, these notions had even penetrated academia, with revisionist scholars arguing that Wilson's diplomacy had not been beyond reproach. In 1934, the Senate established a Special Committee on Investigation of the Munitions Industry, commonly known as the Nye Committee after its chairman, Gerald Nye of North Dakota. The Nye Committee would conduct ninety-three hearings and question more than two hundred witnesses over the course of eighteen months. The committee's findings fed into the narrative that the American public had somehow been hoodwinked into war, though Nye overstepped the bounds of senatorial propriety when he directly attacked Wilson in 1936. The committee's dissolution did not spell the end of isolationist sentiment. Instead, bipartisan majorities passed a series of neutrality acts in 1935, 1936, 1937, and 1939. The Neutrality Act of 1935 authorized the president to do what Wilson had refused to do some twenty years earlier: he could proclaim that American citizens should refrain from traveling on belligerent ships. Those who traveled despite the president's warning would do so at their own risk. The ghosts of the *Lusitania* would haunt the next American president to confront a naval crisis.

The USS *Panay* under way on the Yangtze River, date unknown.
Naval History and Heritage Command, Photo Archives, NH 11353

3 THE *PANAY* INCIDENT

BACKGROUND TO THE AMERICAN PRESENCE IN CHINA

On August 22, 1937, Admiral Harry Yarnell, commander in chief of the U.S. Asiatic Fleet, dispatched a stern protest to the commander of the Japanese Third Battle Fleet, whose ships were firing on Chinese positions near Shanghai's International Settlement. Yarnell, joined by his British and French counterparts, complained that Japanese destroyers were shooting directly over his flagship and other non-belligerent naval ships. He objected that the Japanese were endangering neutral shipping caught in the crossfire between Chinese and Japanese forces, noting that two days earlier a shell had landed directly on the deck of his flagship, killing one American sailor and wounding eighteen. Admiral Yarnell urged the Japanese admiral to shift his warships to a different anchorage so that the USS *Augusta* and other neutral vessels moored off Shanghai's bustling waterfront, the Bund, would not be further endangered. He explained that he was unable to move his flagship as it was protecting American nationals and needed to stay in communication with the American perimeter of the International Settlement.[1] Yarnell's request was duly conveyed to Tokyo, and while the Japanese government responded reassuringly that it had directed its forces to exercise utmost caution so as to avoid incidentally damaging Western embassies or ships, the reality was that the escalating conflict between Imperial Japan and Nationalist China threatened long-established Western interests.

These interests took many forms, from large international settlements with extraterritorial jurisdiction at dozens of treaty ports along China's coast to factories, railroads, and warehouses throughout the country, to missionary schools and churches tucked deep in the country's hinterland. The British had blasted the path for Western penetration of China in the nineteenth century, using modern firepower and steam-propelled warships to humiliate the Qing Empire during the Opium War of 1839–42. Britain, France, Russia, Germany, and Japan subsequently had extracted additional concessions from the tottering Qing government following Chinese defeats in the Second

Opium War (1856–60), the Sino-Japanese War (1894–95), and the Boxer Rebellion (1898–1900).

Although the United States played a secondary role in these conflicts, bombarding fortifications along the Pearl River and at Taku in 1856, and contributing a contingent to the 18,000-strong Beijing "International Relief Expedition" in 1900, it nevertheless insisted that China grant Americans equivalent rights, privileges, and protections to those it was reluctantly granting to other foreign nationals.[2] To enforce these rights, the United States negotiated permission to patrol the Yangtze River under the terms of the Sino-American Treaty of 1858, with the so-called Boxer Protocol of 1901 further expanding the American military presence in China. In order to forestall Europe's imperial powers and Japan from carving up China into spheres of influence where trade and investment opportunities would be restricted, the United States pronounced that the great powers should implement an "Open Door Policy" toward China. This policy would grant all foreign nations equal access to the Chinese market, with no one country claiming exclusive rights to China as a whole or of portions of the tottering Chinese empire. To demonstrate its commitment to defending American rights and market access, the United States maintained a small military presence in China after the defeat of the Boxers and during the tumultuous period that followed.

By the mid-1930s, the United States had around 2,400 ground troops in China, with 528 marines on station in Beijing, 785 Army troopers posted to Tientsin, and 1,100 marines stationed at Shanghai.[3] In addition, units of the U.S. Asiatic Fleet regularly visited Chinese ports, with Admiral Yarnell's flagship the *Augusta* (a heavy cruiser) anchored conspicuously at Shanghai's Battleship Row throughout the summer and fall of 1937.[4] Lastly, the riverine gunboats of the U.S. Yangtze Patrol provided a reassuring presence deep into the interior of China for the scattered American missionary outposts, schools, trading enclaves, and businesses strung out along South China's major trade corridor, the Yangtze River.

The U.S. Yangtze Patrol dated back to the 1860s, when the U.S. Navy had dispatched two paddle-wheel steamers to China to protect American interests following the American Civil War. These were eventually replaced with former Spanish gunboats salvaged from the bottom of Manila Bay by the U.S. Navy following the Spanish-American War. In 1919, the Department of the Navy designated the assorted river craft it maintained in China as the U.S. Yangtze Patrol, or YangPat. The U.S. Navy gradually replaced the YangPat's hodgepodge of vessels with more modern, specially designed riverboats built in Shanghai's Kiangnan Shipyard. These river gunboats (the USS *Luzon, Guam, Tutuila, Mindanao, Oahu,* and *Panay*), along with two older vessels dating to the First World War (the USS *Monocacy* and the USS *Isabel*), operated from Shanghai on the coast all the way to Chungking (Chongqing), 1,400 miles upriver from the sea. Their mission, enunciated in the

Navy's 1922 Annual Report, was to "protect U.S. interests, lives, and property, and to maintain and improve friendly relations with the Chinese people."[5]

During the 1920s, the gunboats of YangPat seemed to be constantly on call, suppressing river pirates, confronting Chinese warlords who violated American rights, and resisting an assertive, nationalistic Kuomintang movement that was whipping up anti-foreign sentiment as it consolidated its grip on power. U.S. gunboats engaged Chinese military units no fewer than thirty-seven times over the course of 1927–28, upholding treaty rights secured during the waning days of the Qing Empire.[6] Confrontations between the U.S. Yangtze Patrol and Kuomintang forces began to decrease after the Japanese invasion of Manchuria in 1931, as Chiang Kai-shek correctly perceived that Japan posed a greater danger to the Republic of China's long-term viability than did the various Western powers still clinging to treaty rights dating to the nineteenth century. Japan was nearer, had territorial ambitions that remained unfulfilled, and seemed intent on exerting a more extensive dominance over China than Western imperial powers had ever achieved.

In July 1937, Japan launched a full-scale invasion of China following a clash between Chinese and Japanese troops at the Marco Polo or Lugou Bridge southwest of Beijing. Japan demanded that China recognize the Japanese-dominated puppet state of Manchukuo; cease all anti-Japanese activities and propaganda; and suppress communism. Since the Japanese would determine what constituted "anti-Japanese activities," they in effect were demanding a broad veto right over both internal and external Chinese affairs. Japan's goal seemed clear. It was seeking to displace Britain as the most influential power in China.[7] While reassuring the United States that it had no intention of challenging the long-standing U.S. Open Door Policy on China, Japan engaged in military operations designed to secure a position of dominance that would inevitably affect U.S. investments, trade, educational, and missionary activity in China.[8]

As clashes between Kuomintang and Japanese soldiers escalated into a full-fledged (though undeclared) war in July 1937, the environment in which U.S. troop detachments and gunboats operated became increasingly dangerous. The isolated gunboats of the Yangtze Patrol were particularly vulnerable, usually operating as detached units and lacking the firepower to defend themselves from anything more serious than small-arms fire. On August 10, Secretary of State Cordell Hull clarified the mission of the Yangtze Patrol, specifying that both offensive and coercive operations against foreign governments fell outside its mission set. He emphasized that the Yangtze Patrol's primary function was to protect American nationals, with a secondary function to protect American property. American forces in China were

in no sense expeditionary forces. They are not in occupation of an enemy territory nor are they defending [the] territory of the United States. They are expected to protect lives but they are not expected to hold positions regardless of hazards. They would be expected to repel threatened incursions of mobs or of disorganized or unauthorized soldiery, but they would not be expected to hold a position against . . . armed forces of another country acting on express high authority.[9]

By this time, Sino-Japanese fighting had spread from northern China and the Beijing area to Shanghai and the Yangtze River Valley. Americans, other Westerners, and Chinese civilians became caught in the crossfire, with both sides showing a general disregard for non-combatant lives and neutral property. On August 14, the Republic of China (ROC) Air Force attempted to bomb the Japanese cruiser *Izumo*, flagship of a twenty-ship Japanese task force assembled at the mouth of Whangpoo River at Shanghai. The Chinese pilots released their bombs early, dropping their payload over Shanghai's International Settlement. One bomb demolished the upper stories of the sumptuous Palace Hotel; another landed among a throng of refugees crowding the settlement's main road. Over 700 civilians were killed and thousands injured, including many Chinese women and children who had sought refuge in the International Settlement in hopes that both sides would scrupulously avoid bombing it.[10] Two weeks later, Chinese pilots mistook the SS *President Hoover*, a large passenger liner about two-thirds the size of the *Lusitania,* for a Japanese troop transport, bombing the American ship as it waited for the tide to shift so it could move upstream to evacuate American citizens as the fighting intensified around Shanghai. The Chinese Nationalist government expressed its deepest regrets for the incident, and Chiang Kai-shek furiously threatened to execute the Chinese airmen responsible for the attack.[11]

It soon became apparent, however, that Japanese aircraft and artillery were becoming the main threat to American lives and property in China. Relaying a report from the U.S. embassy in Nanking (Nanjing) to the American ambassador in Japan, Secretary of State Hull remarked that "Sooner or later some incident is going to happen resulting in the death or injury of American citizens going about their legitimate occupations within the interior of China where such dangers should not exist." Hull directed Ambassador Joseph Grew to deliver an aide-mémoire to the Japanese Ministry for Foreign Affairs urging Japan to "refrain from attacks upon defenseless cities, hospitals, trains, and motor cars etc." Hull noted that while Japan claimed it was not at war with China, Japanese aircraft were conducting raids deep into the interior of China with "consequent serious damage to the rights of other nations."[12]

Hull's misgivings were justified. As Japan proceeded with military operations around Shanghai and then pushed up the Yangtze River toward the ROC's capital at Nanking, a growing number of complaints reached the U.S. Embassy about incidents in which Americans had been hurt, attacked, or witnessed brutal assaults on Chinese employees and civilian facilities. On September 17, Ambassador Grew lodged an official complaint with the Japanese government, noting that Japanese military forces were showing a reckless disregard for American lives and property. Japanese aircraft, Grew admonished, had even subjected U.S. humanitarian and philanthropic establishments in China to savage attacks. Most recently, three Japanese airplanes had conducted a low-level attack on a U.S. missionary hospital in Kwantung province, completely ignoring the two large American flags prominently displayed. The hospital was miles from the nearest ROC facility, and the attack violated all international norms and standards of conduct.

Ambassador Grew called upon Japanese foreign minister Kōki Hirota three days later, warning him of "the very serious effect which would be produced in the United States . . . if some accident should occur in connection" with the Japanese navy's announced intention to bomb Nanking. Grew recalled that he had employed the most emphatic language, reminding Hirota that "we must not forget history . . . neither the American Government nor the American people had wanted war with Spain in 1898, but when the *Maine* was blown up nothing could prevent war. The American people are the most pacific and patient people in the world. . . . But under provocation we can become the most inflammable people in the world."[13] Ambassador Grew feared that overeager Japanese aviators might attack a U.S. ship or contingent of marines despite directions to exercise utmost caution. He blamed young, hotheaded Japanese aviators for causing trouble, commenting in his diary that "having once smelled blood they simply fly amok and 'don't give a damn whom or what they hit.'"[14]

Grew underestimated the complicity of Japanese political authorities in condoning military operations that would culminate in wholesale murder and mass rape after the fall of Nanking in December, but as he assessed the situation in September 1937, he drew on his knowledge of the past. As first secretary at the U.S. Embassy in Berlin during the *Lusitania, Arabic,* and *Sussex* crises, Grew had witnessed the German government's efforts to selectively employ frightfulness, only to have U-boat commanders ignore or violate orders to avoid sinking neutral ships and passenger liners.[15]

Less than three months after warning Hirota that overeager Japanese aviators might plunge relations between the United States and Japan into a crisis, Grew found himself issuing orders to the American Embassy staff in Tokyo to plan for a hurried departure. The atmosphere reminded him of that which prevailed in the U.S. Embassy in Berlin after the sinking of the *Lusitania* in 1915.[16] The ambassador had received word that Japanese aircraft had sunk the USS *Panay* on December 12 as it lay at anchor upstream of Nanking.

THE INCIDENT

The USS *Panay* was stationed far upriver at Chungking in mid-summer 1937, shifting downriver to Hankow to be closer to the action as it became clear that the latest Sino-Japanese incident had escalated into major warfare. The ship was small, measuring no more than 191 feet in length and designed to operate in shallow waters. Its propellers were enclosed in tunnels to furnish protection from rocks, logs, and debris, with three rudders providing excellent control in the swift currents where the Yangtze narrowed. Drawing less than six feet of water, the *Panay* was lightly armed, equipped with two three-inch guns and ten .30-caliber machine guns.[17] Though the size and armament of the *Panay* and its sister gunboats might suggest that assignment to these units was akin to ostracism from the fleet, a posting to the Yangtze Patrol was highly coveted. The *Panay*'s complement of fifty enlisted men found that their meager pay was sufficient to hire a complement of Chinese "boatmen" who washed their uniforms, prepared their food, polished the ship's metalwork, and provided menial labor for the countless work details that keep a vessel supplied and ready. The bars and brothels of Shanghai, Nanking, and other Yangtze River towns were legendary, and a good many chiefs and petty officers were long-timers who had spent years in the Far East.[18] The U.S. Navy was stricter about rotating the officers of the U.S. Asiatic Fleet back to the United States and to sea duty in one of the U.S. Navy's other numbered fleets, but the five officers assigned to the *Panay* likewise found that the assignment had its benefits. Their paltry interwar salaries went a long way in the China of the 1930s, enabling those with wives and families to taste the privileged life of white expatriates during the sunset days of Western imperialism. Houseboys, cooks, nannies, and a small army of domestics made life ashore a pleasant experience for naval officers and their families during off-duty hours, and the expatriate communities in Shanghai, Nanking, and elsewhere extended a warm welcome to new arrivals from the United States.[19]

The onset of Sino-Japanese warfare put an end to accompanied tours of duty and evenings at the club. In the fall of 1937, the wives

Duty aboard the USS *Panay* and the other vessels of the Yangtze Patrol was coveted by American officers and sailors, with Chinese "boatmen" performing many of the menial tasks.

Naval History and Heritage Command, Photo Archives, NH L45-222

and dependents of the *Panay*'s officers were evacuated by train to Canton, and the *Panay* was dispatched to Nanking so that it could evacuate American nationals and embassy staff should that become necessary. The Yangtze Patrol's flagship, the USS *Luzon*, was already there, as were the British gunboats HMS *Cricket* and *Scarab*. Two additional British gunboats, the HMS *Ladybird* and *Bee*, were positioned approximately fifty miles upriver at Wuhu, with the USS *Oahu* an additional four hundred miles upstream at Kiukiang (Jiujiang).

On November 21, 1937, the Republic of China announced that it was relocating its foreign ministry and other state offices from Nanking to Hankow. Japanese aircraft had been bombing the Chinese capital for more than two months, and following the fall of Shanghai on November 8, Japanese troops were making rapid progress toward Nanking. China's minister for foreign affairs requested that all foreign chiefs of mission leave Nanking as soon as possible. On November 22, the American ambassador and most of the embassy staff boarded the USS *Luzon* for evacuation to Hankow. The *Panay* was ordered to stay at Nanking to serve as a radio relay ship for the skeleton embassy staff that remained, standing by to evacuate remaining embassy personnel and American nationals still in Nanking if so directed. George Atcheson Jr., second secretary of the U.S. Embassy in China, became the acting officer in charge of the diplomatic staff left in Nanking. A hard core of American businessmen and journalists remained in the city despite repeated warnings from the embassy that the situation was becoming increasingly dangerous. These included a handful of Standard Oil (Socony) personnel, a few independent businessmen, and journalists, cameramen, and correspondents bent on covering the war despite the dangers.[20] Atcheson and his staff did their utmost to make sure that all Americans who wished to leave before the maelstrom hit were able to do so.

Norman Alley, a newsreel cameraman for Universal Studios, captured the chaos that pervaded throughout Nanking as the Japanese closed on the capital. Eager to record the Japanese aerial bombardment of the railroad yards that converged on the opposite side of the river, Alley hitched a ride on a sampan putt-putt to Pukow. Upon arriving at the bombed-out terminal, Alley began to take pictures, including an image of a Chinese "coolie widow" clutching an infant while squatting and wailing beside her dead husband. A young boy, who appeared to be around seven, tugged at the distraught woman's sleeve and desperately pleaded that she take cover. Alley recalled,

> Suddenly, from out of the west, came some Japanese war planes . . . these returning planes swooped low as their machine guns spat deadly fire, and proceeded to strafe everything left living. The wretched fugitives didn't have a Chinaman's chance. Hemmed in this high-walled box canyon, herded like sheep on a slaughterhouse runway, they jostled and struggled. It was a mad nightmare, Grand Guignole on a wholesale scale, as back would swing the planes, again and again, death-dealing pendulums. Innocents ran screaming and stumbled, dying, over already smoldering bodies. . . . When the Nipponese fliers had done one of two things—exhausted their ammunition, or thought the job was complete enough—they flew away. Now, we watched the long, tedious, and heartbreaking progress of the still living, as they wended their way, literally, over the bodies of the mangled, dying, and dead. They were two and three deep in many places, and overlapping.[21]

The situation in Nanking became ever more precarious as Japanese ground troops and artillery drew closer. On December 2, George Atcheson sent a circular to all the Americans he could find. He informed them:

> The Embassy has issued repeated warnings to Americans of the increasing danger to those who remain in Nanking. Under telegraphic instructions from the Department of State, this circular is issued as a final warning to all Americans that they should withdraw from Nanking as soon as possible and proceed upriver to a place of greater safety.
>
> The Embassy would be grateful if each American in Nanking would indicate on the accompanying sheet whether he is planning to leave the city by arrangement independent of the Embassy, or whether he desires to take refuge on the "USS *Panay*" when advised to do so by the Embassy, probably within the next few days.[22]

Three days later, Atcheson distributed a final warning to all Americans in Nanking, advising them to assemble at 9:30 the next morning at the Bund (riverfront) if they planned to embark on the *Panay*. Each individual was to bring bedding, with baggage limited to one suitcase per person. By December 7, Japanese forces had reached Tangshan, twenty miles east of Nanking. The American, British, and German embassies decided to order all remaining staff to evacuate the following day. After establishing a temporary embassy office onboard the *Panay*, Atcheson dispatched a message to Japanese authorities on the morning of December 9 listing the names of eighteen Americans who had elected to remain in the city. The Japanese were by then exchanging machine-gun fire with Chinese gunners outside Nanking's Kwangsua gate. Bombs began to fall in the water near the *Panay* that evening, prompting its captain, Lieutenant Commander James Hughes, to move the ship upriver about two miles to San Chia Ho.[23] Two days later, as artillery shells began to splash around the *Panay*, Hughes again ordered the *Panay* to shift anchorage to a position approximately twelve miles upriver from Nanking. The next day, December 12, as shells once again began to send water spouts into the air off the *Panay*'s starboard beam, Hughes weighed anchor and began moving the *Panay* upriver, accompanied by the Standard Oil tankers *Meiping, Meihsia*, and *Meian*.

In addition to its normal complement of five officers and fifty enlisted men, the *Panay* had embarked three groups of Americans: embassy personnel, businessmen, and an assortment of American newsmen and photographers. The U.S. Embassy also permitted the Italian vice-consul, two Italian journalists, and a journalist from the *London Times* to join the American evacuees. The heavy presence of newsmen aboard the *Panay* was remarkable, with Eric Mayell of Fox Movietone, Norman Alley of Universal Newsreel, Jim Marshall of *Collier's Magazine*, Norman Soong of the *New York Times*, and Weldon James of United Press onboard the gunboat.[24]

George Atcheson kept the U.S. consul general in Shanghai and the U.S. ambassador in Hankow informed of the *Panay*'s position and movement. He and others had witnessed how Japanese shells had fallen near HMS *Scarab*, HMS *Cricket*, the British passenger liner *Whangpoo*, and the Jardine-Matheson hulk sheltering British nationals on December 11. In addition to relaying the *Panay*'s position to Japanese authorities, the Americans had taken the precaution of painting two large American flags horizontally on the ship's awning, and the vessel displayed an oversized American ensign at the gaff of the mast.[25] The SS *Meiping, Meihsia*, and *Meian* likewise had painted the U.S. colors horizontally on their superstructures and flew large American flags.

The *Panay* departed its anchorage twelve miles upriver (south) of Nanking at 8:25 A.M. At 9:40, Japanese troops on the north shore of the river signaled that the *Panay* should stop. A motorboat approached, and two Japanese officers and four soldiers with fixed bayonets scrambled onboard the gunship. The Japanese commander, Lieutenant M. Shigeru, asked why the *Panay* was proceeding upriver. Informed that it was doing so to escape shelling, Shigeru then asked whether the *Panay* had sighted Chinese troops and where they were located. When informed that a neutral party could not provide information on troop locations or movements to either belligerent party, the Japanese departed. At 11 A.M., the *Panay* dropped anchor just north of the Hohsien cutoff near an island the Americans called May Queen Island. The Standard Oil tankers followed suit. Atcheson sent a priority radiogram to the U.S. consul general in Shanghai requesting that the Japanese consul general be informed of the ship's change of position. Atcheson's message read:

> Shell fire at nine o'clock this morning caused the *Panay* to move farther upstream and vessel is now anchored twenty-seven miles above Nanking at mileage two twenty one above Woosung. Standard Oil Company's steamers *Meiping*, *Meian*, and *Meihsia* are anchored nearby.
>
> As from this embassy please inform Japanese Embassy of present position of *Panay* and American merchant vessels' names, and request that appropriate instructions be issued to Japanese forces. Please add that circumstances may again cause *Panay* to move either up- or downriver and that *Panay* expects to return downriver to Nanking as soon as feasible in order to reestablish communications with Americans who remained in Nanking and in order that this embassy may as soon as practicable resume its functions ashore. Please state that the American embassy hopes that appropriate steps to facilitate this plan will be taken by all four authorities who may be concerned.
>
> Sent to Shanghai, repeated to Department Hankow, Peking. Peking please repeat to Tokyo with request that Embassy Tokyo communicate to Japanese foreign office.[26]

Having moved the ship almost thirty miles away from the front line, Commander Hughes felt that the *Panay* was well out of the danger zone. The ship's cook prepared to treat crew and guests to a Sunday chicken dinner, and afterward everyone not on duty settled back for a restful afternoon. Hughes felt sufficiently at ease that he gave permission for a small liberty party to depart for the *Meiping*. There they could enjoy a cold beer at a temporary "Navy club" the sailors had established, as alcohol had been prohibited on U.S. naval vessels ever since Secretary of the Navy Josephus Daniels had imposed his teetotaling ways on the Navy in 1914.[27] Onboard the *Panay*, the "mess boys" busied themselves with cleaning the dishes and clearing the galley, as crew members not on watch retired to their favored spots for some "sack time."

At 1:35 P.M., spotters on the bridge passed the word to the skipper that aircraft had been sighted high in the sky to the southeast. Commander Hughes and Chief Quartermaster John Lang headed up to the pilothouse, where the captain raised his binoculars to examine the approaching aircraft. He sighted what appeared to be six planes, then realized that the leading three were rapidly dropping in altitude and appeared to be in a dive. Before he could sound General Quarters, an explosion rocked the *Panay*, throwing the captain across the bridge against the engine order telegraph (E.O.T.) and breaking the femur in his upper thigh. The ship was under attack.

The impact of the first bomb sent men flying like rag dolls. Ensign Dennis Biwerse, who had been standing on the main deck forward, was thrown against the ship's superstructure; the shock wave stripped him of much of his uniform. Two embassy staffers were working in the ship's office when a concussion wave threw them across the room, breaking the embassy code clerk's leg and twisting the leg of Atcheson's second in command. As people began to get back on their feet, another series of blasts and explosions tore at the ship.

The *Panay*'s survivors differed about the precise number of aircraft they sighted and the specific sequence of bomb attacks and low-level strafing runs. They were unanimous, however, in identifying their attackers as Japanese; engineering officer John Geist commented that the dive bombers "came low enough for us to see the red suns on their wings distinctly and we could see the pilots of some of the planes. Even in the excitement they would have had to see our flags."[28] We now know that the *Panay* was attacked by Japanese naval aircraft from the 12th and 13th Air Groups based at Changchow, midway between Shanghai and Nanking. Masatake Okumiya, the only participating Japanese squadron commander to survive World War II, later provided a detailed account of the attack. The high-level bombers in the Japanese attacking formation had released their 60-pound bombs first, and it was the impact of one of these bombs that threw Commander Hughes across the bridge just moments after he noticed the first dive bomber commence its dive.[29] The first group of dive bombers released around twenty additional bombs just seconds before the ordnance from the high-altitude bombers hit, with many of these bombs falling close aboard and spraying fragments around the ship's superstructure. A second group of dive bombers then attacked the *Panay*, and fighter planes subsequently strafed the vessel with machine-gun fire.[30]

The swift sequence of high-altitude bombs, dive-bomb attacks, and strafing runs wreaked havoc on the *Panay*. The first bomb hit forward of the port bow, disabling the forward three-inch gun, wrecking the pilothouse and sick bay, and disabling the radio equipment. Both the main steam line and main fuel line were cut, and when the General Quarters alarm was activated, all the crew could hear was a weak tinkle on the bridge.[31]

Commander Hughes had trained his crew well, with sailors tumbling out of racks, showers, and elsewhere to man their battle stations. The ship's air-defense bill did not entail manning the three-inch guns, so the crew concentrated on bringing as many of the .30-caliber machine guns into action as possible. The executive officer, Arthur "Tex" Anders, was on deck organizing anti-aircraft fire when he heard that the *Panay*'s captain was out of action, his hip shattered and shock setting in. Anders scrambled to the bridge, where a shell fragment pierced his neck and rendered speech impossible. Undeterred and bleeding profusely from the neck, Anders grabbed a pencil and began to write orders on the back of charts and on the pilothouse's white bulkheads.[32] Many others performed with equal valor. Chief Boatswain's Mate Ernest Mahlmann would later be lionized in the American press as the "pantless gunner." At the time of the attack, Mahlmann had been in the forward hold of the boatswain's locker that served as his berthing space. He and the other chief petty officers had given up their quarters to their civilian guests, and Mahlmann was in the midst of putting on his clothes following a Sunday nap when the Japanese attacked. Mahlmann recalled, "As I was about to get into my trousers, the crash came. Everything started to fall, cases of soap and soap powder with many other things that were hung up. The water started rushing in. Instead of finishing the job of getting into my trousers, I thought it would be faster to get them off as there was a ladder to climb." Mahlmann emerged from below decks wearing only his skivvies, a long-sleeved shirt, and his life jacket. He rushed to man one of the .30-caliber guns, and subsequently played an instrumental role in organizing boats and evacuating the wounded while the Japanese strafed the *Panay*. An amateur poet in Kansas later penned an ode to the chief, "The Pantless Gunner of *Panay*," which was picked up by the Associated Press and widely reproduced. While some took it as an attempt at humor, it recognized that Mahlmann had kept his wits while "in the battle's heat, [he] Rushed to his post without his pants, The bomber's dive to meet."[33]

The *Panay*'s Lewis guns chattered away and made a racket, but they proved entirely ineffective. The Japanese aircraft dove and strafed the ship along its length, with the machine guns positioned on the port and starboard sides of the ship unable to fire at their attackers until the Japanese veered off to the side and began to climb back to altitude. Norman Alley later wrote that "the guns of the *Panay* were cap-pistoling against the sun at swiftly moving marks which snapped by at 200 miles an hour. [They were] as effective as swatting at a pestiferous mosquito in the black of the night. Our machine guns, four in number, were old Lewis pieces, vintage of 1917, all right for a comic opera campaign against Chinese river pirates, but never designed for bringing down belligerent aircraft. . . . [T]he seamen on the USS *Panay* didn't have a fighting chance!"[34] If nothing else, however, the ability to shoot back boosted morale, as each gunner hoped he might bring down one of the attacking Japanese aircraft. Their hopes remained unfulfilled. Throughout the twenty-minute attack, they did not shoot down a single Japanese aircraft.

The civilian news photographers and cameramen onboard risked their lives to record the attack. Norman Soong, an American photographer of Chinese extraction, was topside dozing in the sun when the first bomb exploded. He grabbed his camera and immediately began to snap pictures. Soong knew that if he were captured by the Japanese, his chances would be slim. Norman Alley picked his way through the debris toward his quarters, where he had stowed his movie camera and film. He proceeded topside with camera in hand. Alley and Eric Mayell of Fox Movietone News would film much of the attack. Their pictures clearly showed that it was a bright, clear, and sunny day. No clouds or smoke obscured the *Panay*.

The attacking Japanese aircraft had not only targeted the *Panay* but had attempted to sink the *Meihsia*, *Meiping*, and *Meian* as well. The *Meiping* had been anchored about one hundred yards off the *Panay*'s starboard bow that morning, minimizing the boat trip for the eight lucky sailors authorized "liberty" aboard the tanker. Just as the visiting sailors were cracking open bottles of cold beer in the temporary club they had established, the water between the tanker and the *Panay* erupted with water geysers from bombs that had missed their target. The *Meiping*'s captain weighed anchor and made for the north shore before sighting a pontoon wharf on the south shore and steering toward it. Shortly thereafter, the *Meiping* was hit and set ablaze. Its captain was able to bring the ship to the wharf, with many of its terrified Chinese crew streaming off the ship, fearful that the tanker might explode. The *Meihsia* retained maneuverability. When its captain saw that the *Panay* was severely stricken, he steered toward the gunboat to see whether he could take aboard any of its wounded men or passengers. Yet the last thing that the beleaguered *Panay*'s crew wanted was to have a highly combustible tanker come alongside. They vigorously waved off the *Meihsia*, which headed toward the south bank, tying up alongside the smoking *Meiping*.[35] The third Standard Oil tanker, the *Meian*, had been struck by bombs and rendered unmaneuverable. Its captain, C. H. Carlson, had been killed, and the ship drifted in the Yangtze's current until finally grounding on its north bank.

The *Panay*'s liberty party and a firefighting detail sent from the *Meihsia* were so focused on extinguishing the fire on the *Meiping* that they had not noticed the approach of a Japanese army patrol. The Japanese officer in charge was apparently confused to see American flags flying aboard the tankers, and inquired what was happening. When he was told that Japanese aircraft had attacked the tankers and the USS *Panay*, he was baffled. One of his officers queried, "If American gunboat, why [did] it shoot?"[36] The Japanese patrol appeared friendly, and its commander stationed two signalmen at the end of the floating pontoon wharf to ward off further aerial attacks. They desperately waved two small Japanese flags as the attacking aircraft circled around and commenced another bombing run. The Japanese pilots apparently did not see the small figures. Two bombs slammed into the *Meiping*, killing both Japanese signalmen and causing new fires. Everyone ran for shore as the Japanese aircraft circled for another attack. Both ships became engulfed in flames, and those on shore could hear the screams of Chinese crewmen trapped onboard the burning tankers. The explosion of gas drums on the *Meiping* could be heard for hours.[37]

The situation on the *Panay* went from bad to worse while the Japanese aircraft were pounding the *Meiping, Meihsia*, and *Meian*. Water was pouring into the ship through various holes, the main generator was inoperable, and only emergency power was available. "Tex" Anders, unable to speak and growing increasingly weak from the loss of blood, calculated that the ship had taken on at least four feet of water. Writing on the back of a nautical chart, the *Panay*'s executive officer painstakingly communicated his orders. In addition to his neck wound, Anders's hands had been lacerated and blood kept dripping onto the paper. Able to write only a word or phrase at a time before blood smears forced him to shift to a different spot, Anders gave his orders to the ship's chief engineer. Anders laboriously penciled the following on the back of a chart:

>   alongside
> Get all
>   boats
> small
>
> Can we run
> ship aground
>   if not
> Abandon Ship[38]

The *Panay* was equipped with two boats, a 26½-foot motor sampan which served as the captain's gig and a 22½-foot pulling sampan equipped with a small outboard motor. The order to abandon ship was issued around 2 P.M., though the time interval between the initial Japanese attack at 1:38 and the abandon-ship order undoubtedly seemed far longer to those onboard. The severely wounded, including the protesting skipper, were loaded into the sampans first, and they deposited their charges on the western banks of the river in a marshy area selected for the cover provided by tall reeds. The sampans were strafed by Japanese fighter aircraft as they made their way to shore, some of the bullets hitting Storekeeper First Class Charles Ensminger, who had already sustained fragment injuries on-board the *Panay*. The additional bullet wound put him on the edge of death.

The sampans returned to the *Panay* to pick up more men, with those on-board insisting that the weakened executive officer, "Tex" Anders, and the State Department's diplomat in charge, George Atcheson, evacuate. Anders could barely stand and Atcheson departed only after Captain Frank Roberts, the em-bassy's army attaché, informed him that he would use force if necessary to get Atcheson into the boat. By navy regulations, Ensign Dennis Biwerse, still re-covering from the concussion he sustained when the first Japanese bomb flung him across *Panay*'s deck, took command of the ship. Those onboard did what they could to gather medical supplies, food, and other equipment. Anders had reminded them to destroy all codebooks and communication gear prior to leav-ing, but the ship's safe had been blown over on its side and could not be opened. Making a third trip, the sampans returned to the *Panay* to pick up the salvage and demolition parties. Shortly after 3 P.M., Biwerse stepped off the *Panay* and into the ship's sampan. He was the last to leave the sinking vessel.[39]

The ordeal of the *Panay* survivors had only begun. Although no one had been killed during the attack itself, sixteen men had been seriously wounded. Coxswain Edgar Hulsebus had sustained spinal injuries, storekeeper Ensminger had both fragment and bullet wounds, and Sandro Sandri, an Italian journalist on assignment in China for Milan's *Corriere Della Sera*, had been pierced in the abdomen by bomb fragments. Ensminger and Sandri had less than twenty-four hours to live. Hulsebus died a week later from wounds sustained in the attack. Another thirty-five Americans sustained minor injuries, though some of these, such as sprains and severe bruises to joints, made walking painful or impossible.

Anders had selected a riverbank area where the group could hide because he was sure the attack had been deliberate. Shortly after the last men were evacuated, the Americans huddling among the reeds saw two Japanese powerboats filled with soldiers approach the sinking *Panay*. The Japanese boats raked the *Panay* with ma-chine-gun fire before sending a boarding party onto the American gunboat. In his report to the State Department, Atcheson would later explicitly note that "The *Panay*'s flags were flying in plain view at this, as at all times, until the vessel sank."[40] Later in the afternoon, Japanese aircraft buzzed over the marsh, and the sound of bombing was heard in the distance for some time thereafter. The *Panay*'s survivors suspected that the Japanese were attacking the British flotilla anchored down-stream, and they feared that the Japanese were trying to wipe out all eyewitnesses to their attack on the *Panay*. Hiding in the marsh, the group had no way of know-ing whether the United States was now at war with Japan. This seemed doubt-ful, but while it seemed conceivable that the Japanese pilots in the high-altitude bombers had mistakenly attacked the *Panay*, everyone concurred that the strafing attacks could only have been deliberate. There was no way, the survivors believed, that pilots flying as low as 500 feet could have overlooked the large American flags stretched horizontally across the upper-deck awnings. The Japanese soldiers who boarded the abandoned ship after machine-gunning it likewise could not have failed to see the American flag waving at the mast. The *Panay* survivors feared the worst and believed they were being hunted down for elimination.

At 3:54 P.M., shortly after the Japanese boarding party departed, the USS *Panay* rolled over on its starboard side and sank. The Stars and Stripes still hung at the mast as the ship disappeared into the muddy waters of the Yangtze, and the gunboat settled into the river's bottom at a depth estimated somewhere between seven and ten fathoms.

All four of the *Panay*'s naval line officers had been wounded in the attack; Commander Hughes was in a near state of shock and Lieutenant Anders passed out from loss of blood. Hughes decided to designate Captain Frank Roberts, U.S. Army, who had worked at the embassy, as the officer in charge of the assembled survivors. Roberts would earn a Navy Cross for his leadership over the next several days. He faced three challenges: evading detection by the Japanese, establishing communication with the U.S. Embassy, and securing food, shelter, and care for the group.

Roberts sent out several of the ship's Chinese supernumeraries ("boatmen" and "mess boys") to scout the area, calculating that they knew the language and could pass for locals if stopped by Japanese patrols. Yuan Te Erh, a mess attendant, returned with the information that a small walled town named Hohsien lay approximately eight miles upriver. Roberts dispatched a larger scouting party to the town to see whether they could hire some stretcher bearers. Among the scouting party was the embassy staff's second in command, Robert Paxton. Paxton managed to find a Chinese official with a telephone, who contacted his superior with the request that he inform the U.S. Embassy in Hankow that the *Panay* had been attacked and that its survivors were gathering in Hohsien. Paxton pressed on by rickshaw and car to establish direct contact with the embassy. Meanwhile, the rest of the scouting party managed to secure stretchers and bearers, and returned to the main body of survivors.

Struggling through the night in the cold and muck, the survivors and stretcher bearers made their way to Hohsien. As he approached the town, Secretary Acheson recalled that he was met by a Chinese employee of the Standard Vacuum Oil Company. The man proved very helpful, introducing the diplomat to the local magistrate. Much to Acheson's surprise, the magistrate spoke fluent English, and he informed Atcheson that he had studied at Syracuse University in upstate New York. Both men did their utmost to help the Americans, putting the town hospital at the disposal of the *Panay*'s doctor and securing quarters for those who simply needed rest. The ship's doctor did what he could, administering morphine to those in severe pain, and cleaning, dressing, and bandaging wounds. Ensminger and Sandri were beyond help. Both died in Hohsien's hospital on December 13.

The group was utterly exhausted, but their ordeal was not over. Japanese aircraft had flown over the town at low level several times, and when Roberts received word from the magistrate that Japanese troops had landed only a few miles downstream from Hohsien, he made the decision to move the group farther inland. The group pooled their money and made arrangements to be towed up a canal twenty miles to the small village of Hanshan. The journey took more than ten hours, as towing was done by crews of Chinese laborers hauling the barges up the canal one step at a time in the darkness of night. Arriving at Hanshan as dawn was breaking, the Americans received word from Rear Admiral Holt of the Royal Navy that they should return to Hohsien. The Japanese were claiming the entire episode had been an accident. HMS *Bee* and HMS *Ladybird* were standing by in Hohsien to transport the group down to Shanghai, where Admiral Harry Yarnell eagerly awaited them.

The USS *Panay* had been in the midst of transmitting a routine message to the USS *Luzon* in Hankow when the first Japanese bomb struck the ship at 1:42 P.M. on Sunday, December 12.[41] The radio officer on the *Luzon* was not unduly concerned when the signal stopped in mid-transmission, as generator problems and battery malfunctions were fairly common. Yet as the afternoon progressed and they heard nothing from the *Panay*, the American ambassador and the commander of the Yangtze Patrol became increasingly concerned. That night, the U.S. ambassador to China, Nelson T. Johnson, learned from his British colleague that the Japanese had deliberately bombed the British gunboats *Scarab* and *Cricket* and the passenger ship *Whangpoo*. He telegraphed the information to the secretary of state and informed Admiral Yarnell and the U.S. consuls in Beijing and Shanghai as well. Johnson added a warning at the end of the telegram: "unless the Japanese can be made to realize that these ships are friendly . . . a terrible disaster is likely to happen."[42] The warning came too late—by then, the *Panay* had been sunk and its survivors were struggling toward Hohsien. At 9:30 A.M. (China time) on Monday, Johnson received an urgent phone call from an American missionary physician resident in Anking. The physician told Johnson that he was relaying a message from George Atcheson Jr., senior American diplomat on board the *Panay*. The *Panay* had been bombed and sunk. Fifty-four persons onboard had survived, of whom fifteen were wounded. After hanging up the phone, Johnson relayed the news to the commander of the U.S. Yangtze Patrol, Rear Admiral John Marquart. Marquart immediately telegraphed the U.S. Chief of Naval Operations, Admiral Leahy. The ambassador likewise notified the secretary of state.[43] Before Washington had a chance to react, the U.S. ambassador in Japan received a telephone call indicating that Japan's foreign minister was on his way to the embassy. This was unprecedented. Grew realized that "something terrible had happened" and immediately thought of the *Panay*.[44]

CONTEXT

ISOLATIONISM, FOREIGN POLICY, AND THE SINO-JAPANESE WAR

At the time the *Panay* was sunk, there was a deep vein of isolationist sentiment in the United States. With the benefit of hindsight, policymakers, strategists, and historians have concluded that isolationism was shortsighted and counterproductive, tying the hands of the Roosevelt administration at precisely that point in time when the weight of American influence might have deterred Japan in the Far East and stiffened the resolution of Britain and France in Europe.[45] The populism of Charles Lindbergh and the America First Committee during the critical period 1940–41 reinforces this image of isolationists as insular, naïve, and ill-informed, for by then Hitler and the Third Reich posed a deadly menace not just to Britain, its empire, and the Commonwealth but also to the broader principles of liberalism, international law, and Judeo-Christian values.

Yet it is misguided to breezily dismiss isolationists as country bumpkins whose provincialism had run amok. Rather, isolationism grew out of a reassessment and backlash against the Wilson administration's prewar policies from 1914 to 1916. By the early 1930s, a growing cadre of respected academics, influential journalists, and progressive intellectuals were coming to the conclusion that America's entry into the First World War had been a mistake. These opinion-makers stoked popular support for initiatives intended to ensure that the mistakes of the past would not be repeated again. They failed to recognize that Hitler had very different ambitions from Wilhelm II, and that Japan and Italy dreamed of overturning rather than simply readjusting the power structures of the Far East and Mediterranean. Knowing what we now know, it is hard to empathize with the American isolationists of the 1930s. Yet people tend to draw upon the lessons of *their own* past when dealing with the crises of the present, and by the mid-1930s there was growing uneasiness with the choices the Wilson administration had made prior to intervention in the First World War.

Twenty years after the *Lusitania* disaster and eighteen years after Congress declared war on Germany, some 50,000 American veterans staged a march through downtown Washington on April 6, 1935, to show their support for peace. The following week, roughly 175,000 American college students staged sit-down strikes in Boston, New York, Washington, and Los Angeles, demanding that the government spend money on schools rather than on battleships.[46] Progressives and conservatives joined together in opposing American interventionism abroad. Cordell Hull, reflecting on those events after World War II, remarked that America's isolationist sentiment tangled relations with the very countries the United States should have been supporting in the tumultuous years preceding the Second World War. He was sure that Hitler, Mussolini, and Japanese militarists took comfort knowing that they could proceed unconcerned with their designs because public opinion in the United States ran strongly against American intervention of any sort.[47]

Numerous accounts trace the origins of isolationism to the bitter debates of 1919–20 and the Senate's refusal to join the League of Nations. Yet the Senate's rejection of the Treaty of Versailles and its provision of a League of Nations had more to do with contrasting visions of America's role in the world than with a repudiation of all American interests overseas. Henry Cabot Lodge, who as chairman of the Senate Foreign Relations committee had played a key role in undermining Wilson's postwar vision, can hardly be characterized as an isolationist. He had been at the forefront in arguing for American intervention in Cuba in 1898–99 and had chafed at Wilson's perceived weakness and hesitancy when Europe went to war in 1914. Rather, the confrontation over the League entailed different visions of what an active American foreign policy entailed, with Wilson advocating an idealist international-institutional approach while Lodge insisted on a realist national-constitutional approach. A careful look at the foreign policies of the Harding, Coolidge, and Hoover administrations indicates that isolationism gained strength at the close of the 1920s, accelerating after Wall Street's crash and the onset of the Great Depression.

Isolationist sentiment grew stronger as a result of retrospection and soul-searching that pertained to the "web of circumstances" that led the United States down the paths of war in 1898 and 1917. It represented a rebirth of the anti-imperialist critique of the Spanish-American War and a postmortem revival of William Jennings Bryan's conception of impartial neutrality. Peace organizations such as National Council for the Prevention of War, the Women's

International League for Peace and Freedom, and S.O.S. (Stop Organized Slaughter) spurred efforts to isolate the United States from conflict abroad once hopes for global peace agreements faded.[48] Their first target was the munitions industry and the trade in arms, with echoes of the arms-embargo debate of the First World War gaining a new lease on life.

Twenty years after the start of the First World War, a bevy of books appeared that claimed to reveal the nefarious role that arms manufacturers had played in creating and profiting from the armaments race that culminated in World War I. In 1930, an American publisher translated German peace activist Otto Lehmann-Russbüldt's *Die Blutige Internationale der Rüstungsindustrie*, titling it *War for Profit*.[49] The piece created a stir, with freelance reporter George Seldes's longer study *Iron, Blood, and Profits: An Exposure of the World-Wide Munitions Racket* vying for readership alongside Helmuth Engelbrecht and Frank Hanighen's *Merchants of Death: A Study of the International Armament Industry* in 1934.[50] The Book-of-the-Month Club selected *Merchants of Death* as its book for April 1934, and *Harper's*, the *New Republic*, and even the generally pro-business *Fortune* magazine all published exposés of the armaments industry that year. The perspective of these pieces can be gleaned from a selection that appeared in *Fortune* in March 1934. It claimed that "Big Business men" had made a fortune in the First World War and continued to do so, selling weapons and ammunition to all buyers. The commentary, written by staff writers, explained that "Killing is their business. Armaments are their stock in trade; governments are their customers. . . . [E]very time a burst shell fragment finds its way into the brain, the heart, or the intestines of a man in the front line, a great part of the $25,000 [cost to kill a soldier], much of it profit, finds its way into the pocket of the armament maker."[51]

Many of these analyses rested on hearsay, dubious statistics, and anti-capitalist convictions, but the suspicion that the munitions industry was fueling war was not limited to peace activists susceptible to sensational critiques of the arms industry. In January 1933, Secretary of State Henry L. Stimson wrote President Hoover that "it is becoming more and more evident that the international traffic in arms must be supervised and controlled by national and international action." His predecessor, Frank B. Kellogg, expressed a similar sentiment, writing in 1934 that "In my opinion there is no question whatever that the world munition manufacturers are adding their influence and in every way trying to prevent disarmament."[52] When the War Policies Commission created by Congress in 1930 failed to stir any action, a frustrated Dorothy Detzer, executive secretary of the Women's International League, turned to Senators George W. Norris of Nebraska and Robert La Follette Jr. of Wisconsin for redress. Norris, along with La Follette's father, had been one of the six senators who had voted against

America's entry into World War I; and although they had been roundly exco-
riated for their stance against intervention in 1917, by the early 1930s public
sentiment had swung in the other direction. Detzer pleaded with Norris and
La Follette to take on the arms industry. Norris, too sick and feeble to lead the
charge himself, steered Detzer toward a younger progressive Republican, Gerald
P. Nye of North Dakota. On February 8, 1934, Nye introduced a resolution that
the Senate appoint a committee to investigate individuals and corporations engaged in the manufacture, sale, distribution, import, and export of munitions.
Only intense lobbying by the Women's International League and other peace
organizations saved Nye's resolution from being buried in committee indefinitely. On April 12, 1934, the Senate passed Senate Resolution 206 directing the
vice president to appoint a seven-member committee to examine the munitions
industry.

In a bid to show bipartisanship, the four Democrats appointed to the "special
committee to investigate the munitions industry" nominated Nye, one of the
three Republicans on the committee, to serve as chair. This, according to the
secretary of state, "was a fatal mistake because the committee, under his chairmanship, proceeded to enlarge the scope of its inquiry into an attempt to prove
that the United Sates had been drawn into the First World War by American
bankers and munition makers." Hull elaborated, "Had I dreamed that an isolationist Republican would be appointed I promptly would have opposed it, but
I expected that a member of the majority party would be named under the usual
practice and that he would keep the investigation within legitimate and reasonable bounds."[53]

Yet Democrats outnumbered Republicans on the committee, and Senator
Bennett Champ Clark (D-Missouri), who would most probably have chaired
the committee if the "usual practice" had been observed, heatedly rejected
the charge that the committee had veered beyond its mandate. Rebutting the
angry snarl of Senator Thomas Connally (D-Texas) that the committee was
besmirching the memory of President Wilson and his secretaries of state by
asking probing questions about American neutrality in the First World War,
Clark insisted that it was right and proper "for us to soberly and dispassion-
ately examine the facts in connection with the web of circumstances which
brought us into the World War." Only by studying "the events of those tragic
years [1915–1917] to draw such lessons as may be possible" could one devise
remedies to prevent the creation of another "web of circumstances" that
might draw the United States into a future war. The Great War, after all,
had been the "greatest calamity" to ever befall the United States, according
to Clark.[54]

Senators Gerald P. Nye (seated, far left) and Homer T. Bone (seated, far right) of the Senate Munitions Committee discussing the day's events with members of the press, September 3, 1935.

Library of Congress, Prints and Photographs Division LC-DIG-hec-39410

The Nye Munitions Committee convened its first hearing on September 4, 1934. Over the course of ninety-three hearings, it examined the manufacture and sale of munitions, the activities of major U.S. shipbuilders, plans for reducing corporate and individual profits in the event of a new war, and the economic circumstances of America's entry into the First World War.[55] The committee hearings made front-page news, the chamber was always packed, and the American public initially relished the spectacle of shipbuilders and financiers squirming under questioning. The hearings "made some useful disclosures concerning the traffic in arms," Cordell Hull conceded, but "its effect was to throw the country into deepest isolationism at the very moment when our influence was so vitally needed to help ward off the approaching threats of war abroad."[56]

One of the key contentions in Engelbrecht and Hanighen's *Merchants of Death* was that the armament industry profited from war, with arms merchants inciting arms races and military conflict. Though little evidence was presented to confirm the latter contention, many witnesses spoke in favor of some sort of law that would equalize the burden of war. It somehow seemed unfair to many that industrialists were making millions while the common soldier risked his life for a pittance. If the average citizen was to be asked to make sacrifices, then surely one might ask munition makers to do the same. John T. Flynn, an influential financial writer and editor, remarked to the committee that a law against wartime profiteering might be unpopular, but "I rather think that the man who is disposed to be very sensitive, if some Japanese lieutenant fails to take his hat off in the presence of the American flag some place in Manchukuo, will not be so sensitive" if such a law were in effect.[57]

Senators sympathetic to banking and shipping interests had stifled their concerns when the Nye Committee called bankers and industrialists to the stand, but the Nye Commission's foray into historical revisionism provided an opening for a counterattack. On January 17, 1936, following several sessions that explored whether J. P. Morgan had pressured Wilson to overturn his ban on wartime loans in August 1915, Senator Carter Glass of Virginia exploded. Pounding his desk until the skin of his knuckles cracked, Glass exclaimed, "Oh, the miserable demagogy, the miserable and mendacious suggestion, that the house of Morgan altered the neutrality course of Wilson. . . . [W]hat I feel like saying here or anywhere else to the man who thus insults the memory of Woodrow Wilson is something which may not be spoken here, or printed in the newspapers, or uttered by a gentleman."[58] A good many Democrats still held Wilson in great esteem, and Glass's outburst served as a rallying cry for bringing the committee's investigations to a close. The Senate refused to appropriate additional funding for the committee beyond the paltry sum of an additional $7,369, which would allow it to wrap up investigations and submit a report. On February 20, 1936, Chairman Nye adjourned the munitions hearings.

The outrage that Nye's hearings provoked among those who admired Wilson, coupled with Hull's extremely negative portrayal of his chairmanship, might lead one to conclude that Nye had badgered witnesses, skewed evidence, and overstepped his mandate. Yet this was not so. While Nye could be inflammatory when interviewed by the press or when on the radio, his conduct of the hearings was generally fair and measured.[59]

The achievements of the Nye Munitions Committee were meager. Congress did not move to nationalize the arms industry, nor did it pass any legislation to effectively limit wartime profits. By the time the Nye Committee turned to examining the economic circumstances of America's entry into World War I, the Senate Foreign Relations Committee had begun considering legislation related to American neutrality in times of war. The Nye Committee had mobilized support for new legislation that would ensure American neutrality in future wars, but deferred the task of drafting the appropriate bills to the Senate Foreign Relations Committee.[60]

The Nye Committee fanned the home fires of isolationism, but the sentiments expressed by Gerald Nye, Bennett Champ Clark, and the other isolationists on the committee reflected widely held views. Even before the committee turned to the controversial subject of war loans, munition sales, and American neutrality in the First World War, a number of mainstream journalists and scholars had begun to question Wilson's strict neutrality. Walter Millis, a staff writer for the *New York Herald Tribune*, published a 460-page bestseller titled *Road to War: America 1914-1917* in the spring of 1935. The book received rave reviews, establishing Millis as a respected military historian and commentator. Millis had little truck for the conspiracy theories of Engelbrecht and Hanighen (*Merchants of Death*), and he dismissed the charge that the House of Morgan had somehow played the Wilson administration as a puppeteer does a puppet. Instead, he advanced a more subtle argument: the Wilson administration had gradually shifted from strict neutrality to policies that favored the Allies in fact, if not by intention.[61] War loans, the sale of munitions, and the American response to British and German maritime warfare had transformed the United States into "silent partner of the Entente" by 1917. The crucial turning point in this drift away from strict neutrality was Wilson's acceptance of William Jennings Bryan's resignation and the elevation of Robert Lansing to secretary of state. Commenting on the matter, Millis wrote:

> What the President did not see was that Mr. Bryan was essentially right. . . . He [Bryan] never had a detailed understanding of the intricate issues by which he was surrounded; his mind was too slow and too unfamiliar with the office to make effective the attitude to which his instincts compelled him. But that instinct was so much surer than that of the bemused intellectuals, lawyers and politicians who decried him. . . . It led him to a failure, but a failure which enshrines him in one of the more honorable niches of our history.[62]

Millis's study was historical, but its implications for ongoing debates about neutrality legislation were readily apparent. Charles A. Beard, a progressive historian who had taught at Columbia University, helped found The New School for Social Research in Greenwich Village, and served as president of both the American Polical Science Association (1926) and the American Historical Association (1933), moved beyond implications and commented directly on the neutrality legislation then under consideration. In early 1935, he wrote in the

New Republic that "We tried once to right European wrongs, to make the world safe for democracy. Even in the rosiest view the experiment was not a great success. Mandatory neutrality may be no better, for aught anyone actually knows. But we nearly burnt our house down with one experiment; so it seems not wholly irrational to try another."[63]

By 1935, the international environment appeared increasingly menacing, and hopes for international schemes for general disarmament were fading. During the 1920s, peace activists had hoped that international agreements, arms-limitation conferences, and collective renunciations of war might make the world a better place, but these dreams foundered as Japanese militarism, Italian fascism, and German Nazism challenged the postwar order. In 1933, Japan withdrew from the League of Nations after it was condemned for its invasion and occupation of Manchuria. In October 1934, Germany announced that it would no longer participate in the General Disarmament Conference and gave notice that it, too, was withdrawing from the League of Nations. Two months later, Japan notified fellow signatories of the Washington Naval Treaty that it would no longer be bound by the naval limitations agreed upon in 1922. During the spring of 1935, Mussolini's Italy began to massively increase its military presence in Eritrea and Italian Somaliland, following a border clash between Italian-led forces and Ethiopians in the Ogaden. War seemed to be in the air, and the ineffectual response of the League of Nations and the Western democracies to the "Abyssinian Crisis" was underlined when Hitler announced the formation of a German Air Force and the introduction of conscription in February and March 1935.

The reaction of many American progressives and peace advocates was to distance and disassociate the United States from the unfolding crises abroad. In May, the monthly publication of the National Council for the Prevention of War spoke out in favor of some sort of neutrality legislation that would prevent the United States from becoming embroiled in distant conflicts. An alliance of twenty-eight peace organizations staged a massive anti-war rally for peace that month at New York's Carnegie Hall, featuring Nye, Clark, and other members of the Nye Commission as guest speakers. Other groups such as the Federal Council of Churches and the Women's International League for Peace and Freedom joined the chorus, with newsletters, radio broadcasts, and letter-writing campaigns whipping up support for congressional action.[64]

Congressmen and senators from Ohio, Texas, and Missouri responded by introducing various bills in the spring of 1935 that would prohibit Americans from providing loans, credits, munitions, and arms, and advising Americans who insisted on traveling in declared war zones or aboard belligerent vessels that they did so at their own peril. The administration was lukewarm about these various proposals, as they threatened presidential freedom of action. Over the course of the summer, the administration made the case that neutrality legislation should be discretionary, enabling the president to punish aggressors with sanctions and embargoes while still allowing the victims of aggression to draw upon American industry to strengthen their defenses.

Yet public sentiment ran strongly in the direction of neutrality laws applied impartially to all belligerents, reinforced by the perception that Wilson's very different response to German and British violations of U.S. neutrality had contributed to a slide toward intervention in the First World War. The "intellectuals, lawyers and politicians"—to use Millis's language—who shaped foreign policy and advised American presidents too often mistook their own views for those of the American people, and the whole point of neutrality legislation was to make sure that in the future all belligerents would be treated similarly in order to keep the United States out of foreign wars that did not involve its vital interests. President Roosevelt attempted to deflect neutrality legislation, first pushing allies in the House Foreign Affairs Committee to sit on resolutions, then arguing that other matters had legislative priority, and finally attempting to seek some sort of compromise that would provide FDR with a degree of flexibility. The exasperated chairman of the Senate Foreign Relations Committee eventually warned the White House that if the president "insists on designating the aggressor in accordance with the wishes of the League of Nations . . . he will be licked as sure as hell."[65] The president's last hope—that Congress would adjourn before passing the bill—was dashed when a group of senators threatened to filibuster any Senate adjournment move until it had put neutrality resolutions to a vote. Senator Arthur Vandenberg, a conservative Republican from Michigan, argued in favor of a strict neutrality law because the United States had been "sucked into" World War I owing to the absence of neutrality legislation. Senator Homer Bone, a progressive Democrat from Washington State, grew more excited, lecturing his colleagues that:

> Everyone has come to recognize that the Great War was utter social insanity, and was a crazy war, and we had no business in it at all. Oh yes, we heard a great deal of talk about freedom of the seas. Whose seas? The seas upon which were being shipped munitions of war which served only to enrich a comparatively small group of men, and whose enrichment cost this country a staggering price. The enrichment of this group brought down upon our heads the terrible economic problems with which we wrestle here today and we find it well-nigh impossible to solve some of them.

Freedom of the seas! Out with such nonsense. For the sake of this fantastic theory that could at best serve the few and not the many, thousands have died, and our hospitals are filled with insane boys who had a right, under God's providence, to live their lives in peace. What a distortion![66]

On August 21, 1935, the Senate passed Senate Joint Resolution 173, prohibiting the export of munitions to belligerents and declaring that Americans who chose to enter war zones or travel on belligerent ships did so at their own risk. Two days later, the House passed an amended form of the bill that made no substantive changes but directed that the bill would expire after six months. The Senate passed the amended resolution with a 77–2 vote, giving the president no choice but to sign the bill into law.

The provisions of the Neutrality Act of 1935 were renewed in 1936 and made permanent in January 1937; the 1936 and 1937 Neutrality Acts strengthened and expanded the 1935 Act, rather than weakening it. Among the numerous provisions of the Neutrality Act of 1937, four clearly show the lingering ambivalence about Wilson's decision making in the First World War. Henceforth, once the president proclaimed that a state of war existed between or among two or more foreign states, it would be unlawful for any American vessel to carry any arms, ammunition, or implements of war to any belligerent state; Americans would be prohibited from traveling on belligerent-owned vessels; the export of arms, ammunition, or implements of war to any belligerent state would be prohibited; and Americans were forbidden from purchasing, selling, or exchanging bonds, securities, or other obligations of belligerent governments.

With the outbreak of the Spanish Civil War, the 1937 Neutrality Act expanded these earlier provisions to cover civil wars as well, providing the president only slim space for maneuvering. The administration negotiated one small window of wiggle room: the president could authorize belligerent nations to acquire nonmilitary materials from the United States so long as they paid for these purchases in cash and shipped their purchases on non-American vessels (a procedure known as "Cash and Carry").[67]

By late 1937, peace activism, historical revisionism, and the Nye Committee hearings had generated an intense public conviction that the United States should not embroil itself in foreign quarrels that did not directly threaten U.S. security. The Neutrality Laws of 1935, 1936, and 1937 translated this general attitude into legal guidelines that made it difficult, if not illegal, for the president to support one side over the other in Ethiopia, Spain, and China. While few Americans had much sympathy for Mussolini's Italy, Franco's Nationalists, or Japanese militarists, the lesson that the great majority of Americans drew from the First World War was to steer clear of conflicts that did not directly involve the United States.

Franklin Delano Roosevelt and his advisers were keenly aware of the strengths of isolationism as they attempted to forge a coherent strategy for dealing with Japanese aggression in East Asia during the 1930s. Though the U.S. Senate had declined to join the League of Nations after World War I, the United States had played a key role in forging international agreements designed to stabilize the situation in East Asia in the 1920s. The Nine Power Treaty, signed in Washington, D.C., in February 1922, pledged its signers to respect the sovereignty, independence, and administrative integrity of China. In addition, the signatory powers (the United States, Japan, China, France, Great Britain, Italy, Belgium, Netherlands, and Portugal) promised that they would refrain from claiming any special rights, privileges, and monopolies that would deprive the nationals of other powers from undertaking legitimate trade or industry in China.

The Kellogg-Briand Pact (1928) obliged signatory states, including the nine powers most intimately interested in the Far East, to resolve differences peacefully, renouncing the recourse to war as an instrument of national policy. Following Japan's invasion and occupation of Manchuria in 1931, the Hoover administration issued a note, the so-called Stimson doctrine, to Japan and China instructing both parties that the United States had no intention of recognizing any situation, treaty, or agreement brought about by the force of arms. Yet as Stanley Hornbeck, the chief of the State Department's Division of Far Eastern Affairs, conceded in an internal memorandum analyzing the Manchurian crisis for the incoming Roosevelt administration in the spring of 1933, "The United States has not much to lose. The principles of our Far Eastern policy and our ideals with regard to world peace may be further scratched and dented . . . and our trade prospects may be somewhat further impaired; but from the point of view of material interests there is nothing there [in North China] that is vital to us."[68]

The United States refused to acknowledge Japan's conquest of Manchuria, but did little beyond cautioning Japan and the Republic of China to resolve their differences as the Kuomintang (KMT), Mao's communist forces, and various Chinese volunteer and regional forces battled one another and the Japanese throughout the decade. Chinese and Japanese units clashed at Shanghai in February 1932 and along the Great Wall in Jehol province in 1933, and communist guerillas harassed Japanese occupation forces in Manchuria after the defeat of various Chinese volunteer militia armies in the early 1930s. The outbreak of major fighting between KMT and Japanese forces in July 1937 threatened American interests more directly, as fighting spread from Beijing and northern China to Shanghai and the Yangtze River Valley. More than one thousand marines were stationed in Shanghai as part of the international contingent guarding Shanghai's International Settlement, with the gunboats of the Yangtze

River Patrol scattered up and down South China's main corridor of commerce. Thousands of American businessmen, missionaries, and dependents worked, lived, and owned property in Shanghai, along the Chinese coast, and on the banks and tributaries of the Yangtze River.

Cordell Hull, FDR's secretary of state, claimed that in the spring and early summer of 1937, the United States had contemplated relinquishing its extraterritorial rights in China, and had contacted the British to begin exchanging views on the topic of restoring full sovereignty to China.[69] The outbreak of fighting put the matter of the American military presence in China on the front burner, where it would remain until the *Panay* was sunk in December. Harold Ickes, FDR's secretary of the interior, recorded in his diary how both the president and the vice president were ambivalent, to say the least, about the presence of American troops in China. According to Ickes, Vice President John Nance Garner had asked the secretary of state why he had not removed American troops prior to the latest outbreak of fighting. On being told that this might have been seen as a sign of weakness, Garner had snapped, "Are we going to keep our troops in China for twenty or fifty or a hundred years?"

For Garner, the issue was clear. The United States "oughtn't to have soldiers and marines in foreign countries." The Texan continued, "we wouldn't take it in good part if Japan insisted on having marines in San Francisco." FDR was circumspect, asking Admiral Leahy how many marines were in Shanghai, and then sighing that "he wished they were not there." When Leahy pointed out that the marines were protecting four thousand Americans in the city, the president countered that "there were about twenty-five thousand Americans in Paris and not a single Marine." Ickes recorded that the president reluctantly agreed with Hull and Leahy that the marine contingent could not be removed given the present situation. He confided to his diary that "It is the old case of not doing something when it can be done and then when a crisis arises, deciding that it can't be done then."[70] Roosevelt predicted that some Americans were going to get hurt, and instructed Leahy to work out plans to evacuate those Americans who wished to leave.

If the president, vice president, and secretary of the interior were frustrated that outdated treaty rights dating back to the Boxer Rebellion had put American forces in a vulnerable position from which it was difficult to withdraw without appearing weak, isolationist congressmen and senators were appalled. Immediately after the outbreak of fighting in China in July, Representative Hamilton Fish of New York announced to the press that he would introduce legislation forcing the administration to relinquish extraterritorial rights in China. Fish challenged his fellow House members to come up with a single good reason for maintaining American troops and gunboats in China.[71] As the situation in China deteriorated, congressmen and senators took to the floor demanding a withdrawal of American forces in China.[72]

Isolationist sentiment in Congress began to crystallize around the contention that the president had the duty to invoke the Neutrality Act, even if China and Japan had not formally declared war against one another. The situation did not replicate that of 1914–16: although Chinese and Japanese troops were engaged in combat, the two governments had not broken diplomatic relations at this point and technically were not at war. The Chinese, according to Secretary of State Hull, believed that the Japanese government had lost control of its military, and feared that breaking diplomatic contacts would only strengthen the hand of Japanese militarists. The Japanese, for their part, claimed that the invasion was a punitive expedition and indicated that they were perfectly willing to enter peace negotiations as soon as the Chinese recognized the Japanese-dominated puppet state of Manchukuo, ceased all anti-Japanese activities and propaganda, and suppressed communism.[73] Japan and China, in short, had hundreds of thousands of troops fighting each other, but neither had declared war. For isolationists in Congress, this was beside the point. On August 19, twenty-four members of the House issued a joint pronouncement declaring that the president had the duty

Secretary of State Cordell Hull arrives at the White House to discuss the Far Eastern situation in August 1937.

Library of Congress, Prints and Photographs Division
LC-DIG-hec-23201

to invoke the Neutrality Act. Two days later, Congress went into recess, leaving the matter at the president's discretion.

With Congress blustering but unwilling to force the president's hand in 1937, FDR had some time to ponder whether to invoke the Neutrality Act. He clearly had the authority to do so, but his first inclination was to gather advice and deliberate about whether it would be wise to do so. In the meantime, State Department cables and press reports painted an ever-worsening situation in China. On August 15, Admiral Yarnell requested an additional 1,000 marines to reinforce the American contingent in Shanghai. Stanley Hornbeck, chief of the State Department's Division of Far Eastern Affairs, strongly endorsed the request. Hornbeck noted that while he was "not oblivious of the fact that political considerations within the United States need to be taken into account," there were more than 40,000 foreign nationals, including women and children, in Shanghai along with tremendous capital investments. Hornbeck advised his boss that "A complete abandonment of the port, leaving the city to be fought over and fought for by China and Japan, would be calamitous to the whole world both from the economic and from the political points of view."[74]

Hull and Leahy advised the president to authorize the reinforcements, which FDR did, but he took pains to explain to the press that his long-term objective was to "get our marines completely out of China as fast as it is a practical thing to do."[75] FDR emphasized that the marines were there for the sole purpose of protecting Americans, and that the administration was organizing evacuation transports for those Americans wishing to leave China. Hull made the same point, explaining that the administration was trying to steer a middle course between those who advocated some sort of international intervention and isolationists who wanted to tell Americans overseas that their government would do nothing to protect them.[76]

Senator Key Pittman, chairman of the Committee on Foreign Relations, defended the administration's reluctance to simply order Americans out of China. Speaking on the subject of neutrality and the Far Eastern crisis at a forum organized by the *Washington Evening Star*, Pittman explained,

China is an enormous country. It is larger than the United States. We have missionaries and teachers, explorers and business men, in the most remote territory. Transportation is difficult and slow. In many places they have no protection through the military or police forces of either China or Japan. The outcry coming even as it does from some intelligent sources that we should immediately withdraw our army and navy and have our citizens in China without protection is cowardly and unpatriotic and reflects upon the dignity and glory of our country. No such request comes either from China or Japan.[77]

Public opinion was divided on the matter. On August 5, Gallup conducted a poll asking whether the United States should withdraw all troops from China in order to keep from getting involved in the fighting, or keep them there to protect American rights. Fifty-four percent of those polled answered "withdraw"; forty-six percent responded "remain." Yet when the president remarked to some journalists that same day that Americans in China had been urged to leave and those who decided to remain did so "at their own risk," hundreds of messages poured into the White House from missionary leaders and businessmen stunned at the statement.[78] English-language newspapers in China, such as the *Shanghai Evening Post and Mercury,* the *China Weekly Review,* and the *North China Daily News,* reflecting the sensibilities of the American expatriate community in China, ascribed the president's remark to an overestimation of isolationist opinion in the country.

With Congress out of session, the administration might have avoided deciding whether to invoke the Neutrality Act for weeks, but two developments re-energized the debate. On August 25, Japan declared that it was closing some 800 miles of the Chinese coast to Chinese maritime traffic, extending the measure to embrace much of the remaining coast on September 5. The Japanese limited the blockade to Chinese ships, reassuring third parties that they had no intention of interfering with their peaceful commerce. Less than a week after the initial Japanese declaration, the story broke that the SS *Wichita* was leaving Baltimore en route to China with a cargo of nineteen Bellanca cargo aircraft rumored to have been purchased by the Chinese Air Force with the intent of converting them to bombers. Crew members of the *Wichita* were threatening to stage a sit-down strike if they did not receive a "war zone" bonus for the final leg of their voyage.[79] After having been reassured by the administration that the situation in China was entirely different from that of 1914–16, many felt duped. The Emergency Peace Campaign—an umbrella group of six peace organizations— seized upon the issue in order to force the administration's hand. The group's strategy board bombarded newspapers with letters urging the administration to invoke the Neutrality Act. To make the connections between past and present clear, the group published a pamphlet titled "Deadly Parallels—A Warning to United States Citizens on Keeping This Country out of War with Asia," emphasizing how trade, loans, and credits to belligerents had pulled the United States into the First World War.[80] The Neutrality Act of 1937 prohibited these sorts of activities, and would insulate America from the widening conflict in East Asia.

Aware of the public's extreme sensitivity to the issue of neutral rights, the shipment of contraband, and maritime blockades, FDR addressed the matter before it spiraled out of control. Secretary of State Hull instructed Joseph Green of the Office of Arms and Munitions Control to discreetly telephone the shipping company operating the SS *Wichita*. Green warned the company that if the *Wichita* proceeded to carry the planes to China, it might encounter grave difficulties and place the government in an embarrassing situation. He told the shipper that the president was about to issue a statement, and he suggested that the "owners might wish to remove the airplanes in San Pedro before proceeding with the voyage across the Pacific." The shipper replied that he would tell the owners to make any excuse they wished to delay the ship, suggesting that unforeseen engine troubles might necessitate repairs lasting several days.[81]

On September 14, following a conference with the secretary of state and the chairman of the U.S. Maritime Commission, Roosevelt declared that merchant vessels owned by the government of the United States would not be permitted to transport any arms, ammunition, or implements of war to either China or Japan. Any other merchant vessel flying the American flag that attempted to transport these articles did so at its own risk.[82] The presidential directive imposed fewer restrictions on the export of munitions than would have been the case if he had invoked the Neutrality Act, but it showed that the president understood that many Americans were concerned that the country might once again be dragged into a war over the issue of neutral rights, the sale of munitions, and blockades.

Three months after reassuring the public that U.S.-owned ships would not be involved in transporting munitions to belligerents, FDR quietly instructed the Treasury Department to purchase Chinese silver in exchange for dollar credits, directing Henry Morgenthau to justify the measure in terms of stabilizing the dollar. The real purpose, however, was to provide China with a foreign exchange loan so it could purchase war supplies. Commenting on a State Department recommendation that the Treasury make future purchases contingent on questions of neutrality, FDR snorted that the State Department memorandum was "the most stupid . . . I have ever read" and would play directly into the hands of isolationists.[83] The purchase went ahead in the form of a technical measure related to monetary stabilization.

The president had to reconcile the wishes and recommendations of his foreign and security policy advisers with the realities of the political situation at home. When Admiral Yarnell requested additional marines to reinforce the marine detachment in Shanghai in mid-August, the president had endorsed the request in the face of considerable pressure. But when Yarnell and Hornbeck, the former the on-scene military commander in Shanghai and the latter the State Department's East Asia expert, asked for two additional cruisers (watered down from an initial request of four cruisers), FDR turned down the request emphatically.[84] And when Yarnell issued a statement to the press explaining that American forces had the duty and obligation to protect American citizens in China even at the risk of being exposed to danger, the president curtly instructed Leahy that "hereafter any statement regarding 'policy' contemplated by the Commander-in-Chief Asiatic Fleet must be referred to the Secretary of the Navy for approval."[85]

FDR's muzzling of Yarnell highlights the limited and secondary role that the Navy and War Departments played in shaping foreign policy in the mid- to late 1930s. This was particularly apparent when one examines the disconnect between war planning and crisis management.[86] Admiral James Richardson, the assistant chief of naval operations in 1937 and later commander in chief, U.S. Fleet, recalled that "From 1919 thru the early and middle 1930's, the whole subject of war planning was a tabu one with the American people. . . . In order to keep the Navy as a whole from knowledgeable violation of this peculiar isolationist and pacifist tabu, the very existence of our Naval War Plans was a very closely held secret with the Naval Service during the period 1919–1937."[87]

Naval planners were wise to keep their deliberations internal, for the plans they developed would have encountered a storm of criticism, not just from an isolationist public but also from the State Department, Congress, and the cabinet. Throughout the 1920s and into the 1930s, the navy envisioned that in the event of war with Japan it would rapidly dispatch the fleet to the Far East where, after defeating the Japanese navy, it would impose a blockade that would strangle Japan and force it to seek terms. The concept reflected Mahan's proposition that the best method of using sea power to isolate an enemy's economy was by defeating the enemy's fleet and securing command of the seas through which trade flowed. Commerce warfare by means of submarines, trade sanctions, or blockading Japanese imports at their source was deemed no substitute for a full-blown blockade of the Japanese islands enforced by American naval and airpower operating from bases in the Marshall, Caroline, and ultimately the Ryukyu Islands. By the mid-1930s, plans to rapidly thrust the fleet through to the Philippines, Guam, or some other base in the western Pacific at the outset of war had been abandoned, with the U.S. naval plan for war with Japan (War Plan Orange) instead calling for an offensive that would secure the Marshall Islands within a little over a month and the Caroline Islands within three months. From these bases, the navy would then gradually force its way to the Ryukyus, from which it could impose a devastating blockade, with air bombardment of the Japanese islands ratcheting up the pressure.

General Stanley Dunbar Embick, director of the Army's War Plans Division, warned the president that the navy's opening gambit in the event of war with Japan was extremely aggressive and might lead to a "national disaster" if implemented. He cautioned that the United States should assume a defensive posture in the Pacific and focus on defending the Western Hemisphere.[88] Admiral

Franklin D. Roosevelt had been Assistant Secretary of the Navy during the First World War, and as president, he remained keenly interested in "his" navy. He particularly enjoyed the naval perquisites of his office, among them the presidential yacht *Potomac* and ship visitations.
Library of Congress, Prints and Photographs Division LC-DIG-hec-47146

Richardson, assistant chief of naval operations, would later concede that naval planners had lost sight of the political and military realities of the time. His post–World War II memoirs asserted that throughout the interwar period, naval planners predicated their plans on what "they would like to have had, rather than on the Navy they actually had, and on what the planners would like to have occur in the event of war, rather than on what more likely did occur."[89] More to the point, the naval planners concentrated largely on what to do in the event of major war with Japan. They provided little in the way of helpful insights on how one might apply naval and economic tools to put pressure on Japan short of major war.[90]

Roosevelt understood that the American people were in no mood to threaten Japan militarily over the escalating Sino-Japanese War. Yet he was frustrated and groping for alternatives. In July, he revealed to Under Secretary of State Sumner Welles that he was considering the idea of imposing a trade embargo on Japan, enforced by British and American ships stationed at "strategic points in the Pacific." Welles, a confidant of the president, asked whether this might not lead to war. The president responded that he did not think so, commenting that the

Japanese were heavily committed to the ongoing war in China and that Japan's economy was "stretched to the breaking point." Welles then asked FDR why he thought the British government would go along with "so radical a policy." FDR retorted that he hoped that Prime Minister Neville Chamberlain and Foreign Minister Anthony Eden would have more "guts" than their predecessors. Welles wrote that the president then chuckled and remarked that "British financial interests at least must realize that they would lose their vast commercial holdings in the Far East if Japan were permitted to make Asia a Japanese colony."[91]

Welles recalled that the president abandoned the concept shortly after mentioning it to him. Welles speculated that the secretary of state and "most of the ranking admirals in the Navy Department" advised the president against the concept, as it might lead to a war the public opposed and the navy was not prepared to fight. Roosevelt, always sensitive to public opinion, surely understood that any signs of joint Anglo-American diplomatic initiatives would provoke a storm of protest. Chamberlain wrote his sister in August, "I tried to get them [the Americans] to come in on China and Japan but they were too frightened of their own people."[92]

Secretary of the Interior Harold Ickes, a political animal and one of the key implementers of the New Deal, shared the prevailing view that what was happening in China was not America's affair. Writing in his private diary, Ickes commented,

> There isn't any doubt that we are in a bad spot so far as the Sino-Japanese situation is concerned. When the President some time ago warned all Americans to leave China or to stay there at their own risk, a great protest went up, especially from the American Chamber of Commerce in Shanghai. As usual, Americans who went abroad to engage in business because of the big profit that they thought they might make expect us to sacrifice thousands of lives if necessary and millions of treasure in an attempt to protect their investments when we can't do it anyhow. It all seems so stupid to me. . . . After all, there is no compulsion to invest money in foreign enterprises and it ought to be at the risk of the investor. Certainly we oughtn't to be expected to go to war, with all the dreadful consequences involved, to protect people who are doing something they want to do and are doing [so] voluntarily.[93]

Roosevelt presided over a back-and-forth struggle between isolationists and internationalists, between those who would do nothing and those who wanted some sort of response short of war. FDR attempted to steer a course that would enjoy public support, opposing recommendations he feared would result in a backlash but resisting calls to invoke the full panoply of restrictions embedded in the Neutrality Act. The counsel he received from members of the cabinet was divided, as were the inputs they received from their subordinates. Secretary of State Hull, for example, cabled the American ambassadors to Japan and China soliciting their opinions on whether the administration should invoke the Neutrality Act during the SS *Wichita* brouhaha. From Tokyo, Ambassador Joseph Grew advised that the administration should do so if the American government was seeking to reduce the likelihood of the United States becoming ensnared in the ongoing Sino-Japanese conflict. Grew believed that there was a grave risk that Japanese naval forces would infringe on American rights, and that the prospects for continued peaceful commerce with China were poor and diminishing.[94] From Nanking, Ambassador Johnson warned that the Chinese government would resent the restrictions associated with the Neutrality Act, concluding that China's leaders would interpret any application of the neutrality laws as an attempt to disable China as it defended itself.[95] Roosevelt and Hull determined that they would not apply the act in the Far East until circumstances forced them to do so, ignoring rumblings from out-of-session congressmen that Congress might initiate impeachment proceedings when it reconvened if the administration continued to delay implementing the law.[96]

The administration had to tread very carefully when dealing with the Sino-Japanese conflict in the summer and fall of 1937. Isolationist sentiment expressed itself not only in calls for the rapid withdrawal of U.S. military units in China and in demands that FDR implement the Neutrality Act but also in a deep-seated skepticism toward any joint, multinational, or international response to the crisis. At the very outset of the crisis in July, the British government had suggested that Britain, France, and the United States should jointly approach the Japanese and Chinese governments and request that the belligerents suspend troop movements and negotiate an end to the conflict. In November, Foreign Minister Eden again expressed the conviction that Britain and the United States needed to stand "shoulder to shoulder" to confront the deteriorating situation in China. Roosevelt was uninterested, aware that isolationists in the United States viewed China as a British problem.[97]

The British ambassador delivered an urgent message in late November to Under Secretary of State Sumner Welles, noting that the British government had concluded that the Japanese were determined to disregard the interests of all third parties in China. His government desired to know whether the United States would be disposed to join in assembling an "overwhelming display of naval force" that would strengthen their hand in dealing with the crisis in East Asia. Welles dryly noted that British authorities had repeatedly advised their American counterparts over the past months that the British government was not in the position to dispatch naval forces to the Far East, given tensions in Europe and the Mediterranean. The overwhelming display of naval force that the British were recommending was really an overwhelming display of American naval force, a distinction that Welles pointed out was very important. Britain's suggestion that the two governments immediately initiate staff conversations "to consider appropriate and adequate combined steps" as they related to the situation in the Far East was ignored.[98] The Americans turned down the British initiative, with suspicions running deep in the State Department that Eden was trying to dragoon American power to defend British imperial interests.

As with many generalizations, there was an element of truth to the American perception that Britain had more at stake in the Far East than did the United States, and that the British government wanted to shift the burden of deterring the Japanese from itself to the United States. Anchored in Shanghai and Hong Kong, the British presence in China was extensive. Economically, firms such as Butterfield & Swire and Jardine Matheson & Company owned railways, tea plantations, shipyards, petroleum facilities, breweries, and more, with hundreds of smaller British firms owning mines, factories, and other enterprises throughout the country. Institutionally and socially, the British were first among equals in the various concession ports and international settlements, providing the bulk of personnel for the international Shanghai Volunteer Corps, serving in senior positions in the Chinese Maritime Customs Service, and dominating the expatriate social scene. More directly, the British presence in China reflected and interacted with the broader British imperial system, supported by and linked to British holdings in Singapore, Malaya, Burma, India, and the dominions of Australia and New Zealand.

American perceptions that the British Empire was capable of containing the Japanese were illusory. By 1937, Britain clearly faced serious challenges in the Mediterranean and in continental Europe; it simply could not deal with the strategic dilemma of responding to Nazi Germany, fascist Italy, and militarist Japan at the same time. As late as November 1938, the first sea lord continued to assure the Australian high commissioner in London that Britain would dispatch seven capital ships to the Far East in the event of war with Japan.[99] Whether Britain would have contributed a significant naval detachment to a demonstration of force in the fall of 1937 is unknown, as FDR did not put the British to the test. He understood that given their revisionist take on U.S. intervention in World War I, isolationists and peace activists would not tolerate anything that smacked of pulling British chestnuts from the Sino-Japanese fire.

If Roosevelt consistently rejected British calls for bilateral and joint action in the Far East in 1937, he was willing to test whether the American public would support some broader international response. On October 5, in Chicago,

Roosevelt delivered what came to be known as the "Quarantine Speech." After remarking about the signs of economic recovery he had seen around the country, Roosevelt addressed the international situation. He commented gravely that the high aspirations expressed in the Briand-Kellogg Peace Pact had given way to haunting fears of calamity, describing how civilians, including vast numbers of women and children, were being ruthlessly murdered with bombs from the air. Warning his fellow Americans that they could not expect to live tranquilly if the peace-loving nations of the world simply tolerated barbarity, Roosevelt exclaimed:

> The peace, the freedom and the security of ninety percent of the population of the world is being jeopardized by the remaining ten percent who are threatening a breakdown of all international order and law. Surely the ninety percent who want to live in peace under law and in accordance with moral standards that have received almost universal acceptance through the centuries, can and must find some way to make their will prevail. . . . It seems to be unfortunately true that the epidemic of world lawlessness is spreading. When an epidemic of physical disease starts to spread, the community approves and joins in a quarantine of the patients in order to protect the health of the community against the spread of the disease. . . .
>
> War is a contagion, whether it be declared or undeclared. It can engulf states and peoples remote from the original scene of hostilities. We are determined to keep out of war, yet we cannot insure ourselves against the disastrous effects of war and the dangers of involvement. We are adopting such measures as will minimize our risk of involvement, but we cannot have complete protection in a world of disorder in which confidence and security have broken down. If civilization is to survive the principles of the Prince of Peace must be restored. Trust between nations must be revived.[100]

The initial press and public reaction to Roosevelt's speech was mildly favorable; on October 6, the *New York Times* ran an article headlined "Roosevelt Speech Widely Approved."[101] Yet within days, opinion began to shift, driven by fears that Roosevelt might translate his general denunciation of aggression and international passivity into concrete measures. In particular, when the League of Nations condemned Japanese military actions on October 6, and issued a call that member nations who were signatories to the Nine Power Treaty should convene a conference to address the ongoing Sino-Japanese hostilities, isolationists began to fear that Roosevelt's quarantine speech had been testing the waters for some sort of U.S. leadership role. They reacted vociferously, with the Hearst newspapers leading the charge. Throughout October and into November, the *Chicago Tribune* attacked the idea of any sort of American role in mediating the conflict, with banner headlines proclaiming, "Whatever It's Called It's War" and "It's Britain's War."[102] The *Tribune* was relentless in publishing interviews with isolationist congressmen and senators, with Senator William Borah thundering that if the United States participated in some scheme to sanction Japan, it would be "just the same as initiating war," a view echoed by Vandenberg, La Follette, and others in somewhat less inflammatory language.[103] Venting privately to Harold Ickes, FDR remarked how he found it particularly outrageous how Hearst was stirring up public opinion, commenting, "one of these days, I'm going to remind Mr. Hearst that he had been responsible for an absolutely unjustifiable war with Spain."[104]

Hull, writing after World War II, observed that the backlash to FDR's Quarantine Speech set back any support for international cooperation by at least six months, as the Veterans of Foreign Wars launched a campaign to secure 25 million signatures on a petition to "Keep America Out of War."[105] The business community, with the exception of those firms with direct interests at stake in China, was firmly against any sort of intervention or sanctions, and the *Wall Street Journal* ran a front-page editorial titled "Stop Foreign Meddling; America Wants Peace." The *Journal* advised the president to give all conflicts a wide berth, a sentiment echoed by the *Commercial and Financial Chronicle*.[106] A telephone poll of congressional opinion conducted by the *Philadelphia Inquirer* showed that Congress was attuned to the public's reluctance to become involved in the Far East, with two out of three respondents indicating that they opposed any sort of common action with the League of Nations.

With the passage of time, it has become tempting to characterize the isolationists as know-nothing provincials, Republican holdouts embittered by the New Deal, or the offspring of the midwestern "hyphenated Americans" who had opposed Wilson's tilt to the Entente in World War I. Yet isolationist sentiment was widespread even in the circles most enthusiastic about the New Deal; college professors, ministers, and many intellectuals warned against any administration scheme that envisioned the United States taking the lead in organizing a collective response to overseas aggression. Charles Beard serves as an example of a progressive, highly educated isolationist. Writing in the *Political Quarterly* that fall, Beard commented that "With much twisting and turning, the American people are renewing the Washington tradition and repudiating both the Kiplingesque imperialism of Theodore Roosevelt and the universal philanthropy of Woodrow Wilson." They are showing a "firm resolve not to be duped by another deluge of propaganda—right, left, or centre."[107] While Beard supported the administration's New Deal and was sympathetic to its domestic activism, he opposed FDR's Chicago agenda of international cooperation against nations violating international law and human decency. Responding to the internationalist argument, Beard wrote in the *New Republic* that:

> It is easy to get into a great moral passion over the distant Chinese. It costs nothing now, though it may cost the blood of countless American boys. It involves no conflict with greedy interests in our own midst. It sounds well on Sunday. . . . [But] Anybody who feels hot with morals and is affected with delicate sensibilities can find enough to do at home, considering the misery of the 10,000,000 unemployed, the tramps, the beggars, the sharecroppers, tenants and field hands right here at our door.[108]

A few voices pushed back against the strong current of isolationism in the fall of 1937. Senator M. M. Logan of Kentucky advised the administration to act more forcefully, telling journalists that "I am opposed to war, but I am also opposed to running for a hole every time anyone says 'boo.' I think the fleets of a group of nations blockading Japan would stop the present hostilities. But it would have to be collective action by several nations."[109] Admiral Leahy, the chief of naval operations, forwarded a proposal from Admiral Harry Yarnell in Shanghai sketching out how one might economically strangle Japan.[110] FDR's secretary of the navy, Claude Swanson, told the president in a cabinet meeting that the navy staff was of the opinion that "if it was considered necessary to put Japan in its place, this was the right time to do it, with Japan so fully occupied in China." The president ignored Logan's public call, pocketed the Yarnell proposal, and smilingly chided Swanson that he [FDR] was a pacifist and had no intention of making any warlike moves.[111]

The instructions that FDR gave the American representative sent to the conference convened in November 1937 to address the ongoing undeclared war in the Far East are telling. Ignoring isolationist critics who had opposed even sending an American representative to the Nine Powers Conference held in Brussels on November 3–24, 1937, FDR sent Norman Davis. Yet his instructions to Davis made clear that he envisioned no leading role for the United States. Davis was to make clear to the other attendees that:

a. The United States is in no way, and will not be in any way, a party to joint action with the League of Nations.
b. United States policy does not envisage the United States being pushed out in front as the leader in, or suggestor of, future action.

c. That on the other side of the picture, the United States cannot afford to be made, in popular opinion at home, a tail to the British kite, as has been charged and is now being charged by the Hearst press and others.[112]

The Brussels Nine Powers Conference accomplished nothing. In China, there had been great hopes that the Western signatory powers might somehow bring pressure to bear on Japan to end hostilities. But this was not to be. Japan declined two invitations to attend. Great Britain and France were intently focused on crises closer to home, and sought to pass responsibility for dealing with the Far East to the United States. The smaller nations in attendance feared that using economic sanctions to pressure Japan would disproportionately burden them. And the United States refused to take the lead. After issuing a declaration that the attending powers were firmly convinced force could not provide a just and lasting solution for disputes between nations, the delegates suspended the conference indefinitely on November 24. By then, Shanghai had fallen and Japanese armies were closing on Nanking. Three days later, the Chinese commander in chief in Nanking issued a bulletin instructing foreign residents to leave the city as he could no longer guarantee their safety. Most of the American Embassy staff had already evacuated Nanking the previous week aboard the USS *Luzon*. The gunboat *Panay* was en route to Nanking, where it was ordered to stand by to evacuate the few staff members the embassy had left behind, along with American journalists and businessmen who had ignored earlier warnings to leave the city. The president's prediction that some Americans were going to get hurt—expressed four months earlier at the start of the war—was about to come true, though not in the form he anticipated. The *Panay* was about to be sunk and hundreds of thousands of Chinese would be brutally massacred and raped as Japanese troops overwhelmed the Chinese defenders of Nanking and occupied the city in December 1937.

THE IMMEDIATE REACTION

THE PUBLIC, THE PRESS, AND CONGRESS

Japanese naval aircraft attacked the USS *Panay* in the early afternoon of Sunday, December 12, 1937, and the ship sank beneath the muddy surface of the Yangtze River shortly before four in the afternoon. The initial attack destroyed the ship's transmitter, and the *Panay*'s survivors hid in the riverbank reeds until nightfall, as they feared that the Japanese intended to kill them. As word reached the commander of the U.S. Yangtze Patrol and the American ambassador to China that British gunboats had been subjected to Japanese artillery and air attacks that Sunday afternoon, a sense of alarm began to grip State and Navy Department personnel in Hankow. At 9:30 on Monday morning (Sunday evening in Washington), the American ambassador in Hankow received a telephone call from an American missionary doctor in Anking relaying the information that the *Panay* had been sunk. The ambassador and the commander of the U.S. Yangtze Patrol rushed to inform their respective superiors, and by late Sunday evening, Eastern Standard Time, the secretary of state and chief of naval operations had received the news. Hull telegraphed Grew in Tokyo shortly before midnight and instructed him to immediately contact the Japanese foreign minister and "impress upon him the gravity of the situation and the imperative need to take every precaution against further attacks on American vessels or personnel."[113]

Even as Hull's cable was in transmission, the Japanese government sought to defuse the situation by immediately apologizing for the incident at multiple levels and across time zones.[114] In Tokyo, Foreign Minister Hirota broke with diplomatic protocol by personally visiting the American Embassy to express his regret for the incident. Hirota explained that he had received a Dōmei News Agency dispatch from Shanghai indicating that Japanese planes, intent on attacking remnants of the Chinese army, had instead accidentally bombed three Standard Oil vessels and sunk the USS *Panay*. Hirota indicated that while he had not yet received any official reports, he wanted to extend his government's profound apology immediately, commenting that "I cannot possibly express how badly we feel about this."[115] The Japanese navy minister meanwhile sent his senior aide to the U.S. naval attaché in Tokyo to convey the navy minister's "sincerest regret to this unhappy accident," and the chief of staff of the Japanese China Area Fleet paid a formal call on Admiral Yarnell aboard the flagship *Augusta* in Shanghai to apologize and offer medical assistance.[116] In Washington, the Japanese ambassador requested an urgent meeting with the U.S. secretary of state, intent on conveying his government's full and sincere apologies for the "very grave blunder" that had occurred.

The barrage of apologies from Japanese officials gave the administration little time to digest what had happened to the *Panay*, let alone conduct protracted internal debates before responding. Secretary of State Hull put off meeting the Japanese ambassador until 1 P.M. on Monday so that he could first consult with the White House. Hull had conferred with officers of the Far Eastern Division the previous evening, and met with them again early Monday morning to discuss

Ambassador Hirosi Saito poses for photographers while waiting to express Japan's regrets for the *Panay* incident to Secretary of State Hull, December 13, 1937.
Library of Congress, Prints and Photographs Division LC-DIG-hec-23766

what response the State Department should recommend. The initial consensus was that Japan's behavior had been outrageous, but given isolationist sentiment, the United States was in "no position to send sufficient naval forces . . . to require the Japanese to make the fullest amends and resume something of a law-abiding course."[117] Admiral Leahy, the chief of naval operations, participated in the discussion Sunday evening, and was not impressed. Rather than focusing on an effective response, he wrote privately that "The Department of State seems to be interested principally in getting the written record of this incident so complete as to provide defense against criticism." On Monday, he advised the president that it was "time to get the fleet ready for sea, to make an arrangement with the British Navy for joint action, and to inform the Japanese that we expect to protect our nationals."[118] Secretary of State Hull's recommendation was more restrained: public opinion in the United States would not support a war with Japan, and the United States should press Japan diplomatically to issue an apology, pay indemnity, and punish the officers involved in the attack. In addition, Japan needed to assure the United States that similar incidents would not happen again. Hull apparently never considered breaking relations with Japan, given the readiness of the Japanese to apologize and his assessment that the American people did not want war.[119]

The president thus received a variety of counsel from his inner circle as the crisis broke. Perhaps to stiffen Hull's backbone, he insisted on giving the secretary of state written guidance before he met with the Japanese ambassador. Roosevelt called his stenographer into the room and dictated the following memorandum:

Please tell the Japanese Ambassador when you see him at one o'clock:

(1) That the President is deeply shocked and concerned by the news of indiscriminate bombing of American and other non-Chinese vessels on the Yangtze, and that he requests that the Emperor be so advised.

(2) That all facts are being assembled and will shortly be presented to the Japanese Government.

(3) That in the meantime it is hoped the Japanese Government will be considering definitely for presentation to this Government:

    a. Full expressions of regret and proffer of full compensation.

    b. Methods guaranteeing against a repetition of any similar attacks in the future.[120]

The president's instinct to express shock, demand an apology, but wait until all the facts were assembled before offering more precise terms of settlement served him well. The Japanese, while apologizing profusely, attributed the attack to a terrible mistake on the part of its forces in the field. Citing reports that it had received from military commanders in China, the Japanese government explained that Japanese pilots had mistaken the *Panay* and the Standard Oil tankers for Chinese ships, as poor visibility and smoke had obscured distinguishing marks identifying the ships as American.[121] *Panay* survivors, however, told a very different story. The day had been clear and bright, the *Panay* and the three tankers all had large American flags prominently displayed across their upper decks. Although it would take George Atcheson and the Naval Court of Inquiry a week to file their official accounts of what had happened, the journalists who had been onboard the *Panay*—in particular, Colin MacDonald for *The Times* of London and Norman Soong for the *New York Times*—worked on faster deadlines. Even before they arrived in Shanghai with the other dazed and wounded *Panay* survivors, MacDonald and Soong somehow managed to send the first eyewitness accounts of the bombing. Over the coming days, more survivor accounts would make their way into the papers, and by the close of the month, the *San Francisco Chronicle* would run a front-page pictorial spread headlined "All Flags Flying!" It depicted exactly how the *Panay* had displayed the Stars and Stripes at the time it was attacked, with Norman Alley's motion-picture footage of the attack providing a clear visual to American movie-goers during the first weeks of 1938. By then, the Roosevelt administration had largely settled the issue after weighing a number of different options.

Did the *Panay*'s destruction alter the domestic isolationist mood, enabling the president to embark on a more activist foreign policy? Did the ship's sinking generate cries of "Remember the *Panay*" on a par with earlier campaigns to "Remember the *Maine*" and "Remember the *Lusitania*"? Did it galvanize Congress as did the naval incidents of 1898 and 1915? More broadly, was the president pushed to take action, or did he retain freedom of action to respond as he deemed appropriate?

Generalizing about press opinion during this period is difficult, as hundreds of local and independent regional papers still flourished alongside the great metropolitan flagship papers and newspaper conglomerates. Editors might support the administration's domestic agenda while remaining suspicious of external entanglements, or vigorously attack the New Deal while reluctantly supporting the administration's foreign policy. Editorial opinion concerning the *Panay* was divided. Many of the editors at smaller regional papers questioned why the *Panay* had been in the middle of a war zone; the *Portland Oregonian,* for example, commented that while the ship's destruction had been tragic, "The United States government should address a sharp note of protest to itself for having permitted the gunboat to be in that exposed position." These isolationist editors asserted that the administration should have withdrawn American forces from China before the incident. The *Richmond Times-Dispatch* thundered, "The blowing up of the gunboat *Panay* is just what we said was going to happen if this country persisted in keeping fighting ships in the Far Eastern danger zone." The *St. Louis Post Dispatch* cut to the point, remarking that the administration should "protest to Japan and obtain compensation but remove our forces.[122]

A number of papers advised against withdrawal, with both the *Chicago Tribune* and the *Chicago Daily News* opposed to simply abandoning American rights in China. The *Chicago Daily News* warned its readers that "every backward step, every withdrawal, every surrender, only brings the eventual point of conflict that much nearer to our own shores. We strongly urge the Administration to convince the Japanese of their error." The *New York Times* and the *New York Herald Tribune* supported Roosevelt's decision to keep naval forces in China, and the *Washington Post* lectured Tokyo that it would be gravely mistaken if it assumed that professional pacifists were representative of American public opinion. The *Post* warned the Japanese government that "it would be highly dangerous for them to assume that Uncle Sam will swallow a long series of calculated affronts indefinitely."[123]

The *New Republic*, in an editorial titled "From *Lusitania* to *Panay*," laid out the contradictions of the situation for its readers on December 22. Acknowledging that "there is no question that the men who executed the attack against the *Panay* and the Standard Oil tankers, as well as those who fired at the British gunboats in another part of the river, knew perfectly well what they were doing," the journal concluded that the Japanese government "cannot control the men who fly its planes and shoot its guns." Roosevelt, by refusing to invoke the Neutrality Act, had put American forces in harm's way. Countering the administration's claim that invoking the act would harm the victims of aggression more than the perpetrators of violence, the *New Republic* noted that American fuel was powering the Japanese military. Under the Neutrality Act, the president could direct that fuel exports to belligerents be limited to "cash and carry" purchases. Since Japan did not have enough tankers and cash to transport and pay for the fuel its military needed, the measure could help halt the "rape of China and the bombing of hospitals and civilians."[124]

Both isolationist and internationalist editors comforted themselves with the thought that their views represented those of the silent majority of Americans. A Gallup poll conducted in January 1938 suggests that the editors of the smaller, regional papers expressing isolationist viewpoints were more in line with public opinion than were the editors of the internationalist-leaning papers of New York, Boston, and Washington, D.C. In August 1937, some 54 percent of those polled favored a complete American withdrawal from China. By January 1938, one month after the attack on the *Panay*, 70 percent favored a complete withdrawal. The Women's International League for Peace and Freedom wrote to the president after the *Panay*'s destruction that "the incident of the *Lusitania* and the cry of the American people may be repeated if America does not act at once."[125] And by action, the league meant withdrawal and de-escalation, not ultimatums, blockades, or escalation.

Given the wide range of opinion in editorial pages across the country, the administration might have taken up the *Washington Post*'s refrain that the "professional pacifists" of the Women's International League and Emergency Peace Campaign did not reflect the broader American public. But FDR could not ignore Congress. He had summoned Congress back into session in November in order to pass four major domestic bills that the president believed would help spur the economy out of recession: an agriculture bill, a wage bill, an executive reorganization bill, and a planning bill. Though Democrats still dominated the House and Senate by wide majorities, FDR's attempt to reform the Supreme Court earlier that year had significantly weakened his influence in Congress. (Frustrated by Supreme Court rulings against New Deal legislation, FDR had urged Congress to give him the authority to add new justices to the court. His proposal was derided as a "court packing plan," and recalcitrant Democrats joined Republicans in the Senate to stymie the initiative in July.) Congress was keen to show its independence, and the press reported that congressional Democrats were in rebellion.[126] The sinking of the *Panay* energized isolationists from both parties who had been aggrieved that the president had not put the Neutrality Act of 1937, passed by a Senate margin of 66 to 6 that spring, into effect.

FDR had been able to avoid activating the Neutrality Act because the language of the law required that he do so only if a state of war existed between two or more states, or if civil strife abroad was of such a magnitude that the export of arms, ammunition, and implements of war from the United States would threaten or endanger the peace of the country. Yet neither Japan nor China had declared war against one another, and FDR had been content to merely warn American-flagged vessels transporting war materials to China that they did so at their own risk. Congressional isolationists found the president's reluctance to activate the law infuriating. With Congress back in session, isolationist representatives and senators took up the arguments they had made in the summer—namely, that the president should withdraw U.S. forces from China and fulfill his duties as laid out in the Neutrality Acts.

The day after the sinking of the *Panay*, Secretary of State Hull received a letter from Senator William Smathers of New Jersey, urging the immediate withdrawal of American ships and citizens from China.[127] Senator Ashburn of Arizona warned the administration that not a single senator would vote for war. Hamilton

Fish of New York went even further. He declared that even a commercial boycott of Japan went too far. Senator Borah, an outspoken isolationist, crisply informed one of his constituents that "I am not prepared to vote to send our boys into the Orient because a boat was sunk which was travelling in a danger zone. That which happened might be expected to happen under such circumstances."[128]

Congressional isolationists wanted the president to invoke the Neutrality Act and insulate the United States from the fighting in China. Yet forcing the president to do what he did not want to do was difficult. To put pressure on him, a steady trickle of congressmen from both parties signed on to the Ludlow Amendment. Introduced in 1935 by Democratic congressman Louis Ludlow of Indiana, the Ludlow Amendment, if adopted, would have subjected any congressional declaration of war to a national referendum before it took effect. Ludlow's resolution stalled in the powerful House Judiciary Committee during the 74th Congress. Only seventy-four congressmen signed on to the discharge petition, which would have forced the Judiciary Committee to put the matter before the House.

Ludlow reintroduced the resolution with minor modifications when the 75th Congress convened in January 1937.[129] Again, it stalled in the Judiciary Committee, despite Ludlow's impassioned pleas that it should be put to a vote. Ludlow attempted to force it out of committee, working to acquire the 218 House signatures that would force the committee chair to release the resolution to the House for a vote. By the end of November, he had gathered 194 signatures; another eleven trickled in during the first week of December. The *Panay*'s sinking did not generate any sort of mass hysteria within the House in favor of the Ludlow Amendment. It did, however, prompt thirteen additional congressmen to sign the discharge petition posthaste as alarm mounted about how the administration might react.[130]

The signal was clear. FDR could delay implementing the Neutrality Act if he wished, but Congress not only retained the prerogative of declaring war but also was considering amending the Constitution to share that power directly with the American people. More than two-thirds of the House Republican minority signed the discharge petition (fifty-five out of ninety Republicans), almost half of the House Democratic majority (151 of 328 Democrats), and almost all the Progressives and Farmer-Laborites in the House (12 of 13). The House leadership scheduled a full vote on the discharge resolution for January 10, 1938.[131] FDR and his political advisers understood that too assertive a response to the *Panay*'s destruction would galvanize support for the Ludlow Amendment, while too timid a response might send the signal to Japan that it could run roughshod over American interests in the Far East.

The public, the press, and Congress reacted very differently to the sinking of the *Panay* than they had to the destruction of the *Maine* and the *Lusitania*.

Though American diplomats, naval officers, and internationalist editors recalled these earlier episodes and anticipated a strong reaction from the administration, the loudest voices in the public sphere and in Congress were those who warned against letting the incident drag the United States into a faraway war. Seventy percent of the public believed that the First World War had been a mistake, and Congress seemed determined to block any measures that increased the risk of an American entanglement abroad.[132] Many remembered the *Maine* and the *Lusitania*, but few wanted any repeat of 1898 or 1915.

The response of the Japanese government and the Japanese people to the sinking of the *Panay* reinforced isolationist arguments against escalation. The Japanese government apologized for the incident even before details of what had happened percolated across the Pacific. In addition, Japanese newspapers and editorials were more conciliatory in tone than had been the case with the German press in 1915, echoing their government's expressions of profound apologies rather than seeking to justify the incident or to shift blame.[133] Ambassador Grew in Tokyo summarized the public sentiment in Japan in his diary:

> Ever since the first news of the *Panay* disaster came, we have been deluged by delegations, visitors, letters, and contributions of money—people from all walks of life, from high officials, doctors, professors, businessmen down to school children trying to express their shame, apologies, and regrets for the action of their own Navy. One well-dressed Japanese woman stepped behind a door in the chancery and cut off a big strand of her hair and gave it to us with a carnation—the old-fashioned gesture of mourning for the loss of a husband. Another Japanese broke down and cried at his country's shame. Wherever we go, people try to express their apologies.[134]

Despite these public apologies and repeated references to the accidental nature of the incident, both the American and British governments suspected that there was more to the bombing of the USS *Panay*, the shelling of British gunboats, and other incidents affecting Western interests than miscalculation and misidentification. The president believed that the attack had been deliberate, undertaken to diminish American prestige, discourage the Chinese, make a continued Western presence in the Yangtze River Valley uncomfortable, and eventually force the Western powers out of China.[135]

FDR'S OPTIONS AND RESPONSE

FDR's initial response to the Japanese government had been to express his shock, insist that the Japanese emperor be made aware of the crisis, and direct the Japanese government to apologize, offer compensation, and provide guarantees against any repetition of similar attacks in the future. As the president and his advisers awaited the findings of the Naval Court of Inquiry convened to investigate the sinking of the *Panay*, they discussed several options that might convey American displeasure. These ranged from imposing a distant blockade on Japan to organizing a joint demonstration of naval force with the British, to using financial instruments to punish the Japanese. But after careful consideration, each option was shelved or watered down.

Secretary of the Navy Claude Swanson, though old and in poor health, was enraged by the attack and "shouted for war in his feeble voice" during the cabinet meeting held on December 17, 1937.[136] Swanson made his case forcefully despite difficulty speaking, arguing that war with Japan was inevitable. Given this unfortunate reality, it was better to fight Japan while its military was bogged down in China rather than wait until Japan had consolidated its hold on the mainland.[137] Returning to a point he had made three months earlier, Swanson pointed out that Japan was highly dependent on imports and therefore vulnerable to naval pressure. Roosevelt then shared the concept he had mentioned to Welles months earlier—that the United States might impose a trade embargo on Japan, enforced by U.S. and British ships positioned at key points in the Pacific and South China Seas. The president viewed a distant blockade as less drastic than fleet action, and remarked that the U.S. Navy could blockade Japan from the Aleutian Islands to Hawaii to Guam, with the British taking over the blockade from there to Singapore. FDR asserted that a blockade was a "comparatively simple task which the Navy could take care of without having to send a great fleet." He believed that a joint Anglo-American blockade would bring Japan to its knees within a year.[138] The concept, however, required collaboration with the British Navy, and put the thousands of American civilians still in China; the U.S. troop detachments at Beijing, Shanghai, and Tientsin; and the weak U.S. Asiatic Fleet at risk. FDR realized that while many Americans were appalled by the Japanese behavior in the Far East, few wanted to go to war with Japan over American gunboats on the Yangtze or Japanese atrocities in Shanghai, Nanking, or elsewhere. Admiral Leahy, the chief of naval operations, advised the president to take the precaution of sending the ships of the fleet to navy yards "without delay to obtain fuel, clean bottoms, and take on sea stores preparatory for a cruise at sea."[139]

If imposing a naval blockade went too far and constituted an act of war, sending a powerful naval force to the area to show the flag offered an alternative. The British had suggested a joint display of force back in November, only to be rebuffed by the Americans. As news of the Japanese attacks on the HMS *Ladybird*, HMS *Bee*, and the USS *Panay* reached London, the British government sounded out the Americans once again. Noting that they were "fully aware" that the American government was unable to participate in "joint actions," the British

Chief of Naval Operations Admiral William D. Leahy, who joined Secretary of the Navy Claude Swanson in recommending a strong response to Japan's attack on the USS *Panay*.
Naval History and Heritage Command, Photo Archives, NH 50873

suggested that their two governments might synchronize their responses, since the Japanese attacks on vessels of both nations "could not possibly have been the result of accident," according to their sources.[140] The British government attached great importance to creating a unified Anglo-American front, urging the Americans to move their fleet and assuring them that "in such circumstances Great Britain would undoubtedly increase her own Far Eastern naval contingent."[141] The message delivered by the British ambassador to Cordell Hull the next day was somewhat more circumspect; while reiterating that the British believed the Japanese were following a policy of firing upon the nationals and warships of other nations in the most "reckless, criminal, and deliberate manner," the British government conceded that it was doubtful whether either Great Britain or the United States could assemble a naval force sufficiently impressive to deter the Japanese from further outrageous behavior. London continued to believe that it was important that Western powers make a show of force in the Far East, but noted that Britain was not in the position to do so at that point in time, given commitments in Europe. The British government anticipated that it would be prepared to make a show of force "on each side of the planet" within a number of months.[142]

The British position, in short, was much the same as it had been back in November. Britain encouraged the United States to take a strong stance toward Japan, desired joint action, but was unable to contribute to the strong display of force it advocated. On the evening of the December 16, Roosevelt met with British Ambassador Sir Ronald Lindsay and Secretary of State Hull to explore the matter of naval cooperation more fully off the record. Returning to the concept of a naval blockade or "quarantine" of Japan, FDR grew increasingly enthusiastic as he outlined the concept to the British ambassador. If Japan committed another outrage, the British and American navies should implement a cruiser blockade of Japan, keeping their battleships to the rear. The French and Dutch would have to be brought onboard, with the blockade supplemented by a general embargo of Japanese goods. Roosevelt elaborated that there was no need for the British to send a fleet; the dispatch of cruisers, destroyers, and submarines would suffice, perhaps backed by one or two battleships. Reporting on the conversation to Foreign Minister Eden, Lindsay concluded:

> From the foregoing you may think that these are the utterances of a harebrained statesman or of an amateur strategist, but I assure you that the chief impression left on my own mind was that I had been talking to a man who had done his best in the Great War to bring America speedily on the side of the Allies and who now was equally anxious to bring America in on the same side before it might be too late.[143]

Roosevelt had first considered the idea of blockading Japan back in July, but had shelved it without explanation. The sinking of the *Panay* caused him to resurrect the concept and check with the British whether they were willing and able to participate in such an endeavor. The president concluded that Japanese militarists were determined to subjugate China over the protests of the United States, the League of Nations, and the British government. FDR realized that considerable discussion would be needed to transform the concept into a plan, and he sought to explore the option of joint naval and economic coercion off the record. In his mind, a blockade did not equate to a declaration of war, hence his use with the British ambassador of the more innocuous term he had tested the previous October, that of a "quarantine."

British officials from the prime minister on down, no doubt drawing upon their experience in the First World War, were skeptical of the distinction. The Foreign Office favored a joint demonstration of force, a concept it had advocated months before. Both options required a modicum of staff discussions between the U.S. Navy and the Royal Navy, though the administration knew that even a whiff of such discussions would cause an uproar in Congress and the public. On December 23, FDR asked Admiral Leahy and Captain Royal E. Ingersoll, director of the U.S. Navy's War Plans Division, to attend a secret meeting at the White House, along with the secretaries of state and treasury. Ignoring Hull's misgivings, FDR instructed Ingersoll to go to London for the purpose of making "preliminary arrangements, if we could, with the British for joint action in case of war with Japan."[144]

Domestic realities made it difficult for the president to openly engage in coercive diplomacy. In groping for a way to respond to aggression without resorting to war, FDR toyed with the idea of using U.S. economic power to exert pressure without force. This would be particularly useful if the Japanese either refused to pay indemnities for their attack on the *Panay* and the Standard Oil tankers, or if they dragged their feet and quibbled about the damages demanded. During the first cabinet session after the *Panay*'s destruction, FDR asked Henry Morgenthau what legal rights he had to "take possession of all the worldly goods that belong to the Japanese Government and their citizen and hold it for damages done," commenting "There are lots of ways of declaring war. In the old days, sinking of an American battleship would be a declaration of war. Today it is not considered such."[145] Morgenthau consulted his senior legal adviser, general counsel Herman Oliphant, and reported the next day that a 1933 amendment to the Trading with the Enemy Act empowered the president to issue regulations that prohibited or restricted exchange transactions if the president declared a national emergency. FDR was delighted, and instructed Morgenthau to develop the concept further.

Oliphant put the Treasury Department's top lawyers through their paces, directing them to complete a draft legal justification of the concept as quickly as possible.[146] Assistant Secretary of the Treasury Wayne Taylor pushed for more deliberation during a departmental review, asking under what circumstances the United States could impose the rules and for how long. Morgenthau remarked that those decisions would be up to the president, with restrictions removed when the Japanese agreed to "be good boys." When Taylor argued that the proposed regulations might lead to war, Morgenthau shot back that "they've sunk a United States battleship [*sic*] and killed three people. . . . You going to sit here and wait until you wake up here in the morning and find them in the Philippines, then Hawaii, and then in Panama? Where would you call halt?" Taylor, reflecting the opinion of most Americans, said he would wait quite a while.[147] When Morgenthau snapped that he could see no reason to wait for the Japanese to strike again, Taylor blurted out, "Well, of all the cockeyed things in the world that we can do that would be more cockeyed than the last World War we got into, this would be it." The exchange reveals how extensive isolationism was even within a department headed by one of Roosevelt's most dynamic, interventionist confidants. Morgenthau's reply to Taylor's outburst sheds light on the president's thinking and illustrates how pervasive was the tendency among policymakers to equate the *Panay* with the *Maine*, though the latter ship was far larger and its loss had cost the lives of hundreds. Morgenthau told Taylor:

> I think it's a time to call a halt when a United States battleship has been sunk and three of our people have been killed. For us to let them put their sword into our insides and sit there and take it and like it, and not do anything about it, I think is un-American and I think we've got to begin to inch in on those boys, and that's what the President is doing. . . . How long are you going to sit there and let these fellows kill American soldiers and sailors and sink our battleships?[148]

One of the major stumbling blocks to the Treasury plan was that Japan might sell or convert its assets before they could be frozen. To render the plan workable, the British would have to be brought onboard. The president directed Morgenthau to contact Sir John Simon, Chancellor of the Exchequer, directly, bypassing the usual diplomatic channels and keeping the matter secret.[149] The British response was cautious, and by the time Treasury had completed drafting the regulations on December 21, Roosevelt had cooled toward the proposal. The chancellor's remarks, which Morgenthau must have shared with the president, only served to dampen enthusiasm for the idea further. Simon noted that the British government lacked powers equivalent to those found in the Trading with the Enemy Act, and that Chamberlain's government would have to request special legislation from Parliament before it could cooperate in any joint monetary action against Japan. Furthermore, Simon remarked, long-term economic pressure would not produce any immediate response from the Japanese, while immediate and drastic pressure was indistinguishable from "other forceful devices." Internally, a senior civil servant at the British treasury was more candid. Commenting on American proposals, Sir Warren Fisher wrote: "Over and above the imbecility of economic sanctions, we sh[oul]d find ourselves left in the lurch sooner or later by the U.S.A. (who incidentally have no very special stakes in Asia) and Japan w[oul]d scoop Hong Kong. Sh[oul]d we then add the fatal folly of going to war with Japan and so committing suicide in Europe?"[150]

An earlier internal British study of the utility of trade boycotts or sanctions had concluded that they would take months to be effective and might force Japan to resist economic pressure by occupying the Dutch East Indies, Cochinchina (southern Vietnam), the Philippines, and perhaps parts of Malaya. It had warned that "Half measures are far worse than useless and full measures mean war."[151] Morgenthau correctly concluded that the British were politely but emphatically opposed to exerting serious economic pressure on Japan. FDR had hoped that using economic pressure would be an alternative to using military pressure. Yet without British cooperation, the economic instrument of power was blunt and difficult to deploy.

Roosevelt was left to rely on diplomatic negotiations to resolve the crisis. Secretary of State Hull had always believed that diplomacy was the only option, given the strength of isolationist sentiment in Congress, and FDR had deliberately bypassed Hull and used back channels to explore his naval and economic options. But resolving the crisis through noncoercive diplomacy required Japanese cooperation. There was considerable anxiety in the White House, at the State Department, and at the American Embassy in Tokyo that the Japanese might fail to respond appropriately. This sense of anxiety mounted as the administration received information that undermined the initial Japanese narrative of an accidental attack under conditions of restricted visibility. On December 16, Hull directed Ambassador Grew in Tokyo to call upon the Japanese minister of foreign affairs as soon as possible. Grew was to tell Hirota that the American government had received disturbing new details concerning the attack. Particularly troubling were reports that while survivors were escaping the sinking *Panay*, Japanese airplanes had dived and strafed its lifeboats at extremely low altitudes. In addition, two Japanese army motorboats had machine-gunned the ship, boarded it, and searched the vessel while the American colors still hung clearly visible at the gaff. Lastly, on reaching the shore, the *Panay*'s survivors had reported that Japanese planes flew repeatedly over the area where they were hiding in an apparent effort to exterminate them. Hull concluded that these new reports raised two questions in addition to those of acknowledging, apologizing, and paying damages. How did Tokyo intend to deal with those responsible for the incident? And what specific steps would the Japanese take to ensure that American nationals, interests, and property in China would not be subjected to further attacks or unlawful interference from Japanese forces and authorities?[152]

The following day, matters threatened to boil over when the Japanese ambassador called upon the secretary of state to deny that the *Panay* or any of its survivors had been fired upon by Japanese military boats. Hull interrupted him, insisting that the American government had incontrovertible proof to that effect. Turning to the matter of punishment, Hull lectured the Japanese ambassador that "if Army or Navy officials in this country were to act as the Japanese had over there, our Government would quickly court martial and shoot them."[153] In Tokyo, Ambassador Grew wrote in his diary on December 20 that, as evidence began to mount that the attack may have been deliberate, "My first thought was that this might result in a breach of diplomatic relations and that Saito [Japan's ambassador to the United States] would be given his passports and that I would be recalled home, for I 'remembered the *Maine*.'"[154]

Had the Japanese government been intransigent and argued that the American government had only itself to blame for putting the *Panay* in a dangerous situation—as a number of isolationists in the United States were claiming—Grew's fears of a diplomatic rupture might have materialized. Instead, on December 15, Vice Minister of the Japanese Navy Isoroku Yamamoto informed the American ambassador that he had relieved Rear Admiral Teizo Mitsunami, commanding officer of naval air forces in the Shanghai region, of command. The next day, Japan's navy minister announced that the Imperial Navy would render a salute of honor to the victims of the *Panay* at the site of the attack. In addition, he extended the apologies of every member of the Japanese navy to the U.S. Navy. The Japanese government moved quickly to share the information it had received from the investigations it had initiated. The Japanese navy and army conducted separate and independent investigations. The two investigations diverged in several significant matters—in particular, on the role that Japanese army launches had played in the incident. Indicative of the serious interservice rivalries that plagued Japan during this period and throughout the Second World War, the Japanese government was never able to fully reconcile the conflicting reports it received.[155] Nonetheless, a high-level Japanese delegation, led by Vice Minister of the Navy Yamamoto (who in 1941 as commander in chief of the Japanese Combined Fleet would plan the Pearl Harbor attack) spent three hours on the evening of December 23 briefing Ambassador Grew and his team on the Japanese investigations. Grew reported to Washington that the effort had been thorough, with maps strewn all over his office. All the American attendees, Grew noted, had been impressed "with the apparently genuine desire and effort of both [the Japanese] Army and Navy to get at the undistorted facts."[156]

Grew had not yet received a copy of the U.S. Naval Court of Inquiry findings when the Japanese presented their briefing, and he told them that based on the information he possessed, the Japanese account did not tally completely with the evidence. Grew reminded his high-level visitors that the American government was still waiting for a full reply to the American notes of December 14 and 17—that is, to Roosevelt's initial demand that Japan express regret, offer full compensation, and provide assurances, and to Hull's follow-on note reiterating these points and inquiring how Tokyo would deal with those responsible.[157]

The next day, the Japanese foreign minister handed Grew his government's official response. The Japanese note maintained that the incident had been "entirely due to a mistake," and explained that thorough investigations had fully established that the attack had been "entirely unintentional." The Japanese note reaffirmed Japan's deep regret and willingness to pay indemnities, adding that the Japanese navy had been issued strict orders to "exercise the greatest caution in every area where warships and other vessels of America or any other third power are present, in order to avoid a recurrence of a similar mistake, even at the sacrifice of a strategic advantage in attacking Chinese troops." Furthermore, Hirota continued, the commander of the flying force concerned had been removed from his post for failing to take the fullest precautions. Staff officers, the commander of the flying squadron, and all others responsible for the attack would be dealt with duly according to law.[158]

By the time Washington received the note at noon on December 24, the administration was digesting Secretary Atcheson's preliminary report on the bombing of the *Panay* and the U.S. Naval Court of Inquiry findings.[159] Both were damning, leaving little doubt that the *Panay*'s survivors felt the attack had been deliberate. Atcheson, commenting on his experience hiding in the marsh, stated that the *Panay* survivors had "every reason to believe that the Japanese were searching for us to destroy the witnesses to the bombing." The navy report did not speculate on Japanese intentions, confining itself to listing thirty-six findings of fact. These spoke for themselves, in particular the finding that a Japanese powerboat filled with armed Japanese soldiers had approached close to the *Panay*, opened fire with a machine gun, and boarded the vessel after the air attacks had subsided. The naval board report included a concluding opinion broken down into eight subsections. Contradicting the Japanese investigations, the U.S. Navy Court of Inquiry concluded that while the first Japanese bombers might not have been able to identify the USS *Panay* on account of their altitude, "it was utterly inconceivable that the six light bombing planes coming within about six hundred feet of the ships and attacking for over a period of twenty minutes could not be aware of the identity of the ships they were attacking."[160]

The Atcheson report and the Naval Court of Inquiry opinion made it difficult for the administration to accept the Japanese position that the entire incident had been accidental. They were uncertain, however, whether the Japanese government was itself directly responsible or whether "wild, runaway, half-insane Army and Navy officials" in China had initiated the attack.[161] The American ambassador in Tokyo believed that the Japanese army and navy were "running amok, and perpetrating atrocities which the Emperor himself cannot possibly desire or sanction."[162] As for the Japanese government, it had substantially met the four demands FDR and Hull had communicated. Given that the president had no proof that the Japanese government had instigated the attack, he decided to settle the matter. On the afternoon of Christmas Day, Hull sent a note to Tokyo indicating that the United States regarded the Japanese note as "responsive" to American requests. Hull made clear, however, that the United States would rely on the findings of its own Naval Court of Inquiry rather than the Japanese investigations into the *Panay* incident. Japan was provided with a copy of the findings of facts, and there the matter rested.

When Grew communicated the American acceptance of the Japanese note to Foreign Minister Hirota, he recorded that Hirota's eyes filled with tears. The Foreign Minister remarked to Grew that "I heartily thank your Government and you yourself for this decision. I am very, very happy. You have brought me a splendid Christmas present."[163] The *Panay* crisis was over.

On Friday, December 31, a small group assembled in a darkened room in Washington to view the film that cameraman Norman Alley had taken of the attack. Alley's negatives had been rushed under strict security across the Pacific, and had been developed at Fort Lee the previous day. Alley was on hand as Secretary of the Navy Claude Swanson, Secretary of War Harry Woodring, and Senator Key Pittman, chairman of the Senate Foreign Relations Committee, watched the reel in silence. The film showed Japanese aircraft high above the *Panay*, Chief Boatswain's Mate Mahlmann manning the guns in his skivvies, and the destruction onboard.[164] The mood was grim. Harold Ickes, FDR's secretary of the interior, writing after the president had decided to accept the Japanese Christmas note, probably captured the sentiments of others in the cabinet who likewise wished the president had been more forceful. Ickes's diary entry recorded that in his view:

We didn't get the satisfactory apology from Japan that we asked for. . . .
In its note Japan distinctly negatived [*sic*] any charge of responsibility for

Norman Alley talks with Assistant Secretary of the Navy Charles Edison on December 31, 1937, following a restricted screening of his footage of the attack on the *Panay*.
Library of Congress, Prints and Photographs Division LC-DIG-hec-23823

other than an unpremeditated incident. This we have accepted, despite the fact that we know, and are apparently in a position to prove, that the attack was deliberate and wanton. It may be that the President thinks public opinion would not support him if he should go any further just now, but he proposes to be ready if another incident occurs. . . . Much as I deprecate war, I still think that if we are ever going to fight Japan, and it looks to me as if we would have to do so sooner or later, the best time is now.[165]

After the Second World War, a number of historians asserted that the *Panay* crisis brought the United States to the brink of war with Japan four years before Pearl Harbor.[166] Despite the rumblings of Ickes, Swanson, Leahy, and others, this seems to be an overstatement.[167] The president pushed his advisers to give him a range of options, asking Morgenthau to look into the legality of seizing Japanese assets and directing Leahy to initiate conversations with the British Admiralty. Yet Roosevelt was keenly aware of public and congressional opinion, telling a friend after the hostile reaction to his "Quarantine Speech" the previous

October that "It's a terrible thing to look over your shoulder when you are trying to lead and find no one there."[168]

The Japanese, by apologizing, paying an indemnity, and providing assurances they would not repeat their outrageous behavior, made it difficult and unnecessary for the president to buttress his diplomatic requests with coercive measures. Furthermore, while FDR and his advisers found it hard to believe that the attack had been entirely accidental, they had no proof to substantiate their suspicion that the attack had been authorized by the Japanese government. Indeed, decoded Japanese message traffic suggested otherwise, with the Japanese consul in Shanghai informing Foreign Minister Hirota on December 13 that a Japanese navy flier had mistaken the *Panay* and the Standard Oil tankers for Chinese vessels and had sunk them.[169] Decoded messages from the Japanese foreign ministry provide no confirmation that the Japanese government was trying to deliberately mislead the Americans or cover up a sanctioned attack.[170] If there was any deception on the part of the Japanese, then the Japanese government was being deceived by its own commanders in the field. On December 20, the *New York Times* ran a story that Colonel Kingoro Hashimoto of the Imperial Japanese Army had instigated the machine-gun attack on the *Panay*.[171] Hashimoto was a right-wing firebrand, an anti-Western nationalist, and a participant in various extremist coup attempts against the Japanese government. Hallett Abend, the China correspondent who wrote the piece, would later expand upon this initial charge, claiming that Hashimoto had deliberately misled navy fliers into staging an air strike on the *Panay*. No proof has ever surfaced of either charge. Masatake Okumiya, the only naval squadron leader involved in the attack to survive World War II, pointedly rebutted the claim in a *US Naval Institute Proceedings* interview in the 1950s.[172] The Japanese claimed at the time that the shelling of HMS *Ladybird* and *Bee*, aerial attacks on HMS *Cricket* and *Scarab*, and the sinking of the *Panay* were all unfortunate blunders.

Secretary of State Hull captured the administration's assessment crisply in the memoir he published ten years after the event. Drawing upon memoranda, conversations, and his recollections, Hull characterized Japanese claims that the incident was entirely accidental as "the lamest of lame excuses." He explained,

> That some members of the Foreign Office had no hand in it may be true. Hirota himself professed to be genuinely disturbed and sincerely regretful. That the Japanese people did not like it also seemed to be true, to judge from the thousands who expressed their sympathy to the Embassy and offered contributions for the families of the victims and for the survivors. But that the Japanese military leaders, at least in China, were connected with it, there can be little or no doubt. In any case, it was their business to keep their subordinates under control.

On this side our people generally took the incident calmly. There were a few demands that the Fleet should be sent at once to the Orient. There were many more demands that we should withdraw completely from China. . . . It was a serious incident; but, unless we could have proven the complicity of the Japanese Government itself, it was not an occasion for war."[173]

AFTERMATH, CONSEQUENCES, AND REFLECTIONS ON THE *PANAY* INCIDENT

The American press and public generally viewed Roosevelt's handling of the *Panay* crisis favorably. He had been firm, but not provocative. He had presented the Japanese government with clear requirements, but had not threatened to break relations or blustered about war. His examination of coercive measures, both naval and economic, had been conducted behind the scenes, with the administration reassuring the public that it had no intention of defending British interests in the Far East. It seemed that Roosevelt had achieved all that Wilson had in the aftermath of the *Lusitania* incident, but without the threats, ultimatums, and biased neutrality that set into motion the slide toward American intervention in World War I. While the *Panay* settlement felt unsatisfactory to some of Roosevelt's advisers, to most Americans it seemed a wise middle course between imprudent threats of punishment and submissive disengagement from the region. The former seemed provocative and lacked popular support; the latter appeared spineless and sent the wrong message.

Parts of the settlement were straightforward. The Japanese government's apology left something to be desired, in that it insisted the incident had been entirely accidental, yet it expressed deep regret; and by expressing its willingness to pay damages, it implicitly owned up to its responsibility for the incident. On March 22, the American ambassador in Tokyo informed the Japanese government that damages related to property losses associated with the *Panay* and the Standard Oil tankers totaled $1,945,670.01. Indemnities connected to the deaths and personal injuries amounted to an additional $267,337.35.[174] The Japanese government, while requesting an itemized breakdown of the claim, did not quibble about the claim. Moving at a deliberate pace, on April 22 it delivered a check for the full amount requested.

Other parts of the settlement promised to be more complicated. The Japanese navy removed Vice Admiral Teizo Mitsunami from command of the Second Combined Naval Air Group and issued letters of reprimand to the naval lieutenants in command of the four squadrons of aircraft that participated in the attack. The letters of reprimand, in a departure from the usual practice, were issued and signed directly by the minister of the navy. The Japanese army, however, did little to discipline its forces. On January 17, the American government again felt compelled to bring to the attention of the Japanese government repeated incidents in which Japanese forces had entered American facilities, removed goods, and committed other "acts of depredation." In almost every case, the property had been marked by American flags, which Japanese soldiers not only ignored but in numerous incidents tore down, burned, and otherwise mutilated.[175] On January 21, the president told his cabinet that he had received reports of Japanese atrocities that were so terrible in their detail that he could not read them aloud. Japanese soldiers had been breaking into American missions and businesses, carrying off Chinese female employees, and "raping Chinese women without limit."[176] Three days later, John Allison, third secretary of the U.S. Embassy, was slapped in the face by Japanese soldiers while investigating the rape of a Chinese female employee of the American University in Nanking. Allison reported that when gendarmes tried to intervene, the Japanese soldier assaulting him and his colleague became "livid with rage," ranting against Americans. The Japanese commanding officer, arriving at the scene, joined in shouting at the Americans in an "offensive manner." The Japanese foreign ministry was in the midst of assuring the American government that orders had been given to its forces in China to show the utmost care and caution regarding American persons and properties. Reports from China suggested that the Japanese army either was ignoring these instructions or could not enforce discipline among its ranks.

Ambassador Grew warned the Japanese foreign ministry that "facts mean more than statements."[177] The facts in China suggested that even as the Japanese foreign ministry was in the midst of settling the *Panay* crisis, soldiers and officers of the Japanese Imperial Army were running roughshod over American and British rights while subjecting Chinese civilians to rape and mass executions. On February 9, 1938, Admiral Harry Yarnell, commanding the U.S. Asiatic Fleet, invited the American director of the International Committee for the Nanking Safety Zone, George Ashmore Fitch, to lunch on his flagship. Yarnell recorded in his diary how Fitch had informed him that reports about massacres in Nanking had not been exaggerated but, rather, understated. There had been:

> Slaughter of men, ex-soldiers and others, by the thousands. Innumerable cases of rape, and in many cases, murder and mutilation of women afterwards. Wholesale looting indulged in by the officers and men alike. Little control exercised over the men by the officers. Men were rounded up and machine-gunned in droves, then gasoline poured over dead & wounded

& set on fire. Other prisoners used for bayonet practice. Mr Fitch said that he never dreamed that any so-called civilized race of people could show the inhumanity and sadism shown by the Jap. Troops in Nanking.[178]

The *Panay* incident itself may not have been ordered from on high, but the behavior of the Japanese military in China confirmed Roosevelt's assessment that Japan was on a rampage. The Japanese army meant to reduce Western influence in China, utilizing intimidation, brutality, and force as necessary. It was employing terror as a tool to demoralize the Chinese, and was intent on becoming the dominant actor in mainland China.

Roosevelt faced a two-way struggle in responding to the broad challenge posed by Japanese militarists, Italian fascists, and Hitler's Germany. Before he could move internationally, FDR had to turn the tide of isolationism within the United States. The *Panay* incident can be seen as a high point of isolationism. A better assessment, however, is that the *Panay* incident represented the culminating point of isolationism. The president used the episode to begin to claw back presidential power and prerogatives. Isolationism remained powerful, and had it not been for France's sudden and unexpected defeat in June 1940, and Britain's tenacity in the Battle of Britain, it was by no means a foregone conclusion that isolationist sentiment would have yielded to the president's desire to help a beleaguered Great Britain in 1941. In three areas, the administration seized the initiative in January 1938 and laid the groundwork for Roosevelt's later policies.

The administration's first signal accomplishment in the shadow of the *Panay*'s sinking was to defeat the Ludlow Amendment. Ludlow's supporters had hoped to use the fear of war and entanglement in the Far East to secure passage of the amendment when it came up for a vote in the House in January. Shortly before Christmas, they organized a National Committee for the War Referendum. The National Committee, supported by the same groups that had successfully pushed through the Neutrality Act of 1937, organized speeches, rallies, and letter-writing campaigns in support of the amendment. Americans were reminded that war was a dire business, and they were told that they ought to have the right to vote on a declaration of war directly, rather than counting on Congress to reflect the popular will.

House and Senate isolationists such as Herbert Bigelow of Ohio and Robert La Follette of Wisconsin spoke out in support of the amendment. Bigelow warned that "When the Government by act of a President and the votes of 267 men in Congress, puts you on transports and ships you to foreign lands, to fight and die on foreign soil and shoots you if you protest, there is just one name to give to that—it is mass slavery."[179] The chairman of the National Committee for the War Referendum, retired Army Major General William Rivers, wrote to the *New York Times* on December 15 that the *Panay* case and that of the battleship *Maine* were excellent illustrations of why the Ludlow Amendment was necessary. The press, he explained, had nurtured the idea that the Spaniards had blown up the *Maine* when able officers in the navy had privately speculated that the explosion was internal. Having served in the West during "Indian troubles," in Santiago during the Spanish-American War, in the Philippines during the insurrection, and in France during WWI, Rivers recalled that concentrated propaganda could be directed at the five hundred men who made up the two houses of Congress. He claimed that convincing the American population as a whole of the merits of war would be more difficult, and he concluded that "War is too vital a matter to be left entirely to the old methods. . . . New methods should be tried in the important efforts to minimize wars."[180]

Yet if arguments like this had swept all before them as Congress adopted the Neutrality Acts of 1935, 1936, and 1937, fissures began to appear within the isolationist ranks as supporters and opponents of the Ludlow Amendment made their case. Robert McCormick's isolationist *Chicago Daily Tribune* supported the president's handling of the *Panay* crisis, explaining that the United States had not caused the crisis and arguing that pacifism was no answer. Senator Arthur Vandenberg, an ardent isolationist, conceded that requiring a referendum on war would be as sensible as requiring "a town meeting before permitting the fire department to put out a blaze."[181] William Allen White, whose small but influential *Emporia Gazette* claimed to speak for the common man, distanced himself from the proposal. White had been an early supporter of Ludlow's amendment, but became convinced during the course of December that the president's firm response to Japan would have been undermined if the amendment had been in effect. On the eve of the vote, White editorialized against it, arguing that "We should support the President while he is facing the gangster of Japan. But when the crisis passes—that will be another day."[182]

The president's measured handling of the *Panay* crisis garnered support from other directions as well. Internationalist-leaning papers such as the *New York Times, Washington Post*, and *Christian Science Monitor* pointed out that the Ludlow Amendment would endanger American security. Journalists such as Arthur Krock and Walter Lippmann, who would rally support for Britain during the early days of World War II, argued firmly against the resolution. They explained to the public that an amendment requiring not only a congressional declaration of war but also a public referendum on war would undermine American foreign policy. It would send signals all over the world that militarists could do as they pleased.

The *New Republic*, a liberal and progressive journal, laid out the arguments for and against the Ludlow Amendment for its readers in its December 29, 1937, edition. Proponents of the measure, the *New Republic* noted, claimed that the United States had made a mistake in participating in the First World War, and that the miseries and costs of modern war are so great that there was no good reason for fighting save in the defense of the country from invasion. Opponents, on the other hand, argued that the government needed the ability to make threats if the United States aimed to play a major world role. Without resorting to international relations theory and jargon, the *New Republic* painted the opponents of the Ludlow Amendment as realists who believed that "Force is the ultimate basis of power." The *New Republic* conceded that both arguments had merit.

> No interest in trade or finance, no moral conceptions, no sympathy for other people can possibly involve issues so important as to outweigh the certain losses of war. Most wars do not win what they are fought for . . . and it is certainly true that people can be precipitated by governments into wars that those people do not want. On the other hand, power politics of the traditional kind is much hampered if the fear of force is removed from the diplomatic background. . . . If we are going to get angry enough to fight because of injuries to our ships or trade or citizens abroad, then it is more prudent to try to prevent those injuries by making ourselves feared and respected before the injuries become too serious.[183]

Having laid out both positions, the editors endorsed the Ludlow Amendment, advocating that the United States should adopt an attitude "which is exemplified not by a great military or naval power, but by Holland, or Denmark, or Norway."

The administration strongly opposed the Ludlow Amendment; the president wrote the Speaker of the House on January 6 advising Congress that, if adopted, the amendment would "cripple any President in his conduct of our foreign relations, and it would encourage other nations to believe that they could violate American rights with impunity.[184] In making the case against the Ludlow Amendment, the administration was able to draw on support from across the political aisle. A number of mainstream Republicans were becoming alarmed by the radical isolationism and populism of La Follette and other Republican progressives. Henry L. Stimson, who had served as secretary of war under President Taft and secretary of state under Hoover, denounced the concept as an untried, fantastic panacea.[185] Alfred M. Landon, the 1936 Republican candidate for the presidency, sent a telegram to Roosevelt supporting FDR's position.

When the House voted on the matter on January 10, fifty-five representatives who had signed the discharge petition decided, upon reflection, against voting for the amendment itself. The final vote of 209 against and 188 in favor of the amendment was a significant setback to the isolationist cause, with Roosevelt's adept handling of the *Panay* crisis contributing to the amendment's defeat. Yet Roosevelt had little cause for celebration: fully half of the representatives from states in the Midwest, the Plains, the Rockies, and the West voted for the amendment.[186] Roosevelt may have checked the rising tide of isolationism, but he would have a bitter struggle before he rolled back its signature achievement, the Neutrality Act of 1937.

Even as he was beating back the Ludlow Amendment, Roosevelt continued to explore the option of joint Anglo-American naval and economic measures. This second initiative, unlike the administration's very public offensive against the Ludlow Amendment, was secretive, with the administration doing what it could to explore its options without attracting unwanted congressional scrutiny and public debate. As noted earlier, FDR had decided to send Captain Ingersoll, director of the navy's War Plans division, to London in the midst of the *Panay* crisis. FDR did not abort the Ingersoll mission after he had settled the incident with Japan but, rather, instructed Ingersoll to explore three topics while in London. First, Ingersoll was to conduct talks of a technical nature on the qualitative restrictions to which Britain and the United States had bound themselves in 1936. The *Giornale d'Italia* had published an article in December indicating that Japan was building three super-battleships of 45,000 tons and mounting sixteen-inch guns. Since the British and Americans had agreed to limit the size of their battleships to 35,000 tons, with guns no larger than fourteen inches, joint discussions concerning self-imposed qualitative restrictions were necessary. In addition, these "technical discussions" provided good cover for Ingersoll's second, more sensitive assignment. In London, Ingersoll was to exchange information and coordinate naval plans in the event of war with Japan. Ingersoll's third assignment was rather odd for a navy man. He was to follow up on Morgenthau's earlier conversation with the Chancellor of the Exchequer, and see whether the British would cooperate with the Treasury Department's idea of freezing Japanese credit. Morgenthau, after his disappointing telephone conversation with Sir John Simon, told Ingersoll to put on the British the burden of discussing the concept in more depth. The Exchequer made no effort to contact Ingersoll.[187]

The main purpose of the Ingersoll mission was not to discuss the merits of fourteen-inch versus sixteen-inch naval gunnery but, rather, to follow up on the exchange between Roosevelt and Ambassador Lindsay regarding joint coercive naval measures. Ingersoll was not empowered to enter into any sort of formal agreement, but was directed to "obtain naval information on which to plan and to base decisions, if necessary, for future action."[188] Meeting with Foreign Minister Eden, Under Secretary for Foreign Affairs Alexander Cadogan, and the U.S. chargé d'affairés, Herschel Johnson, on January 1, Ingersoll was asked whether his mission related to near-term naval action or long-term planning. Ingersoll evaded the question, noting that both required an exchange of information. His subsequent meetings with First Sea Lord Sir Ernle Chatfield, Deputy Chief of Naval Staff Vice Admiral William James, and the director of the Admiralty's Plan Division, Captain Thomas Phillips, went far beyond what the administration publicly admitted. Ingersoll and Phillips explored the president's idea of a distant blockade in operational terms, discovering that the blockade line would have to run from Indonesia and Australia to Fiji and on to the Hawaiian Islands. Both officers assessed the effectiveness of a distant blockade as low, given the great distances involved.[189] Turning to more practical matters, they agreed to make arrangements to exchange code books, radio call letters, and ciphers in the event that both countries became involved in a war against Japan. More broadly, the two sides briefed each other on the composition, state of readiness, and initial movements of their fleet in the Indo-Pacific region. Ingersoll advised the British that the U.S. Navy envisioned sending an advance force of cruisers, destroyers, and submarines to Hawaii immediately after the president declared a National Emergency, with the main force of nine battleships ready to sail within ten to fifteen days. The British indicated that they envisioned sending most of their fleet to the Far East within ten to fourteen days after mobilization.[190]

While Ingersoll was in London in January, the Foreign Office received news that Japanese soldiers had beaten four British police officers who were performing their duties inside Shanghai's International Settlement. The British were furious, as the Japanese government had issued apologies and assurances to Great Britain similar to those it had given the United States. The British informed Washington that it was considering putting its fleet on a war footing, and inquired whether the United States would be willing to join Britain in some sort of strong, tangible demonstration of force.[191] The British asked for clarification as to what specific actions the Americans were willing to take. Prime Minister Chamberlain wrote to his sister,

> I am trying to jolly them along with a view to making some sort of joint (or at least "parallel") naval action. They are incredibly slow and have missed innumerable buses. . . . I do wish the Japs would beat up an American or two! But of course the little d-v-ls [*sic*—devils] are too cunning for that, and we may eventually have to act alone and hope the yanks will follow before it's too late.[192]

The president's response was cautious yet mildly encouraging. He was unwilling to engage in any open, joint displays of force directed against Japan, but he was willing to send three American cruisers to Singapore; announce that the vessels of the Pacific Fleet would have their hulls scraped so as to be ready for sea; and move up the date for the annual Pacific Fleet maneuvers.[193]

The Admiralty had advised the prime minister and foreign secretary that sending the fleet to the Far East would only be possible by weakening the British Mediterranean Fleet. After carefully considering what the Americans were willing to offer, the Chamberlain government decided against escalation. The British realized that threatening Japan with imminent naval mobilization would be an escalatory step that might embarrass the British government if it then failed to follow through. As Britain's under-secretary for foreign affairs informed the prime minister,

> it certainly has to be remembered that if the fleet were to sail in three or four weeks, that might be just at the time when we are trying to come to terms with Mussolini, who might choose to think that he was in a stronger position for dealing with us if the fleet were removed from home waters and the Mediterranean. . . . There arises the question whether the present incidents are of sufficient gravity to justify starting along this road.[194]

Given the geopolitical realities of the time, the British government decided to send a stern warning to the Japanese government. The British were under no illusion that their protest note would carry much weight in Tokyo, but given the strategic dilemma they faced, they decided to play for time in the hope that Chamberlain's appeasement policy would ease the situation in Europe.

Once news of Roosevelt's modest initiatives in the area of joint planning and possible joint displays of force leaked to the press, the administration backed away from them. It denied that either Ingersoll's visit or the Singapore port call had anything to do with Japan. In response to questions from the press whether Captain Ingersoll had been sent to London to initiate naval staff talks related to the Far East, high-level American diplomats responded off the record that the administration was "not that crazy," given the mood on Capitol Hill.[195] Likewise, when questioned by a Republican congressman whether the administration was trying to send signals to Japan by directing the cruisers *Memphis*, *Milwaukee*, and *Trenton* to visit Singapore, Leahy replied, "It is a friendly visit of our cruisers to a friendly port. They are on a courtesy mission, nothing more. Singapore is not much out of the way since the cruisers are to return home [from a visit to Australia] via Manila."[196]

When Senator Hiram Warren Johnson of California submitted a resolution on January 5 asking specifically whether or not any alliance, agreement, or understanding existed or was contemplated with Great Britain relating to war or the possibility of war; whether or not there was any understanding or agreement, express or implied, for the use of the navy of the United States in conjunction with any other nation; and whether or not there was any understanding or agreement, express or implied, with any nation, that the U.S. Navy, or any part of it, should police or patrol or be transferred to any particular waters or any particular ocean, Secretary of State Hull responded with an emphatic no, no, and no.[197] The answer, if not quite a lie, was certainly not the whole truth.[198]

Admirals Leahy and Yarnell had recommended joint action to the president, special adviser Norman Davis had advocated the same, and FDR's naval emissary had just returned from London where he had discussed potential naval cooperation—in particular, the idea of a distant blockade of Japan—in some detail with top officials in the Admiralty. These talks had been of an exploratory and informational nature, but FDR was clearly exploring his options. Once Congress and the press caught wind of the Ingersoll mission and the planned courtesy port calls to Singapore, FDR backed away from using what his distant cousin Teddy had called "the big stick" that supported America's diplomacy.[199]

The defeat of the Ludlow Amendment retarded the tide of isolationism, and the Ingersoll mission laid the groundwork for future Anglo-American naval cooperation. But FDR's most important initiative in reaction to the sinking of the *Panay* crisis was his request for a 20 percent expansion of the U.S. Navy in January 1938. Throughout the fall of 1937, FDR had privately remarked that he believed the U.S. Navy needed to be strengthened. He was convinced that Japan would continue to trample Western interests in China. More broadly, as he had indicated in his "Quarantine Speech," he believed that regimes greedy for power and supremacy were endangering the global order. The United States could not simply ignore the breakdown of stability, as the modern world was interconnected. The *Panay* incident strengthened this conviction.

In late December, FDR contacted the chairman of the House Appropriations Committee about expanding naval construction, indicating at a press conference on December 29 that he intended to ask Congress to increase the size of the navy. After meeting with Admiral Leahy and the chairman of the House Naval Affairs Committee, Carl Vinson, in early January 1937, the president decided that the fleet needed to be increased. On January 28, Roosevelt sent a special message to Congress pushing for a substantial increase in naval power.

FDR understood that he would have to fight to strengthen the navy. One of the signal accomplishments of the Republican administrations that succeeded Woodrow Wilson had been to negotiate naval limitation treaties that had saved the American taxpayers untold millions. By the early 1930s, the fiscal incentive for restraining naval expenditures had been supplemented by the argument that arms expenditures cause war, and therefore were morally suspect. Books like Engelbrecht and Hanigen's *Merchants of Death* and congressional investigations such as the Nye Committee had portrayed the armaments and shipbuilding in the worst light, undermining efforts to increase military spending. FDR's request for a 20 percent expansion of the fleet, coming days after Congress approved a navy budget of $547 million for 1938–39, was sure to run into a stiff headwind in Congress. In justifying his request, Roosevelt named no specific countries that endangered the United States, but simply noted that it was his constitutional duty to report that U.S. national defenses were "inadequate for purposes of national security" in light of the increasing armaments of other nations. Furthermore, he warned that Americans could not assume they would only be challenged in one ocean. Adequate defense meant that the United States needed the ability to keep any potential enemy hundreds of miles away from America's continental limits.

The president's request immediately set off a storm of public debate, forcing Americans to debate what sort of navy they required and what its duties entailed.[200] Many midwestern editors and letter writers doubted the necessity for a larger navy, with numerous commentators suggesting that Roosevelt was exploiting the nation's anger about the *Panay* in order to resurrect the internationalist agenda that lurked behind his Quarantine Speech. The *Minneapolis Tribune* editorialized that Roosevelt's arms program was "more a move in the international chess game of a war-minded diplomacy than it is an effort at meeting an open threat against national security." The *Butte Standard* proclaimed that it was "not necessary, sound, or logical for us to match ship for ship, gun for gun, and man for man with the mad-dog governments of the world." Tying the president's request to the *Panay* incident, the *New Republic* charged that the administration was asking for a larger navy "so that a vast American armada can steam across the Pacific and blow up the Japanese island" if another such incident loomed.[201]

Yet if many heartland papers stuck to the narrative put forth by Engelbrecht and Hanighen, Nye, and various peace organizations, most papers located near the nation's two seaboards supported the idea of strengthening the navy. The *New York Times*, the *Boston Globe*, the *Philadelphia Inquirer*, and the *Los Angeles Times* all supported the president's request, as did a number of important midwestern America papers, including the *Cleveland Plain Dealer*, the *Indianapolis Star*, the *Chicago Tribune*, and the *Chicago Daily News*. The *San Francisco Chronicle* put it as follows: "We are neither imperialistic nor militaristic, but we must be prudent. We cannot by weakness invite attack."[202]

The president could request an increase in the size of the navy, but Congress held the power of the purse. Over the course of the first four months, Congress conducted various hearings and debated whether the president's request was justified. Senator Vandenberg of Michigan wondered why the nation suddenly needed a larger navy, and bristled at the suggestion that the navy was an instrument of diplomacy. Representative Henry Carl Luckey of Nebraska denounced building up the navy beyond its currently authorized strength, arguing that doing so would propel the United States into the power politics of East Asia and Europe. He doubted that Japan had any intention of attacking the United States. Senator Borah of Idaho made the same point in the upper chamber, declaring that "I do not think the danger is any greater today. I do not think Japan wants war with the United States and I do not think she is so situated that she could make war if she wanted to do so." Borah believed that Japan's involvement in China made it less likely that Japan would start another war, commenting that "Japan will have no time in which to send a single battleship out of her waters for the next 50 years, with 400,000,000 people in China and 170,000,000 Russians in her front yard. Need we anticipate any immediate trouble from that source?"[203]

Congressional opponents of increased naval spending could draw upon respected experts to support their position. Thomas Healy, dean of Georgetown's School of Foreign Service, testified that American interests in the Far East were insufficient to justify the cost of expanding the navy. Healy told senators soliciting his learned opinion that "I see no substantial reason why the United States should become involved in the Far East as long as we mind our own business and do not go out of our way to start a war about matters which are of little concern to us."[204] Brigadier General Stanley Dunbar Embick, who served as the commander of the Manila harbor defenses in 1933 and then as director of the army's War Plans Division in 1936, was likewise convinced that the United States should reduce its liabilities in the Far East, and had earlier commented that building a formidable navy capable of regaining "worthless possessions" on the other side of the Pacific would be a waste of resources.[205]

The naval expansion plan was bitterly attacked by representatives and senators who feared that a strengthened navy might tempt the president to supplement diplomacy with the threat of force. The administration's supporters went out of their way to refute this suspicion, and a number of isolationists broke ranks to support the bill. Progressive Republican George Norris of Nebraska conceded that the administration was right to be concerned about Japanese naval expansion—in particular, reports that it was building super-battleships with larger-caliber guns than any battleship in the U.S. Navy. He could not understand why Japan needed such ships except for aggression, and believed that it was only prudent for the United States to be ready for such a contingency. Louis Ludlow, author of the earlier-mentioned war referendum amendment proposal, found no contradiction in pushing for his amendment while strengthening the nation's defenses. He claimed that voting for naval expansion would "cause warring nations to think twice before attacking us."[206] Representative Carl Vinson of Georgia, who together with Senator Park Trammel of Florida crafted the language of the bill and shepherded it through Congress, was masterful in dispelling the concerns of his colleagues. The administration was not asking for a stronger navy so that it could engage in a more activist, coercive foreign policy. Instead, the administration needed a stronger navy to defend the United States. Vinson reassured his colleagues and the public, "We have no desire to police the world. We are not building the Navy to get entangled in any alien quarrels. This bill is not here for the purpose of building a navy to make China and Japan or any other nation safe for democracy. It is here for the purpose of insuring peace for America."[207]

After months of debate and testimony, the House and Senate voted on the Naval Expansion Act of 1938 in April and May. The margins by which the bill was approved—294 to 100 in the House and 56 to 28 in the Senate—signaled the abandonment of the thesis that weapons and ships made war more likely. Japan's aggression in China, the ongoing Spanish Civil War, Italy's attack on Ethiopia, and most recently Germany's annexation of Austria in March 1938 all suggested that the world was becoming a more dangerous place. Isolationists hoped that strength might keep America out of war. Internationalists anticipated that naval power would give the United States the confidence to support friendly nations that were the targets of aggression.

President Roosevelt might have responded more forcefully to the sinking of the *Panay* had public opinion, the media, and Congress either urged for intervention, as they generally did 1898, or ceded the president considerable freedom of action, as they did in 1915 despite the best efforts of "hyphenated Americans." Yet in 1937–38, both the public and Congress were determined to impose boundaries on the executive branch when it came to responding to international crises and naval incidents. FDR played his hand as best he could. He settled the matter on terms most Americans found firm but not reckless. He stopped the forward momentum of isolationism and defeated the Ludlow Amendment. He secretly explored the possibility of joint naval and economic coercion of Japan, though off the record and only in the form of nonbinding discussions. Most important, he began to strengthen the nation's defenses, doing so in a manner that garnered support from many isolationists who had previously been generally hostile to military expenditures. While FDR was entirely oblivious of Sunzi's ancient *The Art of War*, he in effect was attempting to transform the configuration of power both domestically and internationally.

If this attempt was marginally successful domestically, it was less so internationally. As FDR anticipated, the *Panay* settlement did nothing to resolve continuing differences about Japanese policies toward China, nor diminish the pattern of Japanese attacks against American citizens, property, and facilities in China. Before a month had elapsed, Japanese soldiers were slapping an American diplomat and trampling American flags in China. In early June, a drunken Japanese soldier killed Dr. Frederick Scovel, a Presbyterian missionary in Tsining. In July, Japanese officials prevented the U.S. Yangtze Patrol gunboat *Monocacy* from refueling and attempted to restrict its movements. Admiral Leahy once again recommended a firm response: "It is my opinion that this action by Japan is for the deliberate purpose of injuring the prestige of America in the Orient, and that it has no other action. . . . Some strong stand by this government is, in my opinion, necessary to preserve what little prestige America now has in the Orient."[208]

Yet FDR understood that he could not take a strong stand. Instead, he ordered the Fifteenth Infantry Regiment and the Sixth Marines home from China. The U.S. ambassador to Japan, Joseph Grew, reflected on his fruitless efforts to convince the Japanese government to respect U.S. interest in China. Noting eight months after the *Panay* sinking that the Japanese continued to give assurances "in plenty," he concluded that they would not alter their behavior in China unless the United States was willing to "do something about it."[209] Yet Roosevelt perceived correctly that in 1938 the American people were not willing to "do something" about Japanese aggression in distant China. He could build up the navy, he could warn of gathering storm clouds, and he could start thinking about the options he might employ in the future when and if the tide of public and congressional opinion turned. But unlike Presidents McKinley and Wilson, he could not start a war or threaten to break diplomatic relations with another country over a naval incident that most Americans believed did not affect the nation's vital interests.

The *Panay* incident stands separate and distinct from the naval incidents of 1941, which reflected Roosevelt's effort to incrementally steer a reluctant American public and Congress from strict neutrality to non-combatant belligerency in the widening conflict that became the Second World War. The sinking of the U.S. merchant ship *Robin Moore* in May 1941, the attacks on the USS *Greer* and USS *Kearny* in September and October, and the sinking of the USS *Reuben James* on October 31 were all part of an "undeclared war" that Roosevelt waged in the Atlantic against Nazi Germany with the aim of sustaining Great Britain against the Third Reich after the fall of France.[210] While Roosevelt had alluded to the rising danger posed by Japan, Italy, and Germany in his "Quarantine Speech" in October 1937, most Americans did not yet perceive the connections between Japanese aggression in China, Mussolini's dream of transforming the Mediterranean into a Mare Nostrum, and Hitler's threats against Austria, Czechoslovakia, and Poland. They had confidence that the British and French empires were more powerful than these revisionist powers, and they noted that the Soviet Union was more directly challenged by the Anti-Comintern Pact than was the United States. To draw direct connections between Roosevelt's important but modest initiatives in the spring of 1938—the defeat of the Ludlow

Amendment, his discreet exploration of joint naval and economic measures, and his request to strengthen the U.S. Navy—and his much bolder initiatives in 1940 and 1941 overstates the significance of the *Panay* incident. By then, Europe was at war and the geo-strategic situation was quite different. But to point out the indirect links and second-order connections between the *Panay* incident and American neutrality in World War II is reasonable. The *Panay* incident clearly highlights the interconnections that bedeviled the president later. The incident underlines the connectivity between the domestic and the foreign spheres; between the Far East, the Mediterranean, and European theaters; and between the diplomatic, military, and economic realms.

Domestic realities clearly imposed constraints on the president's freedom of action internationally. Revisionist interpretations of the First World War, disillusionment over the inequities of burden sharing during the war, peace activism, and the Nye Committee investigation all generated pressure for legal restrictions intended to prevent another incremental slide toward intervention. The Neutrality Acts of 1935 and 1936 addressed these concerns, with the Neutrality Act of 1937 rendering the various restrictions of the earlier acts permanent. Roosevelt's defeat of the Ludlow Amendment in January 1938 stopped the forward momentum of isolationism, but to borrow Churchill's rhetoric, this small victory should not be interpreted as the end of isolationism, nor even the beginning of the end of isolationism.[211] It was merely the end of isolationism's expansion. Likewise, Congress's endorsement of FDR's request for a larger navy did not signal any support for an activist, interventionist foreign policy. But it did signal a turn away from the idea that peace is best served by disarmament, and that military appropriations increase the likelihood of war.

Roosevelt had been able to evade invoking the Neutrality Act of 1937 in the Far East because Japan and China had not formally declared war against each other. Yet Roosevelt had no choice but to invoke the Neutrality Act when war broke out in Europe in September 1939, as the belligerents had formally declared war against one another. His sympathies were entirely with the Allies, but the Neutrality Act of 1937 made it illegal to export arms, ammunition, or implements of war to belligerents. Arguing that this arms embargo served only aggressor nations that had been building up their militaries for years, rather than the victims of aggression who desperately required military equipment to defend themselves, FDR argued that the Neutrality Act should be amended to allow belligerents to purchase military goods on a strictly "cash and carry" basis. This amendment would allow Britain and France to purchase vital military supplies, but it retained firewalls to prevent American banks, businesses, and shipping companies from making loans, providing credits, or transporting war materials for them.[212] FDR's request to amend the Neutrality Act created a furious uproar, with many of the same senators and congressmen who had called for a with-drawal from China in 1937–38 now rallying against amending the law. Roosevelt encouraged pro-Allied editors and intellectuals to speak out. William Allen White and Clark Eichelberger then organized the Non-Partisan Committee for Peace through Revision of the Neutrality Act to generate support. Roosevelt secured a revision of the Neutrality Act in October 1939; the Senate approved the amended bill by a margin of 63 to 30 and the House by 243 to 181.

White and Eichelberger's Non-Partisan Committee for Peace through Revision of the Neutrality Act re-emerged as the Committee to Defend America by Aiding the Allies (CDAAA) in May 1940, arguing that the president should move beyond the "cash and carry" provision to aid the Allies more directly. Roosevelt remained cautious, however, throughout the spring, given the domestic strength of isolationism. The rapid fall of France in the summer of 1940 changed his calculus, in that German control of the French and Norwegian coasts changed the geo-strategic situation much to the disadvantage of Great Britain. Roosevelt's subsequent steps, from the Two Ocean Navy Expansion Act of July 1940 to the Destroyer for Bases deal in September, to the reintroduction of conscription, sought to build up American strength, help Great Britain to the extent possible, and keep the United States out of the war.

These measures galvanized isolationists to form their own grassroots campaign, and Yale Law School student R. Douglas Stuart Jr. launched the America First Committee in September 1940. Claiming more than 800,000 members at its height, the American First Committee railed against intervention, vigorously objected to renewed Anglo-American naval talks, and opposed the president's Lend-Lease proposal in 1941. Charles Lindbergh Jr., who had been awarded the Medal of Honor by a special act of Congress in December 1927 for his bravery in completing the first nonstop transatlantic flight, became a spokesman for the isolationist agenda of the American First Committee. He spoke to overflowing crowds at Madison Square Garden and Chicago's Soldier Field, vigorously attacking Roosevelt's support for Great Britain.

Roosevelt's foreign policy remained constrained by public and congressional opinion throughout 1940–41. Claims that he misled the public about his intentions have a grain of truth to them, though one senses that the American people endorsed his efforts to support Great Britain to the extent possible short of war. Roosevelt carefully looked over his shoulder to see whether the public and Congress supported him, and opinion polls in the fall of 1941 indicate that they did.[213] FDR's gradual, step-by-step intervention in the ongoing Battle of the Atlantic, from the stationing of U.S. forces in Newfoundland, Bermuda, and Trinidad to ordering U.S. Navy ships to escort merchant shipping within the Neutrality Zone, to ordering U.S. ships to "shoot at sight" German submarines following the *Greer* incident, was made possible only by a sustained campaign against congressional isolationists and America Firsters. This domestic struggle over the direction of foreign possible was bitter, divisive, and sustained, but by mid-1941 the president had chipped away at many of the restrictions that limited his freedom of action. In November 1941, Congress repealed the remaining provisions of the Neutrality Act. By then, Hitler's troops were on the outskirts of Moscow; the mass murder of Jews, gypsies, and Polish intellectuals was in high gear; and the situation in the Far East had deteriorated dramatically.[214]

The *Panay* crisis highlights the interconnections between the domestic and foreign spheres, foreshadowing FDR's struggle against congressional isolationists and the America First movement in 1940 and 1941. In addition, it demonstrated the global dynamics that would become apparent during the same period. Great Britain was especially troubled by the prospect that regional crises that might be dealt with individually—such as Japan's occupation of Manchuria, Italy's attack on Ethiopia, and Germany's remilitarization of the Rhineland—might coalesce into an insoluble global challenge. This is evident in Britain's efforts in the fall of 1937 and in January 1938 to convince the United States to assume the burden of deterring Japan. The American public, and much of the administration, believed that Britain was trying to maneuver the United States into pulling its chestnuts out of the Far Eastern fire, pointing out that Britain had more at stake in China than did the United States. This was undoubtedly true. But the fact of the matter was that Britain could face down the Japanese in the Far East only by weakening its Mediterranean fleet. The British government was not prepared to weaken its position in Europe for the sake of its position in the Far East. Most of the American public believed that the United States had no vital interests in the Far East and resented suggestions that the United States should take the lead in deterring Japan. But as they would discover, fires have a way of spreading. The strategic problems of the Far East were connected with those of the Mediterranean, and those of the Atlantic with those of the Pacific. The *Panay* crisis provided an early warning of the global dynamics of the coming war. While most Americans still believed in insulating the United States from troubles overseas in 1938, by 1941 there was a growing recognition that Roosevelt had not been wrong in warning that the triumph of Axis powers would pose a threat to the Western Hemisphere in the long term.[215]

Lastly, the *Panay* crisis provides insight into FDR's thinking about war and the use of force. In grappling with the crisis, Roosevelt remarked on numerous occasions that he was trying to devise an American response to Italian, German, and Japanese methods of fighting undeclared wars. He believed that the United States and Britain should be able to use their geographic positions and economic power to deter aggression without the direct application of force. The distant blockade he outlined to the cabinet in December 1937 rested on four geographic anchorpoints (Hawaii, Guam, Australia, and Singapore), with destroyer and cruiser forces enforcing the blockade in the confident conviction that Japan would back down within a year. FDR likewise overestimated the effectiveness of financial and economic pressure in deterring and dissuading adversaries. Already in 1938, he had contemplated freezing Japanese assets to compel Japan to apologize and pay damages for the destruction of the *Panay*. The British had warned that blockades and economic sanctions were indistinguishable from war. Roosevelt would have been well advised to remember this when he ratcheted up the economic pressure on Japan in 1940 and 1941. But he was not alone in believing that Japan was extremely vulnerable to financial and economic pressure. The leading economic and financial advisers in the Treasury Department, the Commerce Department, and on Wall Street projected that Japan would run out of funds to sustain its aggression in the near future.[216]

Some have interpreted Roosevelt's use of sanctions and embargoes in 1941 as a devious plot on the part of the president to create a backdoor path to intervention in the Second World War, forcing Japan to choose between backing down or attacking the United States, with full knowledge that the Japanese would choose the latter. Yet the evidence points in the opposite direction. The president protested Japanese aggression in China for four years, and was well informed by the interception of Japanese diplomatic traffic that Japan was eager to exploit the opportunities Hitler's defeat of France and his occupation of the Netherlands had opened up. Roosevelt hoped to deter Japan from further aggression after its occupation of French Indo-China, but if that was impossible, he was resolved that American steel and petroleum would not fuel the Japanese war machine.[217] FDR hoped to use a combination of economic, naval, and airpower in the Pacific to deter Japan while focusing on aiding Great Britain in its battle in the Atlantic against Germany. If Japan would not be deterred and was determined to widen the war, FDR was ready for that eventuality. He coaxed an enormous naval expansion bill out of Congress in July 1940, resumed naval talks with the British in October, and tightened export controls over steel and petroleum to Japan in 1941. All these measures had been explored in a more modest form in 1938, but were abandoned due to the domestic climate of opinion. By the fall of 1941, FDR had altered the domestic equation substantially and was creating an international situation that blocked further German and Japanese expansion in the Atlantic and in East Asia. Japan had a choice whether to back down or choose war. Prodded on by the Third Reich, Japan chose war.

4 ANTICIPATING THE UNEXPECTED

The explosion of the battleship *Maine*, the sinking of the passenger liner *Lusitania*, and the air attack on the gunboat *Panay* all generated major crises that threatened U.S. relations with a significant foreign power. Those who experienced the three crises drew mental connections between them, fearing that history was about to repeat itself. This was most apparent with the isolationists of the 1930s, who established committees and devised neutrality laws with the express purposes of preventing the missteps they perceived in Wilson's handling of German and British economic warfare in the First World War. Yet one detects a similar tendency on the part of presidential advisers who wished that President Roosevelt had been more assertive in responding to the attack on the *Panay*. Images of the battleship *Maine* wafted in the background as FDR's advisers discussed how the United States should respond to a blatant assault on a symbol of American rights, privileges, and obligations in the Far East. If FDR was looking over his shoulder to see whether Congress and the public were willing to follow him in late 1937, in the distance he would have perceived the shadows of the *Maine* and *Lusitania*.

Yet while the images of the *Maine* and *Lusitania* lingered in the background, many participants in the public and behind-the-scenes debates of the 1930s realized that the issues, adversaries, and domestic context of 1898, 1915, and 1937 were quite different. They cautioned against drawing direct parallels. With the passage of time, the differences between the three cases have become apparent, as we interpret these crises with an enhanced awareness of how they played out. Hindsight gives us a more precise understanding of how diplomatic signals were interpreted, how Congress reacted, and how the public responded. McKinley, Wilson, and Roosevelt acted without this retrospective certainty. They knew only how earlier crises had unfolded. Each responded quite differently to the calamity he confronted, as the adversaries and international issues involved had changed. They reacted differently because the domestic environment, despite having the same institutions, had shifted with the passage of time and in reaction to the past.

Context, in short, remains the most important component of understanding how presidents respond to naval incidents that threaten to veer into major international crises. Context is all about particularities and specifics, about the constellation of domestic politics, public opinion, press commentary, and presidential leadership. Furthermore, context means that all states do not react in the same manner to similar crises, and that specific foreign powers will react differently based on *their* domestic politics, public opinions, press commentaries, and perceptions of the antagonist.

The primacy of context means that theories, models, and approaches that seek to provide general insights and lawlike propositions are of limited value for understanding past and future naval incidents. It mattered that Congress had been urging McKinley for months to do something about Cuba, when a coal bunker explosion blew the ship sky-high during the course of a port visit. It mattered that Wilson had staked out a maximalist position on American rights and a minimalist position on American responsibilities (arms exports) months before the *Lusitania* was attacked. And it very much mattered that Congress had tied Roosevelt's hands with the Neutrality Act and was in the midst of considering the Ludlow Amendment when Roosevelt grappled with the *Panay* incident.

One might well argue that the *Maine, Lusitania*, and *Panay* incidents were so different in their causes, context, and resolution that they have little in common. But this misses the point: decision makers, journalists, and much of the public drew comparisons between these and other naval incidents as they struggled to understand what had happened and assess how to respond to the disaster. They thought in terms of types and categories, even if on closer examination these "naval incidents" were different in their cause, conduct, and consequences.

The *Maine, Lusitania*, and *Panay* incidents had one thing in common. Each incident was wrapped in uncertainty and suspense, with elements of the unknown lingering into the present. McKinley knew that the USS *Maine* had suffered a calamitous explosion, but for weeks he did not know the cause of the explosion or whom to hold responsible for the disaster. The Sampson Board of Inquiry arrived in Havana six days after the *Maine* exploded, and required almost a month to interview survivors, conduct dives, examine evidence, and reach a conclusion. While the board went about its business, pressure grew in Washington as McKinley, Congress, and the American people anxiously awaited the results of the inquiry. The De Lôme scandal and the Proctor Report added kindling to interventionist agitation during the interlude, and the clamor to do something grew louder. Yet nagging doubts about the Sampson Board's conclusion resurfaced after the Spanish-American War. These misgivings led to another formal Naval Court of Inquiry a decade later (the 1911 Vreeland Board) and subsequent re-examinations of the incident by Admiral Rickover (1971) and the National Geographic Society (1998). Each investigation has questioned the findings of its predecessor, and closure remains elusive.

The *Lusitania* incident likewise was immediately enveloped with uncertainties and debates. Some of the allegations were introduced and carefully cultivated by the German government, and were soon disproved. The *Lusitania* was not carrying deck guns, nor were Canadian troops embarked on the ship. But others proved true and raised questions that lingered for decades. The ship was carrying small-arms ammunition and shell casings, as the British government acknowledged in its July 1915 Board of Trade investigation (the Mersey Inquiry). Was it right to insist that Americans should expect safe passage on a passenger ship carrying munitions through a war zone? Were there other munitions onboard beyond those listed on the cargo manifest, and if so, had they contributed to the ship's rapid sinking? Why had the captain slowed the ship and why wasn't he zigzagging as the Admiralty claimed it had recommended? The German-American press kept these questions in circulation as Wilson contemplated how to respond to the *Lusitania* and *Arabic* incidents, and revisionist historians resurrected these questions a decade later. Even after the passage of a century, wealthy American skeptics continue to fund dives to the wreck in the hope of finding evidence that will confirm conspiracy theories that refuse to die.

One might think the *Panay* incident would have been immune to these types of uncertainties. After all, in addition to the detailed reports compiled by Secretary Atcheson and the Naval Court of Inquiry, a handful of top-notch reporters had been onboard the ship when it was attacked; Norman Alley had filmed the incident as it happened. But here, too, it becomes apparent that eyewitness accounts and photography do not entirely lift the fog of war. The *Panay* was in the midst of transmitting a message when attacked at 1:35 P.M. on Sunday, December 12, 1937; superiors in China were fearful but uncertain about what had happened for almost twenty hours.

Even after reports filtered back to Washington that the ship had been sunk, the picture remained unclear. Japan immediately apologized and claimed the attack was accidental. Roosevelt suspected there was more to the story than that. Japanese planes and artillery, after all, had attacked British gunboats as well, and the U.S. ambassador to Japan had been warning Tokyo for months that something was bound to happen unless the Japanese government exercised tighter control over its military forces in China. Though the eyewitness accounts, photographs, and film left little room for debate about what had happened, uncertainty still clung to the question of why it had happened. Given the domestic situation, Roosevelt settled the matter diplomatically. The Americans and Japanese agreed to disagree about the accidental nature of the attack.

The *Maine, Lusitania,* and *Panay* incidents were very different, but what they had in common was a high degree of uncertainty. In each case, the president could pause for a brief period while awaiting official findings, allowing him to consider various options and giving him time to assess the domestic and international environments. The official findings provided some answers, but they did not close the book on speculations about culpability and intent. If there is one generalization that seems to hold true, it is that presidents dealing with naval incidents must reach decisions in an environment where the facts are not yet fully established.

The *Maine, Lusitania*, and *Panay* incidents were superficially similar, in that they involved sunken ships, dead Americans, and urgent calls to "do something." They involved utterly different types of ships and numbers of casualties, but despite this, the first reaction of journalists and decision makers was to think about the parallels and similarities of these incidents. This brings us back to the argument that context and specifics matter. One can try to categorize naval incidents and devise general propositions about presidential crisis decision making, but typologies, theories, and models provide only limited insights into naval incidents and the decision for war. One can best understand naval incidents as a phenomenon by approaching them with a historical mindset that values the particular, the interplay between foreign and domestic affairs, and the role of chance, friction, and uncertainty.

CATEGORIZING NAVAL INCIDENTS

Social scientists who value theory seek to examine incidents, events, and conflict by categorizing them into types and then searching for patterns and trends. One might do this for naval incidents, but the very process of categorizing incidents can obscure interconnections and blur important contextual influences. Consider, for example, three different approaches to categorizing naval incidents. Each provides a useful lens, but each, in the end, is flawed and limited.

First, one might use the benefit of hindsight to categorize naval incidents on the basis of whether they became major inter-state disputes and whether these disputes in turn escalated into military confrontation and war. This method of categorization may appear attractive, as it lends itself to quantitative analysis. Naval incidents occur with sufficient frequency that they appear to be amenable to a quantitative, "rigorous," and scientific examination. The British diplomat and scholar James Cable spent decades researching the use or threat of limited naval force, compiling a representative list of naval confrontations short of war that stretched to fifty-three pages.[1] David Winkler, director of programs at the U.S. Naval Historical Foundation, has assembled a thirty-three-page chronology of more than 450 incidents at sea during the cold war period, ranging from low-level overflights (buzzing) of ships to collisions at sea, to the purposeful downing of aircraft and the seizure of ships.[2] Naval historians can rattle off dozens of naval incidents that had the potential to lead to military hostilities or war. For the United States, these would include various incidents associated with the Quasi-War with France in the 1790s, naval incidents preceding the War of 1812, and incidents such as the *Trent* affair of 1861, when a Union warship intercepted a British mail ship with Confederate emissaries onboard, sparking outrage in the United Kingdom. In addition to the *Maine, Lusitania*, and *Panay* incidents, one can add German attacks on the USS *Greer* and the *Reuben James* to cover the period 1898 to 1941.

More recently, one could point to the Gulf of Tonkin incident in 1964, the Israeli attack on the USS *Liberty* in 1967, North Korea's seizure of the *Pueblo* in 1968, the *Mayaguez* incident of 1975, and various air and sea incidents associated with the Iran-Iraq War, al-Qaeda's campaign against the United States, and disputes in the South China Seas.[3] Yet despite the allure of categorizing incidents in terms agreeable to quantitative analysis, this sort of categorization is fraught with problems. How, for example, would one categorize the *Lusitania* incident? Wilson did not respond to the incident by declaring war, and in the short term his policy of threatening Germany if it did not abandon unrestricted submarine warfare succeeded. Coding the incident as a major crisis resolved short of war fails to recognize the connections between the *Lusitania* incident and the entry of the United States into the First World War in 1917. Likewise, coding the *Maine* incident as an incident that escalated to war would be extremely simplistic.[4] The connections between the *Maine* disaster and the Spanish-American War may appear direct, but it remains debatable whether the *Maine* incident was either a necessary or sufficient cause for the U.S. intervention in the ongoing Spanish-Cuban War. To the best of our knowledge, the *Maine* incident was caused by the chance explosion of a coal bunker; the *Maine* might have been blown to smithereens as unexpectedly while at anchor in Charleston, South Carolina, or Key West, Florida. Interconnectivity, chance, and ambiguity fade away when categorizing incidents in terms of their immediate connection to war.

A second approach to categorizing naval incidents would be to group them in terms of the legal issues and rights at stake. International law derived in good measure from medieval and early modern efforts to codifying the rights and responsibilities of states, kingdoms, and mercantile republics on the high seas during times of peace and war. Initially, international treaties dealt with such matters as the distinction between privateers and pirates, the disposition of seized vessels, and the functioning of Prize Courts, but by the nineteenth century they began to nail down the rules related to blockades, the seizure of contraband, and the rights of neutral shipping in times of war.[5] Wilson framed his policy toward Germany in the First World War around the principle of neutral rights and international law, rather than in terms of the global balance of power and the threat that an over-mighty Germany might pose to U.S. interests should Britain be defeated.

The *Lusitania* incident provides a glimpse of how the defense of maritime rights can escalate into war. Wilson, cognizant that he could not confront both Britain and Germany, objected to British infringements of U.S. neutral rights but refrained from backing his protests with actions and consequences. His policy toward Germany was much sterner, and the president backed himself into a corner by explicitly warning the German government that further attacks on American lives and shipping would have dire effects. Wilson waved off various

German attempts at establishing some sort of modus vivendi that would enable Germany to continue attacking British merchant shipping without surfacing, boarding, and inspecting them. Wilson's uneven enforcement of neutral rights angered the German-American community in particular, and by the early 1930s what had once been lauded as a principled stand was widely perceived as a legalistic defense of American rights in a manner that favored the Entente at the expense of the Central Powers.[6] By the late 1930s, the notion that submarines were obliged to observe the rules of cruiser warfare began to appear outmoded and questionable. After Japan attacked the United States, the U.S. Navy quietly set about waging a submarine campaign in the Pacific in a manner that paid little heed to the legal requirements that Wilson had so adamantly insisted should be observed even at the cost of endangering submarine crews.[7]

In recent decades, the rights and legal issues that so concerned Presidents James Madison and Woodrow Wilson have faded into the background and have been replaced by new issues, rights, and legal points of disputation. Few Americans worry that a foreign navy will station ships just outside U.S. territorial waters for the purpose of intercepting American ships, seizing contraband goods, and impressing American citizens into naval service, as occurred between 1805 and 1812.[8] Few believe it likely that America's major trading partners will resort to seizing or sinking each other's ships, declaring certain sections of the high seas closed to merchant shipping, and demanding that neutral powers abide by various restrictions they impose on trade, as happened between 1914 and 1917. Yet we do fret that other nations may attempt to set limits on the principle that all nations have the right to operate ships freely on the high seas, with disputes over the boundaries of exclusive economic zones (EEZs) growing in salience. China's attempt to legitimize its claims in the South China Sea by converting reefs into islands has alarmed its neighbors. In 2015, the United States began to deliberately contest Chinese claims by sending U.S. Navy ships on "Freedom of Navigation" (FON) exercises to demonstrate its commitment to principles, rights, and international law.

Categorizing naval incidents in terms of specific rights and issues can lead to one-dimensional analyses that fail to capture the complexity of the confrontation. Numerous FON exercises, for example, couple the defense of a principle with a broader coercive agenda. Freedom of Navigation exercises across Muammar Gaddafi's self-declared "Line of Death" in the mid-1980s, for example, had more to do with displaying U.S. power than defending the principle that all nations have the right to operate vessels on the high seas. In 1973, Gaddafi announced that the Gulf of Sidra between Benghazi and Misrata was Libyan territorial waters, threatening foreign navies that crossed his "Line of Death" with dire consequences. Over the next decade, Gaddafi became an increasingly obnoxious threat to American interests, hosting terrorist training camps, funding terrorist groups around the world, and sending thousands of Libyan soldiers into northern Chad. President Reagan decided that the United States had to send Gaddafi a message, ordering ships and aircraft from the Sixth Fleet to cross Gaddafi's "Line of Death" in 1981 and 1986. These operations, described as Freedom of Navigation exercises, were meant to showcase American military might. Gaddafi played into Reagan's hand by sending out Libyan jet fighters, which were promptly shot down when they fired air-to-air missiles at F-14 Tomcats defending the American carrier battle group. Commenters in the United States were quick to claim that Gaddafi had been taught a lesson. It was not the lesson intended.

Gaddafi's response to the spring 1986 Sixth Fleet FON exercise was to strike back at the United States unconventionally. On April 5, 1986, an explosion ripped through a West Berlin disco frequented by American servicemen, killing two U.S. servicemen and a Turkish woman, and injuring more than 200 young people. The FBI eventually traced the La Belle discotheque bombing back to Libya. The nexus between U.S. and Libyan foreign policy, the Gulf of Sidra, and terrorism becomes lost if one focuses too intently on the right to operate on the high seas. The United States initiated its FON exercises to send Gaddafi a signal related to his incursion into Chad, his support of terrorist groups around the world, and his efforts to secure nuclear weapons. Gaddafi, humiliated conventionally, responded asymmetrically.[9]

The Gaddafi case illustrates the broader point that while some naval incidents can be categorized as arising from specific maritime rights and issues of contention, others spring from grievances that have little to do with freedom of navigation, neutral rights at sea, conflicting maritime claims, or overlapping EEZs. FDR sensed that the attack on the *Panay* was part of a broader effort to undermine American and British prestige in the Far East. More recently, the terrorist attack on the USS *Cole* in 2000 reflects the same logic. The *Cole* was attacked not because of differences between the al Qaeda leadership and the United States over specific rights and maritime issues, but because of al Qaeda's deep resentment of American influence in the region. Bin Laden's 1998 message "Jihad against Jews and Crusaders" listed his grievances, ranging from the presence of American troops in the Arabian Peninsula to ongoing UN sanctions against Iraq, to U.S. support of Israel. None of these related to maritime matters, and one might note, the withdrawal of American forces from Saudi Arabia in 2003 and Iraq in 2012 did little to diminish the resentment of successor organizations such as ISIL (the self-designated al Qaeda offshoot "Islamic State in Iraq and the Levant") toward the United States. The USS *Cole*, a warship flying the American flag in a region deemed vital to U.S. interests, was a symbol of American power and forward presence. Categorizing naval incidents in terms of disagreements over specific maritime rights and issues may be informative in some cases, but it fails to capture the dynamics at work in other cases.

This brings us to a third approach, categorizing naval incidents in terms of the purpose served. James Cable's *Gunboat Diplomacy*, first published in 1971 and updated in 1981 and 1994, provides an original if somewhat problematic alternative to classifying naval incidents in terms of outcomes or of the rights, laws, and specific issues. Focusing on the use of naval force short of war, Cable sets out to examine *"the use or threat of limited naval force, otherwise than as an act of war, in order to secure advantage or to avert loss, either in the furtherance of an international dispute or else against foreign nationals within the territory or the jurisdiction of their own state."*[10]

Cable's study has resonated only marginally with American international relations scholars, as he wrote from a British point of view, was a practitioner of diplomacy rather than being an academic, and used the rather off-putting term "gunboat diplomacy" in his initial study. He would later broaden his analysis to diplomacy at sea and the political influence of naval forces, exploring concepts such as coercion, compromise, and compliance in his studies of naval power.[11] Cable's interest in naval diplomacy is shared by a number of other prominent British or British-educated political scientists and historians, with Geoffrey Till, Lawrence Freedman, Nicholas Rodger, Paul M. Kennedy, and Edward Luttwak among the most prominent.[12] In contrast, much of the U.S. literature on coercion and coercive diplomacy focuses on airpower.[13] This interest in coercive airpower spilled over into a handful of books and articles on "carrier diplomacy," but Alfred Thayer Mahan and Julian Corbett still cast powerful shadows over most studies of naval power.[14] This paucity of American scholarship on the intersection of naval power and coercive diplomacy is remarkable, as the United States still tends to react to crisis situations by dispatching carrier groups rather than using land-based airpower. Navies, unlike air forces, can operate for months on the global commons, with no need to negotiate tiresome basing agreements with friends, allies, and partner nations.[15]

Cable suggested that coercive naval power tends to serve four general purposes. As a *definitive force*, naval power can be used to create a fait accompli. By this, Cable means that naval power can be applied at the appropriate level to create a situation that the opposing side must simply accept because it either lacks the capability to respond or lacks the will. As examples, Cable cites the British seizure of the German merchant ship *Altmark* in Norwegian territorial waters over the objections of Norwegian authorities in February 1940. British intelligence believed that the Germans were in the midst of transporting hundreds of British POWs to Germany using the merchant ship. Churchill gave the order to liberate the POWs before the *Altmark* came within the protective range of German aircraft, with the British naval forces moving into Norwegian territorial waters and accomplishing this objective. The British correctly calculated that the Norwegian government had no desire to go to war with Britain, and by employing sufficient force (five destroyers and a cruiser) to intimidate the Norwegians, the British rescue operation succeeded without conflict.[16]

The second purpose that limited naval force can serve is to change the policy or character of a foreign government or some organized group. Cable terms this *purposeful force*. It is analogous to Shelling and George's concept of coercive force. An example of purposeful force would be John F. Kennedy's threat to intervene in the Dominican Republic in November 1961.[17] Rafael Trujillo's son and brothers were brutally attempting to maintain their family's grip on power following the assassination of "el Jefe" (the boss) Trujillo in May. Kennedy signaled his displeasure with the situation by sending two American carriers and some 1,800 marines off the coast of the Dominican Republic. Faced with a military uprising and the threat of American intervention, the Trujillo clan chose to flee rather than to test American resolve.

Cable's third and fourth categories are the most interesting, because they capture the less clearly defined notions of presence, assurance, and flag showing. These sorts of operations have hazier objectives than definitive and purposeful displays of naval power, but policymakers find them attractive because they provide options and have low political costs. Cable designates the decision to send naval forces into troubled areas the use of *catalytic force*. The exact mission of the force is unclear at the outset, but as he puts it, there is a sense that "something is going to happen, something that somehow might be prevented if force were available at the critical point."[18] This sort of deployment may be anathema to modern military planners, schooled to establish clear objectives and defined end-states before committing forces into action. But historically, great naval powers have deployed ships and maintained naval "presence" for precisely this sort of ill-defined reason.[19]

If the use of naval force for *catalytic* purposes seems vague, then its employment for expressive purposes is even vaguer. Cable defines *expressive force* as the employment of naval forces to "emphasize attitudes, to lend verisimilitude to otherwise unconvincing statements, or to provide an outlet for emotion." Most commonly, the expressive use of naval power is described in terms such as "showing the flag," sending messages, and providing "assurance." McKinley's decision to send the *Maine* to Havana is a good example of the expressive use of naval power. In his December 1897 State of the Union address, McKinley argued that Spain should be given a "reasonable chance to realize her expectation" that clemency, less brutal military tactics, and the promise of autonomy would lead to the end of the Cuban uprising. If Spanish hopes proved illusory, or if Spain backtracked on its new, gentler approach to the Cuban insurgency, then the United States reserved the option of taking "further and other action," which McKinley did not specify. Sending the *Maine* responded to congressional pressure to do something and underlined the message that McKinley had been sending Spain for months: the fighting in Cuba must come to an end. How exactly this was to be done remained unclear, but the dispatch of the *Maine* underscored McKinley's message that American patience was running low.

Cable's categories embrace the often vague, ill-defined, and contingent uses of naval power. But as his lengthy descriptive accounts of each category make clear, the different purposes of naval coercion meld and morph into one another in practice.[20] Turning to his own example of British naval power in the Baltic Sea as the Russian Revolution unfolded, one sees how the British government initially sent ships to the area to "show the British flag" (expressive force), then kept them there while the cabinet debated whether, and in support of whom, the British naval force should be used (catalytic force), and finally—after British ships had already fired on Bolshevik forces on several occasions—provided the admiral in charge with more specific instructions about which groups he should support (purposeful force). One type of naval action may evolve into another, making Cable's categories too indistinct for quantitative scholars to use.

More problematic, however, is that Cable's typology does not embrace the full range of naval incidents. Not all naval incidents derive from the coercive use of naval power. One can make a persuasive case that McKinley sent the *Maine* to Havana to emphasize U.S. concern about Cuba (expressive force). But FDR had no such agenda with the *Panay*. As fighting between Japanese and Chinese troops widened in August 1937, the president remarked to his cabinet that he wished American troops (and presumably gunboats) were not in China. But he was stuck with commitments and decisions made decades earlier. He felt that he could not withdraw U.S. troops and gunboats without conveying the false impression to Japanese leaders that they had carte blanche to do as they liked. As for the *Lusitania* crisis, even critics of President Wilson concede that he had not sought out a confrontation with Germany. The ongoing war in Europe—in particular, British and German decisions to use naval power to attack each other's economies—affected American trade, lives, and interests. Wilson and the United States were the targets of British and German coercion, with the British effort smarter, less harmful, and less outrageous to American pride and American pocketbooks than the brutal and diplomatically disastrous German war on British commerce.

Numerous other methods for categorizing naval incidents might be devised, from categorizing incidents in terms of the size of the forces involved to focusing on the sort of operations that resulted in incidents (convoy operations, blockade duties, surveillance missions, carrier operations, etc.). No one single method is entirely satisfactory, with each subject to its own limitations. Using typologies may be helpful when trying to analyze particular sorts of incidents, though quantitative studies tend to provide bland, uninformative insights on the causes of war.[21] One gains a much better sense of types and range of incidents when one studies several incidents in depth, analyzing causes, possible responses, and outcomes within their historical and geopolitical contexts.

VALUING THE PARTICULAR

Theories, models, and quantitative studies all generate insights that can help policymakers assess contemporary problems. Yet as one prominent scholar concluded after thirty years of researching and writing about international relations theory, "academic theory has had relatively little direct or indirect impact on actual state behavior."[22] Policymakers, he elaborated, are not so much interested in knowing what happens "most of the time" but, rather, "what is most likely to happen in the particular case at hand."[23] Upper-level international relations theories generate diametrically opposed prescriptions on major policy questions ranging from how to respond to the rise of China, to whether to support Arab Spring protests against pro-American but repressive regimes. Quantitative studies yield probability statistics on the generic correlates of war, but shed little light on how to resolve particular "bones of contention."[24] While social scientists have supplied much of the vocabulary employed in foreign policy debates, with references to the "clash of civilizations," "soft power," "interdependence," and "deterrence" abounding, policymakers have little patience for theory and models. Instead, they turn to internalized worldviews, gut feelings, ideology, and "the lessons of the past" to interpret contemporary crises and assess policy alternatives.

Thucydides hoped that his *History of the Peloponnesian War* would be "judged useful by those inquirers who desire an exact knowledge of the past as an aid to the understanding of the future."[25] This notion—that by understanding the past we are better equipped to deal with the future—has persisted for millennia, with Bismarck allegedly remarking that "fools learn by experience, wise men learn by other people's experience."[26]

History books clutter the nightstands and summer reading lists of presidents, politicians, military officers, and diplomats. Some, like Serbian president Slobodan Milošević, use history in a cynical and self-serving way to stir up nationalism and anchor their political fortunes. Others, like Adolf Hitler, drew on the past to nurse grievances, cast blame, and reorder the world through war and genocide. Yet many policymakers turn to the past for more benign, practical purposes. They seek to orient themselves. They seek to understand other regions and cultures. They look to the past to provide insights into how to respond to the pressing problems of the present.

While it is widely recognized that policymakers draw upon history to understand contemporary challenges, many argue that they tend to use the remembered past ineffectively. In his highly regarded 1976 study *Perception and Misperception*, Robert Jervis took on the charge that politicians simply use history to bolster preexisting viewpoints, reinforce established patterns, and convince others to support decisions already made. The reality is more subtle. Politicians may indeed use history to manipulate, to court, and to convince.[27] But even when they do not resort to the deliberate abuse of history, firsthand experiences and generational memory are powerful forces that shape perceptions and worldviews. Traumatic events such as war, revolution, and crises burn themselves into the memory of individuals and groups, creating a prism through which contemporary issues and challenges are perceived.

This tendency to interpret the present in terms of the past can lead to simplistic analogies that mislead as often as they inform.[28] President Johnson's advisers drew on Munich and Dien Bien Phu to make their case for and against American military intervention in South Vietnam. As Ernest May, Richard Neustadt, and Yuen Foong Khong have shown, Johnson's advisers used history uncritically to support their recommended course of action in Vietnam in 1965. Little serious thought was given to assessing whether and how the analogies drawn were applicable. Since then, the U.S. war in Vietnam has itself become a key reference point whenever U.S. presidents contemplate foreign interventions, with those cautioning against intervention in Yugoslavia, Afghanistan, and Iraq pointing out dangerous parallels.[29]

This tendency to seize on historical parallels and analogies certainly pertains to naval incidents with the potential for escalation. During the summer and fall of 1937, isolationists in Congress, on editorial boards, and in the public warned the president that he should apply neutrality legislation to the widening war in China. They worried that some incident in the Far East might draw the United States into a war on the other side of the globe in defense of British interests. In their mind, Roosevelt's refusal to apply neutrality laws in the Far East was setting up a dangerous situation that paralleled that of 1914–15. The sinking of the *Panay* raised all sorts of warning flags among isolationists, with newspapers warning against ultimatums, coercion, or hints of escalation. Internationalist advisers, in contrast, remembered the *Maine* and chomped at the bit waiting for more assertive American leadership on the international stage. But internationalist voices were few and far between in the United States of 1937.

FDR's measured response, the Japanese apology, and continued isolationist vigilance against foreign entanglements made comparisons between the *Panay* incident and the *Lusitania* and *Maine* incidents seem less important over time. But the tendency to make parallels and analogies, particularly if one has first-hand experience, is almost irresistible. Should another major naval incident occur, one can expect a rash of analogies likening the incident to the last such incident or to one that seems at the surface alike. But the *Chesapeake* (1807) and *Trent* (1861) affairs; the *Maine, Lusitania*, and *Panay* incidents; and the attacks on the *Liberty, Pueblo, Stark*, and *Cole* naval ships were each unique and different in terms of causes, issues, and resolutions. Efforts to establish generic "lessons learned" are ill-advised, and strict analogies are simplistic. But rather than echo Henry Ford's assessment that "history is bunk," it is worth thinking about how one can better use history to improve crisis decision making and policy selection.

History can be used to help policymakers and the reading public understand contemporary challenges and issues. First, it can be used to acquire strategic depth and vertical knowledge.[30] This requires moving beyond individually experienced history, generational collective memory, and vague notions of tradition. It requires study and reading. By studying history, one acquires the skills to trace a chain of events to its origin. One becomes accustomed to thinking about cause and effect. One grasps that wars, conflicts, and incidents have multiple causes that interact with one another over the short, medium, and long term. History teaches us to trace back from immediate, proximate causes and search for the root and ultimate causes. It embraces complexity, interaction, interdependence, and chance. When a theory, model, or method stresses the overriding importance of a few variables and offers general, nomothetic laws to diagnose new situations and anticipate future developments, these theories and models will not be a good guide to the changing world. History provides no clear guidance, but it trains the mind to analyze complexity, embrace chance and opportunity, view problems from multiple perspectives, and think critically.

Acquiring strategic depth means cultivating an understanding of a specific region's history, culture, values, and experience. George H. W. Bush's foreign policy team of Brent Scowcroft, James Baker, Robert Zoellick, Condoleeza Rice, and Philip Zelikow understood the fears and sensibilities of their German, Russian, and European interlocutors during the waning days of the cold war. They knew of the Soviet Union's immense sacrifices in the Second World War and understood that Russian security interests must be addressed. They remembered the commitments that had been made to Adenauer decades earlier, and they valued German-American friendship. While the situation they faced was unlike any other, their knowledge of European history helped them avoid blunders as they navigated their way through the final rapids of the cold war. In contrast, as McNamara conceded *In Retrospect*, American misjudgments of the situation in Vietnam in the 1960s reflected a "profound ignorance of the history, culture, and politics of the people in the area, and the personalities and habits of their leaders." "We viewed the people and leaders of South Vietnam," McNamara elaborated, "in terms of our own experience. . . . We totally misjudged the political forces within the country."[31] The Gulf of Tonkin incident did not cause the American escalation in Vietnam, but a better understanding of Vietnamese history might have precluded sending the USS *Maddox* into the Gulf of Tonkin in the first place.[32]

If acquiring strategic depth for every region is impossible, then one should at least aspire to a horizontal knowledge of history. This second use of history provides policymakers and the concerned public with a sense of the linkages between issues, across regions, and transecting the systemic, institutional, and political "levels of analysis."[33] It connects the domestic and regional to the international, the cultural to the political, and the economic to the military dimension. One might turn to the *Panay* incident for an illustration of these sorts of interconnections. Though the incident involved an American gunboat stationed in China, analyzing how and why Roosevelt responded as he did entails more than an in-depth knowledge of U.S. policy in the Far East in the 1930s. It involves understanding the domestic debates within the United States about arms embargoes, loans, and neutral rights during the First World War. It involves recognizing the backlash of "hyphenated Americans" and midwesterners against East Coast elites in the late 1920s and mid-1930s. It connects historical revisionism and the Nye Committee to the Neutrality Laws and Ludlow Amendment. And as both Roosevelt and the British understood, it involves recognizing how developments in Europe, the Mediterranean, and Africa closed off certain options in regards to confronting Japan in 1938.

History serves a third practical purpose. It can help provide a sense of the range of options. This can be quite mundane, in that one can look at previous crises and incidents that seem analogous, and examine various courses of action submitted for presidential consideration. But historical study can also show how previous presidents created new options, pushing their subordinates to examine options they had overlooked and laying the ground for future courses of action. Roosevelt pushed Henry Morgenthau to come up with some sort of economic form of warfare in answer to Japanese aggression well before Congress and the public were willing to recognize that isolationism would not keep the United States safe in the long run. He dispatched Captain Royal E. Ingersoll to London to explore options that were never exercised yet might have been had Chamberlain's appeasement policy in Europe succeeded. FDR pushed his subordinates to provide him a wider range of options than would have been the case without his prodding and backdoor diplomacy.

Historical study provides insights into options and option creation, but it can do more. It exposes different modes of thinking, alternative forms of organization, and dissimilar perceptions of reality.[34] By reading history, we become aware that the modern nation-state was indeed constructed, and that other forms of political organization have existed before and may yet develop after the nation-state. By examining the "past as a foreign land," we become aware that things were not always as they are, and that the future may be very different from the world in which we live. This widens one's aperture of understanding, and used constructively, prompts one to consider roads less traveled and options unexplored. It warns one that rosy predictions of the end of history are oblivious to alternative developments and unanticipated challenges.[35]

Fourth, history can provide policymakers and the concerned public with a sense of bureaucratic intelligence and institutional guidance. By understanding how political bargains are struck, how policies are crafted, how interdepartmental differences are settled, and how presidents interact with Congress, one can educate oneself about processes, leadership, and negotiations. Presidents, National Security Council principals, generals, and diplomats read biographies and histories not simply for pleasure, but because they seek insights into how others in similar position have acted. In part these decision makers turn to biography for relief from the pressures of the moment, but they also seek to understand how successful predecessors delivered on promises made.

Lastly, history teaches a sense of humility and skepticism. Historical study reveals how often predictions have been off the mark. It confirms that chance, sudden deaths, unexpected developments, and even the weather can intervene to make the improbable succeed and render the near certain a failure. In addition to recognizing the interplay of chance and reason, of purpose, preparation, and luck, the historical method provides a corrective to "rigorous" scientific studies of international relations that claim to be entirely objective. Historians have long recognized that subjectivity, perception, and perspective not only shape interpretations but also shape the selection of facts, the construction of narratives, and how events are categorized. As E. H. Carr commented well over half a century ago,

> Study the historian before you begin to study the facts. . . . When you read a work of history, always listen out for the buzzing. If you can detect none, either you are tone deaf or your historian is a dull dog. The facts are really not at all like fish on the fishmonger's slab. They are like fish swimming about in a vast and sometimes inaccessible ocean; and what the historian catches will depend, partly on chance, but mainly on what part of the ocean he chooses to fish in and what tackle he chooses to use. . . . By

and large, the historian will get the kind of facts he wants. History means interpretation.[36]

One might add the same words of caution to think-tank consultants, international relations scholars, and those who determine policy. Listen for the buzzing and be aware of studies and recommendations that claim to be based solely on the hard, objective facts of the matter.

Marc Bloch once cautioned his fellow historians that "the scholar who has no inclination to observe the men, the things, or the events around him will perhaps deserve the title . . . of useful antiquarian."[37] Contemporary concerns prompted this study of the interplays between naval incidents, presidential decision making, and the decision for war. The *Maine, Lusitania*, and *Panay* incidents drive home the point that context trumps theory, and that the particular is at least as important as the general.

Rather than using history to provide direct analogies and "lessons learned," students of foreign affairs should employ history to gain strategic depth, study interconnections, examine what sort of options past presidents considered, and think about why they acted as they did. The challenges of the contemporary world are very different from those of 1898, 1915, and 1937. In the Far East, a rising China is becoming more assertive about claims in the South and East China Seas, while American allies look anxiously to the United States to balance against China. In an arc spanning from the western Sahara into the Indian Ocean, radical jihadi groups wage war against their neighbors and attack U.S. targets, often relying on suicide bombing to terrorize their opponents. In the Baltic and Black seas, NATO has enhanced its naval and air presence in order to reassure vulnerable member states against an awakening Russia that still thinks in terms of spheres of influence.

Historians, social scientists, and members of the intelligence community do well analyzing and assessing long-term trends, but they have a poor track record predicting sudden change. Revolutions, market collapses, and naval incidents can be explained in retrospect, but are rarely pinpointed before the event.[38] Yet one can hone critical thinking skills by studying the past and applying these faculties when and if future naval catastrophes generate cries that we must "do something." History provides no clear lessons of what we should do, but by dissecting the past we develop familiarity with complexity, interdependence, and the role of chance, fog, and friction. By understanding the multiple forms that naval incidents may take, by analyzing the interplay of foreign and domestic forces, and by examining the interplay of forces at work in the *Maine, Lusitania*, and *Panay* incidents, this work aims to contribute to debates concerning the future, as well as those centered on the past.

NOTES

INTRODUCTION

1. Marc Léopold Benjamin Bloch, *The Historian's Craft* (New York: Knopf, 1953), 44–45.
2. Ibid., 37.
3. John A. Lynn, "The Embattled Future of Academic Military History," *Journal of Military History* 61, no. 4 (1997): 777–89.
4. For a small sampling, see Robert D. Kaplan, *Asia's Cauldron: The South China Sea and the End of a Stable Pacific* (New York: Random House, 2014); Stephan Frühling. *Defence Planning and Uncertainty: Preparing for the Next Asia-Pacific War* (London: Routledge, 2014); Geoff Dyer, *The Contest of the Century: The New Era of Competition with China—and How America Can Win* (New York: Alfred A. Knopf, 2014); David L. Shambaugh, *Tangled Titans: The United States and China* (Lanham, MD: Rowman & Littlefield, 2013); Andrew J. Nathan and Andrew Scobell, *China's Search for Security* (New York: Columbia University Press, 2012); Edward Luttwak, *The Rise of China vs. The Logic of Strategy* (Cambridge, MA: Belknap Press of Harvard University Press, 2012); Geoffrey Till and Patrick C. Bratton, eds., *Sea Power and the Asia-Pacific. The Triumph of Neptune?* (New York: Routledge, 2012); Philip C. Saunders et al., *The Chinese Navy. Expanding Capabilities, Evolving Roles* (Washington, DC: Institute for National Strategic Studies, 2011).
5. See the unclassified summary of the classified Air-Sea Battle Concept, version 9.0, dated May 12, and the Air-Sea Battle Master Implementation Plan (FY13), dated September 12, entitled *Air-Sea Battle: Service Collaboration to Address Anti-Access & Area Denial Challenges* (Washington, DC: Air-Sea Battle Office, May 2013), www.defense.gov/pubs/ASB-ConceptImplementation-Summary-May-2013.pdf; Sam J. Tangredi, *Anti-Access Warfare: Countering A2/AD Strategies* (Annapolis, MD: Naval Institute Press, 2013); Anthony H. Cordesman and Bryan Gold,

The Gulf Military Balance: The Missile and Nuclear Dimensions. A Report of the CSIS Burke Chair in Strategy (New York: Rowman & Littlefield, 2014); "Ballistic and Cruise Missile Threat (Nasic-1031-0985-13)," (Wright Patterson AFB, OH: National Air and Space Intelligence Center, 2013); Andrew S. Erickson, *Chinese Anti-Ship Ballistic Missile Development: Drivers, Trajectories and Strategic Implications* (Washington, DC: Jamestown Foundation, 2013).

6. Frederick Jackson Turner, *The Early Writings of Frederick Jackson Turner; with a List of All His Works Compiled by Everett E. Edwards* (Madison: University of Wisconsin Press, 1938), 52.

7. While I employ a similar methodology to that recommended by George in terms of selecting and structuring historical case studies, my aim is not to generate theory and general principles. It is to highlight the important of context and the particular. Alexander L. George and Andrew Bennett, *Case Studies and Theory Development in the Social Sciences* (Cambridge, MA: MIT Press, 2005).

8. Jack S. Levy, "Explaining Events and Developing Theories: History, Political Science, and the Analysis of International Relations," in *Bridges and Boundaries: Historians, Political Scientists, and the Study of International Relations*, ed. Colin Elman and Miriam Fendius Elman (Cambridge, MA: MIT Press, 2001).

9. John Lewis Gaddis is particularly biting in his assessment of the tendency toward reductionism among his social scientist colleagues. He recalled attending a conference at "a distinguished American university with an equally distinguished group of political scientists." The subject of the conference was the use of case studies, and Gaddis became so exasperated with the incessant call that one needed to "tease out" independent from dependent variables that he finally objected: "How, apart from God if he or she exists, can there ever be such a thing as an independent variable? Aren't all variables dependent on other variables?" Entire chapters of *The Landscape of History* should be read as a not so subtle counteroffensive against the international relations theorists and political scientists who now dominate the field of security studies. John Lewis Gaddis, *The Landscape of History: How Historians Map the Past* (Oxford: Oxford University Press, 2002), 53–54. One might note that Dean Acheson had made the same point some forty years earlier, remarking that "his already low estimate of political science was lowered still more when he saw a study that treated him as a dependent variable. 'At the very least,' he said, 'I thought I was an independent variable.'" Robert Jervis, "Navies, Politics, and Political Science," in *Doing Naval History: Essays toward Improvement,* ed. John B. Hattendorf (Newport, RI: Naval War College Press, 1995), 45.

10. Stephen Pelz, "Toward a New Diplomatic History: Two and a Half Cheers for International Relations Methods," in *Bridges and Boundaries: Historians, Political Scientists, and the Study of International Relations*, ed. Colin Elman and Miriam Fendius Elman (Cambridge, MA: MIT Press, 2001), 105; Alan Beyerchen, "Clausewitz, Nonlinearity, and the Unpredictability of War," *International Security* 17, no. 3 (1992/93).

11. Hew Strachan, *The Direction of War: Contemporary Strategy in Historical Perspective* (Cambridge: Cambridge University Press, 2013), 253.

12. George Santayana, *The Life of Reason, or, the Phases of Human Progress* (New York: Scribner's, 1954), 82.

13. Cohen's short essay on the historical mind touches on a topic developed more fully in the concluding chapter—how policymakers can use both theory and history. Eliot A. Cohen, "The Historical Mind and Military Strategy," *Orbis* 49, no. 4 (2005); William Inboden, "Statecraft, Decsion-Making, and the Varieties of Historical Experience: A Taxonomy," *Journal of Strategic Studies* 37, no. 2 (2014); Francis Gavin, "History and Policy," *International Journal* 63, no. 1 (Winter 2007-08); Hattendorf, *Doing Naval History*; Richard E. Neustadt and Ernest R. May, *Thinking in Time: The Uses of History for Decision-Makers* (London: Collier Macmillan, 1986); Ernest R. May, *"Lessons" of the Past; the Use and Misuse of History in American Foreign Policy* (New York: Oxford University Press, 1973).

14. For some thought-provoking essays on the dismal record that military leaders and academics have when it comes to predicting future crises and trouble spots, see Micah Zenko, "100% Right 0% of the Time. Why the U.S. Military Can't Predict the Next War," *Foreign Policy* [blog], October 16, 2012, www.foreign-policy.com/articles/2012/10/16/why_the_military_cant_predict_the_next_war; Sam J. Tangredi, *All Possible Wars? Towards a Consensus View of the Future Security Environment, 2001-2025*, McNair Paper 63 (Washington, DC: National Defense University: November 2000); and Laura Lee, "Forecasts That Missed by a Mile," *The Futurist*, September-October 2000, 20–25.

15. Gaddis, *Landscape of History*, xi, 63–64.

16. Philip De Souza, *Piracy in the Graeco-Roman World* (Cambridge: Cambridge University Press, 1999).

17. Douglas C. Peifer, "Maritime Commerce Warfare: The Coercive Response of the Weak?," *Naval War College Review* 66, no. 2 (2013).

18. Michael Eliot Howard, *War in European History* (London: Oxford University Press, 1976), ch. 3, 38–53. For a broader discussion of naval power during this period, see the excellent collection edited by John B. Hattendorf and Richard W. Unger, *War at Sea in the Middle Ages and the Renaissance, Warfare in History* (Rochester, NY: Boydell Press, 2003) and N. A. M. Rodger, *The Safeguard of the Sea: A Naval History of Britain, 660-1649* (New York: Norton, 1998).

19. Robert Finlay, "The Voyages of Zheng He: Ideology, State Power, and Maritime Trade in Ming China," *Journal of the Historical Society* 8, no. 3 (2008); Hing Hui Chun, "Huangming Zuxun and Zheng He's Voyages to the Western Oceans. (English)," *Journal of Chinese Studies* 51(2010).

20. For a fuller discussion of gunboat diplomacy and coercive airpower, see Douglas Peifer, "Risk-Free Coercion? Technological Disparity and Coercive Diplomacy," *European Security* 18, no. 1 (2009).

21. MacGregor Knox and Williamson Murray, *The Dynamics of Military Revolution, 1300-2050* (New York: Cambridge University Press, 2001).

22. Hilaire Belloc and Basil Temple Blackwood, *The Modern Traveller* (London: Edward Arnold, 1898), 41.

23. For a fascinating look at the internal debates over the proper role of the United States in world affairs, and the appropriate naval force structure for an emerging world power, see Kenneth J. Hagan, *American Gunboat Diplomacy and the Old Navy, 1877-1889* (Westport, CT: Greenwood 1973).

24. Robert Shufeldt letter to Leopold Morse on the topic "The Relation of the Navy to the Commerce of the United States," 1878, cited in Kenneth J. Hagan, *American Gunboat Diplomacy and the Old Navy, 1877-1889* (Westport, CT: Greenwood, 1973), 37.

25. See Marius B. Jansen, *The Making of Modern Japan* (Cambridge, MA: Belknap Press, 2000), 257–371, for a discussion of the Perry Mission, the fall of the Tokugawa, and the Meiji Revolution.

26. James Cable, *Gunboat Diplomacy, 1919-1991*, 3rd ed. (New York: St. Martin's, 1994), 159–213.

27. See the National Security Agency Public Information website at www.nsa.gov/public_info/declass/uss_pueblo/ for the November 20, 2012, "USS Pueblo Release Summary" and relevant documents. These newly released documents are in the midst of first-generation analysis, with John Prados and Jack Cheevers of George Washington University's National Security Archive providing some broad commentary in Electronic Briefing Book No. 453 at www2.gwu.edu/~nsarchiv/NSAEBB/NSAEBB453/.

28. The veil is starting to lift on the internal deliberations related to the *Pueblo* and *Liberty* episodes, but the picture is still very incomplete regarding other, more recent incidents. For these two exceptions, see A. Jay Cristol, *The Liberty Incident Revealed: The Definitive Account of the 1967 Israeli Attack on the U.S. Navy Spy Ship* (Annapolis, MD: Naval Institute Press, 2013); Jack Cheevers, *Act of War: Lyndon Johnson, North Korea, and the Capture of the Spy Ship Pueblo* (New York: NAL Caliber, 2013); Richard A. Mobley, *Flash Point North Korea: The Pueblo and EC-121 Crises* (Annapolis, MD: Naval Institute Press, 2003); Mitchell B. Lerner, *The Pueblo Incident: A Spy Ship and the Failure of American Foreign Policy* (Lawrence: University Press of Kansas, 2002).

29. Larry Tart and Robert Keefe, *The Price of Vigilance: Attacks on American Surveillance Flights* (New York: Ballantine, 2001), 13–14. David Lednicer's comprehensive website "Aircraft Downed during the Cold War and thereafter" lists over 200 incidents, but includes Allied aircraft other missions than ISR; see http://sw.propwashgang.org/shootdown_list.html for details. Several other books provide overviews of these confrontations. See William E. Burrows, *By Any Means Necessary: America's Secret Air War in the Cold War* (New York: Farrar, Straus and Giroux, 2001); Norman Polmar, *Chronology of the Cold War at Sea,*

1945-1991 (Annapolis, MD: Naval Institute Press, 1998); David F. Winkler, *Cold War at Sea: High-Seas Confrontation between the United States and the Soviet Union* (Annapolis, MD: Naval Institute Press, 2000); Roy A. Grossnick and Naval Historical Center (U.S.), United States Naval Aviation, 1910-1995 (Washington, DC: Naval Historical Center, Dept. of the Navy, 1997); Appendix 34, "Cold War Incidents Involving U.S. Navy Aircraft."

30. Text available at www.state.gov/t/isn/4791.htm.

31. One of the complicating factors following China's downing of an EP-3 surveillance aircraft south of Hainan Island was the absence of a hot line. This has since been remedied, but has rarely been used. John McLaughlin, a former deputy director of the CIA, examines these and other troubling parallels in his essay "How 2014 Is Strikingly Similar to 1914," published by the digital newsmagazine *Ozy. com*; www.ozy.com/c-notes/the-spy-who-told-me-its-been-a-century-since-wwi-began/32057.article.

PART ONE

1. In his transmittal to Congress of the report of the Naval Court of Inquiry, McKinley characterized the *Maine*'s visit as a "symbol of good will." See "Message from the President of the United States Transmitting the Report of the Naval Court of Inquiry Upon the Destruction of the United States Battle Ship Maine in Havana Harbor, February 15, 1898, Together with the Testimony Taken before the Court, 55th Congress, 2d Session, Document 207" (Washington, DC: Government Printing Office, 1898), 225 [hereafter "Report of the Naval Court of Inquiry"].

2. Magaret Long, ed. *The Journal of John D. Long* (Rindge, NH: Richard R. Smith, 1956), 214; Charles D. Sigsbee, *The "Maine": An Account of Her Destruction in Havana Harbor* (New York: Century, 1899), 32.

3. In testimony, Sigsbee recalled no demonstrations of animosity on shore but recalled that some spectators returning from a bullfight in Regla whistled and made derisive catcalls when their water taxi passed the *Maine*. "Report of the Naval Court of Inquiry," 13.

4. Sigsbee, *The "Maine,"* 64.

5. James Rankin Young and J. H. Moore, *History of Our War with Spain, Including Battles on Sea and Land. To Which Is Added a Full Account of the Conquest of Spain in America, Naval Battles of the United States, Etc., Etc.* (Philadelphia: National Publishing, 1898), 59–61.

6. Letter from Lt. Blow to his wife, February 16, 1898, available at The Spanish-American War Centennial, http://spanamwar.com/blowlet1.htm; http://span-amwar.com/action.htm.

7. Sworn statements of witnesses given to the Naval Court of Inquiry, February 24, 1898, in "Report of the Naval Court of Inquiry," 53, 58.

8. John Patrick Chidwick, *"Remember the Maine!" An Historical Narrative of the Battleship Maine as Told by Its Chaplain, the Right Reverened [!] Monsignor John P. Chidwick* (Winchester, VA: Winchester Printers and Stationers, 1935). From Peggy Samuels and Harold Samuels, *Remembering the Maine* (Washington, DC: Smithsonian Institution Press, 1995), 106. For a gripping compilation of the disaster as experienced by the *Maine*'s crew, see John Edward Weems, *The Fate of the Maine* (New York: Holt, 1958).

9. Sigsbee, *The "Maine,"* 71.

10. "Report of the Naval Court of Inquiry," 287, app. A.

11. *The "Maine,"* 80–81, app. G and H.

12. M. Long, *Journal of John D. Long,* 215.

13. Lewis L. Gould, *The Presidency of William McKinley* (Lawrence: Regents Press of Kansas, 1980), 74.

14. Charles Henry Brown, *The Correspondents' War: Journalists in the Spanish-American War* (New York: Scribner's, 1967), 120–21; Evan Thomas, *The War Lovers: Roosevelt, Lodge, Hearst, and the Rush to Empire, 1898* (New York: Little, Brown, 2010), 208–09.

15. M. Long, *Journal of John D. Long,* 215.

16. Theodore Roosevelt et al., *Letters* (Cambridge, MA: Harvard University Press, 1951), 1:775.

17. John L. Offner, *An Unwanted War: The Diplomacy of the United States and Spain over Cuba, 1895-1898* (Chapel Hill: University of North Carolina Press, 1992), 128; Hyman George Rickover, *How the Battleship Maine Was Destroyed* (Washington, DC: Naval History Division, Dept. of the Navy, 1976), 63–64, 70.

18. Brown, *The Correspondents' War,* 144.

19. See "Message from the President of the United States Transmitting the Report of Board convened at Habana, Cuba, by order of the Secretary of the Navy, to inspect and report on the wreck of the 'Maine' (Old)," 62nd Congress, 2[d] Session, Document No. 310 (December 1911).

20. Rickover, *How the Battleship Maine Was Destroyed,* 91.

21. Thomas Allen, "A Special Report. What Really Sank the Maine," *United States Naval Institute Naval History,* March/April 1998: 30–39. Dana Wegner, who participated in the Rickover report, was livid that the Advanced Marine Enterprise team did not seek the collaboration of the Rickover team, and dismisses their analysis as reflecting "poor historical research and/or bad engineering." See Dana Wegner, "New Interpretations of How the USS *Maine* Was Lost," in *Theodore Roosevelt, the U.S. Navy, and the Spanish-American War,* ed. Edward J. Marolda (New York: Palgrave, 2001).

22. "The Destruction of USS *Maine,"* Naval History and Heritage Command, www.history.navy.mil/browse-by-topic/disasters-and-phenomena/destruction-of-uss-maine.html.

23. Rickover, *How the Battleship Maine Was Destroyed*, 46–50, 76–79. While Roosevelt clearly wished for a finding that pointed toward an external source, his efforts to discourage naval officers from speculating about the causes of the *Maine*'s destruction in the press before the Naval Court of Inquiry had completed its analysis hardly constitutes interference with board deliberations.

24. Henry Cabot Lodge conveys contemporary American skepticism of the Spanish investigation, characterizing it as nothing more than an insult lacking substantial evidence and perfunctory in the extreme. Henry Cabot Lodge, *The War with Spain* (New York: Harper & Brothers, 1900), 30–31.

25. During the period that the board was in session, the Secretary of the Navy recorded in his private journal that "I believe that war will be averted, for I am satisfied that the Spanish government is not responsible for the disaster." M. Long, *Journal of John D. Long*, 220. Long notes furthermore on February 28 that the U.S. consul in Havana, General Lee, was "very clearly of the opinion that the Spanish government had no connection with or participation in the disaster."

26. For an overview of the literature on U.S.-Cuban-Spanish relations throughout the nineteenth century, with an emphasis on Cuban agency, see Louis A. Pérez, *The War of 1898: The United States and Cuba in History and Historiography* (Chapel Hill: University of North Carolina Press, 1998).

27. Lodge, *The War with Spain,* 13. In addition to the role he played as "the most powerful official advocate, by position and conviction" of U.S. imperialism, Lodge sought to write the history of the Spanish-American War. He depicted the conflict between Spain and the United States as the latest manifestation of the struggle between Anglo-Dutch people who "stood for civil and religious freedom and those who stood for bigotry and tyranny." Joseph A. Fry, "The Architects of the 'Large Policy' Plus Two," *Diplomatic History* 29, no. 1 (2005): 186.

28. While ponderously ideological, Foner's work on the Spanish-Cuban-American War remains an important English-language guide to the Cuban War of Independence and America's intervention into the Spanish-Cuban war. For a more recent analysis which takes on the myth of the inevitable success of Cuban revolutionaries, see John Lawrence Tone, *War and Genocide in Cuba, 1895-1898* (Chapel Hill: University of North Carolina Press, 2006). Philip Sheldon Foner, *The Spanish-Cuban-American War and the Birth of American Imperialism, 1895-1902* (New York: Monthly Review Press, 1972), vol. 1, 14–118; Louis Pérez provides a fine sense of Spanish, Cuban, and American literature on the matter. Pérez, *War of 1898.*

29. Pérez bemoans the pervasive absence of the Cuban perspective in most accounts of the Spanish-American War, arguing that rebel forces were on the verge of attaining independence even in the absence of U.S. intervention. Taking on this myth of inevitability, Tone argues that by 1897 the Cuban insurgency was in a "nearly terminal condition and had no chance of victory without outside aid." He argues that Spanish decisions, outside pressure, and Cuban perseverance turned the tide in 1898. Pérez, *War of 1898,* 8–10; Tone, *War and Genocide in Cuba,* xii, 179–92.

30. Foner, *The Spanish-Cuban-American War,* 32.

31. Ibid., xx–xxiv; Tone, *War and Genocide in Cuba,* 31–41.

32. George W. Auxier, "The Propaganda Activities of the Cuban Junta in Precipitating the Spanish-American War, 1895-1898," *Hispanic American Historical Review* 19, no. 3 (1939); Foner, *The Spanish-Cuban-American War,* 17–18.

33. Charles and Mary Beard, Julius Pratt, and Joseph Wisan all argued in the 1920s and 1930s that press rivalries and sensationalism had forced the McKinley administration to take action, with Wisan quoting Hearst's admonition to Frederick Remington that "You furnish the pictures and I'll furnish the war." More recent studies assert that much of the press outside New York was more circumspect in its coverage, and that furthermore, McKinley paid little attention to the press. For first-wave interpretations, see Charles A. Beard and Mary Ritter Beard, *The Rise of American Civilization* (New York: Macmillan, 1930); Julius William Pratt, *Expansionists of 1898; the Acquisition of Hawaii and the Spanish Islands* (Baltimore, MD: Johns Hopkins University Press, 1936); Joseph E. Wisan, *The Cuban Crisis as Reflected in the New York Press (1895–1898)* (New York: Columbia University Press, 1934). For more recent counterarguments, see W. Joseph Campbell, *Yellow Journalism: Puncturing the Myths, Defining the Legacies* (Westport, CT: Praeger, 2001); Piero Gleijeses, "1898: The Opposition to the Spanish-American War," *Journal of Latin American Studies* 35 (2003).

34. Elbert Jay Benton, *International Law and Diplomacy of the Spanish-American War* (Baltimore, MD: Johns Hopkins University Press, 1908), 26; Lodge, *The War with Spain,* 17.

35. Charles H. Brown, *The Correspondents' War,* 26–27; Bonnie Goldenberg, "Imperial Culture and National Conscience: The Role of the Press in the United States and Spain During the Crisis of 1898," *Bulletin of Hispanic Studies* 77, no. 3 (2000): 176–81.

36. For documents and commentary regarding Spanish military policy, see Benton, *International Law and Diplomacy,* 27–28.

37. Tone, *War and Genocide in Cuba,* 218.

38. Goldenberg, "Imperial Culture and National Conscience," 174.

39. State of the Union address, December 6, 1897, William McKinley, *Messages, Proclamations, and Executive Orders Relating to the Spanish-American War,* Project Gutenberg, October 29, 2004 [EBook #13893]). doi:www.gutenberg.net. For a detailed discussion of civilian casualty figures in the Cuban Revolution, see Tone, *War and Genocide in Cuba,* 209–24.

40. Offner, *An Unwanted War,* 46–47.

41. George W. Auxier, "Middle Western Newspapers and the Spanish American War, 1895-1898," *Mississippi Valley Historical Review* 26, no. 4 (1940).

42. Ivan Musicant, *Empire by Default: The Spanish-American War and the Dawn of the American Century* (New York: Holt, 1998), 84.

43. American concern about German adventurism in the Caribbean and South America may seem overblown when viewed with the benefit of hindsight, but did not seem unfounded at the time. See Holger H. Herwig, *Germany's Vision of Empire in Venezuela, 1871-1914* (Princeton, NJ: Princeton University Press, 1986); also, Holger H. Herwig, *"Luxury" Fleet: The Imperial German Navy, 1888-1918* (Atlantic Highlands, NJ: Ashfield Press, 1987); Miriam Hood, *Gunboat Diplomacy, 1895-1905: Great Power Pressure in Venezuela* (Boston: Allen & Unwin, 1983); Gerhard Wiechmann, *Die preussisch-deutsche Marine in Lateinamerika 1866-1914: eine Studie deutscher Kanonenbootpolitik* (Bremen: H.M. Hauschild, 2002).

44. Ernest R. May, *Imperial Democracy; the Emergence of America as a Great Power* (New York: Harcourt, 1961), 85.

45. For a sense of the relentless stream of letters between the State Department and Spanish officials concerning the fate of Americans imprisoned in Cuba, see the correspondence related to the maltreatment of Manuel Jóse Delgado, the death of Ricardo Ruiz, and the imprisonment of Charles Scott. *Papers Relating to the Foreign Relations of the United States. . . 1896* (Washington, DC: Government Printing Office, 1896), 582–615; *Papers Relating to the Foreign Relations of the United States. . . 1897* (Washington, DC: Government Printing Office, 1897), 483–87 [hereafter *FRUS*]. The Hearst and Pulitzer papers made the miserable fate of Americans imprisoned in Cuba a staple of their coverage, with the Ruiz case in particular receiving extensive treatment. *FRUS 1896.*

46. Grover Cleveland, A*nnual Message of the President Transmitted to Congress December 7, 1896*, in *FRUS 1896*, xxxi.

47. Benton, *International Law and Diplomacy*, 42.

48. Ibid., 42–44. For a broader discussion of Spanish-American diplomacy and the issue of American aid to Cuban insurgents, see Ernest R. May, *Imperial Democracy; the Emergence of America as a Great Power* (New York: Harcourt, 1961), 86–89.

49. For a detailed discussion of various court rulings on filibustering, see Benton, *International Law and Diplomacy*, 46–62.

50. Gerald G. Eggert, "Our Man in Havana: Fitzhugh Lee," *Hispanic American Historical Review* 47, no. 4 (1967): 468–69. Eggert exposes that Lee had no compunction about pursuing private "investment" opportunities in Cuba that hinged on the end of Spanish rule.

51. Ibid., 470, 73.

52. May, *Imperial Democracy*, 104–06.

53. Musicant, *Empire by Default*, 94–95; Offner, *An Unwanted War*, 32–33.

54. Grover Cleveland, *Annual Message of the President Transmitted to Congress December 7, 1896*, in *FRUS 1896*, xxxv.

55. May, *Imperial Democracy*, 112.

56. William McKinley: Inaugural Address, March 4, 1897. Online by Gerhard Peters and John T. Woolley, *The American Presidency Project*, www.presidency.ucsb.

edu/ws/?pid=25827. McKinley made similar remarks privately, informing Carl Schurz shortly after becoming president that "You may be sure there will be no jingo nonsense under my administration." Lewis L. Gould, *The Spanish-American War and President McKinley* (Lawrence: University Press of Kansas, 1982), 11.

57. For explanations that emphasize ultimate over proximate causes—and thereby have a rather deterministic flavor—see Foner, *The Spanish-Cuban-American War*; George C. Herring, *From Colony to Superpower: U.S. Foreign Relations since 1776* (New York: Oxford University Press, 2011); Walter A. McDougall, *Promised Land, Crusader State: The American Encounter with the World since 1776* (Boston: Houghton Mifflin, 1997); Pérez, *The War of 1898*. Pérez in particular seems appalled by the "chance theory of history," leading one to ask if chance plays no role? Is history entirely predetermined? For a useful overview of contending interpretations, see Thomas G. Paterson, "United States Intervention in Cuba, 1898: Interpretations of the Spanish-American-Cuban-Filipino War," *History Teacher* 29, no. 3 (1996); and Edward Crapol, "Coming to Terms with Empire: The Historiography of Late Nineteenth-Century American Foreign Relations," in *Paths to Power: The Historiography of American Foreign Relations*, ed. Michael J. Hogan (Cambridge: Cambridge University Press, 2000).

58. See Richard F. Hamilton, *President McKinley and the Coming of War, 1898* (New Brunswick, NJ: Transaction, 2006), 119–33; John Offner, "United States Politics and the 1898 War over Cuba," in *The Crisis of 1898: Colonial Redistribution and Nationalist Mobilization*, ed. Angel Smith, Dávila Cox, and Emma Aurora (New York: St. Martin's, 1999), 30–32; John L. Offner, "McKinley and the Spanish-American War," *Presidential Studies Quarterly* 34, no. 1 (2004): 52.

59. May, *Imperial Democracy*, 159. For a broader discussion changes in American diplomacy and power, see Robert L. Beisner, *From the Old Diplomacy to the New, 1865-1900* (Arlington Heights, IL: Harlan Davidson, 1986).

60. Offner, *An Unwanted War*, xi.

61. May, *Imperial Democracy*, 124–26; David F. Trask, *The War with Spain in 1898* (New York: Macmillan, 1981), 18–20.

62. For IR literature on coercion theory and coercive diplomacy, see Robert J. Art and Patrick M. Cronin, *The United States and Coercive Diplomacy* (Washington, DC: United States Institute of Peace Press, 2003); Daniel Byman and Matthew C. Waxman, *The Dynamics of Coercion: American Foreign Policy and the Limits of Military Might* (New York: Cambridge University Press, 2001); Alexander L. George, *Forceful Persuasion: Coercive Diplomacy as an Alternative to War* (Washington, DC: United States Institute of Peace Press, 1991); Alexander L. George et al., *The Limits of Coercive Diplomacy* (Boulder, CO: Westview, 1994); Peter Viggo Jakobsen, *Western Use of Coercive Diplomacy after the Cold War: A Challenge for Theory and Practice* (New York: St. Martin's, 1998); Thomas C. Schelling, *Arms and Influence* (New Haven, CT: Yale University Press, 1966).

63. Having taught coercion theory for over a decade to senior and mid-career military officers, it has become increasingly clear to me that Schelling's dichotomy between brute force and coercive force is problematic, placing both threats and such massive use of force as the August 1945 dropping of atomic bombs on Japan in the same category, that of coercion. One has to look long and hard to find wars where one side had no concern for the other's reaction to threats and violence.

64. George, *Forceful Persuasion*, 18.

65. Note of United States to Spain, September 23, 1897, in *FRUS 1898*, 571.

66. See Offner, *An Unwanted War*, 68–86.

67. Note of United States to Spain, September 23, 1897, in *FRUS 1898*, 572.

68. George addresses nine "variables" in his study of coercive diplomacy, but given McKinley's imprecision about the consequences of Spanish inaction, I restrict commentary to those factors relevant to the note. George's nine variables are: (1) Clarity of the Objective, (2) Strength of Motivation, (3) Asymmetry of Motivation, (4) Sense of Urgency, (5) Strong Leadership, (6) Adequate Domestic and International Support, (7) Unacceptability of Threatened Escalation, (8) Clarity Concerning the Precise Terms of Settlement of the Crisis, (9) Image of the Opponent. A younger coercion theorist tinkers with George's variables, settling on a slightly different list of conditions essential to coercive diplomacy: (1) clear demands, (2) use of ultimatum, (3) low cost (4) usable military options, (5) strong leadership, (6) domestic support, (7) international support, (8) assurance against future demands, and (9) use of carrots. George, *Limits of Coercive Diplomacy*, 10–11, 270–291; Peter Viggo Jakobsen, "The Strategy of Coercive Diplomacy: Refining Existing Theory to Post–Cold War Realities," in *Strategic Coercion: Concepts and Cases*, ed. Lawrence Freedman (Oxford: Oxford University Press, 1998), 61–85.

69. Kapur argues that most accounts of the origins of the Spanish-American War overlook McKinley's deep-seated, if misplaced, faith in the process of arbitration and mediation. Nick Kapur, "William McKinley's Values and the Origins of the Spanish-American War: A Reinterpretation," *Presidential Studies Quarterly* 41, no. 1 (2011); John Davis Long, *The New American Navy*, vol. 1 (New York: Outlook, 1903), 134.

70. Foner, *The Spanish-Cuban-American War*.

71. For an analysis of how the U.S. Navy transformed the North Atlantic Squadron from a motley array of ships operating as single units into a force capable of fighting and winning a fleet action, see James C. Rentfrow, *Home Squadron. The U.S. Navy on the North Atlantic Station* (Annapolis, MD: Naval Institute Press, 2014). For a broader discussion of the development of the U.S. Navy during this period, see Benjamin Franklin Cooling, *Gray Steel and Blue Water Navy: The Formative Years of America's Military-Industrial Complex, 1881-1917* (Hamden, CT: Archon, 1979); and Kenneth J. Hagan, *This People's Navy: The Making of American Sea Power* (New York: Free Press, 1991).

72. McKinley, *Messages, Proclamations, and Executive Orders.*

73. Gould, *Spanish-American War*, 32.

74. James Cable, *Gunboat Diplomacy 1919-1991: Political Applications of Limited Naval Force* (New York: St. Martin's, 1994), 7–64.

75. Eggert, "Our Man in Havana: Fitzhugh Lee," 477; Foner, *The Spanish-Cuban-American War*, 223–25.

76. Sigsbee, *The "Maine,"* 10; Weems, *The Fate of the Maine*, 31.

77. Offner notes that during the riot, Lee had offered Spanish authorities two cruisers from Key West to restore order. Offner, *An Unwanted War*, 95.

78. Eggert, "Our Man in Havana: Fitzhugh Lee," 480.

79. Brown, *The Correspondents' War.*

80. M. Long, *Journal of John D. Long*, 110.

81. Robert R. Hitt (representative from Illinois), Remarks on Cuba, *Congressional Record* 31, Pts. 1–2 (55th Congress, 2nd Session, Wednesday, January 19, 1898), 768–69.

82. Offner, *An Unwanted War*, 98–99.

83. McKinley had appointed aged William Sherman as the Secretary of State for political purposes, relying on William Day to run the department once Sherman's infirmities became apparent.

84. Lodge, *The War with Spain*, 28; Offner, *An Unwanted War*, 98–99.

85. Sigsbee, *The "Maine,"* 22–23.

86. Offner, *An Unwanted War*, 99.

87. Senator Frank Cannon of Utah, Remarks to Senate, February 9, 1898, *Congressional Record*, 55th Congress, 2nd session, 1575.

88. Goldenberg, "Imperial Culture and National Conscience," 173.

89. Joseph Smith, "From Coast Defense to Embalmed Beef: The Infuence of the Press and Public Opinion on McKinley's Policymaking During the Spanish-American War," in *The US Public and American Foreign Policy*, ed. Andrew Johnstone and Helen Laville (London: Routledge, 2010); Auxier, "Middle Western Newspapers," 531.

90. See Offner, "United States Politics," 41n23, for list of dissertations, articles, and books on U.S. regional press coverage of the Cuban Revolution.

91. For an elaboration of these consistent themes, see Goldenberg, "Imperial Culture and National Conscience," 173–83.

92. For a vivid summary of the Evangelina Cisneros story, see Thomas, *The War Lovers*, 179–85.

93. Gleijeses, "1898," 685, 707–19. Offner sees the same pattern in presidential correspondence, with few letters volunteering military service during the interim between the *Maine*'s destruction and the release of the Naval Court of Inquiry report on March 28, and a flood of letters volunteering immediately after the board's findings became public. Offner, "United States Politics," 32. Hamilton's assessment of the press and public opinion likewise finds that both were more differentiated

and less enthused about military intervention than often portrayed. Richard F. Hamilton, *President McKinley*, 149–70, 213–38.

94. Remarks of Senator Frank J. Cannon of Utah to the Senate, February 9, 1898, *Congressional Record*, 55th Congress, 2nd session, 1575.

95. Ibid, 1575.

96. Ibid, 2919.

97. Offner, "United States Politics," 33. Alger's fears were well-founded insofar as they concern McKinley's diminished control of his own party: in January 1898, the Ohio state Republican League passed a resolution favoring recognizing the independence of Cuba by a margin of 437 to 283 over the president's objections. May, *Imperial Democracy*, 138.

98. For a discussion of who constituted the elite that determined American policy, see Lloyd C. Gardner, Walter LaFeber, and Thomas J. McCormick, *Creation of the American Empire* (Chicago: Rand McNally, 1976).

99. May, *Imperial Democracy*, 118; Musicant, *Empire by Default*, 96. Among the works that question the proposition that American industry had shifted its sight from domestic to foreign markets based on the perceived existence of a demand glut are William H. Becker, *The Dynamics of Business-Government Relations: Industry & Exports, 1893-1921* (Chicago: University of Chicago Press, 1982); David M. Pletcher, *The Diplomacy of Trade and Investment: American Economic Expansion in the Hemisphere, 1865-1900* (Columbia: University of Missouri Press, 1998); David M. Pletcher, *The Diplomacy of Involvement: American Economic Expansion across the Pacific, 1784-1900* (Columbia: University of Missouri Press, 2001); and Hamilton, *President McKinley*. See also James Fields's critique of the prevalence of neo-Marxist interpretations for American imperialism in his "American Imperialism: The Worst Chapter in Almost Any Book," *American Historical Review* 83, no. 3 (June 1978).

100. Walter LaFeber, "The American Search for Opportunity, 1865-1913," in *The New Cambridge History of American Foreign Relations*, vol. 2, ed. William Earl Weeks et al. (New York: Cambridge University Press, 2013), 385. Offner notes that while key industrialists and financiers such as J. P. Morgan, John Jacob Astor, William Rockefeller, and Stuyvesant Fish began to favor intervention by mid-March 1898, many smaller businessmen remained resistant to clamors for intervention. Offner, *An Unwanted War*, 31.

101. This revisionist line of scholarship is well represented in Louis A. Pérez, *Cuba between Empires, 1878–1902* (Pittsburgh, PA: University of Pittsburgh Press, 1983), 178.

102. For a convincing exemplar of this school of thought, see Offner, *An Unwanted War*.

103. Tone, *War and Genocide in Cuba,* 237, 70–71, 80.

104. Those arguing that the Spanish army was on the verge of laying down its arms in March 1898 need to explain its tenacious defense of El Caney and the San Juan

Heights in July 1898 against an enemy far better equipped in terms of artillery and Gatling guns than was the Cuban Army of Liberation. See David F. Trask, *The War with Spain in 1898* (Lincoln: University of Nebraska Press, 1996), 194–257.

105. Goldenberg, "Imperial Culture and National Conscience," 182–85.

106. Trask, *The War with Spain in 1898*, 32.

107. Gould, *The Presidency of William McKinley*, 76.

108. Ibid.

109. Offner, *An Unwanted War*, 128; Rickover, *How the Battleship Maine Was Destroyed*, 63–64, 70.

110. Pérez, *The War of 1898*, 5.

111. Woodford to McKinley, March 19, 1898, in *FRUS 1898*, 693.

112. Trask, *The War with Spain in 1898*, 33.

113. Woodford to McKinley, March 2, 1898, in *FRUS 1898*, 684.

114. Trask, *The War with Spain in 1898*.

115. Day to Woodford, March 26, 1898, in *FRUS 1898*, 704.

116. Woodford to Day, March 27, 1898, and Day reply to Woodford, March 28, 1898, in *FRUS 1898*, 713.

117. Day to Woodford, March 27, 1898, in *FRUS 1898*, 711–12.

118. Woodford to McKinley, March 9, 1898, in *FRUS 1898*, 682.

119. Woodford to McKinley, March 18, in *FRUS 1898*, 689.

120. Message to Congress, April 11, 1898, in McKinley, *Messages, Proclamations, and Executive Orders*.

121. Lodge, *The War with Spain*, 36. Gould ventures that Speaker Reed, a McKinley ally and opponent of war, drafted the resolution. Gould, *The Presidency of William McKinley*, 158.

122. Text of Joint Resolution of Congress approved by McKinley, April 20, 1898. McKinley, *Messages, Proclamations, and Executive Orders*.

123. John A. Garraty, *Henry Cabot Lodge, a Biography* (New York: Knopf, 1953), 169.

124. In 1909, Henry S. Pritchett published an article summarizing a candid retrospective assessment that McKinley had shared with him after a game of cribbage at the White House on Sunday evening, May 2, 1899. Pritchard, as superintendent of the Coast and Geodetic Survey, had furnished all the maps and charts necessary for McKinley to follow the flow of operations during the Spanish-American War. He gradually became a trusted subordinate, and after commenting to the president that one year earlier he had been setting up the White House "map room," McKinley shared some thoughts with him on why he had led the nation into war, and after its successful conclusion, opted to retain Puerto Rico and the Philippines. Regarding his decision for war, Pritchett recalls that the president mused that he could have settled matters peacefully but for the "stampeding of Congress under the impression that the country was demanding immediate hostilities." As for the territorial

acquisitions, McKinley made no mention of economic considerations and market motivation, instead reflecting that he gradually came to the decision that the United States had the responsibility to retain the Philippines, given the difficulties the alternatives would entail. Henry S. Pritchett, "Some Recollections of President McKinley and the Cuban Intervention," *North American Review* 189, no. 640 (March 1909): 400–01.

PART TWO

1. For a comprehensive collection of passenger lists, ship characteristics, cargo manifests, and various primary documents and memoirs, see The Lusitania Resource website, www.rmslusitania.info; the Lusitania Online website, www.lusitania.net; and the Board of Trade Wreck Commissioner's Inquiry into the loss of the Lusitania, www.titanicinquiry.org/Lusitania/Report/Rep01.php.

2. The Board of Trade Wreck Commissioner's Inquiry into the sinking of the *Lusitania* lists the number of passengers on board the ship when it sailed as 1,257, with a crew complement of 702. Many authors cite this figure in their monographs. Yet if one takes into account the three stowaways and various double counts, the figure is more likely 1,960. For a detailed discussion of passenger and crew statistics, see www.rmslusitania.info/people/statistics/ and Mitch Peeke, Kevin Walsh-Johnson, and Steven Jones, *The Lusitania Story* (Annapolis, MD: Naval Institute Press, 2002), 111–54, app. I. Note that the detailed listings of the Lusitania Resource website and Peeke et al., differ on the size of the engineering, deck, and victualing departments. I draw upon the searchable, downloadable listing of the Lusitania Resource website.

3. Diana Preston, C-Span *Booknotes* transcript, www.booknotes.org/Watch/170043-1/Diana+Preston.aspx.

4. David Ramsay, *Lusitania: Saga and Myth* (London: Chatham, 2001), 62.

5. Spelling as is from the original, *New York Tribune,* May 1, 1915, 3, available from *Chronicling America: American Historic Newspapers,* Library of Congress, http://chroniclingamerica.loc.gov/.

6. Thomas Andrew Bailey and Paul B. Ryan, *The Lusitania Disaster: An Episode in Modern Warfare and Diplomacy* (New York: Free Press, 1975), 81.

7. Ibid., 82.

8. Ramsay, *Lusitania: Saga and Myth*, 62.

9. For a sense of the ship's interior, see the photo essays depicting first-, second-, and third-class dining and accommodations in Robert D. Ballard and Spencer Dunmore, *Exploring the Lusitania: Probing the Mysteries of the Sinking That Changed History* (New York: Warner Books, 1995).

10. Diana Preston, *Lusitania: An Epic Tragedy* (New York: Walker, 2002), 122.

11. Ibid., 46.

12. Ibid., 108.

13. Bailey and Ryan, *The Lusitania Disaster*, 131–32; Preston, *Lusitania: An Epic Tragedy*, 132.

14. For detailed descriptions of Turner's actions, or lack thereof, on May 7, see Bailey and Ryan, *The Lusitania Disaster*, 77–82; Preston, *Lusitania: An Epic Tragedy*, 167–86; Ramsay, *Lusitania: Saga and Myth*, 77–88.

15. Admiralty Instructions were advisory, not mandatory, but if instructions were ignored, War Risk Insurance might be invalidated. Patrick Beesly, *Room 40: British Naval Intelligence 1914-1918* (Oxford: Oxford University Press, 1984), 88.

16. As with so many other matters concerning the *Lusitania*, there is considerable controversy about whether Turner received the Admiralty instruction that merchant skippers should zigzag their ships while in danger zones. Beesly believes it was highly unlikely that Turner ever received the instructions, as they were only signed on April 25, with distribution outside of the Admiralty commencing on the May 13, days after the *Lusitania* was sunk. He believes that Turner was manipulated into agreeing that he was aware of such guidance, but provides no evidence. Beesly, *Room 40*, 97.

17. German Admiralty proclamation as communicated from the Ambassador in Germany (Gerard) to the Secretary of State, February 4, 1915, and Memorandum of the German government concerning retaliation against Great Britain's illegal interference with trade between neutrals and Germany, February 4, 1915, in *Papers Relating to the Foreign Relations of the United States, 1915* (Washington, DC: Government Printing Office, 1915), suppl., 94–97 [hereafter, *FRUS 1915*].

18. On May 1, U-30 sank the French Steamer *Europe* and the British steamer *Edale* west of the Scilly Isles; on May 5–6, U-20 sank the British sailing ship *Earl of Lathom* and the steamers *Candidate* and *Centurian* south-southwest of Kinsale. For a daily list of U-boat sinkings broken down by vessel type and nationality, see "Ship Hits during WWI," http://uboat.net/wwi/ships_hit/search.php.

19. Bailey and Ryan, *The Lusitania Disaster*, 143–44.

20. Walter Schwieger did not survive the war, going down in the U-88 in September 1917. The quote derives from a postwar interview with one of Schwieger's fellow U-boat commanders, Max Valentiner, who recalled Schwieger's account. Lowell Thomas, *Raiders of the Deep* (Annapolis, MD: Naval Institute Press, 2004), 97.

21. Beesly, *Room 40*, 84.

22. Preston, *Lusitania: An Epic Tragedy*, 195, 198.

23. Bailey and Ryan, *The Lusitania Disaster*, 132.

24. Preston, *Lusitania: An Epic Tragedy*, 210; Ballard and Dunmore, *Exploring the Lusitania*, 99.

25. Preston, *Lusitania: An Epic Tragedy*, 207.

26. In addition to the ship's twenty-two large wooden lifeboats, the *Lusitania* was equipped with thirty-four smaller collapsible lifeboats and eleven life rafts; a

number of these were successfully deployed. For details, see the lifeboat page at the Lusitania Resource webpage, www.rmslusitania.info/lifeboats/.

27. Preston, *Lusitania: An Epic Tragedy*, 244.

28. Ramsay, *Lusitania: Saga and Myth*, 88.

29. Preston, *Lusitania: An Epic Tragedy*, 269.

30. Preston, Bailey, and Ramsay all give slightly different numbers. The most accurate number seems to be that listed in "Passenger and Crew Statistics," www.rmslusitania.info/people/statistics/. Note that four of the survivors died within days, so one might put the number of survivors at 764. Others died months or years later of the aftereffects of exposure and hypothermia.

31. For an example, see the *New York Times* picture section, Sunday, May 30, 1915, available at the Library of Congress Newspaper Pictorials collection, http://memory.loc.gov/cgi-bin/np_item.pl.

32. "Riots All Over England," *New York Times,* May 12, 1915.

33. Arthur Stanley Link, *Wilson: The Struggle for Neutrality 1914-1915* (Princeton, NJ: Princeton University Press, 1960), 373.

34. As noted in part 1, in 1998, the National Geographic Society commissioned a fourth technical analysis of the matter by Advanced Marine Enterprise, which reopened the possibility that the initial inquiries may have been correct. The weight of informed opinion, however, is that Rickover's analysis still makes more sense.

35. Bailey and Ryan, *The Lusitania Disaster*, 229.

36. Survivors were among the first to raise these questions, with the *Morning Post* quoting Welsh millionaire and Member of Parliament David on May 10: "Why were we not protected. . . . Other ships have been, why were not we? Then also, why were we going so slowly? . . . There was absolute panic." Preston, *Lusitania: An Epic Tragedy*, 292.

37. For one of the harshest assessments of the Mersey Inquiry, see Beesly, *Room 40*, 112–14. For a more empathetic account, see Preston, *Lusitania: An Epic Tragedy*, 315–31.

38. For an extensive discussion of the manipulation of witnesses and evidence, see Bailey and Ryan, *The Lusitania Disaster*, 192–226; Ramsay, *Lusitania: Saga and Myth*, 126–59.

39. Ramsay, *Lusitania: Saga and Myth*, 107.

40. Bailey and Ryan, *The Lusitania Disaster*, 198.

41. Lord Mersey had been in charge of the *Titanic* inquiry in 1912.

42. A transcript of the Wreck Commissioner's Inquiry into the loss of the *Lusitania* is at www.titanicinquiry.org/Lusitania/Report/Rep01.php.

43. "Verdict on the Sinking of Lusitania Delivered with Impressive Gravity," *New York Times,* July 17, 1915.

44. While a recent documentary purports to reveal "new clues on the *Lusitania's* Sinking," the presence of some 4,000 crates of small-arms ammunition aboard the *Lusitania* was known at the time and acknowledged in the Mersey Inquiry. Conspiracy theories have posited that the *Lusitania* may have carried high

explosives in addition to the listed small-arms cartridges, but there is no evidence to support the assertion. Anne Goodwin Sides, "New Clues in *Lusitania*'s Sinking," *Science Friday*, NPR broadcast, November 22, 2008, www.npr.org/templates/story/story.php?storyId=97350149. .

45. See Beesly, *Room 40*, 113; Hans Joachim Koerver, ed., *German Submarine Warfare 1914-1918 in the Eyes of British Intelligence* (Berlin: LIS Reinisch, 2010).

46. Beesly claims that he was shown "conclusive evidence that the shells [listed in *Lusitania*'s manifest] were not empty shells; they were filled but not fused." He received this information from John Light, an American diver who also claimed that the *Lusitania*'s bow was nearly severed from the rest of the hull. Robert Ballard's 1983 dive photographed the gaping hole Light had described, but note that it was aft of the fully intact area where the shell casings were stowed. Beesly, *Room 40*, 114–15; Ballard and Dunmore, *Exploring the Lusitania*, 190–95.

47. Bailey and Ryan, *The Lusitania Disaster*, 219.

48. Opinion of Court, U.S. District Court, Southern District of New York—In the matter of the petition of the Cunard Steamship Company, Limited, as owners of the Steamship "Lusitania," for limitation of its liability, August 23, 1918; www.rmslusitania.info/primary-docs/mayer-opinion/. According to Ramsay, Weimar Germany eventually paid $2,531,000 in compensation to *Lusitania* claimants—far short of the $15.5 million jointly agreed by the claims commission. Ramsay, *Lusitania: Saga and Myth*, 167.

49. This continues to this day. See Eric Nelson, Dave Harding, and Raymond Bridges, "Dark Secrets of the Lusitania" [video recording] (Washington, DC: National Geographic Society, 2012), distributed by Warner Home Video; Erin Mullally, "Lusitania's Secret Cargo," *Archaeology* 62, no. 1 (2009); Sides, "New Clues in Lusitania's Sinking"; Patrick O'Sullivan, *The Lusitania: Unravelling the Mysteries* (Dobbs Ferry, NY: Sheridan House, 2000). *National Geographic*'s 2012 documentary is better than its sensational title suggests, providing an accurate assessment of the findings of Gregg Bemis's 2011 wreck dive and follow-on explosive tests at the Lawrence Livermore National Laboratory.

50. Examples of survivor accounts and initial assessments include Frederick D. Ellis, *The Tragedy of the Lusitania* (Philadelphia: National, 1915); C. E. Lauriat, *The "Lusitania's" Last Voyage* (Boston: Houghton Mifflin, 1915). Among the dozens of memoirs and histories written by those directly involved in planning naval operations or shaping the response to the *Lusitania* disaster are Johann Heinrich Bernstorff and Eric Sutton, *The Memoirs of Count Bernstorff* (London: Heinemann, 1936); Theobald von Bethmann-Hollweg and George Young, *Reflections on the World War* (London: Butterworth, 1920); Winston Churchill, *The World Crisis* (London: Butterworth, 1923); John Arbuthnot Fisher, *Memories* (London: Hodder and Stoughton, 1919); James W. Gerard, *My Four Years in Germany* (New York: George H. Doran, 1917); Alfred Peter Friedrich von Tirpitz, *My Memoirs* (London: Hurst & Blackett, 1919).

51. Thomas was by no means a German sympathizer but, rather, an Anglophile, with his wartime reports from the Middle East transforming T. E. Lawrence into "Lawrence of Arabia." After the war, Thomas exploited his connection with Lawrence via film (*With Allenby in Palestine and Lawrence in Arabia*, 1919) and in print (*With Lawrence in Arabia*, 1924). The success of Thomas's books on the German naval heroes shows how American public opinion was swinging away from wartime depictions of Germans as Huns and barbarians, and embracing more favorable views of its defeated foe. Lowell Thomas, *Count Luckner, the Sea Devil* (Garden City, NY: Doubleday, Page, 1927); Thomas, *Raiders of the Deep*.

52. Hoehling and Hoehling's riveting 1956 narrative of the *Lusitania*'s final voyage drew upon an extensive collection of published memoirs, interviews with survivors, newspaper and magazine articles, and secondary literature published since the event. They were not, however, able to access Admiralty records still sealed in the Public Records Office. A. A. Hoehling and Mary Duprey Hoehling, *The Last Voyage of the Lusitania* (New York: Holt, 1956).

53. The British journalist Colin Simpson and American diver John Light published a series of articles in the *Sunday Times, Life, Sports Illustrated*, and *Reader's Digest* in the early 1970s, advancing controversial claims that have not stood up to scrutiny. John Light conducted some forty-two dives to the *Lusitania*'s wreck, and concluded that the ship had been sunk by an internal explosion and may well have carried deck guns. Colin Simpson, a correspondent for the *London Sunday Times*, went further, asserting in a series of articles, TV documentaries, and a book that the Admiralty had deliberately exposed the *Lusitania* in order to draw the United States into war. Both allegations were thoroughly debunked by Bailey and Ryan in the mid-70s, only to be revived by Patrick Beesly in 1982. The latest scholarship tends to support Bailey and Ryan's interpretation given the unwillingness of John Light to subject his collection of damning letters and secret records to public scrutiny. See Colin Simpson, *Lusitania* (London: Longman, 1972); Bailey and Ryan, *The Lusitania Disaster*; Beesly, *Room 40;* Preston, *Lusitania: An Epic Tragedy*; Ramsay, *Lusitania: Saga and Myth*.

54. The works by Bailey and Ryan, *The Lusitania Diaster*; Preston, *Lusitania: An Epic Tragedy*; and Ramsay, *Lusitania: Saga and Myth,* stand out.

55. Using three remotely controlled submersibles and a small manned submersible, Robert Ballard—who previously led dives to the wrecks of the *Titanic* and *Bismarck*—photographed and filmed the site in 1993, with Gregg Bemis conducting an even more thorough exploration of the wreck in 2011 (following up on numerous less elaborate dives in 1999, 2000, 2001, and 2008). Ballard and Dunmore, *Exploring the Lusitania*; "Last Voyage of the Lusitania" [videorecording] (Washington, DC: National Geographic Society, 2003), distributed by Warner Home Video; Nelson et al., "Dark Secrets of the Lusitania."

56. George Sylvester Viereck's English-language New York newspaper the *Fatherland* went so far as to claim that the liner had been equipped with twelve six-inch guns.

Justus D. Doenecke, *Nothing Less Than War: A New History of America's Entry into World War I* (Lexington: University Press of Kentucky, 2011), 73.

57. For a detailed debunking of the allegation that the *Lusitania* was armed, an allegation actively fostered by Germany's ambassador in Washington, see Bailey and Ryan, *The Lusitania Disaster*, 186–90.

58. The 1903 agreement between Cunard and the Admiralty can be found in app. II of Peeke et al., *The Lusitania Story*, 155–66.

59. Julian Stafford Corbett and Henry John Newbolt, "Naval Operations," in *History of the Great War Based on Official Documents, by Direction of the Historical Section of the Committee of Imperial Defence* (London: Longmans, Green, 1920), 1:29–31. One might note that Alfred Booth, chairman of Cunard, addressed the matter head-on in the *New York Tribune*, commenting that "*Lusitania* was not armed in any way. She was built under the company's agreement with the British Government, under which she could be requisitioned for service as an armed cruiser. As a matter of fact, she was never so used at any period of her career, and no guns of any description were ever put on board the ship." *New York Tribune*, May 10, 1915, quoted in Ramsay, *Lusitania: Saga and Myth*, 184.

60. In late January 1915, the Admiralty had used the *Transylvania* and *Ausonia*, the former under the command of Captain Turner, to transport several large-caliber guns it had purchased from Bethlehem Steel Works. They could clearly be seen lashed down on the forward decks of the liners when the ships diverted into Queenstown on January 31 and February 3, respectively. The guns were not operational, and neither ship had operational deck guns, but this would have been difficult to determine from afar. The British began converting a number of merchant ships into decoy submarine entrapment killers (Q-ships) by mounting hidden guns on them; and while the first clash between a U-boat and a Q-ship occurred weeks after the *Lusitania*'s destruction, orders for the program had been given in November 1914, with two Q-ships entering into service in 1914 and an additional 29 in 1915. Beesly, *Room 40*, 93; Ramsay, *Lusitania: Saga and Myth*, 46–47. "Decoy Q-Boats," *Inside Out*, BBC broadcast, June 23, 2003; www.bbc.co.uk/insideout/southwest/series3/qships_submarine_firstworldwar.shtml.

61. Preston, *Lusitania: An Epic Tragedy*, 94, 136, 211–12, 346, 92.

62. Reply of the German government to the *Lusitania* note, transmitted by the Ambassador in Germany (Gerard) to the secretary of state, May 29, 1915, in *FRUS 1915*, suppl., 420.

63. Preston, *Lusitania: An Epic Tragedy*, 111.

64. The *Lusitania*'s supplementary cargo manifest from crossing 202, courtesy Franklin D. Roosevelt Presidential Archive, www.rmslusitania.info/downloads/crossing202_supplementary_cargo_manifest.pdf. For a breakdown of the size and insurance value of each consignment, consult Daniel Allen Butler, *The Lusitania: The Life, Loss, and Legacy of an Ocean Legend* (Mechanicsburg,

PA: Stackpole, 2000), 267–69. Butler concludes that over half the cargo carried was, by British definition, contraband.

65. Each small-arms crate held 1,000 rounds, each shrapnel box held 4 shrapnel cases. The *Lusitania,* therefore, carried over 4 million rounds of small-arms ammunition (.303 caliber), almost 5,000 shrapnel shell casings, and 3,240 brass percussion fuses. Using a calculus of 100 rounds = 1 dead soldier, outlets sympathetic to the German cause estimated that the *Lusitania* carried sufficient ammunition to kill 40,000 German soldiers. Given the profligate expenditure of ammunition in WWI, the estimate is probably inflated, but that misses the point. The *Lusitania* was carrying ammunition destined for use against German soldiers.

66. Bailey and Ryan, *The Lusitania Disaster*, 100–01. Ramsay asserts that *Lusitania's* previous skipper, Captain Daniel Dow, had asked to be relieved of command in March 1915, informing Cunard's chairman that he could not accept the responsibility of carrying munitions or contraband on a passenger liner. Ramsay provides no specific citation for this claim, though his bibliography suggests that he consulted numerous record groups in the Cunard archives at the University of Liverpool. Ramsay, *Lusitania: Saga and Myth*, 49.

67. Letter to the Editor, from Dudley Field Malone, *The Nation* 116, no. 3 (January 3, 1923). Link, *Wilson: The Struggle for Neutrality*, 161–69.

68. Simpson's revisionist account found multiple outlets, from newspaper articles to popular magazines, to a book, since republished in 1983. One can assess the appeal of revisionism by looking at customer, rather than academic, reviews of the book. Despite being thoroughly debunked by Bailey and Ryan shortly after publication, the Simpson book has been republished and continues to receive far more favorable than unfavorable customer reviews on Amazon.com. Simpson, *Lusitania*; Bailey and Ryan, *The Lusitania Disaster*.

69. Nelson et al., "Dark Secrets of the Lusitania."

70. One should note that survivors were very inconsistent in describing the time delay between the first and second explosions, and that humans have a very poor record of discerning elapsed time when under stress. Maienschein's certainty does not seem to take the vagaries of memory and the impact of stress into account.

71. Video-recorded conclusion of Dr. Jon Maienschein, director of the Lawrence Livermore National Laboratory Energetic Materials Center, upon the conclusion of the LLNL's 2011 tests and computer modeling of the Lusitania's destruction, quoted in Nelson et al., "Dark Secrets of the Lusitania."

72. For a detailed rebuttal of the myth of Canadian soldiers, see Bailey and Ryan, *The Lusitania Disaster*, 110–13.

73. One can search the entire passenger list at www.rmslusitania.info/lusitania-passenger-list/.

74. "Admiral Lord Fisher. His Maxims in War," *New Zealand Herald*, April 9, 1910, 5; http://paperspast.natlib.govt.nz/cgi-bin/paperspast?a=d&d=NZH19100409.2.116.52.

75. Randolph S. Churchill and Martin Gilbert, *Winston S. Churchill, 1914-16* (London: Heinemann, 1973), 3:501; Preston, *Lusitania: An Epic Tragedy*, 76.

76. "Hobson Sees British Plot to Thrust U.S. into War," *New York Tribune*, May 15, 1015, 4; http://chroniclingamerica.loc.gov/lccn/sn83030214/1915-05-15/ed-1/seq-4/. Hobson's Medal of Honor was awarded for extraordinary courage in carrying out orders to sink the USS *Merrimac* at the entrance to the fortified harbor of Santiago de Cuba on June 3, 1898. Joining Hobson in expressing skepticism about Wilson's reaction to the *Lusitania* in 1915 was fellow Spanish-American veteran and naval officer Rear Admiral French Chadwick. Link, *Wilson: The Struggle for Neutrality*, 25.

77. O'Sullivan, *The Lusitania: Unravelling the Mysteries*; Simpson, *Lusitania*.

78. Patrick Beesly uncovered so much negligence on the part of the Royal Navy that he was "reluctantly driven to the conclusion that there was a conspiracy deliberately to put the *Lusitania* at risk in the hopes that even an abortive attack on her would bring the United States into the war." Yet as noted, Beesly drew back speaking of a plot, as the odds against it were so great. Beesly, *Room 40*, 121.

79. Preston, *Lusitania: An Epic Tragedy*, 318.

80. Link, *Wilson: The Struggle for Neutrality*, 375.

81. Ibid., 7.

82. Many Jewish-American groups initially favored the Central Powers, given tsarist Russia's persecution of its Jewish population, while Armenian Americans favored the Entente, as they viewed Russia as an ally in their struggle against Ottoman despotism.

83. The size estimates, terminology, and composition of these three groups derive from Link, *Wilson: The Struggle for Neutrality*.

84. Ibid., 13.

85. The term "Whiggish history" refers to interpreting the past as a progressive, inevitable move away from absolutism toward constitutional governance, with Scottish historian and philosopher Thomas Carlyle epitomizing this perspective. While most Americans were unaware of and indifferent to the development of British government, American elites who attended boarding schools, Ivy League colleges, and top law schools received a heavy dose of the Whiggish perspective.

86. Link, *Wilson: The Struggle for Neutrality*, 14.

87. For a discussion of the German-American community, especially how the *Lusitania* disaster undermined its solidarity and coherence, see Frank Trommler, "The *Lusitania* Effect: America's Mobilization against Germany in World War I," *German Studies Review* 32, no. 2 (2009); Reinhard R. Doerries, *Imperial Challenge: Ambassador Count Bernstorff and German-American Relations, 1908-1917* (Chapel Hill: University of North Carolina Press, 1989), 41–76.

88. Doenecke, *Nothing Less Than War*, 20; Ernest R. May, *The World War and American Isolation, 1914-1917* (Cambridge, MA: Harvard University Press, 1959), 36.

89. Link, *Wilson: The Struggle for Neutrality*, 30.

90. Woodrow Wilson: "Message on Neutrality," August 19, 1914, available at Gerhard Peters and John T. Woolley, *The American Presidency Project*, www.presidency.ucsb.edu/ws/?pid=65382.

91. LeRoy Ashby, *William Jennings Bryan: Champion of Democracy* (Boston: Twayne, 1987), 143–52.

92. William Jennings Bryan and Mary Baird Bryan, *The Memoirs of William Jennings Bryan* (Chicago: John C. Winston, 1925), 376.

93. "Wilson against U.S. Loans to Nations at War," *The* [New York] *Sun,* August 16, 1914; available at *Chronicling America: Historic American Newspapers,* Library of Congress, http://chroniclingamerica.loc.gov/lccn/sn83030272/1914-08-16/ed-1/seq-1/.

94. Annual Estimates of Unemployment in the United States, 1900–1954, National Bureau of Economic Research Study (1957), www.nber.org/chapters/c2644.pdf.

95. Link, *Wilson: The Struggle for Neutrality*, 136, 616. In August 1915, the administration abandoned its opposition to granting war loans entirely, opening the way for massive financing of the Allied war effort. For a full discussion of this, see John Milton Cooper Jr., "The Command of Gold Reversed: American Loans to Britain, 1915-1917," *Pacific Historical Review* 45, no. 2 (1976).

96. Proclamations of Neutrality and Appeal by the President of the United States to the citizens of the Republic, in *Papers Relating to the Foreign Relations of the United States, 1914* (Washington, DC: Government Printing Office, 1914), suppl., 550–51 [hereafter, *FRUS 1914*].

97. Public circular issued by the Secretary of State, October 15, 1914, regarding neutrality and trade in contraband, in *FRUS 1914*, suppl., 573–74.

98. Memorandum by the Counselor for the Department of State (Lansing) on Professor Hugo Müsterberg's Letter to President Wilson of November 19, 1914. *Papers Relating to the Foreign Relations of the United States: The Lansing Papers, 1914-1920,* II:169; http://digital.library.wisc.edu/1711.dl/FRUS.FRUS19141920v1 [hereafter, *Lansing Papers*].

99. For a detailed discussion of the German-organized propaganda office established in New York, and the efforts of Bernhard Dernburg, Heinrich Albert, and George Sylvester Viereck, see Doerries, *Imperial Challenge,* 41–76. For an overview of indigenous German-American initiatives, see Clifton J. Child, "German American Attempts to Prevent the Exportation of Munitions of War, 1914-1915," *Mississippi Valley Historical Review* 3 (1938).

100. Link, *Wilson: The Struggle for Neutrality,* 166.

101. Link, *Wilson: The Struggle for Neutrality,* 354.

102. Johann Heinrich Bernstorff, *My Three Years in America* (New York: Scribner's, 1920), 30.

103. In terms of number of ships, the British merchant fleet was ten times larger than the U.S. merchant fleet, which in turn was considerably smaller than the German

merchant fleet. Nicholas A. Lambert, *Planning Armageddon: British Economic Warfare and the First World War* (Cambridge, MA: Harvard University Press, 2012), 239; Link, *Wilson: The Struggle for Neutrality*, 81–82.

104. For a detailed discussion of British efforts to derail the bill, see Lambert, *Planning Armageddon*, 245–50.

105. Lambert notes that the British objections to the scheme stemmed from the realization that "these ships would be added to the U.S. registry and therefore become available to transport a flow of U.S. goods to Europe (and Germany)," with the British Cabinet realizing that the risks of an Anglo-American confrontation would increase dramatically. Lambert, *Planning Armageddon,* 243–44.

106. Link, *Wilson: The Struggle for Neutrality*, 147.

107. Lodge for his part confided with Roosevelt that "I never expected to hate any one in politics with the hatred which I feel toward Wilson." Link, *Wilson: The Struggle for Neutrality*, 151, 158.

108. Sir Edward Grey put it as follows to Ambassador Page: the chief weapon that England has against any enemy is her navy and that navy may damage an enemy in two ways: by fighting and by economic pressure, explaining that under present conditions economic pressure was at least as important as fighting. In *FRUS 1915*, suppl., 682.

109. See Churchill memorandum to Grey in Lambert, *Planning Armageddon*, 241–45.

110. For a detailed analysis of prewar British planning to use sea power and finance to strangle Germany, see Lambert, *Planning Armageddon*.

111. Article 56 of the 1909 Declaration of London expressly prohibited the "transfer of a belligerent vessel to a neutral flag in a case where such vessel finds herself shut up in a neutral port from which she has no chance of escaping under the belligerent flag." Wilson may have reasoned that the British could hardly invoke one article of the Declaration of London while simultaneously ignoring and reinterpreting other articles.

112. For an excellent discussion of how Britain sought to control neutral shipping through the use of black and white lists, see Patrick Devlin, *Too Proud to Fight: Woodrow Wilson's Neutrality* (New York: Oxford University Press, 1975), 180–86.

113. Lambert, *Planning Armageddon*, 179. Lambert's work contradicts earlier assessments arguing that the decision to fight a continental war reduced the Royal Navy to a secondary role. For an example of this earlier assessment, see John W. Coogan, *The End of Neutrality: The United States, Britain, and Maritime Rights, 1899-1915* (Ithaca, NY: Cornell University Press, 1981), 148–68.

114. Lambert, *Planning Armageddon*, 178, 181.

115. Lambert notes that while the concept had been endorsed by the Committee on Imperial Defence, "the precise means to achieve the agreed ends were not yet settled [and] . . . powerful interest groups remained violently opposed to economic

warfare, especially the Treasury and Board of Trade." His monograph focuses as much on the internal strife and debates within the British government as it does the diplomatic row that ensued internationally as Britain moved to implement the strategy in 1914–16. Lambert, *Planning Armageddon*, 181.

116. Ibid., 99.

117. Ambassador in Austria-Hungary (Penfield) to the Secretary of State, August 13, 1914; Ambassador in Great Britain (Page,) to the Secretary of State, August 26, 1914; Ambassador in Germany (Gerard) to the Secretary of State, September 2, 1914. In *FRUS 1914*, suppl., 217–18, 224.

118. The full text of the "Declaration concerning the Laws of Naval War" (London, February 26, 1909), available at the Treaties and Documents collection of the International Committee of the Red Cross, www.icrc.org/ihl/INTRO/ 255?OpenDocument.

119. See Articles 24–29 and 33 of the "Declaration concerning the Laws of Naval War."

120. One might note that the Royal Navy began to seize grain shipments bound for Rotterdam well before the cabinet settled on the fiction of German government control of all foodstuffs (not yet established in August 1914) to declare food-stuffs a conditional contraband. For a full discussion, see Devlin, *Too Proud to Fight,* 191–96.

121. Ambassador in Great Britain (Page) to the Secretary of State, August 5, 1914; British Order-in-Council 20 August 1914. In *FRUS 1914*, suppl., 215–16, 219–20.

122. Telegram, Acting Secretary of State to the Ambassador in Great Britain (Page), September 26, 1914, in *FRUS 1914*, suppl., 236.

123. Ambassador in Great Britain (Page) to the Secretary of State, September 29, 1914; British Proclamation specifying certain additional articles which are to be treated as contraband of war, September 21, 1914, attached to telegram from Ambassador in Great Britain (Page) to the Secretary of State, September 30, 1914. In *FRUS 1914*, suppl., 233, 237.

124. Link, *Wilson: The Struggle for Neutrality*, 112–14.

125. The Ambassador in Great Britain (Page) to the Secretary of State [Telegram], October 16, 1914, in *FRUS 1914*, suppl., 248–49.

126. Norway asked the United States to join the protests that it and other northern neutrals had issued at Britain's novel step of declaring whole sections of inter-national waters as a war zone. The United States declined to join the protest. Devlin, *Too Proud to Fight*, 199–200.

127. Link, *Wilson: The Struggle for Neutrality*, 173.

128. Note to Great Britain of December 26 Protesting Against Seizures and Detentions Regarded as Unwarranted, in *FRUS 1914*, suppl., 373–75.

129. *New York Tribune*, December 29, 1914, available at *Chronicling America: American Historic Newspapers*, Library of Congress, http://chroniclingamerica. loc.gov/.

130. Link, *Wilson: The Struggle for Neutrality*, 175.

131. Edward Grey, Viscount of Fallodon, *Twenty-Five Years, 1892-1916* (New York: Frederick A. Stokes, 1925), 2:107. Grey's wartime interaction with his Cabinet colleagues confirms the priority he assigned to maintaining good Anglo-American relations. See May, *The World War and American Isolation*, 8, 16–18.

132. Joseph P. Tumulty, *Woodrow Wilson as I Know Him* (Garden City, NY: Doubleday, Page, 1922); www.gutenberg.org/ebooks/8124.

133. For discussions of the *Dacia* and *Wilhelmina* cases, see Doenecke, *Nothing Less Than War*, 65–68; Link, *Wilson: The Struggle for Neutrality*, 179–90. For an in-depth discussion of Anglo-American maritime differences, see Coogan, *The End of Neutrality*, 169–256.

134. See Memorandum from German Embassy to the Department of State, February 7, 1915, and follow-on discussions, in *FRUS 1915*, suppl., 95, 102.

135. Devlin, *Too Proud to Fight*, 187–88, 207–08; Link, *Wilson: The Struggle for Neutrality*, 179–90.

136. For a critique of Link's labored defense of Wilsonian impartiality as applied to the British maritime system, see Robert W. Tucker, *Woodrow Wilson and the Great War: Reconsidering America's Neutrality, 1914-1917* (Charlottesville: University of Virginia Press, 2007), 80–87.

137. The first indication that the German navy was even considering the possibility of using submarines against British merchant shipping was a lower-echelon study prepared in May 1914 by Kapitänleutnant Ulrich-Eberhard, and verbally briefed to von Tirpitz before the start of WWI. Blum concluded that Germany would require 222 submarines to successfully wage a campaign against British shipping, explaining von Tirpitz's initial skepticism of Hermann Bauer's October 1914 proposal. For a full discussion, see Arno Spindler, *Der Handelskrieg mit U-Booten: Der Krieg zur See, 1914–1918* (Berlin: E.S. Mittler, 1932), 1:1–10, 153–57, 177–183.

138. At the start of World War I, the German navy had only twenty-five submarines capable of high-seas operations, of which fifteen were gasoline powered and of limited range. The much ballyhooed Handelskrieg mit U-Booten was launched on February 24, 1915, with only six U-boats. Andreas Michelsen, *Der U-Bootskrieg, 1914-1918* (Leipzig: K.F. Koehler, 1925), 2; Spindler, *Der Handelskrieg mit U-Booten*, 1:152–53.

139. Spindler, *Der Handelskrieg mit U-Booten*, 1:v–vii, 384; May, *The World War and American Isolation*, 113–36; Link, *Wilson: The Struggle for Neutrality*, 312–20.

140. German Admiralty proclamation as communicated from the ambassador in Germany (Gerard) to the secretary of state, February 4, 1915; and Memorandum of the German government concerning retaliation against Great Britain's illegal interference with trade between neutrals and Germany, February 4, 1915, in *FRUS 1915*, suppl., 94–97.

141. Wilson's cabinet met on Friday, February 5, the day after the German Admiralty proclamation of unrestricted submarine warfare. Its first order of business was to discuss the German statement and the danger it posed to American shipping. The second order of business was to discuss what to do about Werner von Horn, who had been apprehended by American authorities after his failed effort to blow up a Canadian Pacific railway bridge over the St. Croix River. See E. David Cronon, ed., *The Cabinet Diaries of Josephus Daniels, 1913–1921* (Lincoln: University of Nebraska Press, 1963). For the particulars of this and other cases, see Graeme S. Mount, *Canada's Enemies: Spies and Spying in the Peaceable Kingdom* (Toronto: Dundurn Press, 1993), 31–33.

142. Link, *Wilson: The Struggle for Neutrality*, 321.

143. American Note to the German Government, February 10, 1915, in *FRUS 1915*, suppl., 98–99.

144. Note to Great Britain of December 26 Protesting Against Seizures and Detentions Regarded as Unwarranted, in *FRUS 1914*, suppl., 373–75; American Note to the German Government, February 10, 1915, in *FRUS 1915*, suppl., 98–99.

145. The Secretary of State to President Wilson, February 15, 1915, in *Lansing Papers,* 1:353–54. One should note that the German proposal represented the views of the chancellor and Foreign Ministry, with the German navy opposed to the idea. But in the spring of 1915, the former still determined policy. See May, *The World War and American Isolation*, 127–28.

146. Translation of German reply to American proposal, Ambassador in Germany (Gerard) to the Secretary of State, March 1, 1915, in *FRUS 1915*, suppl., 129–30.

147. Link, *Wilson: The Struggle for Neutrality*, 335.

148. British and French Declaration Prohibiting All Trade with Germany, March 1, 1915, in *FRUS 1915*, suppl., 127–28. The British Order in Council translating the declaration into policy was issued on March 11. For extended analyses of the American response to British and German naval measures aimed at merchant shipping, see Doenecke, *Nothing Less Than War*, 58–92; Tucker, *Woodrow Wilson and the Great War*, 88–108; Link, *Wilson: The Struggle for Neutrality*.

149. Doenecke, *Nothing Less Than War*, 65.

150. Secretary of State to the Ambassador in Great Britain (Page), March 30, 1915, in *FRUS 1915*, suppl., 152–56.

151. Woodrow Wilson to William Jennings Bryan, March 24, 1915, in *Lansing Papers,* 1:288–89.

152. Doenecke, *Nothing Less Than War*, 63.

153. As Patrick Devlin notes in an important study of Wilson's neutrality, "an American ship could be identified and action avoided, but no submarine commander could detect the presence of an American on an Allied ship. For Germany to agree to spare American ships would be a hindrance to the campaign; an agreement to spare American lives would make it impossible." Devlin notes that Lansing appreciated the distinction, suggesting that British ships

carrying American passengers should hoist an American flag to indicate their presence. The impracticality of the scheme, given the Admiralty's instruction to British merchant captains to hoist neutral colors if threatened, is striking. Devlin, *Too Proud to Fight*, 211.

154. See, for example, the coverage in *The* [New York] *Sun*, April 2, 1915; available at *Chronicling America: Historic American Newspapers,* Library of Congress, http://chroniclingamerica.loc.gov/lccn/sn83030272/1915-04-02/ed-1/seq-2/.

155. Counselor for the Department of State (Lansing) to the Secretary of State, April 5, 1915, in *Lansing Papers*, 1:369.

156. The Secretary of State to President Wilson, April 7, 1915, in *Lansing Papers*, 1:374.

157. One should note that this division between hawks and doves did not align one department against another, but was replicated within departments, with Assistant Secretary of the Navy Franklin Roosevelt and State Department Counselor Robert Lansing favoring harder positions than did their superiors. See Lee Craig, *Josephus Daniels. His Life and Times* (Chapel Hill: University of North Carolina Press, 2013), 306.

158. Suggestion of outline of note to the German government, President Wilson to the Secretary of State, April 22, 1915, in *Lansing Papers*, 1:377–78. A recent biography of Wilson's secretary of the navy dryly remarks that Wilson "underappreciated the efficacy of compromise" and was in the "habit of wrapping his opinions in a self-righteousness that he confused with noble idealism." Craig, *Josephus Daniels*, 213.

159. Secretary of State Bryan to President Wilson, April 3, 1915, in *Lansing Papers*, 1:378.

160. Secretary of State Bryan to President Wilson, April 3, 1915, in *Lansing Papers*, 1:378–79; Wilson's secretary of the navy, Josephus Daniels, had similar misgivings and sympathized with Bryan's position. Yet Daniels was unwilling to break openly with the president, calculating that the Democratic Party needed Wilson more than Bryan. For details on Daniels decision to stifle his reservations for the good of the party, see Craig, *Josephus Daniels*, 306–14.

161. John Milton Cooper Jr., "The Shock of Recognition: The Impact of World War I on America," *Virginia Quarterly Review* 76 (2000); Mark Sullivan, *Our Times; the United States, 1900-1925* (New York: Scribner's, 1926).

162. Link, *Wilson: The Struggle for Neutrality*, 379–87.

163. Assistant Secretary of the Treasury (Peters) to the Counselor for the Department of State (Lansing), May 8, 1915, in *Lansing Papers*, 1:385–86. The reply indicates some uncertainty, indicating the shipment from Remington consisted of 2,400 [4,200?] cases of metallic packages [cartridges].

164. Ambassador in Great Britain (Page) to the Secretary of State, May 8, 1915, in *FRUS 1915*, suppl., 385.

165. Consul at Cork (Frost) to the Secretary of State, May 9, 1915, in *FRUS 1915*, suppl., 386–87.

166. House had been in Europe in the summer of 1914, and he believed that American efforts at mediation might have averted the war. Wilson encouraged House to explore the prospects for mediation more fully in 1915, establishing a parallel conduit for U.S. diplomacy largely outside of Bryan's supervision. For details of House's 1915 mission, see Link, *Wilson: The Struggle for Neutrality*, 191–231; Devlin, *Too Proud to Fight*, 252–96.

167. House to Wilson, May 9, 1915, quoted in Nicholas Ferns, "Loyal Advisor? Colonel Edward House's Confidential Trips to Europe, 1913–1917," *Diplomacy & Statecraft* 24, no. 3 (2013). House's postwar papers confirm how his increasingly pro-British views made it difficult for him to render objective, impartial assessments of British and German claims. Edward Mandell House and Charles Seymour, *The Intimate Papers of Colonel House* (Boston: Houghton Mifflin, 1926).

168. Secretary of State to President Wilson, May 9, 1915, in *Lansing Papers*, 1:386–87.

169. Counselor for the Department of State (Lansing) to the Secretary of State, May 9, 1915, in *Lansing Papers,* 1:387–88.

170. Memorandum by the Counselor for the Department of State (Lansing) on the Sinking of the *"Lusitania,"* May 10, 1915, in *Lansing Papers*, 1:389.

171. Lansing's exact wording was that the German government guarantee "that in the future ample measures will be taken to insure the safety of the lives of American citizens on the high seas unless they are traveling on a vessel of belligerent nationality, which is armed or being convoyed by belligerent war craft." I have taken the liberty of spelling out the implications of Lansing's carefully chosen words. Counselor for the Department of State (Lansing) to the Secretary of State, May 10, 1915, in *Lansing Papers*, 1:391–92.

172. Wilson did find time to write three letters to Edith Galt between May 9 and May 11, later even asking her to read the draft of his second protest note to Germany (June 3). For an examination of how Wilson's courtship of Edith Galt intersected with the unrestricted submarine crisis and Secretary of State Bryan's resignation, see Phyllis Lee Levin, *Edith and Woodrow. The Wilson White House* (New York: Scribner's, 2001), 74–87.

173. Devlin, *Too Proud to Fight*, 288.

174. Link, *Wilson: The Struggle for Neutrality*, 382.

175. Ibid., 43.

176. Edwin Alderman, President of the University of Virginia, to Walter Page, U.S. Ambassador to Great Britain, May 12, 1915, in Link, *Wilson: The Struggle for Neutrality*, 375.

177. Doenecke, *Nothing Less Than War*, 73. Another study notes that "out of 1,000 newspaper editors who took part in a telegraph poll, only six called for war." John Milton Cooper Jr., "The United States," in *The Origins of World War I*, ed. Richard Hamilton and Holger Herwig (Cambridge: Cambridge University Press, 2003), 432.

178. Cooper, "The United States," 73–74; Link, *Wilson: The Struggle for Neutrality*, 375–77.

179. One might also note how Wilson behaved very differently from recent presidents, holding no press conferences at all between July 1915 and late 1916. Doenecke, *Nothing Less Than War*, 5; Link, *Wilson: The Struggle for Neutrality*.

180. Devlin, *Too Proud to Fight*, 306.

181. Arthur Stanley Link, *Wilson the Diplomatist: A Look at His Major Foreign Policies* (Baltimore, MD: Johns Hopkins University Press, 1957), 33.

182. President's Draft Instruction to the Ambassador in Germany (Gerard), attached as an enclosure to Message from the Counselor for the Department of State (Lansing) to the Secretary of State, May 12, 1915, in *Lansing Papers*, 1:395–98.

183. Ibid.

184. For a summary of cabinet discussions, see "Cabinet's Long Session," *New York Times*, May 12, 1915, 2; Link, *Wilson: The Struggle for Neutrality*, 384–85; May, *The World War and American Isolation*, 149–50.

185. Devlin, *Too Proud to Fight*, 290–91; Link, *Wilson: The Struggle for Neutrality*, 388–89.

186. "Cabinet's Long Session," *New York Times*, May 12, 1915, 2.

187. Spindler, *Der Handelskrieg mit U-Booten*, 2:89–90.

188. Ambassador to Berlin (Gerard) to the Secretary of State, May 10, 1915, in *FRUS 1915*, suppl., 389.

189. Ibid., 396.

190. Ambassador to Berlin (Gerard) to the Secretary of State, May 17, 18, and 19, 1915, in *FRUS 1915*, suppl., 398–402.

191. Lane was born on Prince Edwards Island, with his family moving to California when he was seven. Link, *Wilson: The Struggle for Neutrality*, 390.

192. President Wilson to the Secretary of State, May 20, 1915, in *Lansing Papers*, 1:411.

193. German reply to First U.S. *Lusitania* note, May 28, 1915, in *FRUS 1915*, suppl., 419–21.

194. Link, *Wilson: The Struggle for Neutrality*, 411.

195. Secretary of State Bryan to President Wilson, June 5, 1915; President Wilson to the Secretary of State, June 5, 1915, in *Lansing Papers*, 1:437–38.

196. Wilson's marked-up draft is attached to the letter from Counselor Lansing to the Secretary of State, June 7, 1915, in *Lansing Papers*, 1:440–45. For the final version delivered to Germany, see telegram from the Secretary of State ad interim to the Ambassador in Germany (Gerard), June 9, 1915, in *FRUS 1915*, suppl., 436–38.

197. Bryan and Bryan, *Memoirs of William Jennings Bryan*, 411.

198. Link, *Wilson: The Struggle for Neutrality*, 409; Spindler, *Der Handelskrieg mit U-Booten*, 2:98–103.

199. Note from the German Foreign Office to Ambassador Gerard, July 8, 1915, forwarded by Gerard to the Secretary of State July 8, 1915, in *FRUS 1915*, suppl., 463–66.

200. Secretary of State to the Ambassador in Germany (Gerard), July 8, 1915, in *FRUS 1915*, suppl., 462.

201. For a detailed discussion of internal debates relating to the third *Lusitania* note, see Link, *Wilson: The Struggle for Neutrality*, 438–55.

202. Ibid., 449. "Berlin Press Assails Our Note as Unneutral and Threatening," *New York Times*, July 26, 1915, 1, 5.

203. "London Commends President's Note," *New York Times*, July 26, 1915, 1.

204. Bernstorff and Sutton, *The Memoirs of Count Bernstorff*, 144.

205. Link, *Wilson: The Struggle for Neutrality*, 567–68.

206. "President to Dismiss von Bernstorff if *Arabic* Sinking Is Proved Deliberate; May Then Call Congress for Defense," *New York Times*, August 23, 1915. For context, see Link, *Wilson: The Struggle for* Neutrality, 567–69.

207. Ibid., 580–87, 645–67.

208. The best English-language account of the struggle between the German Admiralty and the German chancellor remains Holger H. Herwig, *"Luxury" Fleet: The Imperial German Navy, 1888-1918* (Atlantic Highlands, NJ: Ashfield Press, 1987). Retired Rear Admiral Arno Spindler's courageous postwar study on *Der Handelskrieg mit U-Booten* concluded that the politically imposed restrictions on Germany's submarine campaign were less burdensome than the German Admiralty perceived, and that the German navy could have abided by the restrictions if it had wished to do so. Moreover, Spindler drew a lesson that his fellow naval officers had been loath to acknowledge during the war: political considerations should trump operational consideration, a point that Clausewitz had made over a century before. Spindler, *Der Handelskrieg mit U-Booten*, 1:vi–vii; 2:290–91.

209. Lansing's scathing initial draft is reproduced in the *Lansing Papers*, 1:540–42. Wilson directed that it be moderated in tone, but still threatened that if Germany did not abandon its "present methods of submarine warfare against passenger and freight-carrying vessels," then the United States would sever diplomatic relations with the German empire altogether. Instructions from the Secretary of State to the Ambassador in Germany (Gerard), April 18, 1916, in *FRUS 1916*, suppl., 232–34. For context, see Arthur S. Link, *Wilson: Confusions and Crises 1915-1916* (Princeton, NJ: Princeton University Press, 1964), 222–79.

210. An Address by William Jennings Bryan, "The War in Europe and its Lessons for Us," Washington, D.C., November 1, 1915. Digital copy of pamphlet available at http://catalog.hathitrust.org/Record/009608286.

211. Link, *Wilson: The Struggle for Neutrality*. Bryan in return had lambasted the Eastern press as journalistic mosquitoes affecting a British accent. He claimed that the Appalachians were a godsend that served as a dike against East Coast interventionism. See Ashby, *William Jennings Bryan: Champion of Democracy*, 161.

212. For details of the Konstantin Dumba affair, the Heinrich Albert espionage case, and sabotage schemes ranging from plots to blow up train lines to efforts to plant explosives on merchant ships docked in the United States, see Doerries, *Imperial Challenge*.

213. "Bryan Extols President, Draws Volleys of Cheers from Throng by Praise of Wilson," *New York Times*, June 16, 1916, 1.

214. Holger Herwig, "Total Rhetoric, Limited War: Germany's U-Boat Campaign 1917-1918," in *Great War, Total War: Combat and Mobilization on the Western Front, 1914-1918*, ed. Roger Chickering and Stig Förster (Cambridge: Cambridge University Press, 2000); Holger H. Herwig, *Politics of Frustration: The United States in German Naval Planning, 1889-1941* (Boston: Little, Brown, 1976), 122–33.

215. As late as mid-February, there was little popular support for going to war. The Zimmermann telegraph was dispatched on January 19, intercepted and decoded by the British, and shared with the Wilson administration on February 25. Doenecke, *Nothing Less Than War*, 256, 263–264.

216. In his speech to the Joint Session of Congress on April 2, Wilson claimed that "We enter this war only when we are clearly forced into it because there are no other means of defending our rights." John Coogan comments that "At best this statement indicates Wilson's capacity for self-delusion; at worst it demonstrates his capacity for hypocrisy. The system of international law Wilson claimed to be defending in 1917 had been undermined two years earlier by his own failure to maintain American neutrality." Coogan, *The End of Neutrality*, 236.

217. Alexander Watson, *Ring of Steel: Germany and Austria-Hungary in World War I* (New York: Basic Books, 2014).

218. Arno Spindler's study deserves far more attention than it has received. For a dated but still superb discussion of the Spindler study, see Philip K. Lundeberg, "The German Naval Critique of the U-Boat Campaign, 1915–1918," *Military Affairs* 27, no. 3 (1963); Arno Spindler, "Der Meinungsstreit in der Marine über den U-Bootskrieg 1914–1918," *Marinerundschau* 55 (1958); Spindler, Der Handelskrieg mit U-Booten.

PART THREE

1. The Commander in Chief of the United States Asiatic Fleet (Yarnell) et al., to the Commander of the Japanese Third Battle Fleet at Shanghai, August 22, 1937, *Papers Relating to the Foreign Relations of the United States, Japan: 1931-1941* (Washington, DC: Government Printing Office, 1941), 1:487–88 [hereafter, *FRUS Japan 1931-41*]. A naval inquiry later concluded that the shell that landed in the well-deck where the crew had assembled to watch a movie was a Chinese anti-aircraft shell, but at the time Yarnell believed it was Japanese, with FDR informed

that the AA shell was probably fired by the Japanese. Harold L. Ickes, *The Secret Diary of Harold L. Ickes: The Inside Struggle 1936-1939* (New York: Simon & Schuster, 1954), 199.

2. For an overview of U.S. Navy and Marine Corps involvement in the Second Opium War and the Boxer Rebellion, see David Foster Long, *Gold Braid and Foreign Relations: Diplomatic Activities of U.S. Naval Officers, 1798-1883* (Annapolis, MD: Naval Institute Press, 1988); Trevor K. Plante, "U.S. Marines in the Boxer Rebellion," *Prologue Magazine* 31, no. 4 (1999), www.archives.gov/publications/prologue/1999/winter/boxer-rebellion-1.html and www.archives.gov/publications/prologue/2001/summer/two-japans-1.html.

3. In a response to a Senate request for information, Secretary of State Wells provided a detailed listing of U.S. troops, naval vessels, and military supplies in the Far East at the close of 1937. The United States sent an additional 1,500 marines to Shanghai in the summer of 1937. See Secretary of State to Senator Ernest Lundeen, December 27, 1937, in *FRUS 1937, The Far East* (Washington, DC: Government Printing Office, 1937), 4:420–22 [hereafter *FRUS 1937*].

4. The U.S. Asiatic Fleet was a weak force designed mainly to show the flag. In 1937, it consisted of two cruisers, thirteen destroyers, six submarines, and ten gunboats.

5. Those seeking to explore the roots and history of the U.S. naval presence in China should consult William Reynolds Braisted, *Diplomats in Blue: U.S. Naval Officers in China, 1922-1933* (Gainesville: University Press of Florida, 2009), and Kemp Tolley, *Yangtze Patrol: The U.S. Navy in China* (Annapolis, MD: Naval Institute Press, 2000); Kemp Tolley, "Yangpat—Shanghai to Chunking," *U.S. Naval Institute Proceedings* 89, no. 6 (1963). For a sense of shipboard life and the events of December 1937 as experienced by the *Panay*'s officers and crew, see the various personal recollections posted on the *Panay* Memorial website, www.ussPanay.org/ and Hamilton Darby Perry, *The Panay Incident; Prelude to Pearl Harbor* (New York: Macmillan, 1969).

6. Joseph Bryan Icenhower, *The Panay Incident, December 12, 1937* (New York: Franklin Watts, 1971), 6; Tolley, "Yangpat," 87; Perry, *The Panay Incident*, 1.

7. The reader should not overestimate the status and influence of the United States in China during the 1920s and 1930s. While the United States maintained a significant presence, the British presence was substantially greater, and Britain remained far and away the most influential Western power in China throughout the period. See Robert A. Bickers, *Britain in China: Community Culture and Colonialism, 1900-1949* (Manchester: Manchester University Press, 1999). The retiring U.S. YangPat commander recognized that the eleven gunboats that the British maintained on the Yangtze constituted a "very large part of our strength on the River," in a report to his superior (CINC Asiatic Fleet) in December 1921. Braisted, *Diplomats in Blue*, 66.

8. The U.S. "Open Door Policy," enunciated by Secretary of State John Hay in 1899 following the first Sino-Japanese War, declared that all nations should enjoy equal access to the Chinese market. It rejected the notion that Japan, Britain, Russia, or other powers had the right to establish special spheres of influence in China. For a detailed discussion of U.S. diplomacy and Sino-Japanese conflict in the 1930s, see Dorothy Borg, *The United States and the Far Eastern Crisis of 1933-1938* (Cambridge, MA: Harvard University Press, 1964); Robert Dallek, *Franklin D. Roosevelt and American Foreign Policy, 1932-1945* (New York: Oxford University Press, 1979); Kenneth Sydney Davis, *FDR: Into the Storm, 1937-1940* (New York: Random House, 1993); Rana Mitter, *Forgotten Ally: China's World War II, 1937-1945* (New York: Houghton Mifflin Harcourt, 2013).

9. Secretary of State to the Ambassador in China, August 10, 1937, in *FRUS 1937*, 4:252–53.

10. For an account of the slaughter, see Consul General at Shanghai to the Secretary of State, August 28, 1937, in *FRUS 1937*, 4:294–95, and Norman Alley, *I Witness* (New York: W. Funk, 1941), 172–73.

11. The *President Hoover* had a 30-foot American flag laid out on its top deck. After Chiang Kai-shek discovered that the attack had been organized by Claire Chennault, then working under contract as an air adviser for the Republic of China, he dropped his bluster about executing those involved in the incident. Cordell Hull and Andrew Henry Thomas Berding, *The Memoirs of Cordell Hull* (New York: Macmillan, 1948), 2:540. See also "The Wreck of the SS *President Hoover*," at www.takaoclub.com/hoover/wreck.htm.

12. The Secretary of State to the Ambassador in Japan (Grew), August 30, 1937, in *FRUS Japan 1931-41,* 1:491; Aide-mémoire from the American Embassy in Japan to the Japanese ministry for Foreign Affairs, September 1, 1937, in *FRUS Japan 1931-41*, 1:494–95.

13. The American Ambassador in Japan to the Japanese Minister for Foreign Affairs, September 17, 1937, and Memorandum by the Ambassador in Japan (Grew), September 20, 1937, in *FRUS Japan 1931-41*, 1:498–501; entry for September 20, 1937, in Joseph C. Grew, *Ten Years in Japan: A Contemporary Record Drawn from the Diaries and Private and Official Papers of Joseph G. Grew* (New York: Simon & Schuster, 1944), 217.

14. Grew, *Ten Years in Japan*, 217–18. For a broader discussion of U.S.-Chinese relations during the Sino-Japanese War, see Mitter, *Forgotten Ally*, 27–145.

15. For a discussion of Grew's formative experience in Berlin from 1912 to 1917, see Waldo H. Heinrichs, *American Ambassador: Joseph C. Grew and the Development of the United States Diplomatic Tradition* (New York: Oxford University Press, 1986), 14–34.

16. Grew, *Ten Years in Japan*, 234.

17. Samuel Eliot Morison, *History of United States Naval Operations in World War II*. Vol. 3: *The Rising Sun in the Pacific* (Boston: Little, Brown, 1947), 16.

18. Richard McKenna's novel *The Sand Pebbles* (New York: Harper & Row, 1962) and the Twentieth Century Fox film (released 1966) by the same name capture the atmosphere in which the Yangtze Patrol operated in the 1920s. As noted, armed conflict with the Chinese had faded by the mid-1930s, but practices such as hiring Chinese laborers to perform much of the mundane tasks of shipboard life persisted. For an extended discussion of duty in the Yangtze Patrol from a deckplates perspective, see Tolley, *Yangtze Patrol*; Perry, *The Panay Incident*, 1–28. For a more scholarly account of naval diplomacy during this era, see Braisted, *Diplomats in Blue*.

19. One should note that while expatriate life had its luxuries, it also had its challenges. Muriel Anders, the wife of the *Panay*'s executive officer, recalled that while she and other dependents lived in large homes with ample domestic help, they had no running water or refrigeration. See Muriel Anders's memories of China at the *Panay* Memorial website, www.ussPanay.org/memories_murielAnders.

20. Most accounts refer to Standard Oil or Socony (Standard Oil of New York) personnel and tankers. To be more precise, the tankers and facilities were operated by the Standard Vacuum Oil Corporation following the merger of Socony and the Vacuum Oil Company in 1931. The Standard Vacuum Oil Corporation would eventually become Mobil Corporation.

21. Alley, *I Witness*, 243–44. Grand Guignole was a theater in the Pigalle area of Paris that specialized in naturalist horror shows, with the term used as a synonym for graphic horror until the theater faded from public memory after its closure in 1962.

22. Alley, *I Witness*, 240–41.

23. For a summary of events between November 21 and December 10, 1937, see State Department summary, in *FRUS Japan 1931-41*, 1:517–19. For detailed discussion of the attack itself and the subsequent effort of survivors to evade Japanese strafing attacks, see The Second Secretary of Embassy in China (Atcheson) to the Secretary of State, December 21, 1937, in *FRUS Japan 1931-41*, 1:532–41; Messages between Atcheson and Hull in early December, in *FRUS 1937*, 4:388–94.

24. William Walkowski, "The *Panay* Incident: The Recollections of Assistant Military Attaché Frank N. Roberts 1934-1938," in *Frank N. Roberts Papers* (Independence, MO: Harry S Truman Library, 1973), 8; Icenhower, *The Panay Incident*, 14–16.

25. The details of the attack are drawn from Atcheson's report to the secretary of state dated December 21, 1937, and the Findings of Fact of the Court of Inquiry investigating the bombing and sinking of the USS *Panay*, dated December 23, 1937, both in their entirety in *FRUS Japan 1931-41*, 1:532–47. Additional details drawn from Perry, *The Panay Incident*, 59–113.

26. Ibid., 65–66; and *FRUS Japan 1931-41*, 1:535.

27. General Order 99, June 1, 1914. Perry, drawing upon many interviews, provides the best account of the attack on the *Panay* as seen from the deckplates. Perry, *The Panay Incident*.

28. Ibid., 88.

29. Four squadrons participated in the operation: a squadron of three Type-96 high-level bombers under the command of Lieutenant Shigeharu Murata; a squadron of six Type-96 dive bombers under the command of Lieutenant Masatake Okumiya; a squadron of six Type-94 dive bombers under the command of Lieutenant Ichiro Komaki; and a squadron of nine Type-95 fighters under the command of Lieutenant Ryohei Ushioda. Mastake Okumiya, "How the *Panay* Was Sunk," *U.S. Naval Institute Proceedings* 79, no. 6 (1953).

30. The U.S. Navy Court of Inquiry concluded that the Japanese twin-engine bombers dropped several bombs, of which one or two struck on or very close to the bow of the *Panay*, with the dive bombers dropping about twenty additional bombs, many of which struck "close aboard" and created fragments and damage. Okumiya believed that the high-altitude bombers had scored two direct hits, with the dive bombers dropping perhaps fifteen bombs on the *Panay* and an additional fifteen on the tankers.

31. Perry, *The Panay Incident*, 94.

32. Anders was initially awarded the Navy Cross for extraordinary heroism in combat. The navy withdrew the award, given congressional concern that the award might suggest that the United States was in combat with Japan, which was not the case in December 1937. Anders instead received a Distinguished Service Medal. Following the attack on the *Pueblo* in 1968, Congress revisited the parameters of the combat requirement, reinstating Anders's initial award of the Navy Cross. For details of Anders's heroism, see the *Panay* Memorial website, www.ussPanay.org/crew.shtml; Ronald E. Fischer, "The Navy Cross," *Journal of the Orders and Medals Society of America* 45, no. 2 (March 1994), and Perry, *The Panay Incident*, 103–05.

33. Ibid., 102–03. Note that Mahlmann was awarded the Navy Cross for heroism. While the public may have focused on his lack of pants, fellow crew members recalled that the chief had been instrumental in organizing the ship's defense, the evacuation of wounded, and the final abandon-ship operation with coolness under fire they greatly admired.

34. Alley, *I Witness*, 264.

35. Alley misidentifies the tanker as the *Meiping* in his memoirs, with Atcheson's report stating that it was the *Meihsia* that came up alongside; in *FRUS Japan 1931-41*, 1:537–38; Alley, *I Witness*, 269–70; Perry, *The Panay Incident*, 114–16.

36. Perry, *The Panay Incident*, 118.

37. *FRUS Japan 1931-41*, 1:538.

38. Perry, *The Panay Incident*, 105.

39. Findings of Fact, Naval Court of Inquiry, December 23, 1937, in *FRUS Japan 1931-41*, 1:542–46.

40. *FRUS Japan 1931-41*, 1:537–38.

41. Frank Roberts kept a copy of the *Panay*'s last radio transmission as relayed to Shanghai, with the radio transmission breaking off at 1342. Frank N. Roberts Papers, Box 5, Harry S. Truman Library, Independence, MO.

42. Ambassador in China (Johnson) to the Secretary of State, Hankow, December 12, 1937—10 P.M., in *FRUS 1937,* 4:401.

43. Commander of the United States Yangtze Patrol (Marquart) to the Chief of Naval Operations (Leahy), 10:03 A.M., December 13, 1937, in *FRUS 1937,* 4:488.

44. Ambassador to Japan (Grew) to Secretary of State, December 13, 1937, in *FRUS 1937,* 4:495; Grew, *Ten Years in Japan,* 233–34.

45. Hull and Berding, *The Memoirs of Cordell Hull,* 404.

46. The veteran parade took place on the 18th anniversary of the U.S. declaration of war on April 6, 1917. Dallek, *Franklin D. Roosevelt and American Foreign Policy,* 101–02.

47. Hull and Berding, *The Memoirs of Cordell Hull,* 404.

48. John Edward Wiltz, *In Search of Peace. The Senate Munitions Inquiry, 1934-36* (Baton Rouge: Louisiana State University Press, 1963), 16.

49. Lehmann-Russbüldt was one of the Weimar Republic's leading peace advocates, immigrating to the Netherlands after Hitler was appointed chancellor in 1933.

50. Helmut Carol Engelbrecht and Frank Cleary Hanighen, *Merchants of Death: A Study of the International Armament Industry* (New York: Dodd, Mead, 1934); George Seldes, *Iron, Blood and Profits: An Exposure of the World-Wide Munitions Racket* (New York: Harper & Brothers, 1934).

51. John Edward Wiltz, "The Nye Munitions Committee 1934," in *Congress Investigates: A Documented History, 1792-1974,* ed. Arthur M. Schlesinger and Roger A. Bruns (New York: Chelsea House, 1975), 2740.

52. Wiltz, *In Search of Peace,* 17.

53. Hull and Berding, *The Memoirs of Cordell Hull,* 398.

54. Senate debate over the Nye Committee's work, January 18, 1936, in Wiltz, "The Nye Munitions Committee 1934," 2883, 2887.

55. Ibid., 2745.

56. Hull and Berding, *The Memoirs of Cordell Hull,* 399.

57. Wiltz, "The Nye Munitions Committee 1934," 2752.

58. One might note that Senator Glass had a reputation for being a longtime friend of banking interests. Wiltz, "The Nye Munitions Committee 1934," 2759.

59. According John Edward Wiltz, "Senator Nye and his colleagues never trampled on the constitutional rights of witnesses as subsequent congressional investigating committees were accused of doing." But when Nye was interviewed or talked to the press, he had a tendency to "cast restraint and responsibility to the wind" and become a raving demagogue." Wiltz, "The Nye Munitions Committee 1934," 2764–65.

60. In a rather byzantine maneuver, FDR at one point encouraged Chairman Nye to take up the matter of drafting neutrality legislation, as he feared that the Foreign Relations Committee was preparing a bill he found restrictive. After the Foreign Relations Committee objected to the maneuver, Nye informed the president that

his committee would not take up the matter. Dallek, *Franklin D. Roosevelt and American Foreign Policy*, 102–03.

61. I cite Millis (*Road to War, America 1914-1917* [Boston: Houghton Mifflin, 1935]) because his book was a bestseller. For earlier and later versions of the same argument, see Harry Elmer Barnes, *The Genesis of the World War* (New York: Knopf, 1926); C. Hartley Grattan, *Why We Fought* (New York: Vanguard, 1929); Ray Stannard Baker, *Woodrow Wilson: Life and Letters* (Garden City, NY: Doubleday, Page, 1927), vols. 5 and 6; Charles Callan Tansill, *America Goes to War* (Boston: Little, Brown, 1938). For an overview of this revisionist wave, see Warren I. Cohen, *The American Revisionists: The Lessons of Intervention in World War I* (Chicago: University of Chicago Press, 1967).

62. Millis, *Road to War*, 190–91.

63. Charles A. Beard, "Heat and Light on Neutrality," *New Republic*, February 12, 1936. For a full discussion of the progressive argument for isolationism, see the chapter "Dr. Beard's Garden," in H. W. Brands, *What America Owes the World: The Struggle for the Soul of Foreign Policy* (Cambridge: Cambridge University Press, 1998), 109–42.

64. Dallek, *Franklin D. Roosevelt and American Foreign Policy*, 104. The peace movement embraced dozens of organizations, with the debate leading to the enactment of neutrality laws splitting the movement into two camps, one which continued to favor internationalist, collective responses to aggression and the other favoring isolationist antidotes to war. Attempts to reconcile the two different approaches exacerbated rather than bridged the split. See Borg, *United States and the Far Eastern Crisis*, 342–46.

65. Dallek, *Franklin D. Roosevelt and American Foreign Policy*.

66. Wiltz, *In Search of Peace*, 183. Writing privately to Colonel House, Roosevelt confided that "Some of the Congressmen and Senators who are suggesting wild-eyed measures to keep us out of war are now declaring that you and Lansing and Page forced Wilson into the War! I had a talk with them, explained that I was in Washington myself the whole of that period, that none of them were there, and that their historical analysis was wholly inaccurate." Yet whatever the merits of the argument, by 1937 some 70 percent of Americans polled by Gallup believed that America's entry into the First World War had been a mistake. Dallek, *Franklin D. Roosevelt and American Foreign Policy*, 109; Arthur Scherr, "Presidential Power, the *Panay* Incident, and the Defeat of the Ludlow Amendment," *International History Review* 32, no. 3 (2010).

67. For an exhaustive analysis of the origins, debates, and terms of the Neutrality Acts of the 1930s, see Robert A. Divine, *The Illusion of Neutrality* (Chicago: University of Chicago Press, 1962).

68. Hornbeck memorandum, May 1933, in Borg, *United States and the Far Eastern Crisis,* 569n101.

69. Hull and Berding, *The Memoirs of Cordell Hull*, 566.

70. Description of cabinet sessions of August 7 and 13, 1937, in Ickes, *The Secret Diary*, 186, 192–93.

71. *Congressional Record*, 75th Congress, 1st session, July 24 and August 3, 1937, 8156, 10442.

72. Borg, *United States and the Far Eastern Crisis,* 320–21.

73. Hull and Berding, *The Memoirs of Cordell Hull*, 557; Grew, *Ten Years in Japan*, 223.

74. Three memoranda from Hornbeck to Secretary of State Hull, August 16, 1937, in *FRUS 1937*, 3:420–23.

75. Borg, *United States and the Far Eastern Crisis*, 322.

76. Ibid., 323.

77. Pittman Explains Neutrality Status, *New York Times,* August 24, 1937, 3.

78. Borg, *United States and the Far Eastern Crisis,* 325.

79. "Seamen Demand $250 'War' Bonus Be Granted Before Ship Quits U.S. Waters," *New York Times*, August 31, 1937, 3.

80. The pamphlet appeared in October, but similar points were made in the newsletters and meetings of the six peace organizations that constituted the Emergency Peace Campaign (EPC): the American Friends Service Committee, the National Council for the Prevention of War, World Peaceways, the Women's International League for Peace and Freedom, the Committee on Militarism in Education and the Fellowship of Reconciliation. Borg posits a larger wing of internationalist peace organizations unenthused about neutrality legislation, but the groups she lists—the American Association of University Women, the YWCA, the General Federation of Women's Club—were far less focused than the EPC on the issue of international conflict. Borg, *United States and the Far Eastern Crisis,* 344, 350.

81. Memorandum of Conversations, by the Chief of the Office of Arms and Munitions Control, September 13, 1937, in *FRUS 1937*, 4:527–28.

82. *FRUS Japan 1931-41*, 2:201.

83. Diaries of Henry Morgenthau Jr., December 7–December 13, 1937, 101:70. Entry regarding Conference with the President, December 8, 1937, at FDR Library Digital Collection, www.fdrlibrary.marist.edu/_resources/images/morg/md0132.pdf.

84. Henry Hitch Adams, *Witness to Power: The Life of Fleet Admiral William D. Leahy* (Annapolis, MD: Naval Institute Press, 1985), 98; George C. Dyer, *On the Treadmill to Pearl Harbor. The Memoirs of Admiral James O. Richardson* (Washington, DC: Naval History Division, 1973), 121.

85. Policy statement of the Commander in Chief of the United States Asiatic Fleet, September 22, 1937, in *FRUS 1937*, 4:352–53; Memorandum by the Secretary of State to President Roosevelt, October 4, 1937, in *FRUS 1937*, 4:363–64.

86. While FDR was deeply engaged in naval matters throughout the 1930s, keeping informed of Fleet maneuvers and scrutinizing promotion/assignments at the

higher levels, he did not review or approve the various iterations of the navy's War Plan Orange. The first war plan reviewed and approved at the presidential level was Rainbow One, in October 1939. Edward S. Miller, *War Plan Orange: The U.S. Strategy to Defeat Japan, 1897-1945* (Annapolis, MD: Naval Institute Press, 1991), 10–11, 227, 275.

87. Dyer, *On the Treadmill to Pearl Harbor*, 254–55.

88. Miller, *War Plan Orange,* 214. For a discussion of War Plan Orange as it evolved from a "Through Ticket" to Manila to a more limited thrust toward Truk, see 139–212. For details of the contrasting Army and Navy assessments in 1935–36, see Louis Morton, "War Plan Orange: Evolution of a Strategy," *World Politics* 11, no. 2 (January 1959): 242.

89. Dyer, *On the Treadmill to Pearl Harbor*, 255, 277.

90. Miller examines how some in the navy, in particular James Richardson, had strong reservations about the offensive mindset that dominated naval planning during the interwar years. But he concludes that the "thrusters" warded off calls for more defensive concepts for most of the period, with few alternatives explored that would have provided the president with naval options short of major war. Miller, *War Plan Orange*, 213–32, 267–75.

91. Sumner Welles, "Far Eastern Policy before Pearl Harbor," in his *Seven Decisions That Shaped History* (New York: Harper & Brothers, 1950), 71–72. For a fascinating study that explains the numerous analyses that the president received throughout the period 1937–40 that posited Japan was on the brink of bankruptcy and therefore highly vulnerable to economic pressure, see Edward S. Miller, *Bankrupting the Enemy: The U.S. Financial Siege of Japan Before Pearl Harbor* (Annapolis, MD: Naval Institute Press, 2007), 9–17, 48–74.

92. Malcolm H. Murfett, *Fool-Proof Relations: The Search for Anglo-American Naval Cooperation during the Chamberlain Years, 1937-1940* (Singapore: Singapore University Press, 1984), 48.

93. Diary entry, September 19, 1937, in Ickes, *The Secret Diary*, 209.

94. Ambassador in Japan to the Secretary of State, September 7, 1937, in *FRUS 1937*, 3:515–16.

95. Ambassador in China to the Secretary of State, September 7, 1937, in *FRUS 1937*, 3:516–17.

96. Hull and Berding, *The Memoirs of Cordell Hull*, 557. For examples of impeachment threats, see the cable that Representative George Holden Tinkham (R-Massachusetts) sent Cordell Hull on October 13, 1937, *New York Times,* October 14, 1937, 16; and the statement by Hamilton Fish (R-New York), *New York Times*, October 17, 1937, 40.

97. Jay Pierrepont Moffat and Nancy Harvison Hooker, *The Moffat Papers; Selections from the Diplomatic Journals of Jay Pierrepont Moffat, 1919-1943* (Cambridge, MA: Harvard University Press, 1956), 163–64; Hull and Berding, *The Memoirs of Cordell Hull*, 553.

98. Memorandum by the Under Secretary of State Welles on conversation with the British Ambassador, November 27, 1927, in *FRUS 1937*, 3:724–25. One should note that the British were indeed seriously considering sending a sizable naval force to the Far East, but that the no specifics were provided to Ambassador Lindsay in Washington. For a detailed discussion of the British proposal, in particular internal debates between the Foreign Office and the Admiralty, see Murfett, *Fool-Proof Relations*, 88–103; Lawrence Pratt, "Anglo-American Naval Conversations on the Far East of January 1938," *International Affairs* 47 (October (1972); and James R. Leutze, *Bargaining for Supremacy: Anglo-American Naval Collaboration, 1937-1941* (Chapel Hill: University of North Carolina Press, 1977), 14–19.

99. Prime Minister Neville Chamberlain, in response to further Australian queries, finally conceded in March 1939 that the size of the fleet Britain would dispatch in the event of war with Japan depended substantially on developments in Europe and the Mediterranean. Andrew Field, *Royal Navy Strategy in the Far East, 1919-1939: Preparing for War against Japan* (London: Frank Cass, 2004).

100. For transcript of FDR's Chicago "Quarantine Speech" of October 5, 1937, see the Miller Center, University of Virginia, http://millercenter.org/president/speeches/detail/3310.

101. The *New York Times* reviewed editorial opinion across the country, drawing on sixteen papers. Borg, *United States and the Far Eastern Crisis*, 387–90.

102. Ibid., 395. One might note that the British reaction to Roosevelt's speech was negative, with Prime Minister Chamberlain commenting to the cabinet that he "hoped nothing would come of Roosevelt's idea since it was the most unfortunate time to force Japan's hand," with an economic embargo quite likely causing war. Leutze, *Bargaining for Supremacy*, 14–15.

103. Borg, *United States and the Far Eastern Crisis*, 396.

104. Ickes, *The Secret Diary*, 227.

105. Hull and Berding, *The Memoirs of Cordell Hull*, 545.

106. *Wall Street Journal*, October 6, 1937, 1. Borg, *United States and the Far Eastern Crisis*, 391–92.

107. *Political Quarterly*, October–December 1937, in Brands, *What America Owes the World*, 125.

108. Ibid., 126.

109. *New York Times*, October 14, 1937, 16.

110. John McVickar Haight Jr., "FDR's 'Big Stick.'" *U.S. Naval Institute Proceedings* 106, no. 7 (1980).

111. Ickes, *The Secret Diary*, 211.

112. *FRUS 1937*, 4:85. For a detailed account of the fruitless and frustrating proceedings at Brussels, see Moffat and Hooker, *The Moffat Papers*, 162–95.

113. Secretary of State to the Ambassador in Japan (Grew), 11:45 P.M., December 12, 1937, in *FRUS Japan 1931–41*, vol. 1, 519–20.

114. Ambassador in Japan to Secretary of State, 9 P.M., December 13, 1937, in *FRUS 1937*, 495–96.

115. Ambassador in Japan to Secretary of State, 3 P.M., December 13, 1937, in *FRUS Japan 1931–41*, vol. 1, 521–22.

116. Yarnell to Leahy, and Bemis (Naval Attaché in Japan) to Leahy, December 13, 1937, in *FRUS 1937*, 4:492–93.

117. Hull and Berding, *The Memoirs of Cordell Hull*, 560.

118. Leahy and his wife were dining with the Woodrings (Harry H. Woodring was secretary of war) when he received word of the incident. Leahy excused himself in order to join the small group that Secretary of State Hull had convened for discussions late Sunday evening at his Carlton Hotel apartment. Adams, *Witness to Power*, 101.

119. Hull and Berding, *The Memoirs of Cordell Hull*, 560. Morgenthau commented that "Hull apparently never even considered the possibility that the attack on the *Panay* might lead to a rupture of diplomatic relations or to war," with FDR much more bellicose about the matter. John Morton Blum, *From the Morgenthau Diaries. Years of Crisis, 1928-1938* (Boston: Houghton Mifflin, 1959), 486.

120. White House memorandum for Secretary of State, December 13, 1937, in *FRUS Japan 1931–41*, vol. 1. See Hull's account of the meeting at Hull and Berding, *The Memoirs of Cordell Hull*, 560.

121. See, for example, the note that the director of the American Bureau of the Japanese Ministry for Foreign Affairs handed Ambassador Joseph Grew on December 14, 1937, in *FRUS Japan 1931–41*, vol. 1.

122. Koginos provides an extensive survey of editorial opinion across the nation. Among the papers urging the administration respond to the *Panay*'s sinking by withdrawing from China were the *Portland Oregonian*, the *St. Louis Post-Dispatch*, the *Nashville Banner*, the *Albuquerque Journal*, the *Philadelphia Inquirer*, the *Richmond Times-Dispatch*, and the journals *New Republic* and *Christian Century*. Quotes derive from his analysis. Manny T. Koginos, *The Panay Incident; Prelude to War* (Lafayette, IN: Purdue University Studies, 1967), 31–38. See also Perry, *The Panay Incident*, 167–71.

123. Ibid.

124. "From *Lusitania* to *Panay*," *New Republic* 93, no. 1203 (December 22, 1937):183.

125. Koginos, *The Panay Incident*, 34–35; Scherr, "Presidential Power," 458–62; William W. Lockwood, ed., *Our Far Eastern Record. A Reference Digest on American Policy* (New York: American Council, Institute of Pacific Relations, 1940), 1:45.

126. For a broader discussion of the interplay of domestic and international concerns, see Davis, *FDR. Into the Storm*; David M. Kennedy, *Freedom from Fear* (Oxford: Oxford University Press, 2004).

127. Hull and Berding, *The Memoirs of Cordell Hull*, 565.

128. Koginos, *The Panay Incident*, 45, 47.

129. Ludlow attempted to forestall criticism that his amendment undermined the Monroe Doctrine by adding language to his 1937 resolution exempting any

attacks "by armed forces, actual or immediately threatened, upon the United States or its territorial possessions, or by any non-American nation against any country in the Western Hemisphere."

130. For a detailed discussion of the Ludlow Amendment, see Koginos, *The Panay Incident*, 80–99; Scherr, "Presidential Power."

131. Scherr, "Presidential Power," 481.

132. Gallup polled the public on their assessment of the First World War in April 1937. Scherr, "Presidential Power," 457.

133. Koginos reviews editorial opinion in the *Tokyo Asahi, Tokyo Nichi-Nichi*, the *Japan Times and Mail*, and the *Tokyo Kukumin*, with only the latter questioning why Japan needed to apologize. Koginos, *The Panay Incident*, 43–44.

134. Grew, *Ten Years in Japan*, 236, 241–42. Many Japanese citizens sought to contribute direct donations to the *Panay*'s survivors and dependents, confronting the State Department and U.S. Navy officials with the problem of whether and how to accept these citizen donations. For a full discussion of this other Japan, see Trevor K. Plante, "'Two Japans': Japanese Expressions of Sympathy and Regret in the Wake of the *Panay* Incident," *Prologue Magazine* 33, no. 2 (2001), www.archives.gov/publications/prologue/2001/summer/two-japans-1.html.

135. Ickes recollection of FDR's assessment as expressed during the cabinet meeting of December 17, 1937. Ickes, *The Secret Diary*, 275. One might note that over the past several months, Japanese troopers had on several occasions torn down American and British flags and trampled on them. The most recent incident occurred the day after the *Panay* attack, with troopers tearing down the American flag on a coal junk belonging to the Methodist hospital in Wuhu. Tokyo (Hirota) to Japanese Embassy in Washington, December 27, 1937, National Archives, RG 457, Entry 9032 (HCC), Box 751, Folder 1916, Translations of Japanese Messages Re: *Panay* Incident.

136. Ibid., 274.

137. For an overview of evolving U.S. naval war plans in the event of hostilities with Japan, see Miller, *War Plan Orange*.

138. The concept, as FDR explained to the cabinet, entailed the U.S. Navy blockading Japan from the Aleutian Islands to Hawaii, to Howland, to Wake, to Guam, while the Royal Navy would take over from Guam to Singapore. Ickes, *The Secret Diary*, 274–75; William D. Leahy, *I Was There: The Personal Story of the Chief of Staff to Presidents Roosevelt and Truman* (New York: Whittlesey House, 1950), 64, 128–29; Adams, *Witness to Power*, 101–02.

139. Adams, *Witness to Power*, 101.

140. The Chargé in the United Kingdom (Johnson) to the Secretary of State, December 13, 1937, in *FRUS 1937*, 4:490–91.

141. *FRUS 1937*, 4:494–95.

142. Memorandum by the Secretary of State on conversation with the Ambassador of Great Britain, December 14, 1937, in *FRUS 1937*, 4:499–500.

143. Pratt, "Anglo-American Naval Conversations," 752; Haight, "FDR's 'Big Stick,'" 69–70.

144. For details of the secretive talks between Captain Royal E. Ingersoll, USN, Chief of War Plans Division, and Captain Tom Phillips, his Royal Navy counterpart, see John T. Mason Jr., "The Reminiscences of Admiral Royal E. Intersoll," *Naval History Project of the Oral History Research Office*, Washington, DC, 1964; Alan Harris Bath, *Tracking the Axis Enemy: The Triumph of Anglo-American Naval Intelligence*, Modern War Studies (Lawrence: University Press of Kansas, 1998), 14–16; Gregory J. Florence, *Courting a Reluctant Ally: An Evaluation of U.S./ UK Naval Intelligence Cooperation, 1935-1941* (Washington, DC: Center for Strategic Intelligence Research, Joint Military Intelligence College, 2004), 30–34; Pratt, "Anglo-American Naval Conversations," 745–63; Haight, "FDR's 'Big Stick,'" 71–73.

145. Note from Morgenthau to Oliphant regarding cabinet discussions, December 14, 1937, in Diaries of Henry Morgenthau Jr., 102:2, FDR Library Digital Collection, www.fdrlibrary.marist.edu/_resources/images/morg/md0133.pdf.

146. For an account of the development of the concept that would lead to the establishment of the Foreign Funds Control office of the Treasury Department on April 10, 1940, see Richard D. McKinzie's interview of Bernard Bernstein on July 23, 1975, Oral History Project, Truman Library, www.trumanlibrary. org/oralhist/bernsten.htm. For the full account of how this concept matured into a full press attempt to use economic power to coerce Japan, see Miller, *Bankrupting the Enemy.*

147. Entry record of departmental discussion, December 17, 1937, Diaries of Henry Morgenthau Jr., 103:54–55, FDR Library Digital Collection, www.fdrlibrary. marist.edu/_resources/images/morg/md0134.pdf.

148. Ibid.

149. Borg, *United States and the Far Eastern Crisis,* 495.

150. Memo by Sir Warren Fisher, December 18, 1937, cited in Murfett, *Fool-Proof Relations,* 119.

151. Memo by J. W. Nicholls, Foreign Office, October 8, 1937. The quote derives from a summation of the study by Gladwyn Jebb, in Murfett, *Fool-Proof Relations,* 66.

152. Secretary of State to the Ambassador in Japan, December 16, 1937, in *FRUS Japan 1931–41,* 1:527.

153. Memorandum by the Secretary of State re discussion with Japanese Ambassador, December 17, 1937, in *FRUS Japan 1931–41,* 1:529.

154. Diary entry, December 20, 1937, in Grew, *Ten Years in Japan,* 235. One might note that the Japanese foreign ministry was cognizant of and alarmed by initial press references in the United States referencing the *Maine.* See cable from Tokyo to the Japanese embassy in Washington, December 17, 1037, in National Archives, RG 457, Entry 9032 (HCC), Box 751, Folder 1916, translations of Japanese messages re: *Panay* incident.

155. For specifics on the Japanese Kondo (navy), Takada (navy), Harada (army), and Nishi (army) investigations, see Koginos, *The Panay Incident*, 66–71; Harlan Swanson, "The *Panay* Incident: Prelude to Pearl Harbor," *U.S. Naval Institute Proceedings* 93, no. 12 (1967).

156. The Ambassador in Japan (Grew) to the Secretary of State, December 23, 1937, in *FRUS Japan 1931-41*, 1:547–48. Grew provides an account of the briefing in his diary as well, but places the meeting on the December 22; Grew, *Ten Years in Japan*, 237–39.

157. One has to take note of the time difference between Tokyo and Washington. Instructions dispatched from Washington on the afternoons of December 13 and 16 would be received and acted upon in Tokyo on December 14 and 17, respectively.

158. Copy of Japanese note sent from Grew to the Secretary of State, December 24, 1937, in *FRUS Japan 1931–41*, 1:549–50.

159. The findings of fact of the U.S. Naval Court of Inquiry, along with Atcheson's detailed report to the secretary of state, are available in *FRUS Japan 1931-41*, 1:532–47.

160. Commander in Chief of the United States Asiatic Fleet (Yarnell) to the Secretary of the Navy (Swanson), December 23, 1937, in *FRUS Japan 1931-41*, 1:547.

161. Memorandum of the Secretary of State, December 17, 1937, in *FRUS Japan 1931-41*, 1:529.

162. Diary entry, December 20, 1937, in Grew, *Ten Years in Japan*, 236.

163. Ibid., 240.

164. Hamilton Darby Perry claims that Alley was asked to cut out about 30 feet of film that showed low-level attacks on the *Panay*, presumably because the footage might undercut the diplomatic settlement just reached. Perry indicates that Alley showed him the missing footage, with the story picked up by Kenneth Davis, among others. Alley's 1941 memoir makes no mention of any missing footage, and Universal Studios claimed that the film it ran was "Uncensored!!! Unedited!!!" Perry, *The Panay Incident*, 231–32; Davis, *FDR. Into the Storm*, 158; Alley, *I Witness*, 284–86. The full clip that ran in theaters is available at the Universal Studies archive, https://archive.org/details/1937-12-12_Bombing_of_USS_Panay.

165. Ickes, *The Secret Diary*, 279.

166. Blum, *From the Morgenthau Diaries*, 492; William L. Langer and S. Everett Gleason, *The Challenge to Isolation, 1937-1940* (New York: Council on Foreign Relations, 1952), 24; Swanson, "The *Panay* Incident."

167. Borg, who has written the most detailed examination into FDR's Far East policy during this period, concludes that the president never seriously considered going to war over the matter. Borg, *United States and the Far Eastern Crisis,* 501–03.

168. Davis, *FDR. Into the Storm*, 135.

169. Tokyo to Washington relaying information from Shanghai, December 13, 1937. National Archives, RG 457, Entry 9032 (HCC), Box 751, Folder 1916, translations of Japanese messages re: *Panay* incident.

170. One message even hints that the Japanese government would order Rear Admiral Teizo Mitsunami to commit suicide "if it should turn out that he committed a blunder of such proportions." Tokyo to Washington, December 16, 1937. National Archives, RG 457, Entry 9032 (HCC), Box 751, Folder 1916, translations of Japanese messages re: *Panay* incident. Writing after World War II, Leahy conceded that "the *Panay* was a local incident and the Japanese Government may not have had any advance information about it." Leahy, *I Was There*, 64.

171. Special cable from Hallett Abend to the *New York Times*, "Rift in Army Seen," *New York Times*, December 20, 1937, 1, 16.

172. My search of decoded Japanese message traffic in the National Archive folder of translations of Japanese messages regarding the *Panay* incident revealed no smoking gun to substantiate Abend's allegation, yet given the fact that Frederick Moore, one of the State Department's Far Eastern experts, suspected the same, one cannot rule out the possibility. For a detailed discussion of the purported but unsubstantiated role of Colonel Hashimoto, see Okumiya, "How the *Panay* Was Sunk."; Swanson, "The *Panay* Incident; Frederick Moore, *With Japan's Leaders; an Intimate Record of Fourteen Years as Counsellor to the Japanese Government, Ending December 7, 1941* (New York: Scribner's, 1942), 89.

173. Hull and Berding, *The Memoirs of Cordell Hull*, 563.

174. Secretary of State to the Ambassador in Japan, March 19, 1938. Text of the note delivered by the Ambassador on March 22, 1938, in *FRUS Japan 1931-41*, 1:559.

175. The American Ambassador in Japan (Grew) to the Japanese Minister for Foreign Affairs (Hirota), Tokyo, January 17, 1938, in *FRUS Japan 1931-41*, 1:565–66.

176. Ickes attributes the president's reluctance to read the reports aloud to the presence of Frances Perkins, FDR's female secretary of labor. Ickes, *The Secrety Diary*.

177. See the multiple reports related to attacks on American property, the Allison incident, and the widespread rape of Chinese women by Japanese soldiers, in *FRUS Japan 1931-41*, 1:565–73.

178. Yarnell diary, February 9, 1938, in Stephen Howarth, *To Shining Sea. A History of the United States Navy 1775-1991* (New York: Random House, 1991), 362–63. Fitch, who had served as head of the YMCA branch in Nanking, spent much of 1938 traveling around the United States to raise awareness about Japanese atrocities in China, giving speeches and showing films he had taken in Nanking. For eyewitness accounts, see Kaiyuan Zhang, *Eyewitnesses to Massacre: American Missionaries Bear Witness to Japanese Atrocities in Nanjing* (Armonk, NY: M. E. Sharp, 2001).

179. Koginos, *The Panay Incident*, 285.

180. "Should the People Declare War?: Some Arguments in Favor of Representative Ludlow's Resolution for a Popular Referendum," *New York Times*, December 19, 1937, 70.

181. Scherr, "Presidential Power," 470–72.

182. Ibid., 476.

183. "An Amendment Against War," *New Republic* 93, no. 1204 (December 29, 1937): 212–13.

184. President Roosevelt to the Speaker of the House of Representatives, in *Peace and War. United States Foreign Policy 1931-1941* (Washington, DC: Government Printing Office, 1943), document 101.

185. *New York Times*, December 22, 1937, 1.

186. Koginos, *The Panay Incident*, 96.

187. For a detailed analysis of Anglo-American discussions and the Ingersoll mission, see Murfett, *Fool-Proof Relations*, 128–47.

188. Florence, *Courting a Reluctant Ally*, 43.

189. Mason, "The Reminiscences of Admiral Royal E. Ingersoll."

190. For a copy of the record of conversations, see Pratt, "Anglo-American Naval Conversations," 760–63.

191. Memorandum by Under Secretary of State Welles of a Conversation with the British Ambassador, January 8, 1938, in *FRUS 1938*, 3:7–8. United States Department of State, *Foreign relations of the United States diplomatic papers, 1938. The Far East*, Volume III (Washington D.C.: U.S. Government Printing Office, 1938).

192. Neville Chamberlain to Hilda Chamberlain, January 9, 1938, in Murfett, *Fool-Proof Relations*, 141.

193. Pratt, "Anglo-American Naval Conversations," 757.

194. Memo by Sir Alexander Cadogan for Chamberlain, January 11, 1938, in Murfett, *Fool-Proof Relations*, 145.

195. Adams, *Witness to Power*, 103–04; Borg, *United States and the Far Eastern Crisis,* 497–99, 509, 12, 42; Dallek, *Franklin D. Roosevelt and American Foreign Policy*, 154.

196. Preliminary plans had already been made before the sinking of the *Panay* to send several American ships to Sydney, Australia, for its sesquicentennial celebration in April 1938. FDR wanted to ramp up the port call to four ships and then have them stop by Singapore on the way back, but practical matters resulted in a three-ship package. Leahy quotation in "Leahy Denies Navy Has Ties to British," *New York Times*, February 3, 1938, 6.

197. Secretary of State to the Chairman of the Senate Committee on Foreign Relations (Key Pittman), February 8, 1937, in *FRUS Japan 1931–41*, 1:449–50.

198. The instructions given to Ingersoll, and the responses provided to the British, never crossed the line of formal commitment, but to argue that there were no contemplated, implied understandings seems to stretch the bounds of truthfulness. The more secret parts of the discussions were, according to Alan Bath, never circulated in the ordinary manner and never were forwarded to the U.S. cabinet or the Committee of Imperial Defense at the special request of the United States. Bath, *Tracking the Axis Enemy*, 15. Similar patters of evasion persisted as war clouds gathered in 1939–40. Assistant Secretary of the Navy

Charles Edison, for example, would later tell Congress (February 1939) that "I have never heard discussed, officially or unofficially, any plan . . . that was based on a desire for offensive action. . . . Never, within the Department, in the field or at social gatherings or in personal conversations do I get any other impression. The idea that the Navy seeks defense on the surface and offense in the backroom is simply imaginary and untenable." Miller comments that "Edison was either misinformed or lying through his teeth." Miller, *War Plan Orange*, 13.

199. Leahy had favored joint action as early as December, with Yarnell forwarding various ideas to the president throughout the fall of 1937. Norman Davis, Roosevelt's representative at the Brussels Conference, made the same recommendation at the meeting of presidential advisers on December 16, 1937. The resignation of Foreign Secretary Anthony Eden in February 1938 put an end to continued Anglo-American talks. See Pratt, "Anglo-American Naval Conversations," 750; Leutze, *Bargaining for Supremacy*, 8; and Haight, "FDR's 'Big Stick.' "

200. There is a significant literature on the Vinson-Trammel Act (Naval Expansion Bill) of 1934 and the Naval Act of 1936, with the Vinson-Trammel Act (Naval Expansion Bill) of 1938 often only mentioned as a sequel to these earlier bills. But the two earlier bills only envisioned building up to the quantitative limits established during the Washington Naval and London Naval Treaties of 1921 and 1930. The 1938 Expansion Bill went beyond these treaty limits, and signified a final abandonment of self-imposed construction ceilings.

201. Quotes from Koginos, *The Panay Incident*, 107. One might note that the U.S. Navy had been planning something quite analogous to this from 1906 to 1934, with "thrusters" in the navy planning to send the fleet on a "Through Ticket" to the Philippines immediately after commencement of hostilities. Japan's growing naval strength led to modifications of War Plan Orange thereafter, but despite the reservations of a few individuals, naval planners remained fixated on classical Mahanian conceptions of achieving command of the sea through a decisive naval battle most probably taking place in the eastern Pacific. See Miller, *War Plan Orange,* 86–99, 159–160, 248–09.

202. Koginos, *The Panay Incident*, 108–10.

203. *Congressional Record*–Senate, 75th Congress, 3rd Session, 1938, vol. 83, no. 85 (April 26, 1938): 7639.

204. Koginos, *The Panay Incident*, 121.

205. Miller, *War Plan Orange,* 168, 214–15. Miller notes that Embick warned the president in late 1937 that the navy's War Plan Orange as then envisioned was extremely aggressive, might lead to "national disaster," and violated "the very spirit of America." Embick began advocating that the administration should withdraw U.S. Army units in China in 1936, with the State Department vetoing the plan for diplomatic reasons.

206. Koginos, *The Panay Incident*, 115.

207. Ibid.

208. Adams, *Witness to Power*, 106.

209. Diary entry, August 1, 1938, in Grew, *Ten Years in Japan*, 252. Grew's extensive list of Japanese infringements of American rights and damages to American lives and properties can be found in *FRUS Japan 1931–41*, 1:611–61.

210. Patrick Abbazia, *Mr. Roosevelt's Navy: The Private War of the U.S. Atlantic Fleet, 1939-1942* (Annapolis, MD: Naval Institute Press, 1975); Saul Friedländer, *Prelude to Downfall; Hitler and the United States, 1939-41* (New York: Knopf, 1967); James V. Compton, *The Swastika and the Eagle: Hitler, the United States, and the Origins of the Second World War* (London: Bodley, 1968); William L. Langer and S. Everett Gleason, *The Undeclared War, 1940-1941* (Gloucester, MA: Peter Smith, 1968).

211. The American Committee for Non-Participation in Japanese Aggression, one of the first groups to speak out against isolationism, was only established in August 1938, eight months after the *Panay* incident and the Nanking massacre. For a discussion of the Sino-Japanese War and the beginnings of internationalist sentiment in isolationist America, see Andrew Johnstone, *American Internationalists and the Four Freedoms on the Eve of World War II* (Ithaca, NY: Cornell University Press, 2014), 17–35.

212. While Germany and Italy would be free to buy American materials on a "cash and carry" basis, the president understood that British sea power would prevent them from doing so, as it had in the First World War. So for all practical purposes, the amendment was designed to aid the British and French.

213. For a discussion of Roosevelt's domestic struggle against isolationism and the America First Committee, see David Kaiser, *No End Save Victory. How FDR Led the Nation into War* (New York: Basic Books, 2014); Lynne Olson, *Those Angry Days: Roosevelt, Lindbergh, and America's Fight over World War II, 1939-1941* (New York: Random House, 2013); Divine, *The Illusion of Neutrality*; William L. Langer and S. Everett Gleason, *The Challenge to Isolation; the World Crisis of 1937-1940 and American Foreign Policy* (Gloucester, MA: Peter Smith, 1970); Michael Leigh, *Mobilizing Consent: Public Opinion and American Foreign Policy, 1937-1947* (Westport, CT: Greenwood, 1976); James C. Schneider, *Should America Go to War? The Debate over Foreign Policy in Chicago, 1939-1941* (Chapel Hill: University of North Carolina Press, 1989).

214. Intelligence reports and decrypted Japanese messages indicated that by late 1941, Japanese troops and ships were turning to the south, with the intention of seizing vulnerable French, Dutch, and British holdings in the Far East. For a detailed discussion of the matter, see Gordon William Prange, Donald M. Goldstein, and Katherine V. Dillon, *Pearl Harbor: The Verdict of History* (New York: Penguin Books, 1991); Roberta Wohlstetter, *Pearl Harbor; Warning and Decision* (Palo Alto, CA: Stamford University Press, 1962).

215. For a tour de force that lays bare the global dimensions, and the interconnectivity between theaters, of World War II, see Gerhard L. Weinberg, *A World*

at Arms: A Global History of World War II (New York: Cambridge University Press, 2005).

216. For a detailed discussion of Roosevelt's efforts to use economic means to deter Japanese aggression, see Miller's *Bankrupting the Enemy*. Miller's analysis shows clearly that Roosevelt was not alone in his sanguine hopes that the United States could use economic and financial means—in particular, the authority granted in Section 5(b) of the Trading with the Enemy Act passed in October 1917—to exert pressure on Japan to stop its aggression in China. Ultimately, the economic weapon proved too blunt to convince Japanese militarists to give up their dreams of hegemony in the Far East.

217. Charles Beard, whose isolationist views have been cited earlier, advanced the thesis that FDR maneuvered the United States into an undeclared war with Germany, and then deliberately provoked Japan into attacking the United States in his *President Roosevelt and the Coming of the War, 1941* (New Haven, CT: Yale University Press, 1948), with Tansill and Theobald leveling the same charges in 1947 and 1954. These charges were substantially addressed in Langer and Gleason's masterful analysis of FDR's foreign policy, but have been recently revived by international relations scholars and political scientists. For a sense of the debate, see Charles Callan Tansill, *Back Door to War; the Roosevelt Foreign Policy, 1933-1941* (Chicago: Regnery, 1952); Robert Alfred Theobald, *The Final Secret of Pearl Harbor: The Washington Contribution to the Japanese Attack* (New York: Devin-Adair, 1954); John M. Schuessler, "The Deception Dividend," *International Security* 34, no. 4 (2010); Langer and Gleason, *The Challenge to Isolation*; James William Morley, ed., *The Fateful Choice: Japan's Advance into Southeast Asia, 1939–1941* (New York: Columbia University Press, 1980);

Taiheiyō Sensō Gen'in Kenkyūbu., *The Fateful Choice: Japan's Advance into Southeast Asia, 1939-1941* (New York: Columbia University Press, 1980); Ernest R. May, *American Intervention: 1917 and 1941* (Washington, DC: Service Center for Teachers of History, 1969); Langer and Gleason, *The Undeclared War*; James McAllister et al., "H-Diplo/Issf Roundtabe Exchange on 'Diplomacy, Deception, and Entry into War,'" vol. 5, no. 4 (2013), www.h-net.org/~diplo/ISSF/PDF/ISSF-Roundtable-5-4.pdf; Weinberg, *A World at Arms*.SSS

PART FOUR

1. James Cable, *Gunboat Diplomacy 1919-1991: Political Applications of Limited Naval Force*, 3rd ed. (New York: St. Martin's, 1994), 158–213.

2. David F. Winkler, *Cold War at Sea: High-Seas Confrontation between the United States and the Soviet Union* (Annapolis, MD: Naval Institute Press, 2000), 177–210.

3. In particular, Iraq's attack on the USS *Stark* (May 17, 1987) during the Iran-Iraq War (1980–1988), various Iranian attacks on U.S. protected Kuwaiti tankers

during the so-called Tanker War phase of that war, the shoot-down of Iranian Flight 655 by the USS *Vincennes* on July 3, 1988, and al Qaeda's attacks on the USS *Cole* (October 12, 2000).

4. My general point is that the quantitative studies are less objective than their authors often suggest. The vast databases dazzle with promises of objective, value-free analysis, but one only has to push beneath the surface to see how subjectivity plays a role in defining which incidents merit inclusion in the database, which do not, and what factors are considered.

5. For a broader discussion of maritime law and its roots in the Middle Ages, see John B. Hattendorf and Richard W. Unger, eds., *War at Sea in the Middle Ages and the Renaissance, Warfare in History* (Woodbridge, UK: Boydell Press, 2003); and John B. Hattendorf, "Maritime Conflict," in *The Laws of War: Constraints on Warfare in the Western World*, ed. Michael Eliot Howard, George J. Andreopoulos, and Mark R. Shulman (New Haven, CT: Yale University Press, 1994), 100–01.

6. See Warren I. Cohen, *The American Revisionists: The Lessons of Intervention in World War I* (Chicago: University of Chicago Press, 1967).

7. In response to a query from the defense lawyers representing Grand Admirals Erich Raeder and Karl Doenitz at the Nuremberg Trials after World War II, Admiral Chester Nimitz submitted an affidavit admitting that the U.S. Navy had practiced unrestricted submarine warfare in the Pacific from the first day of hostilities with Japan. *Trial of the Major War Criminals before the International Military Tribunal, Nuremberg*, November 14, 1945 to October 1, 1946 (Nuremberg, Germany: 1947–1949), 17:378–81.

8. Part 2 covers Wilson's defense of American (and neutral) trading rights during the period 1914 to 1917. Those wishing to go further back and examine how the defense of U.S. rights on the high seas contributed to the War of 1812 should consult Jasper M. Trautsch, "The Causes of the War of 1812: 200 Years of Debate," *Journal of Military History* 77, no. 1 (2013); Spencer Tucker and Frank T. Reuter, *Injured Honor: The Chesapeake-Leopard Affair, June 22, 1807* (Annapolis, MD: Naval Institute Press, 1996); Maria Fanis, *Secular Morality and International Security: American and British Decisions About War* (Ann Arbor: University of Michigan Press, 2011), 13–56.

9. David B. Cohen and Chris J. Dolan, "Revisiting El Dorado Canyon: Terrorism, the Reagan Administration, and the 1986 Bombing of Libya," in *Focus on U.S. Presidents, Presidency and Presidential Action*, ed. Robert P. Watson (New York: Nova Science Publishers, 2007); Joseph T. Stanik, *El Dorado Canyon: Reagan's Undeclared War with Qaddafi* (Annapolis, MD: Naval Institute Press, 2003); Brian L. Davis, *Qaddafi, Terrorism, and the Origins of the U.S. Attack on Libya* (New York: Praeger, 1990).

10. Cable, *Gunboat Diplomacy 1919-1991*, 14.

11. See in particular James Cable, *The Political Influence of Naval Force in History* (New York: St. Martin's, 1998); Cable, *Navies in Violent Peace* (New York:

St. Martin's, 1989), and particularly, Cable, *Diplomacy at Sea* (Annapolis, MD: Naval Institute Press, 1985).

12. Geoffrey Till, Lawrence Freedman, Paul M. Kennedy, and Nicholas Rodger were all born British citizens, while Edward Luttwak was not. But Israeli-American Luttwak would certainly have been exposed to British fascination with sea power as a youth attending boarding school in Britain and as an undergraduate at the London School of Economics in the early 1960s. For a sample of the outpouring of British scholarship on sea power and diplomacy, see Geoffrey Till, *Seapower: A Guide for the Twenty-First Century*, 3rd ed. (New York: Routledge, 2013); Lawrence Freedman, *Strategic Coercion: Concepts and Cases* (Oxford: Oxford University Press, 1998); Nicholas Rodger, ed., *Naval Power in the Twentieth Century* (Annapolis, MD: Naval Institute Press, 1996); Paul M. Kennedy, *The Rise of the Anglo-German Antagonism, 1860-1914* (London: George Allen & Unwin, 1980); Edward Luttwak, *The Political Uses of Sea Power* (Baltimore, MD: Johns Hopkins University Press, 1974).

13. One suspects that U.S. scholars focused on airpower's role in coercive diplomacy owing to ongoing debates in the United States during the 1990s over how to respond to ethnic cleansing and conflict in Bosnia and Kosovo without committing "boots on the ground." See Eliot A. Cohen, "The Mystique of U.S. Air Power," *Foreign Affairs* 73, no. 1 (1994); Robert Anthony Pape, *Bombing to Win: Air Power and Coercion in War* (Ithaca, NY: Cornell University Press, 1996); Daniel Byman and Matthew C. Waxman, *The Dynamics of Coercion: American Foreign Policy and the Limits of Military Might* (New York: Cambridge University Press, 2001); Patrick C. Bratton, "A Coherent Theory of Coercion? The Writings of Robert Pape," *Comparative Strategy* 22, no. 4 (2003); Robert Anthony Pape, "The True Worth of Air Power," *Foreign Affairs* 83, no. 2 (2004).

14. Two books on naval diplomacy appeared in the late 1970s; there was a historical study of Teddy Roosevelt's use of the big stick in 2007, as well as an article on the theory of naval airpower in 2014 and chapters in broader studies of sea power in 2004 and 2013. Edward Luttwak and Robert G. Weinland, *Sea Power in the Mediterranean: Political Utility and Military Constraints* (Beverly Hills, CA: Sage, 1979); Bradford Dismukes and James M. McConnell, *Soviet Naval Diplomacy* (New York: Pergamon, 1979); Henry J. Hendrix, *Theodore Roosevelt's Naval Diplomacy: The U.S. Navy and the Birth of the American Century* (Annapolis, MD: Naval Institute Press, 2009); Robert C. Rubel, "A Theory of Naval Airpower," *Naval War College Review* 67, no. 3 (Summer 2014): 63–80; and chapters on "Naval Diplomacy," in Till, *Seapower,*. Rubel's piece ignores coercion theory entirely, instead discussing the "theory of scout bombing," the "theory of fleet defense," and so forth.

15. Cable, *Gunboat Diplomacy 1919-1991*, 13. I do not wish to overstate British domination of the field. For a sample of U.S. works on naval diplomacy, history, and policy, see the essays in John B. Hattendorf, ed., *Doing Naval History: Essays Toward Improvement* (Newport, RI: Naval War College Press, 1995); Hattendorf,

Talking About Naval History: A Collection of Essays (Newport, RI: Naval War College Press, 2011); and the published proceedings of the annual International Seapower Symposium.

16. Cable notes how a weaker naval power can likewise use definitive force, with North Korea's seizure of the USS *Pueblo* a case in point. While the U.S. Navy as a whole was vastly more powerful than that of North Korea, at the point of contact the North Korea's patrol boats outgunned the surveillance ship *Pueblo*. By the time the United States had forces in place to respond, the *Pueblo* was in Wonsan and its crew was captive. The two best accounts of the *Pueblo*'s seizure are Jack Cheevers, *Act of War: Lyndon Johnson, North Korea, and the Capture of the Spy Ship Pueblo* (New York: NAL Caliber, 2013); and Mitchell B. Lerner, *The Pueblo Incident: A Spy Ship and the Failure of American Foreign Policy* (Lawrence: University Press of Kansas, 2002).

17. Cable includes the U.S. invasion of Grenada (Operation Urgent Fury) in 1983 and the overthrow of the Noriega regime in Panama (Operation Just Cause) in 1989 among his examples of purposeful force. Even the smaller of these operations (Operation Urgent Fury) involved a carrier battle group, an amphibious task force, U.S. Army Rangers, the 82nd Airborne Division, and various Air Force Fighter and Airlift Wings. This hardly seems to qualify as the use of limited naval forces "otherwise than as an act of war." Ronald H. Cole, *Operation Urgent Fury: The Planning and Execution of Joint Operations in Grenada, 12 October–2 November 1983* (Washington, DC: Joint History Office, Office of the Chairman of the Joint Chiefs of Staff, 1997).

18. Cable, *Gunboat Diplomacy 1919-1991*, 46. Cohen makes the same point, noting that political objectives are "often ambiguous, contradictory, and uncertain." Eliot Cohen, *Supreme Command. Soldiers, Statesmen, and Leadership in Wartime* (New York: Anchor, 2003), 257–58.

19. Cable points to the British deployment of naval forces in the Baltic from 1919 to 1921 as an example of catalytic force. The British government was extremely vague in the instructions that it provided to the rear-admiral in charge of the Royal Navy Baltic squadron in 1918. His orders were to "show the British flag and support British policy as circumstances dictate." Yet policy had not yet been clearly established. For months, the Foreign Office could not decide whether British forces should back one or more of the White Russian leaders fighting the Bolsheviks; whether they should support the nationalist movements in Finland, Latvia, Estonia, and Lithuania, or whether they should merely observe events. Only as the course of events unfolded did British objectives become clearer, with the British admiral eventually given more specific guidance in January 1919 that his mission was to "prevent the destruction of Estonia and Latvia by external aggression." Cable, *Gunboat Diplomacy 1919-1991*, 46–51; Cable, *Political Influence of Naval Force in History*, 116–17.

20. A number of naval scholars have presented alternative concepts and categories for analyzing naval diplomacy and naval coercion. These range from Luttwak's "theory of suasion" to Ken Booth's triad of prestige, manipulation, and negotiation

through strength, to Geoffrey Till's conception of presence enabling coercion, deterrence, and compellence, to Coutau-Bégarie's multi-level analysis of *diplomatie permanente, diplomatie de crise, diplomatie préventice, diplomatie reactive, diplomatie cooperative, diplomatie coercitive, diplomatie nationale,* and *diplomatie multinationale*. I have selected Cable's typology for discussion as I find it captures the nuance of naval diplomacy well. For alternatives, see Luttwak, *Political Uses of Sea Power*, 1–38; Ken Booth, *Navies and Foreign Policy* (New York: Holmes & Meier, 1979), 16, 26–84; Till, *Seapower*, 221–51; and Hervé Coutau-Bégarie, *Le Meilleur des Ambassadeurs. Théorie et Pratique de la Diplmatie Navale* (Paris: Economica, 2010), 11–21, 45–84.

21. Scholars such as J. David Singer, Melvin Small, Stuart A. Bremer, and John A. Vasquez led the way in compiling quantitative studies assessing the probability of war. On first blush, one might assume that studies with titles like *Explaining War, The War Puzzle,* "Bones of Contention," "Assessing the Steps to War," and "Dangerous Dyads" would have great utility to policymakers concerned with crises decision making, escalation, and naval incidents. Yet the results of these studies tend to be bland, banal, and too broad to cast light on crisis situations. Bremer's groundbreaking study, for example, dazzles the reader with equations for multivariate analysis drawn from the Poisson regression model. Yet his findings are unsurprising. The factor that correlates most directly to the probability of war is that states are contiguous by land or by sea. Put differently, states adjacent to one another are more likely to engage in hostilities with one another than are states widely separated by geography. The second most important factor is that "alliances significantly reduce the likelihood of war between allies, except under special conditions." Put in layman's terms, allies tend not to attack one another. John A. Vasquez, *The War Puzzle Revisited* (Cambridge: Cambridge University Press, 2009); Paul R. Hensel et al., "Bones of Contention: Comparing Territorial, Maritime, and River Issues," *Journal of Conflict Resolution* 52, no. 1 (2008); Paul D. Senese and John A. Vasquez, "Assessing the Steps to War," *British Journal of Political Science* 35, no. 4 (2005); Stuart A. Bremer, "Dangerous Dyads: Conditions Affecting the Likelihood of Interstate War, 1816-1965," *Journal of Conflict Resolution* 36, no. 2 (1992).

22. Stephen M. Walt, "Theory and Policy in International Relations: Some Personal Reflections," *Yale Journal of International Affairs*, vol. 7, nr.2 (September 2012), 35.

23. Ibid., 38.

24. Hensel et al., "Bones of Contention."

25. Robert B. Strassler and Richard Crawley, eds., *The Landmark Thucydides* (New York: Free Press, 1996); see Bk1, Ch22, Sec4, 16.

26. Robert Jervis, *Perception and Misperception in International Politics* (Princeton, NJ: Princeton University Press, 239).

27. In addition to Jervis, *Perception and Misperception*, see Ole Holsti and Alexander George's early work on worldview or, as they term it, the operational code.

Alexander L. George, "The 'Operational Code': A Neglected Approach to the Study of Political Leaders and Decision Making," *International Studies Quarterly* 13, no. 2 (June 1969); Ole Holsti, "The 'Operational Code' Approach to the Study of Political Leaders," *Canadian Journal of Political Science* 3, no. 1 (March 1970).

28. Ernest R. May, *"Lessons" of the Past; the Use and Misuse of History in American Foreign Policy* (New York: Oxford University Press, 1973); Yuen Foong Khong, *Analogies at War: Korea, Munich, Dien Bien Phu, and the Vietnam Decisions of 1965* (Princeton, NJ: Princeton University Press, 1992); Christopher Hemmer, *Which Lessons Matter? American Foreign Policy Decision Making in the Middle East, 1979-1987* (Albany: State University of New York Press, 2000); and Margaret MacMillan, *Dangerous Games: The Uses and Abuses of History* (New York: Modern Library, 2009). One might note that Rusk and Bundy fundamentally misread both the realities of the Munich conference and the "lessons" as they applied to Vietnam. Hitler was quite eager to go to war in 1938, and a tougher stance would not have deterred him. See Gerhard L. Weinberg, "Munich after 50 Years," *Foreign Affairs* 67 (1988): 165–78.

29. McGeorge Bundy did compile a nine-page memorandum for the president dated June 30, 1965, on "France in Vietnam, 1954, and the US in Vietnam, 1965—A Useful Analogy?" Neustadt and May dismiss the analysis as superficial, almost surely written for Johnson so that he had "something to wave at Ball or at some senator or newsman" harkening back to the French experience. Richard E. Neustadt and Ernest R. May, *Thinking in Time: The Uses of History for Decision-Makers* (London: Collier Macmillan, 1986), 81–83. See also Jeffrey Record, *Making War, Thinking History: Munich, Vietnam, and Presidential Uses of Force from Korea to Kosovo* (Annapolis, MD: Naval Institute Press, 2002); and Record, *The Specter of Munich: Reconsidering the Lessons of Appeasing Hitler* (Washington, DC: Potomac Books, 2007).

30. The following draws on the research of Francis Gavin and William Inboden on history, policy, and decision making. Francis Gavin, "History and Policy," *International Journal* 63, no. 1 (Winter 2007-08); William Inboden, "Statecraft, Decsion-Making, and the Varieties of Historical Experience: A Taxonomy," *Journal of Strategic Studies* 37, no. 2 (2014).

31. Robert S. McNamara and Brian VanDeMark, *In Retrospect: The Tragedy and Lessons of Vietnam* (New York: Vintage, 1996), 322. One might add that the same level of historical ignorance and self-deception characterized many of the arguments for invading Iraq. See, for example, Lawrence Kaplan and William Kristol, *The War over Iraq: Saddam's Tyranny and America's Mission* (San Francisco: Encounter Books, 2003).

32. See George Washington University's National Security Archive Electronic Briefing Book No. 132, "The Gulf of Tonkin Incident, 40 Years Later. Flawed Intelligence and the Decision for War in Vietnam," at www2.gwu.edu/~nsarchiv/NSAEBB/NSAEBB132/.

33. While I use the term somewhat differently, I borrow the terminology from Francis Gavin, "History and Policy," 162–177, www.jstor.org/stable/40204495.

34. Inboden distinguishes between "option identification" and "paradigm erosion." I would argue that the latter impacts the former. Inboden, "Statecraft, Decision-Making," 305–06.

35. While Fukuyama's 1992 argument about the "end of history" was not that history itself would end, the widespread debate about his thesis that we were in the midst of the final phase of socio-political development (Western liberal democracy) struck many historians as overly optimistic and historically suspect. Francis Fukuyama, *The End of History and the Last Man* (Toronto: Maxwell Macmillan, 1992).

36. Edward Hallett Carr, *What Is History?* (London: Macmillan, 1961), 23.

37. Marc Léopold Benjamin Bloch, *The Historian's Craft* (New York: Knopf, 1953), 44–45.

38. See, for example, Laura Lee, "Forecasts That Missed by a Mile," *The Futurist*, September-October 2000, 20–25; Sam J. Tangredi, *All Possible Wars? Towards a Consensus View of the Future Security Environment, 2001-2025*, McNair Paper 63 (Washington, DC: National Defense University, November 2000), 15–30 (chs. 2 "Estimates, Forecasts, and Scenarios" and 3 "Using the Future—Some Caveats"); U.S. Commission on National Security/21st Century, *Study Addendum. New World Coming: American Security in the 21st Century* (Washington, DC: Government Printing Office, 1999).

BIBLIOGRAPHY

INTRODUCTION AND PART IV: HISTORY, THEORY,
AND CONTEMPORARY CONCERNS

Allison, Graham T. "Conceptual Models and the Cuban Missile Crisis." *American Political Science Review* 63, no. 3 (September 1969): 689–718.

Allison, Graham T., and Philip Zelikow. *Essence of Decision; Explaining the Cuban Missile Crisis.* New York: Longman, 1999 [orig. 1971].

Art, Robert J., and Patrick M. Cronin. *The United States and Coercive Diplomacy.* Washington, DC: United States Institute of Peace Press, 2003.

"Ballistic and Cruise Missile Threat (NASIC-1031-0985-13)." Wright Patterson AFB, OH: National Air and Space Intelligence Center, 2013.

Beyerchen, Alan. "Clausewitz, Nonlinearity, and the Unpredictability of War." *International Security* 17, no. 3 (1992/93): 59–90.

Bloch, Marc Léopold Benjamin. *The Historian's Craft.* New York: Knopf, 1953.

Booth, Ken. *Navies and Foreign Policy.* New York: Holmes & Meier, 1979.

———. *Strategy and Ethnocentrism.* New York: Holmes & Meier, 1979.

Bratton, Patrick C. "A Coherent Theory of Coercion? The Writings of Robert Pape." *Comparative Strategy* 22, no. 4 (2003): 355.

Bratton, Patrick C., and Geoffrey Till, eds. *Sea Power and the Asia-Pacific: The Triumph of Neptune?* New York: Routledge, 2012.

Bremer, Stuart A. "Dangerous Dyads: Conditions Affecting the Likelihood of Interstate War, 1816-1965." *Journal of Conflict Resolution* 36, no. 2 (1992): 309–41.

Burrows, William E. *By Any Means Necessary: America's Secret Air War in the Cold War.* New York: Farrar, Straus and Giroux, 2001.

Buzan, Barry, Ole Wæver, and Jaap de Wilde. *Security: A New Framework for Analysis.* Boulder, CO: Lynne Rienner, 1998.

Byman, Daniel, and Matthew C. Waxman. *The Dynamics of Coercion: American Foreign Policy and the Limits of Military Might.* New York: Cambridge University Press, 2001.

Cable, James. *Britain's Naval Future*. Annapolis, MD: Naval Institute Press, 1983.

———. *Diplomacy at Sea*. Annapolis, MD: Naval Institute Press, 1985.

———. *Gunboat Diplomacy 1919-1991: Political Applications of Limited Naval Force*. 3rd ed. New York: St. Martin's, 1994.

———. *Navies in Violent Peace*. New York: St. Martin's, 1989.

———. *The Political Influence of Naval Force in History*. New York: St. Martin's, 1998.

———. *The Royal Navy & the Siege of Bilbao*. Cambridge: Cambridge University Press, 1979.

Carr, Edward Hallett. *What Is History?* London: Macmillan, 1961.

Cheevers, Jack. *Act of War: Lyndon Johnson, North Korea, and the Capture of the Spy Ship Pueblo*. New York: NAL Caliber, 2013.

Cohen, David B., and Chris J. Dolan. "Revisiting El Dorado Canyon: Terrorism, the Reagan Administration, and the 1986 Bombing of Libya" In *Focus on U.S. Presidents, Presidency and Presidential Action*, edited by Robert P. Watson. New York: Nova Science, 2007, 121–142.

Cohen, Eliot A. "The Historical Mind and Military Strategy." *Orbis* 49, no. 4 (2005): 575–88.

———. "The Mystique of U.S. Air Power." *Foreign Affairs* 73, no. 1 (1994): 109–24.

———. *Supreme Command. Soldiers, Statesmen, and Leadership in Wartime*. New York: Anchor, 2003.

Cole, Ronald H. *Operation Urgent Fury: The Planning and Execution of Joint Operations in Grenada, 12 October–2 November 1983*. Washington, DC: Joint History Office, Office of the Chairman of the Joint Chiefs of Staff, 1997.

Coutau-Bégarie, Hervé. *Le Meilleur des Ambassadeurs: Théorie et Pratique de la Diplomatie Navale*. Paris: Economica, 2010.

Cristol, A. Jay. *The Liberty Incident Revealed: The Definitive Account of the 1967 Israeli Attack on the U.S. Navy Spy Ship*. 2nd ed. Annapolis, MD: Naval Institute Press, 2013.

Davis, Brian L. *Qaddafi, Terrorism, and the Origins of the U.S. Attack on Libya*. New York: Praeger, 1990.

De Souza, Philip. *Piracy in the Graeco-Roman World*. Cambridge: Cambridge University Press, 1999.

Dismukes, Bradford, and James M. McConnell. *Soviet Naval Diplomacy*. New York: Pergamon Press, 1979.

Doyle, Michael W. "Kant, Liberal Legacies, and Foreign Affairs." *Philosophy and Public Affairs* 12, no. 4 (1983): 323–53.

Dyer, Geoff. *The Contest of the Century: The New Era of Competition with China—and How America Can Win*. New York: Knopf, 2014.

Erickson, Andrew S. *Chinese Anti-Ship Ballistic Missile Development: Drivers, Trajectories and Strategic Implications*. Washington, DC: Jamestown Foundation, 2013.

Fanis, Maria. *Secular Morality and International Security: American and British Decisions About War*. Ann Arbor: University of Michigan Press, 2011.

Fearon, James D. "Domestic Politics, Foreign Policy, and Theories of International Relations." *Annual Review of Political Science* 1, no. 1 (1998): 289.*

———. "Signaling Foreign Policy Interests." *Journal of Conflict Resolution* 41, no. 1 (1997): 68–91.

Finlay, Robert. "The Voyages of Zheng He: Ideology, State Power, and Maritime Trade in Ming China." *Journal of the Historical Society* 8, no. 3 (2008): 327–47.

Freedman, Lawrence. *Strategic Coercion: Concepts and Cases.* Oxford: Oxford University Press, 1998.

Friedman, Thomas L. *The Lexus and the Olive Tree: Understanding Globalization.* 1st Picador, ed. New York: Picador, 2012.

Frühling, Stephan. *Defence Planning and Uncertainty: Preparing for the Next Asia-Pacific War.* London: Routledge, 2014.

Fukuyama, Francis. *The End of History and the Last Man.* Toronto: Macmillan International, 1992.

Gaddis, John Lewis. *The Landscape of History: How Historians Map the Past.* Oxford: Oxford University Press, 2002.

Gavin, Francis J. "History and Policy." *International Journal* 63, no. 1 (Winter 2007-08): 166–67.

———. *Nuclear Statecraft. History and Strategy in America's Atomic Age.* Ithaca, NY: Cornell University Press, 2012.

George, Alexander L. *Forceful Persuasion: Coercive Diplomacy as an Alternative to War.* Washington, DC: United States Institute of Peace Press, 1991.

———. "The 'Operational Code': A Neglected Approach to the Study of Political Leaders and Decision Making," *International Studies Quarterly* 13, no. 2 (June 1969): 190–222.

George, Alexander L., and Andrew Bennett. *Case Studies and Theory Development in the Social Sciences.* Cambridge, MA: MIT Press, 2005.

George, Alexander L., David Kent Hall, and William E. Simons. *The Limits of Coercive Diplomacy; Laos, Cuba, Vietnam.* Boston: Little, Brown, 1971.

George, Alexander L., William E. Simons, David Kent Hall, and Alexander L. George. *The Limits of Coercive Diplomacy.* 2nd ed. Boulder, CO: Westview Press, 1994.

Grossnick, Roy A., and Naval Historical Center (U.S.). *United States Naval Aviation, 1910–1995.* Washington, DC: Naval Historical Center, Dept. of the Navy, 1997.

Haas, Michael. "Deconstructing the Democratic Peace". In *Deconstructing International Relations Theory,* edited by Michael Haas, 127–48. New York: Norton, 2007.*

Haber, Stephen H., David M. Kennedy, and Stephen D. Krasner. "Brothers under the Skin: Diplomatic History and International Relations." *International Security* 22, no. 1 (1997): 34–43.*

Hagan, Kenneth J. *American Gunboat Diplomacy and the Old Navy, 1877–1889.* Westport, CT: Greenwood 1973.

Hattendorf, John B. *Talking about Naval History: a Collection of Essays.* Newport, RI: Naval War College Press, 2011.

Hattendorf, John B., ed. *Doing Naval History: Essays toward Improvement.* Newport, RI: Naval War College Press, 1995.

Hattendorf, John B., and Richard W. Unger. *War at Sea in the Middle Ages and the Renaissance.* Rocherster, NY: Boydell Press, 2003.

Hayton, Bill. *The South China Sea. The Struggle for Power in Asia.* New Haven, CT: Yale University Press, 2014.

Hemmer, Christopher. *Which Lessons Matter? American Foreign Policy Decision Making in the Middle East, 1979-1987.* Albany: State University of New York Press, 2000.

Hendrix, Henry J. *Theodore Roosevelt's Naval Diplomacy: The U.S. Navy and the Birth of the American Century.* Annapolis, MD: Naval Institute Press, 2009.

Hensel, Paul R., Gary Goertz, and Paul F. Diehl. "The Democratic Peace and Rivalries." *Journal of Politics* 64 (2000): 1173–88.

Hensel, Paul R., Sara McLaughlin Mitchell, Thomas E. Sowers II, and L. Thyne Clayton. "Bones of Contention: Comparing Territorial, Maritime, and River Issues." *Journal of Conflict Resolution* 52, no. 1 (2008): 117–43.

Holsti, Ole. "The 'Operational Code' Approach to the Study of Political Leaders," *Canadian Journal of Political Science* 3, no. 1 (March 1970): 123–57.

Howard, Michael Eliot. *War in European History.* London: Oxford University Press, 1976.

Howard, Michael, George J. Andreopoulos, and Mark R. Shulman. *The Laws of War: Constraints on Warfare in the Western World.* New Haven, CT: Yale University Press, 1994.

Hui Chun, Hing. "Huangming Zuxun and Zheng He's Voyages to the Western Oceans" [In English]. *Journal of Chinese Studies* 51 (2010): 67–85.

Ikenberry, G. John. *After Victory: Institutions, Strategic Restraint, and the Rebuilding of Order after Major Wars.* Princeton, NJ: Princeton University Press, 2001.

Inboden, William. "Statecraft, Decision-Making, and the Varieties of Historical Experience: A Taxonomy." *Journal of Strategic Studies* 37, no. 2 (2014): 291–318.

Jakobsen, Peter Viggo. *Western Use of Coercive Diplomacy after the Cold War: A Challenge for Theory and Practice.* New York: St. Martin's, 1998.

Jansen, Marius B. *The Making of Modern Japan.* Cambridge, MA: Belknap Press, 2000.

Jervis, Robert. *The Logic of Images in International Relations.* New York: Columbia University Press, 1989.

———. *The Meaning of the Nuclear Revolution. Statecraft and the Prospect of Armageddon.* Ithaca: Cornell University Press, 1989.

———. *Perception and Misperception in International Politics.* Princeton, NJ: Princeton University Press, 1976.

Kaplan, Lawrence, and William Kristol. *The War over Iraq: Saddam's Tyranny and America's Mission.* San Francisco: Encounter Books, 2003.

Kaplan, Robert D. *Asia's Cauldron: The South China Sea and the End of a Stable Pacific.* New York: Random House, 2014.

Katzenstein, Peter J., ed. *The Culture of National Security: Norms and Identity in World Politics*. New York: Columbia University Press, 1996.

Kennedy, Paul M. *The Rise of the Anglo-German Antagonism, 1860-1914*. Atlantic Highlands, NJ: Ashfield Press, 1987.

Keohane, Robert O. *After Hegemony: Cooperation and Discord in the World Political Economy*. Princeton, NJ: Princeton University Press, 1984.

Keohane, Robert O., and Joseph S. Nye. *Power and Interdependence*. 2nd ed. Glenview, IL: Scott, Foresman, 1989.

Khong, Yuen Foong. *Analogies at War: Korea, Munich, Dien Bien Phu, and the Vietnam Decisions of 1965*. Princeton, NJ: Princeton University Press, 1992.

Kissinger, Henry. *Diplomacy*. New York: Simon & Schuster, 1994.

Knox, MacGregor, and Williamson Murray. *The Dynamics of Military Revolution, 1300-2050*. New York: Cambridge University Press, 2001.

Lerner, Mitchell B. *The Pueblo Incident: A Spy Ship and the Failure of American Foreign Policy*. Lawrence: University Press of Kansas, 2002.

Levy, Jack S. "Coercive Threats, Audience Costs, and Case Studies." *Security Studies* 21 (2012): 383–90.

———. "Explaining Events and Developing Theories: History, Political Science, and the Analysis of International Relations." In *Bridges and Boundaries: Historians, Political Scientists, and the Study of International Relations*, edited by Colin Elman and Miriam Fendius Elman, 39–83. Cambridge, MA: MIT Press, 2001.

———. "Domestic Politics and War." *Journal of Interdisciplinary History* 18, no. 4 (1988): 653–73

Lockwood, William W., ed. *Our Far Eastern Record. A Reference Digest on American Policy*. New York: American Council; Institute of Pacific Relations, 1940.

Lukacs, John. *At the End of an Age*. New Haven, CT: Yale University Press, 2002.

Luttwak, Edward. *The Rise of China vs. The Logic of Strategy*. Cambridge, MA: Belknap Press of Harvard University Press, 2012.

———. *The Political Uses of Sea Power*. Studies in International Affairs, No 23. Baltimore, MD: Johns Hopkins University Press, 1974.

Luttwak, Edward, and Robert G. Weinland. *Sea Power in the Mediterranean: Political Utility and Military Constraints*. Beverly Hills, CA: Sage, 1979.

Lynn, John A. "The Embattled Future of Academic Military History." *Journal of Military History* 61, no. 4 (1997): 777–89.

———. "Reflections on the History and Theory of Military Innovation and Diffusion." Ch. 14 in *Bridges and Boundaries. Historians, Political Scientists, and the Study of International Relations*, edited by Colin Elman and Miriam Fendius Elman, 359–82. Cambridge, MA: MIT Press, 2001.

MacMillan, Margaret. *Dangerous Games: The Uses and Abuses of History*. New York: Modern Library, 2009.

Mansfield, Edward D., and Brian M. Pollins. "The Study of Interdependence and Conflict." *Journal of Conflict Resolution* 45, no. 6 (2001): 834–59.

May, Ernest R. *"Lessons" of the Past: The Use and Misuse of History in American Foreign Policy*. New York: Oxford University Press, 1973.

McNamara, Robert S., and Brian VanDeMark. *In Retrospect: The Tragedy and Lessons of Vietnam*. New York: Vintage Books, 1996.

Mearsheimer, John J. *The Tragedy of Great Power Politics*. New York: Norton, 2001.

Mitchell, Sara McLaughlin, and John A. Vasquez. *Conflict, War, and Peace: An Introduction to Scientific Research*. Thousand Oaks, CA: CQ Press, 2014.

Mobley, Richard A. *Flash Point North Korea: The Pueblo and EC-121 Crises*. Annapolis, MD: Naval Institute Press, 2003.

Morgenthau, Hans J. *Politics among Nations; the Struggle for Power and Peace*. New York: Knopf, 1948.

Nathan, Andrew J., and Andrew Scobell. *China's Search for Security*. New York: Columbia University Press, 2012.

Navias, Martin S., and E. R. Hooton. *Tanker Wars: The Assault on Merchant Shipping During the Iran-Iraq Conflict, 1980-1988*. New York: I.B. Tauris, 1996.

Neustadt, Richard E., and Ernest R. May. *Thinking in Time: The Uses of History for Decision-Makers*. London: Collier Macmillan, 1986.

Nye, Joseph S. *The Paradox of American Power: Why the World's Only Superpower Can't Go It Alone*. Oxford: Oxford University Press, 2002.

O'Rourke, Ronald. "Maritime Territorial and Exclusive Economic Zone (EEZ) Disputes Involving China: Issues for Congress." Washington, DC: Congressional Research Service, 2015.

Oneal, John, and Bruce Russett. "The Classical Liberals Were Right: Democracy, Interdependence, and Conflict 1950-85." *International Studies Quarterly* 41, no. 2 (1997): 267–93.

Orlov, Alexander. "The U-2 Program: A Russian Officer Remembers. A 'Hot' Front in the Cold War." *Studies in Intelligence* (Winter 1998).

Owen, John M. "Give Democratic Peace a Chance? How Liberalism Produces Democratic Peace." *International Security* 19, no. 2 (1994): 87–125.

Pape, Robert Anthony. *Bombing to Win: Air Power and Coercion in War*. Ithaca, NY: Cornell University Press, 1996.

Page, Robert Anthony. "The True Worth of Air Power." *Foreign Affairs* 83, no. 2 (2004): 116–30.

Pedrozo, Raul. "Close Encounters at Sea." *Naval War College Review* 62, no. 3 (Summer 2009): 101–11.

Peifer, Douglas. "Maritime Commerce Warfare: The Coercive Response of the Weak?" *Naval War College Review* 66, no. 2 (Spring 2013): 83–109.

———. "Risk-Free Coercion? Technological Disparity and Coercive Diplomacy." *European Security* 18, no. 1 (2009): 7–31.

———. *The Three German Navies: Dissolution, Transition, and New Beginnings, 1945-1960*. Gainesville: University Press of Florida, 2002.

Pelz, Stephen. "Toward a New Diplomatic History: Two and a Half Cheers for International Relations Methods." In *Bridges and Boundaries: Historians, Political Scientists, and the Study of International Relations*, edited by Colin Elman and Miriam Fendius Elman, 85–110. Cambridge, MA: MIT Press, 2001.

Polmar, Norman. *Chronology of the Cold War at Sea, 1945-1991*. Annapolis, MD: Naval Institute Press, 1998.

Record, Jeffrey. *Making War, Thinking History: Munich, Vietnam, and Presidential Uses of Force from Korea to Kosovo*. Annapolis, MD: Naval Institute Press, 2002.

———. *The Specter of Munich: Reconsidering the Lessons of Appeasing Hitler*. Washington, DC: Potomac Books, 2007.

Rodger, Nicholas A. M. *The Safeguard of the Sea: A Naval History of Britain, 660-1649*. New York: Norton, 1998.

Rodger, Nicholas A.M., ed. *Naval Power in the Twentieth Century*. Annapolis, MD: Naval Institute Press, 1996.

Russett, Bruce M. *Grasping the Democratic Peace: Principles for a Post-Cold War World*. Princeton, NJ: Princeton University Press, 1993.

Santayana, George. *The Life of Reason, or, the Phases of Human Progress*. Rev. ed. New York: Scribner's, 1954.

Saunders, Philip C., Christopher Yung, Michael Swaine, and Andrew Nien-Dzu Yang. *The Chinese Navy. Expanding Capabilities, Evolving Roles*. Washington, DC: Institute for National Strategic Studies, 2011.

Schelling, Thomas C. *The Strategy of Conflict*. Cambridge, MA: Harvard University Press, 1960.

———. *Arms and Influence*. New Haven, CT: Yale University Press, 1966.

Senese, Paul D., and John A. Vasquez. "Assessing the Steps to War." *British Journal of Political Science* 35, no. 4 (2005): 607–33.

Shambaugh, David L. *Tangled Titans: The United States and China*. Lanham, MD: Rowman & Littlefield, 2013.

Slantchev, Branislav. "Audience Cost Theory and Its Audiences." *Security Studies* 21 (2012): 376–82.

Smith, Sheila A. "Japan and the East China Sea Dispute." *Orbis* 56, no. 3 (Summer 2012): 370–90.

Stanik, Joseph T. *El Dorado Canyon: Reagan's Undeclared War with Qaddafi*. Annapolis, MD: Naval Institute Press, 2003.

Strachan, Hew. *The Direction of War: Contemporary Strategy in Historical Perspective*. Cambridge: Cambridge University Press, 2013.

Strassler, Robert B., and Richard Crawley, eds. *The Landmark Thucydides*. New York: Free Press, 1996.

Tangredi, Sam J. *Anti-Access Warfare: Countering A2/AD Strategies*. Annapolis: Naval Institute Press, 2013.

———. *All Possible Wars? Towards a Consensus View of the Future Security Environment, 2001–2025*, McNair Paper 63. Washington, DC: National Defense University, 2000.

Tart, Larry, and Robert Keefe. *The Price of Vigilance: Attacks on American Surveillance Flights*. New York: Ballantine, 2001.

Taylor, Andrew J., and John T. Rourke. "Historical Analogies in the Congressional Foreign Policy Process." *Journal of Politics* 57 (1995): 460–68.

Till, Geoffrey. *Seapower: A Guide for the Twenty-First Century*. 3rd ed. New York: Routledge, 2013.

Trachtenberg, Marc. "Audience Costs: An Historical Analysis." *Security Studies* 21:1 (2012), 3–42.

Trautsch, Jasper M. "The Causes of the War of 1812: 200 Years of Debate." *Journal of Military History* 77 no. 1 (2013): 273–93.

Tucker, Spencer, and Frank T. Reuter. *Injured Honor: The Chesapeake-Leopard Affair, June 22, 1807*. Annapolis, MD: Naval Institute Press, 1996.

Turner, Frederick Jackson. *The Early Writings of Frederick Jackson Turner; Compiled by Everett E. Edwards*. Madison: University of Wisconsin Press, 1938.

Van Evera, Stephen. *Causes of War: Power and the Roots of Conflict*. Ithaca, NY: Cornell University Press, 1999.

Vasquez, John A. *The War Puzzle*. Cambridge: Cambridge University Press, 1993.

———. *The War Puzzle Revisited*. Cambridge: Cambridge University Press, 2009.

Walt, Stephen M. *The Origins of Alliances*. Ithaca, NY: Cornell University Press, 1987.

———. "Theory and Policy in International Relations: Some Personal Reflections." *Yale Journal of International Affairs*, vol. 7, issue 2 (September 2012): 33–43.

Waltz, Kenneth N. "International Politics Is Not Foreign Policy." *Security Studies* 6, no. 1 (1996): 54–57.

———. *Man, the State, and War: A Theoretical Analysis*. New York: Columbia University Press, 1959.

———. *Theory of International Politics*. Boston: McGraw-Hill, 1979.

Weber, Cynthia. *International Relations Theory: A Critical Introduction*. 4th ed. New York: Routledge, 2014.

Wendt, Alexander. "Anarchy Is What States Make of It: The Social Construction of Power Politics." *International Organization* 46, no. 2 (1992): 391–425.

———. *Social Theory of International Politics*. Cambridge: Cambridge University Press, 1999.

Williams, Paul. *Security Studies: An Introduction*. 2nd ed. New York: Routledge, 2013.

Winkler, David F. *Cold War at Sea: High-Seas Confrontation between the United States and the Soviet Union*. Annapolis, MD: Naval Institute Press, 2000.

PART I. THE *MAINE* INCIDENT

Allen, Thomas. "A Special Report: What Really Sank the Maine." *United States Naval Institute Naval History*, vol. 12, nr. 2, April (1998).

Art, Robert J., and Patrick M. Cronin, *The United States and Coercive Diplomacy.* Washington, DC: United States Institute of Peace Press, 2003.

Auxier, George W. "Middle Western Newspapers and the Spanish American War, 1895–1898." *Mississippi Valley Historical Review* 26, no. 4 (1940): 523–34.

———. "The Propaganda Activities of the Cuban Junta in Precipitating the Spanish-American War, 1895-1898." *Hispanic American Historical Review* 19, no. 3 (1939): 286–305.

Beard, Charles A., and Mary Ritter Beard. *The Rise of American Civilization.* New York: Macmillan, 1930.

Becker, William H. *The Dynamics of Business-Government Relations: Industry & Exports, 1893-1921.* Chicago: University of Chicago Press, 1982.

Beisner, Robert L. *From the Old Diplomacy to the New, 1865-1900.* 2nd ed. Arlington Heights, IL: Harlan Davidson, 1986.

Benton, Elbert Jay. *International Law and Diplomacy of the Spanish-American War.* Baltimore, MD: Johns Hopkins University Press, 1908.

Brown, Charles H. *The Correspondents' War. Journalists in the Spanish-American War.* New York: Scribner's, 1967.

Byman, Daniel, and Matthew C. Waxman. *The Dynamics of Coercion: American Foreign Policy and the Limits of Military Might.* New York: Cambridge University Press, 2001.

Cable, James. *Gunboat Diplomacy 1919-1991: Political Applications of Limited Naval Force.* 3rd ed. New York: St. Martin's, 1994.

Campbell, W. Joseph. *Yellow Journalism: Puncturing the Myths, Defining the Legacies.* Westport, CT: Praeger, 2001.

Chidwick, John Patrick. *"Remember the Maine!" An Historical Narrative of the Battleship Maine as Told by Its Chaplain, the Right Reverened [!] Monsignor John P. Chidwick.* Winchester, VA: Winchester Printers and Stationers, 1935.

Cooling, Benjamin Franklin. *Gray Steel and Blue Water Navy: The Formative Years of America's Military-Industrial Complex, 1881–1917.* Hamden, CT: Archon, 1979.

Crapol, Edward. "Coming to Terms with Empire: The Historiography of Late Nineteenth-Century American Foreign Relations." In *Paths to Power. The Historiography of American Foreign Relations*, edited by Michael J. Hogan. Cambridge: Cambridge University Press, 2000, 79–115.

Eggert, Gerald G. "Our Man in Havana: Fitzhugh Lee." *Hispanic American Historical Review* 47, no. 4 (1967): 463–85.

Fields, James A. "American Imperialism: The Worst Chapter in Almost any Book." *American Historical Review*, 83, no. 3 (June 1978): 644–68.

Foner, Philip Sheldon. *The Spanish-Cuban-American War and the Birth of American Imperialism, 1895-1902*. 2 vols. New York: Monthly Review Press, 1972.

Fry, Joseph A. "The Architects of the 'Large Policy' Plus Two." *Diplomatic History* 29, no. 1 (2005): 185–88.

Gardner, Lloyd C., Walter LaFeber, and Thomas J. McCormick. *Creation of the American Empire*. 2nd ed. 2 vols. Chicago: Rand McNally, 1976.

Garraty, John A. *Henry Cabot Lodge, a Biography*. New York: Knopf, 1953.

George, Alexander L. *Forceful Persuasion: Coercive Diplomacy as an Alternative to War*. Washington, DC: United States Institute of Peace Press, 1991.

George, Alexander L., William E. Simons, David Kent Hall, and Alexander L. George. *The Limits of Coercive Diplomacy*. 2nd ed. Boulder, CO: Westview Press, 1994.

Gleijeses, Piero. "1898: The Opposition to the Spanish-American War." [In English]. *Journal of Latin American Studies* 35 (November 2003): 681–719.

Goldenberg, Bonnie. "Imperial Culture and National Conscience: The Role of the Press in the United States and Spain During the Crisis of 1898." *Bulletin of Hispanic Studies* 77, no. 3 (2000): 169–91.

Gould, Lewis L. *The Presidency of William McKinley*. Lawrence: Regents Press of Kansas, 1980.

———. *The Spanish-American War and President McKinley*. Lawrence: University Press of Kansas, 1982.

Hagan, Kenneth J. *This People's Navy: The Making of American Sea Power*. New York: Free Press, 1991.

Hamilton, Richard F. *President McKinley and America's "New Empire."* New Brunswick, NJ: Transaction, 2007.

———. *President McKinley and the Coming of War, 1898*. New Brunswick, NJ: Transaction, 2006.

Herring, George C. *From Colony to Superpower: U.S. Foreign Relations since 1776*. New York: Oxford University Press, 2011.

Herwig, Holger H. *Germany's Vision of Empire in Venezuela, 1871-1914*. Princeton, NJ: Princeton University Press, 1986.

———. *"Luxury" Fleet: The Imperial German Navy, 1888–1918*. Rev. ed. London: Ashfield Press, 1987.

Hogan, Michael J. *Paths to Power. The Historiography of American Foreign Relations*. Cambridge: Cambridge University Press, 2000.

Hood, Miriam. *Gunboat Diplomacy, 1895-1905: Great Power Pressure in Venezuela*. 2nd ed. London: Allen & Unwin, 1983.

Jakobsen, Peter Viggo. "The Strategy of Coercive Diplomacy: Refining Existing Theory to Post–Cold War Realities." In *Strategic Coercion: Concepts and Cases*, edited by Lawrence Freedman, 61–85. Oxford: Oxford University Press, 1998.

———. *Western Use of Coercive Diplomacy after the Cold War: A Challenge for Theory and Practice*. New York: St. Martin's, 1998.

Kapur, Nick. "William McKinley's Values and the Origins of the Spanish-American War: A Reinterpretation." *Presidential Studies Quarterly* 41, no. 1 (March 2011): 18–38.

LaFeber, Walter. *The American Search for Opportunity*, 1865–1913. Edited by William Earl Weeks, Walter LaFeber, Akira Iriye, and Warren I. Cohen. 4 vols. *The New Cambridge History of American Foreign Relations*. Cambridge, New York: Cambridge University Press, 2013.

Lodge, Henry Cabot. *The War with Spain*. New York: Harper & Brothers, 1900.

Long, John Davis. *The New American Navy*. 2 vols. New York: Outlook, 1903.

Long, Magaret, ed. *The Journal of John D. Long*. Rindge, NH: Richard R. Smith, 1956.

May, Ernest R. *Imperial Democracy: The Emergence of America as a Great Power.* New York: Harcourt, 1961.

McDougall, Walter A. *Promised Land, Crusader State: The American Encounter with the World since 1776*. Boston: Houghton Mifflin, 1997.

McKinley, William. *Messages, Proclamations, and Executive Orders Relating to the Spanish-American War.* Project Gutenberg, October 29, 2004 [EBook #13893]. doi:www.gutenberg.net.

"Message from the President of the United States Transmitting the Report of the Naval Court of Inquiry Upon the Destruction of the United States Battle Ship Maine in Havana Harbor, February 15, 1898, Together with the Testimony Taken before the Court, 55th Congress, 2d Session, Document 207." Washington, DC: Government Printing Office, 1898.

"Message from the President of the United States Transmitting the Report of Board convened at Habana, Cuba, by order of the Secretary of the Navy, to inspect and report on the wreck of the 'Maine' (Old)." 62nd Congress, 2^d Session, Document No.310 (December 1911).

Musicant, Ivan. *Empire by Default: The Spanish-American War and the Dawn of the American Century*. New York: Henry Holt, 1998.

Offner, John L. "McKinley and the Spanish-American War." *Presidential Studies Quarterly* 34, no. 1 (2004): 50–61.

———. "United States Politics and the 1898 War over Cuba." In *The Crisis of 1898: Colonial Redistribution and Nationalist Mobilization*, edited by Angel Smith, Dávila Cox and Emma Aurora. New York: St. Martin's, 1999, 18–44.

———. *An Unwanted War: The Diplomacy of the United States and Spain over Cuba, 1895-1898*. Chapel Hill: University of North Carolina Press, 1992.

Papers Relating to the Foreign Relations of the United States. 1896. Washington, DC: Government Printing Office, 1896.

Papers Relating to the Foreign Relations of the United States. 1897. Washington, DC: U.S. Government Printing Office, 1897.

Paterson, Thomas G. "United States Intervention in Cuba, 1898: Interpretations of the Spanish-American-Cuban-Filipino War." *History Teacher* 29, no. 3 (1996): 341–61.

Pérez, Louis A. *Cuba between Empires, 1878-1902*. Pittsburgh: University of Pittsburgh Press, 1983.

———. *The War of 1898: The United States and Cuba in History and Historiography.* Chapel Hill: University of North Carolina Press, 1998.

Pletcher, David M. *The Diplomacy of Involvement: American Economic Expansion across the Pacific, 1784-1900.* Columbia: University of Missouri Press, 2001.

———. *The Diplomacy of Trade and Investment: American Economic Expansion in the Hemisphere, 1865-1900.* Columbia: University of Missouri Press, 1998.

Pratt, Julius William. *Expansionists of 1898: The Acquisition of Hawaii and the Spanish Islands.* Baltimore, MD: Johns Hopkins University Press, 1936.

Pritchett, Henry S. "Some Recollections of President McKinley and the Cuban Intervention." *North American Review* 189, no. 640 (March 1909): 397–403.

Rentfrow, James C. *Home Squadron. The U.S. Navy on the North Atlantic Station.* Annapolis, MD: Naval Institute Press, 2014.

Rickover, Hyman George. *How the Battleship Maine Was Destroyed.* Washington, DC: Naval History Division, 1976.

Roosevelt, Theodore, Elting Elmore Morison, John Morton Blum, and John J. Buckley. *Letters.* 8 vols. Cambridge, MA: Harvard University Press, 1951.

Samuels, Peggy, and Harold Samuels. *Remembering the Maine.* Washington, DC: Smithsonian Institution Press, 1995.

Sigsbee, Charles D. *The "Maine": An Account of Her Destruction in Havana Harbor.* New York: Century, 1899.

Smith, Joseph. "From Coast Defense to Embalmed Beef: The Infuence of the Press and Public Opinion on McKinley's Policymaking During the Spanish-American War." In *The U.S. Public and American Foreign Policy*, edited by Andrew Johnstone and Helen Laville, 13–25. London: Routledge, 2010.

Thomas, Evan. *The War Lovers: Roosevelt, Lodge, Hearst, and the Rush to Empire, 1898.* New York: Little, Brown, 2010.

Tone, John Lawrence. *War and Genocide in Cuba, 1895-1898.* Chapel Hill: University of North Carolina Press, 2006.

Trask, David F. *The War with Spain in 1898.* Lincoln: University of Nebraska Press, 1996.

Weems, John Edward. *The Fate of the Maine.* New York: Holt, 1958.

Wegner, Dana. "New Interpretations of How the USS *Maine* Was Lost." In *Theodore Roosevelt, the U.S. Navy, and the Spanish-American War*, edited by Edward J. Marolda, 7–17. New York: Palgrave, 2001.

Wiechmann, Gerhard. *Die preussisch-deutsche Marine in Lateinamerika 1866-1914: eine Studie deutscher Kanonenbootpolitik.* Bremen: H.M. Hauschild, 2002.

Wisan, Joseph E. *The Cuban Crisis as Reflected in the New York Press (1895-1898).* New York: Columbia University Press, 1934.

Young, James Rankin, and J. H. Moore. *History of Our War with Spain, Including Battles on Sea and Land. . . To Which Is Added a Full Account of the Conquest of Spain in America, Naval Battles of the United States, Etc., Etc.* Philadelphia: National Publishing, 1898.

PART 2. THE *LUSITANIA* CRISIS

Ashby, LeRoy. *William Jennings Bryan: Champion of Democracy.* Boston: Twayne, 1987.

Bailey, Thomas Andrew, and Paul B. Ryan. *The Lusitania Disaster: An Episode in Modern Warfare and Diplomacy.* New York: Free Press, 1975.

Ballard, Robert D., and Spencer Dunmore. *Exploring the Lusitania: Probing the Mysteries of the Sinking That Changed History.* New York: Warner, 1995.

Beesly, Patrick. *Room 40: British Naval Intelligence 1914-1918.* Oxford: Oxford University Press, 1984.

Bernstorff, Johann Heinrich. *My Three Years in America.* New York: Scribner's, 1920.

Bernstorff, Johann Heinrich, and Eric Sutton. *The Memoirs of Count Bernstorff.* London: Heinemann, 1936.

Bethmann Hollweg, Theobald von, and George Young. *Reflections on the World War.* London: Butterworth, 1920.

Bryan, William Jennings, and Mary Baird Bryan. *The Memoirs of William Jennings Bryan.* Philadelphia: John C. Winston, 1925.

Butler, Daniel Allen. *The Lusitania: The Life, Loss, and Legacy of an Ocean Legend.* Mechanicsburg, PA: Stackpole, 2000.

Child, Clifton J. "German American Attempts to Prevent the Exportation of Munitions of War, 1914-1915." *Mississippi Valley Historical Review* 3 (1938): 351–68.

Churchill, Randolph S., and Martin Gilbert. *Winston S. Churchill, 1914–16.* Vol. 3. London: Heinemann, 1973.

Churchill, Winston. *The World Crisis.* 6 vols. London: T. Butterworth, 1923.

Coogan, John W. *The End of Neutrality: The United States, Britain, and Maritime Rights, 1899–1915.* Ithaca, NY: Cornell University Press, 1981.

Cooper Jr., John Milton. "The Command of Gold Reversed: American Loans to Britain, 1915-1917." *Pacific Historical Review* 45, no. 2 (1976): 209–30.

———. "The Shock of Recognition: The Impact of World War I on America." *Virginia Quarterly Review* 76 (2000): 567–84.

———. "The United States." In *The Origins of World War I*, edited by Richard F. Hamilton and Holger H. Herwig, 415–42. Cambridge: Cambridge University Press, 2003.

———. *The Warrior and the Priest: Woodrow Wilson and Theodore Roosevelt.* Cambridge, MA: Harvard University Press, 1983).

Corbett, Julian Stafford, and Henry John Newbolt. "Naval Operations." In *History of the Great War Based on Official Documents*, Direction of the Historical Section of the Committee of Imperial Defence. 5 vols. London: Longmans, Green, 1920.

Craig, Lee A. *Josephus Daniels: His Life & Times.* Chapel Hill: University of North Carolina Press, 2013.

Cronon, E. David, ed., *The Cabinet Diaries of Josephus Daniels 1913-1921.* Lincoln: University of Nebraska Press, 1963.

Devlin, Patrick. *Too Proud to Fight: Woodrow Wilson's Neutrality.* New York: Oxford University Press, 1975.

Doenecke, Justus D. *Nothing Less Than War: A New History of America's Entry into World War I*. Lexington: University Press of Kentucky, 2011.

Doerries, Reinhard R. *Imperial Challenge: Ambassador Count Bernstorff and German-American Relations, 1908–1917*. Supplementary volumes to the Papers of Woodrow Wilson. Chapel Hill: University of North Carolina Press, 1989.

Ellis, Frederick D. *The Tragedy of the Lusitania*. Philadelphia: National Publishing, 1915.

Ferns, Nicholas. "Loyal Advisor? Colonel Edward House's Confidential Trips to Europe, 1913–1917." *Diplomacy & Statecraft* 24, no. 3 (2013): 365–82.

Fisher, John Arbuthnot Fisher. *Memories*. London: Hodder and Stoughton, 1919.

Gerard, James W. *My Four Years in Germany*. New York: George H. Doran, 1917.

Grey, Edward, Viscount of Fallodon. *Twenty-Five Years, 1892-1916*. 2 vols. New York: Frederick A. Stokes, 1925.

Gullace, Nicoletta. "Friends, Aliens, and Enemies: Fictive Communities and the Lusitania Riots of 1915." *Journal of Social History* 39, no. 2 (2005): 345–367.

Hendrick, Burton Jesse. *The Life and Letters of Walter H. Page*. 3 vols. Garden City, NY: Doubleday, Page, 1922–25.

Herwig, Holger H. *"Luxury" Fleet: The Imperial German Navy, 1888-1918*. Rev. ed. Atlantic Highlands, NJ: Ashfield Press, 1987.

———. *Politics of Frustration: The United States in German Naval Planning, 1889-1941*. Boston: Little, Brown, 1976.

———. "Total Rhetoric, Limited War: Germany's U-Boat Campaign 1917-1918." In *Great War, Total War: Combat and Mobilization on the Western Front, 1914-1918*, edited by Roger Chickering and Stig Förster, 189–206. Cambridge: Cambridge University Press, 2000.

Hoehling, A. A., and Mary Duprey Hoehling. *The Last Voyage of the Lusitania*. New York: Henry Holt, 1956.

House, Edward Mandell, and Charles Seymour. *The Intimate Papers of Colonel House*. 4 vols. Boston: Houghton Mifflin, 1926.

Koerver, Hans Joachim, ed. *German Submarine Warfare 1914-1918 in the Eyes of British Intelligence*. Berlin: LIS Reinisch, 2010.

Lambert, Nicholas A. *Planning Armageddon: British Economic Warfare and the First World War*. Cambridge, MA: Harvard University Press, 2012.

"Last Voyage of the Lusitania" [video recording]. Washington, DC: National Geographic Society, 2003. Distributed by Warner Home Video.

Lauriat, C. E. *The "Lusitania's" Last Voyage*. Boston: Houghton Mifflin, 1915.

Levin, Phyllis Lee. *Edith and Woodrow. The Wilson White House*. New York: Scribner's, 2001.

Link, Arthur Stanley. *Wilson: Campaigns for Progressivism and Peace, 1916-1917*. 5 vols. Princeton, NJ: Princeton University Press, 1965.

———. *Wilson: Confusions and Crises 1915-1916*. Princeton, NJ: Princeton University Press, 1964.

———. *Wilson the Diplomatist: A Look at His Major Foreign Policies*. Baltimore, MD: Johns Hopkins University Press, 1957.

———. *Wilson: The Struggle for Neutrality 1914-1915*. Princeton, NJ: Princeton University Press, 1960.

Lundeberg, Philip K. "The German Naval Critique of the U-Boat Campaign, 1915-1918." *Military Affairs* 27, no. 3 (1963): 105–18.

May, Ernest R. *American Intervention: 1917 and 1941*. 2nd ed. Washington, DC: Service Center for Teachers of History, 1969.

———. *The World War and American Isolation, 1914–1917*. Cambridge, MA: Harvard University Press, 1959.

Michelsen, Andreas. *Der U-Bootskrieg, 1914-1918*. Leipzig: K.F. Koehler, 1925.

Mount, Graeme S. *Canada's Enemies: Spies and Spying in the Peaceable Kingdom*. Toronto: Dundurn, 1993.

Mullally, Erin. "Lusitania's Secret Cargo." *Archaeology* 62, no. 1 (2009): 9–19.

Nelson, Eric, Dave Harding, and Raymond Bridges. "Dark Secrets of the Lusitania" [video recording]. Washington, DC: National Geographic Society, 2012. Distributed by Warner Home Video.

Nicoletta, Gullace. "Friends, Aliens, and Enemies: Fictive Communities and the *Lusitania* Riots of 1915." *Journal of Social History* 39, no. 2 (2005): 345–67.

O'Sullivan, Patrick. *The Lusitania: Unravelling the Mysteries*. Dobbs Ferry, NY: Sheridan House, 2000.

Papers Relating to the Foreign Relations of the United States, 1914. Supplement: The World War. Washington, DC: Government Printing Office, 1914.

Papers Relating to the Foreign Relations of the United States, 1915. Washington, DC: Government Printing Office, 1915.

Papers Relating to the Foreign Relations of the United States, 1916. Washington, DC: Government Printing Office, 1916.

Papers Relating to the Foreign Relations of the United States. The Lansing Papers, 1914–1920, 2 vols. Available at http://digital.library.wisc.edu/1711.dl/FRUS. FRUS19141920v1.

Peeke, Mitch, Kevin Walsh-Johnson, and Steven Jones. *The Lusitania Story*. Annapolis, MD: Naval Institute Press, 2002.

Preston, Diana. *Lusitania: An Epic Tragedy*. New York: Walker, 2002.

Ramsay, David. *Lusitania: Saga and Myth*. London: Chatham, 2001.

Sides, Anne Goodwin. "New Clues in Lusitania's Sinking." *Weekend Edition Saturday*, NPR broadcast, November 22, 2008.

Simpson, Colin. *Lusitania*. London: Longman, 1972.

Spindler, Arno. *Der Krieg zur See, 1914–1918*. 2 vols. Berlin: E.S. Mittler, 1932.

———. "Der Meinungsstreit in der Marine über den U-Bootskrieg 1914-1918." *Marinerundschau* 55 (1958): 235–45.

Sullivan, Mark. *Our Times; the United States, 1900-1925*. 6 vols. New York: Scribner's, 1926.

Thomas, Lowell. *Count Luckner, the Sea Devil*. Garden City, NY: Doubleday, Page, 1927.

———. *Raiders of the Deep*. Garden City, NY: Doubleday, Doran, 1928.

Trommler, Frank. "The Lusitania Effect: America's Mobilization against Germany in World War I." *German Studies Review* 32, no. 2 (2009): 241–66.

Tucker, Robert W. *Woodrow Wilson and the Great War: Reconsidering America's Neutrality, 1914-1917*. Charlottesville: University of Virginia Press, 2007.

Tumulty, Joseph P. *Woodrow Wilson as I Know Him*. Garden City, NY: Doubleday, Page, 1922.

Von Tirpitz, Alfred Peter Friedrich. *My Memoirs*. 2 vols. London: Hurst & Blackett, 1919.

Watson, Alexander. *Ring of Steel: Germany and Austria-Hungary in World War I*. New York: Basic Books, 2014.

PART 3. THE *PANAY* INCIDENT

Abbazia, Patrick. *Mr. Roosevelt's Navy: The Private War of the U.S. Atlantic Fleet, 1939-1942*. Annapolis, MD: Naval Institute Press, 1975.

Adams, Henry Hitch. *Witness to Power: The Life of Fleet Admiral William D. Leahy*. Annapolis, MD: Naval Institute Press, 1985.

Alley, Norman. *I Witness*. New York: W. Funk, 1941.

Baker, Ray Stannard. *Woodrow Wilson: Life and Letters*. 8 vols. Garden City, NY: Doubleday, Page, 1927.

Barnes, Harry Elmer. *The Genesis of the World War*. New York: Knopf, 1926.

Bath, Alan Harris. *Tracking the Axis Enemy: The Triumph of Anglo-American Naval Intelligence*. Lawrence: University Press of Kansas, 1998.

Beard, Charles A. "Heat and Light on Neutrality." *New Republic*, 12 February 1936, p. 8.

———. *President Roosevelt and the Coming of the War, 1941: A Study in Appearances and Realities*. New Haven, CT: Yale University Press, 1948.

Bickers, Robert A. *Britain in China: Community Culture and Colonialism, 1900-1949*. Manchester: Manchester University Press, 1999.

Blum, John Morton. *From the Morgenthau Diaries. Years of Crisis, 1928-1938*. Boston: Houghton Mifflin, 1959.

Borg, Dorothy. *The United States and the Far Eastern Crisis of 1933-1938; from the Manchurian Incident through the Initial Stage of the Undeclared Sino-Japanese War*. Cambridge, MA: Harvard University Press, 1964.

Braisted, William Reynolds. *Diplomats in Blue: U.S. Naval Officers in China, 1922-1933*. Gainesville: University Press of Florida, 2009.

Brands, H. W. *What America Owes the World: The Struggle for the Soul of Foreign Policy*. Cambridge: Cambridge University Press, 1998.

Cohen, Warren I. *The American Revisionists: The Lessons of Intervention in World War I*. Chicago: University of Chicago Press, 1967.

Compton, James V. *The Swastika and the Eagle: Hitler, the United States, and the Origins of the Second World War*. London: Bodley, 1968.

Dallek, Robert. *Franklin D. Roosevelt and American Foreign Policy, 1932-1945*. New York: Oxford University Press, 1979.

Davis, Kenneth Sydney. *FDR. Into the Storm, 1937-1940*. New York: Random House, 1993.

Divine, Robert A. *The Illusion of Neutrality*. Chicago: University of Chicago Press, 1962.

Dyer, George C. *On the Treadmill to Pearl Harbor. The Memoirs of Admiral James O. Richardson*. Washington, DC: Naval History Division, 1973.

Engelbrecht, Helmut Carol, and Frank Cleary Hanighen. *Merchants of Death: A Study of the International Armament Industry*. New York: Dodd, Mead, 1934.

Field, Andrew. *Royal Navy Strategy in the Far East, 1919-1939: Preparing for War against Japan*. New York: Frank Cass, 2004.

Florence, Gregory J. *Courting a Reluctant Ally: An Evaluation of U.S./UK Naval Intelligence Cooperation, 1935-1941*. Washington, DC: Center for Strategic Intelligence Research, Joint Military Intelligence College, 2004.

Friedländer, Saul. *Prelude to Downfall; Hitler and the United States, 1939-41*. New York: Knopf, 1967.

Grattan, C. Hartley. *Why We Fought*. New York: Vanguard, 1929.

Grew, Joseph C. *Ten Years in Japan: A Contemporary Record Drawn from the Diaries and Private and Official Papers of Joseph G. Grew, United States Ambassador to Japan, 1932-1942*. New York: Simon & Schuster, 1944.

Haight Jr., John McVickar. "FDR's 'Big Stick.'" *U.S. Naval Institute Proceedings* 106, no. 7 (1980): 68–73.

Heinrichs, Waldo H. *American Ambassador: Joseph C. Grew and the Development of the United States Diplomatic Tradition*. New York: Oxford University Press, 1986.

Howarth, Stephen. *To Shining Sea. A History of the United States Navy 1775-1991*. New York: Random House, 1991.

Hull, Cordell, and Andrew Henry Thomas Berding. *The Memoirs of Cordell Hull*. 2 vols. New York: Macmillan, 1948.

Icenhower, Joseph Bryan. *The Panay Incident, December 12, 1937*. New York: Franklin Watts, 1971.

Ickes, Harold L. *The Secret Diary of Harold L. Ickes: The Inside Struggle 1936-1939*. New York: Simon & Schuster, 1954.

Johnstone, Andrew. *American Internationalists and the Four Freedoms on the Eve of World War II*. Ithaca, NY: Cornell University Press, 2014.

Kaiser, David. *No End Save Victory. How FDR Led the Nation into War*. New York: Basic Books, 2014.

Kennedy, David M. *Freedom from Fear*. Oxford: Oxford University Press, 2004.

Koginos, Manny T. *The Panay Incident; Prelude to War*. Lafayette, IN: Purdue University Studies, 1967.

Langer, William L., and S. Everett Gleason. *The Challenge to Isolation, 1937–1940*. New York: Council on Foreign Relations and Harper, 1952.

——. *The Challenge to Isolation: The World Crisis of 1937-1940 and American Foreign Policy.* 2 vols. Gloucester, MA: Peter Smith, 1970.

——. *The Undeclared War, 1940–1941.* Gloucester, MA: Peter Smith, 1968.

Leahy, William D. *I Was There: The Personal Story of the Chief of Staff to Presidents Roosevelt and Truman, Based on His Notes and Diaries Made at the Time.* New York: Whittlesey House, 1950.

Leigh, Michael. *Mobilizing Consent: Public Opinion and American Foreign Policy, 1937–1947.* Westport, CT: Greenwood, 1976.

Leutze, James R. *Bargaining for Supremacy: Anglo-American Naval Collaboration, 1937–1941.* Chapel Hill: University of North Carolina Press, 1977.

Lockwood, William W., ed. *Our Far Eastern Record. A Reference Digest on American Policy.* New York: American Council, Institute of Pacific Relations, 1940.

Long, David Foster. *Gold Braid and Foreign Relations: Diplomatic Activities of U.S. Naval Officers, 1798-1883.* Annapolis, MD: Naval Institute Press, 1988.

Mason Jr., John T. "The Reminiscences of Admiral Royal E. Ingersoll." *Naval History Project of the Oral History Research Office*, Washington, DC, 1964.

Maurer, John H., and Christopher M. Bell. *At the Crossroads between Peace and War: The London Naval Conference of 1930.* Annapolis, MD: Naval Institute Press, 2014.

May, Ernest R. *American Intervention: 1917 and 1941.* Washington, DC: Service Center for Teachers of History, 1969.

McAllister, James, Marc Trachtenberg, David Kaiser, John Schuessler, and Dan Reiter. "H-Diplo/ISSF Roundtable Exchange on "Diplomacy, Deception, and Entry into War." Vol. 5, no. 4 (2013); https://issforum.org/roundtables/5-4-democracy-deception-war.

Miller, Edward S. *Bankrupting the Enemy: The U.S. Financial Siege of Japan Before Pearl Harbor.* Annapolis, MD: Naval Institute Press, 2007.

——. *War Plan Orange: The U.S. Strategy to Defeat Japan, 1897-1945.* Annapolis, MD: Naval Institute Press, 1991.

Millis, Walter. *Road to War, America 1914-1917.* Boston: Houghton Mifflin, 1935.

Mitter, Rana. *Forgotten Ally: China's World War II, 1937-1945.* New York: Houghton Mifflin Harcourt, 2013.

Moffat, Jay Pierrepont, and Nancy Harvison Hooker. *The Moffat Papers; Selections from the Diplomatic Journals of Jay Pierrepont Moffat, 1919-1943.* Cambridge, MA: Harvard University Press, 1956.

Moore, Frederick. *With Japan's Leaders: An Intimate Record of Fourteen Years as Counsellor to the Japanese Government, Ending December 7, 1941.* New York: Scribner's, 1942.

Morison, Samuel Eliot. *History of United States Naval Operations in World War II.* Vol. 3: *The Rising Sun in the Pacific.* Boston: Little, Brown, 1947.

Morley, James William. *The Fateful Choice: Japan's Advance into Southeast Asia, 1939-1941.* New York: Columbia University Press, 1980.

Morton, Louis. "War Plan Orange: Evolution of a Strategy," *World Politics* 11, no. 2 (January 1959): 221–50.

Murfett, Malcolm H. *Fool-Proof Relations: The Search for Anglo-American Naval Cooperation during the Chamberlain Years, 1937-1940*. Singapore: Singapore University Press, 1984.

Nofi, Albert A. *To Train the Fleet for War: The U.S. Navy Fleet Problems*. Newpor, RI: Naval War College Press, 2010.

Okumiya, Mastake. "How the *Panay* Was Sunk." *U.S. Naval Institute Proceedings* 79, no. 6 (1953): 587–96.

Olson, Lynne. *Those Angry Days: Roosevelt, Lindbergh, and America's Fight over World War II, 1939-1941*. New York: Random House, 2013.

Papers Relating to the Foreign Relations of the United States. Japan: 1931–1941. Washington, DC: Government Printing Office, 1943.

Papers Relating to the Foreign Relations of the United States, 1937. Washington, DC: Government Printing Office, 1937.

Peace and War. United States Foreign Policy 1931–1941. Washington, DC: Government Printing Office, 1943.

Perry, Hamilton Darby. *The Panay Incident; Prelude to Pearl Harbor*. New York: Macmillan, 1969.

Plante, Trevor K. "'Two Japans': Japanese Expressions of Sympathy and Regret in the Wake of the *Panay* Incident." *Prologue Magazine* 33, no. 2 (2001): 109–20; www.archives.gov/publications/prologue/2001/summer/two-japans-1.html.

Plante, Trevor K. "U.S. Marines in the Boxer Rebellion." *Prologue Magazine* 31, no. 4 (1999); www.archives.gov/publications/prologue/1999/winter/boxer-rebellion-1.html.

Prange, Gordon William, Donald M. Goldstein, and Katherine V. Dillon. *Pearl Harbor: The Verdict of History*. New York: Penguin, 1991.

Pratt, Lawrence. "Anglo-American Naval Conversations on the Far East of January 1938." *International Affairs* 47 (October 1972): 745–63.

Scherr, Arthur. "Presidential Power, the *Panay* Incident, and the Defeat of the Ludlow Amendment." *International History Review* 32, no. 3 (2010): 455–500.

Schneider, James C. *Should America Go to War? The Debate over Foreign Policy in Chicago, 1939-1941*. Chapel Hill: University of North Carolina Press, 1989.

Schuessler, John M. "The Deception Dividend." *International Security* 34, no. 4 (Spring 2010): 133–65.

———. *Deceit on the Road to War: Presidents, Politics and American Democracy*. Cornell Studies in Security Affairs. Ithaca: Cornell University Press, 2015.

Seldes, George. *Iron, Blood and Profits: An Exposure of the World-Wide Munitions Racket*. New York: Harper & Brothers, 1934.

Swanson, Harlan. "The *Panay* Incident: Prelude to Pearl Harbor." *U.S. Naval Institute Proceedings* 93, no. 12 (1967): 27–37.

Tansill, Charles Callan. *America Goes to War*. Boston: Little, Brown, 1938.

———. *Back Door to War: The Roosevelt Foreign Policy, 1933-1941.* Chicago: Regnery, 1952.

Theobald, Robert Alfred. *The Final Secret of Pearl Harbor.* New York: Devin-Adair, 1954.

Tolley, Kemp. "YangPat—Shanghai to Chunking." *U.S. Naval Institute Proceedings* 89, no. 6 (1963): 89–94.

———. *Yangtze Patrol: The U.S. Navy in China.* 3rd ed. Annapolis, MD: Naval Institute Press, 2000.

Walkowski, William. "The *Panay* Incident: The Recollections of Assistant Military Attaché Frank N. Roberts 1934-1938." In *Frank N. Roberts Papers.* Independence, MO: Harry S Truman Library, 1973.

Weinberg, Gerhard L. *A World at Arms: A Global History of World War II.* 2nd ed. Cambridge: Cambridge University Press, 2005.

———. *The Foreign Policy of Hitler's Germany.* 2 vols. Atlantic Highlands, NJ: Humanities Press, 1994.

———. "Munich after 50 Years," *Foreign Affairs* 67 (1988): 165–78.

———. *Visions of Victory: The Hopes of Eight World War II Leaders.* Cambridge: Cambridge University Press, 2005.

Welles, Sumner. *Seven Decisions That Shaped History.* New York: Harper & Brothers, 1950.

Wiltz, John Edward. *In Search of Peace. The Senate Munitions Inquiry, 1934-36.* Baton Rouge: Louisiana State University Press, 1963.

———. "The Nye Munitions Committee 1934." In *Congress Investigates: A Documented History, 1792-1974,* edited by Arthur M. Schlesinger and Roger A. Bruns, 2735–919. New York: Chelsea House, 1975.

Wohlstetter, Roberta. *Pearl Harbor; Warning and Decision.* Palo Alto, CA: Stamford University Press, 1962.

Zhang, Kaiyuan. *Eyewitnesses to Massacre: American Missionaries Bear Witness to Japanese Atrocities in Nanjing.* Armonk, NY: M.E. Sharpe, 2001.

INDEX